THE ESSENTIA

The Essential Davidson

DONALD DAVIDSON

with an introduction by
ERNIE LEPORE and KIRK LUDWIG

CLARENDON PRESS · OXFORD

OXFORD

UNIVERSITY PRESS

Great Clarendon Street, Oxford OX2 6DP

Oxford University Press is a department of the University of Oxford.
It furthers the University's objective of excellence in research, scholarship,
and education by publishing worldwide in

Oxford New York

Auckland Cape Town Dar es Salaam Hong Kong Karachi
Kuala Lumpur Madrid Melbourne Mexico City Nairobi
New Delhi Shanghai Taipei Toronto

With offices in

Argentina Austria Brazil Chile Czech Republic France Greece
Guatemala Hungary Italy Japan Poland Portugal Singapore
South Korea Switzerland Thailand Turkey Ukraine Vietnam

Oxford is a registered trade mark of Oxford University Press
in the UK and in certain other countries

Published in the United States
by Oxford University Press Inc., New York

British Library Cataloguing in Publication Data

Data available

Library of Congress Cataloging in Publication Data

Davidson, Donald, 1917–2003
[Selections. 2006]
The essential Davidson / Donald Davidson; with an introduction by
Ernie Lepore and Kirk Ludwig.
p. cm.
Includes bibliographical references and index.
1. Act (Philosophy) 2. Language and languages—Philosophy. I. Title.
B945.D381L47 2006 191—dc22 2005020560

Typeset by Newgen Imaging Systems (P) Ltd., Chennai, India
Printed in Great Britain
on acid-free paper by
Biddles Ltd., King's Lynn, Norfolk

ISBN 0–19–928885–2 978–0–19–928885–4
ISBN 0–19–928886–0 (Pbk.) 978–0–19–928886–1 (Pbk.)

1 3 5 7 9 10 8 6 4 2

Contents

Introduction   1
Ernie Lepore and Kirk Ludwig

PHILOSOPHY OF ACTION AND PSYCHOLOGY

1. Actions, Reasons, and Causes (1963)   23
2. The Logical Form of Action Sentences   37
   with Criticism, Comment, and Defence (1967)   50
3. How is Weakness of the Will Possible? (1969)   72
4. The Individuation of Events (1969)   90
5. Mental Events (1970)   105
   Appendix: Emeroses by Other Names (1966)   119
6. Intending (1978)   122
7. Paradoxes of Irrationality (1982)   138

TRUTH, MEANING, AND INTERPRETATION

8. Truth and Meaning (1967)   155
9. On Saying That (1968)   171
10. Radical Interpretation (1973)   184
11. On the Very Idea of a Conceptual Scheme (1974)   196
12. What Metaphors Mean (1978)   209
13. A Coherence Theory of Truth and Knowledge (1983)   225
    Appendix: Afterthoughts (1987)   238
14. First Person Authority (1984)   242
15. A Nice Derangement of Epitaphs (1986)   251

Contents List of Volumes of Essays by Donald Davidson   267
Bibliography   272
Index   278

Introduction

Ernie Lepore and Kirk Ludwig

Donald Davidson's philosophical program, one of the most influential of the second half of the twentieth century, can be seen as organized around two connected projects. The first is that of understanding the nature of human agency. The second is that of understanding the nature and function of language, and its relation to thought and the world. After a brief overview of Davidson's life and the intellectual background of his work, we will develop these two themes in the context of the present selection of essential papers from Davidson's corpus.

LIFE AND INTELLECTUAL BACKGROUND

Born on 6 March 1917, in Springfield, Massachusetts, Davidson attended Harvard University in 1935, studying English literature for two years before turning to classics and comparative literature. On graduating in 1939, he was awarded a fellowship to pursue graduate studies in classical philosophy at Harvard. During his first year he took a course from W. V. Quine on the logical positivists. He reported later that it changed his view of philosophy. "What mattered to me," Davidson said, "was not so much Quine's conclusions (I assumed he was right) as the realization that it was possible to be serious about getting things right in philosophy—or at least not getting things wrong" (Davidson 1999: 23). Quine was to remain a central influence on Davidson's work. Davidson's graduate studies were interrupted by the Second World War. Davidson volunteered for the navy, and returned to graduate work at Harvard in 1946 after being discharged. He took up a teaching position at Queens College in New York the following year, and after a year on a grant from the Rockefeller Foundation, completed his dissertation on Plato's *Philebus* in 1949 (Davidson 1990). He left Queens for Stanford University in 1951 where he taught for sixteen years before moving to Princeton University in 1967. Subsequently, Davidson taught at Rockefeller University from 1970 until the philosophy unit at Rockefeller was disbanded, at which point he moved in 1976 to the University of Chicago. In 1981, he moved to the philosophy department at the University of California at Berkeley. He died on 30 August 2003.

   The years at Stanford, during which he taught a wide range of subjects, from logic, ancient and modern philosophy, epistemology, philosophy of science, and philosophy of language, to ethics, music theory, and ideas in literature, laid the foundations for his subsequent work. There were four main sources of influence.

The first was experimental work on formal decision theory with Patrick Suppes and J. J. C. McKinsey (Davidson and Suppes 1957). This had an important influence on his views in the philosophy of language, particularly in the theory of radical interpretation. Davidson derived two morals from it. The first was that in 'putting formal conditions on simple concepts and their relations to one another, a powerful structure could be defined.' The second was that the formal theory itself 'says nothing about the world' and that its content is given by how it is interpreted in relation to the data to which it is applied (Davidson 1999: 32).

The second was an invitation to co-author a contribution to the Library of Living Philosophers on Carnap with J. J. C. McKinsey. When McKinsey died, Davidson took up the task alone. This led him to Carnap's work on attitude sentences. When he gave a talk at Berkeley on Carnap's method of intension and extension, Alfred Tarski was in the audience. Tarski gave Davidson a reprint of 'The Semantic Conception of Truth and the Foundations of Semantics' (Tarski 1944). This led him to Tarski's more technical 'The Concept of Truth in Formalized Languages' (Tarski 1934). Tarski's work struck Davidson as providing an answer to a question that had puzzled him about accounts of the semantic form of indirect discourse and belief sentences: how does one tell when an account is correct? The answer, Davidson suggested, was that an account was correct if it could be incorporated into a truth definition for the language in roughly the style outlined by Tarski, or, at least, clearly incorrect if it could not. This would tell one, in the context of a theory for the language as a whole, what contribution each expression in each sentence in the language makes to fixing the sentence's truth conditions. In addition, a theory of this sort would show how finite beings can understand an infinity of nonsynonymous sentences. These insights were the genesis of two foundational papers in Davidson's work on natural language semantics, 'Theories of Meaning and Learnable Languages' (Davidson 1965) and 'Truth and Meaning' (1967, reprinted as Essay 8, this volume). In the former Davidson proposed as a criterion for the adequacy of an analysis of the logical form of a sentence or complex expression in a natural language that it would not make it impossible for a finite being to the learn the language of which it was a part. In the latter, he proposed that a Tarski-style axiomatic truth theory, modified for a natural language, could serve the purpose of a meaning theory for the language, without appeal to meanings, intensions, or the like.

The third influence was an invitation from W. V. Quine to read the manuscript of *Word and Object* while Quine was a fellow at the Center for Advanced Study in the Behavioral Sciences at Stanford in the 1958–9 academic year. *Word and Object* casts the project of understanding linguistic communication in the form of an examination of the task of radical translation. This conception of the basic approach to the problem had a tremendous influence on Davidson. The radical translator constructs a translation manual for another speaker's language solely on the basis of the speaker's dispositions to verbal behavior in response to sensory stimulus. The central idea, that there is no more to meaning than can be gleaned from the standpoint of an interpreter of another speaker, is a central theme of Davidson's philosophy.

The fourth influence was the work on the philosophy of action being done in Oxford in the 1950s, which was transmitted through Davidson's student Dan Bennett, who spent a year at Oxford and wrote a dissertation on action theory inspired by discussions that were going on there. The prevailing orthodoxy was the neo-Wittgensteinian view that action explanation was not causal but functioned rather by redescribing an action in a way that places it in a larger social, linguistic, economic, or evaluative pattern. Davidson famously argued against this orthodoxy in 'Actions, Reasons and Causes' (1963, reprinted as Essay 1, this volume), so successfully as to establish the new orthodoxy that action explanations were both rational and causal explanations.

These influences gave rise to the two main streams in Davidson's philosophy, which were mutually supporting, and interconnected. The first flows from the work on decision theory and the philosophy of action, and is represented by the essays in the first section of this collection on Philosophy of Action and Psychology. The second flows from the work on semantics, and combines the influences of Quine and Tarski, and is represented by the second section in this collection on Truth, Meaning, and Interpretation.

PHILOSOPHY OF ACTION

Davidson's view of the nature of action combines two elements which had been thought to be incompatible, on the one hand the view that action explanations are causal explanations of the movements of our bodies and things that these in turn cause, and on the other hand the view that action explanations have a justifying function, that is, that they show the action to have been done for reasons. In 'Actions, Reasons and Causes', Davidson argued that to explain an action we must cite or indicate a primary reason for it, an appropriately related pair of belief and desire (or 'pro attitude') explained as follows:

C1. *R* is a primary reason why an agent performed the action *A* under the description *d* only if *R* consists of a pro-attitude of the agent towards actions with a certain property, and a belief of the agent that *A*, under the description *d*, has that property. (p. 25)

The primary reason provides the materials to construct a practical syllogism in favor of the action, which shows what was to be said for it from the point of view of the agent. Thus, if *A* waves his hand because he wanted thereby to signal a friend *B* and thought that waving his hand would be a signaling of his friend, the practical syllogism in favor of this action, *W*, is:

Signaling *B* is desirable.
W is a signaling of *B*.
_____

W is desirable.

Each action has a primary reason. Thus, for each action one can construct a practical syllogism that shows what minimally can be said for it from the point of view of the agent. In this sense, each action is minimally rational, that is, shown to be justified from some aspect of the agent's point of view. This leaves it open, though, that in the light of the rest of an agent's attitudes the action might be revealed not to be rational all things considered.

Davidson identified actions with events, and specifically with certain bodily movements. Such actions can be redescribed in terms of their effects. Thus, *A*'s moving his finger may be his flicking the switch, which may be his turning on the light, and alerting a prowler. Actions are intentional or unintentional under a description. *A*'s turning on the light was intentional, but not *A*'s alerting a prowler, though they are one and the same act (see also Davidson 1971).

Davidson combines the view that action explanations provide reasons that justify an action from the point of view of the agent with the view that:

C2. A primary reason for an action is its cause. (p. 30)

The positive argument for C2 goes as follows. An agent may have more than belief–desire pair that provides a justification for an action, though only one of them can be cited in explaining it. Since only one of them explains it, the one that explains the action must stand in some relation to the action beyond that of providing a justification for it, which the other does not. The best candidate is the causal relation. That is, the belief–desire pair that explains the action causes it, while the other does not. Thus, for example, one may wish to notify the bank of a deposit error that adds an extra million dollars to one's checking account because it is the right thing to do, and also because one fears being caught if one does not, but act because it is the right thing to do, rather than out of fear of being caught, or vice versa. Each reason for notifying the bank of the error (constructible from the story) provides a justification for the action, but in either scenario only one explains it. The difference between the one that explains it and the one that does not, Davidson argues, is that the one that explains it is the one that causes it. This argument is combined with a masterful diagnosis of what goes wrong with arguments against the idea that the reasons for which we perform actions (here identified with psychological states of belief and desire which figure in action explanation) are their causes. One principal objection to this idea was that reasons and actions are logically connected, but that causal relations must hold between logically independent events. Davidson pointed out that stating that someone has certain reasons does not entail that he will perform an action which they rationalize, and that describing something as an action does not entail what the reasons were for it. But the more fundamental problem is that the objection rests upon a confusion of events with their descriptions. There is a logical connection between 'the cause of B' and 'B', for it follows from there being a cause of B that B exists. But in this case clearly there can be no objection to the two events described standing in the causal relation. Events stand in the causal relation in virtue of being subsumed by a causal law. Two events are subsumed by a causal law if they have descriptions under which they instantiate the law. It does not follow from this, however, that for any two events e_1 and e_2 and any two descriptions d_1 and d_2 of them, if e_1 and e_2 are subsumed by a causal law, then d_1 and d_2 are descriptions under which they instantiate that law. This is shown by the two descriptions in the example above, 'the cause of B' and 'B'. If the cause of B caused B, there are some descriptions of those events which instantiate a causal law. But they are not the descriptions by which we pick them out in this statement. In sum, events stand in causal relations; their descriptions stand in logical relations. Since events may have many descriptions, they may have some that are logically related, under which, therefore, they do not instantiate a causal law, while at the same time under different descriptions they do instantiate a causal law. Thus, a logical relation between descriptions of events is no bar to those events standing in the causal relation. This observation about the distinction between the descriptions by which we pick out events and the descriptions under which they are subsumed by causal laws turns out to be a key to understanding Davidson's later argument for anomalous monism in 'Mental Events' (1970, reprinted as Essay 5, this volume), an argument which is already hinted at in 'Actions, Reasons and Causes' (p. 35).

The view that actions are events is defended in the 'The Logical Form of Action Sentences' (1967, reprinted as Essay 2, this volume) at the same time that Davidson applies the idea that we judge the correctness of an account of the logical form of a kind of discourse on the basis of how well we can integrate it into a compositional meaning theory for the whole language, which takes the form of an axiomatic truth theory for the language. Davidson starts with the problem of explaining the logical role of adverbial modification in action sentences. In the examples below (2)–(4) evidently follow from (1) as a matter of their form, since it does not matter which two-place action verb stands in the place of 'stabbed'.

(1) Brutus stabbed Caesar with a knife on the Ides of March.
(2) Brutus stabbed Caesar with a knife.
(3) Brutus stabbed Caesar on the Ides of March.
(4) Brutus stabbed Caesar.

We cannot account for this if we take (1)–(4) to involve verbs with a different number of argument places ('a stabbed b with c on d,' etc.). In this case, an argument from (1) to (4), for example, would have the form 'φ (a, b, c, d); therefore, ψ(a, b).' Here we represent the verb in (1) and (4) with different symbols because verbs with different numbers of argument places cannot be synonymous. An argument of this form might be valid, but it would not be formally valid, since it would depend on what the two predicates meant. A formally valid argument must be valid independently of the meaning of the predicates in the sentences which appear in it. The argument from, again, (1) to (4) is clearly formally valid, because it is an instance of a form which we recognize as valid without reference to the content of the predicates: 'A Ved B with a F on G; therefore, A Ved B'. Furthermore, since there is no upper limit to the number of adverbs which can be used to modify a verb, if we treat the addition of an adverb to a sentence such as (4) as involving a new predicate with an additional argument place, we must admit an infinite number of non-synonymous predicates in English (and other natural languages), since we can keep adding adverbs without limit. But this would make the language unlearnable by finite beings such as ourselves (see the section below on 'Truth and Meaning', pp. 11–14, for further discussion).

Davidson's influential suggestion, clearly connected with his independent work in the philosophy of action, was that we treat action verbs as introducing an implicit existential quantifier over events, and treat the adverbs as introducing predicates of the event variable thereby introduced. On Davidson's initial proposal, we would represent (1)–(4) as (1′)–(4′) (ignoring tense).

(1′) $(\exists e)$(stabs(e, Brutus, Caesar) and with(e, a knife) and on(e, the Ides of March)),

(2′) $(\exists e)$(stabs(e, Brutus, Caesar) and with(e, a knife)),

(3′) $(\exists e)$(stabs(e, Brutus, Caesar) and on(e, the Ides of March)),

(4′) $(\exists e)$(stabs(e, Brutus, Caesar)).

This makes transparent how (2)–(4) follow from (1) compatibly with seeing 'stabbed' as making the same contribution to each. In each of (1′)–(4′) 'stabbed' is represented as contributing a three-place predicate relating an event to Brutus and Caesar. Each of (2′)–(4′) follow from (1′) as a matter of form because we know that if something is F and G and H, then something is F and G and something is F and H, and something is F. This shows how we can understand an infinite range of sentences on the basis of finite resources. This analysis has been enormously influential in linguistics. Here the solution to the problem of the logical form of action sentences is supported by Davidson's work in the philosophy of action and in turn provides support for Davidson's view of actions as events.

Any action is at least minimally rational because its explanation shows that there was something to be said for it from the point of view of an agent. But it does not follow that it is rational all things considered. When an agent is faced with incompatible goals each of which he values, he must choose between them. If he ranks one higher than the other but chooses the lesser, then he is guilty of weakness of will. But how is weakness of the will possible? The puzzle arises from an apparent conflict between the thought that what someone actually does intentionally, when he is faced with a choice between two actions, shows what he really wants more, and the thought that when someone judges one thing better than another, he wants it more than the other. Then to rank one action higher than another, intentionally choose the lesser, appears to be a contradiction. Davidson argues for a resolution of this puzzle in 'How is Weakness of the Will Possible?' (1969, reprinted as Essay 3, this volume), which at the same time provides an account of the nature of practical reasoning and its relation to action.

Simply having reasons for an end which show something is to be said for it does not lead directly to action, for practical reasoning requires adjudicating between conflicting ends. So the conclusion of a piece of practical reasoning cannot in general be an action, but must rather be a judgment of some sort. However, it cannot be a judgment that a particular action is correct or flatly good. Eating a particular piece of chocolate may be good insofar as it is sweet, but bad insofar as it contains a lethal dose of arsenic. Davidson argues on these grounds for an analogy between the logical form of practical reasoning and probabilistic reasoning. In the latter, the reasoning takes the form, for example, '*it is probable that* it will rain *given that* the sky is red this morning', and the conclusion of a bit of probabilistic reasoning is not fully detachable from the evidence, for more evidence can overturn the conclusion. Similarly, Davidson argues, the premises of a practical syllogism are of the form, for example, 'That an act is a lie prima facie makes it wrong' (cf. 'that the sky is red this morning *probabilizes* that it will rain'). We can symbolize this as $pf(Wx, Lx)$. The conclusion of a bit of practical reasoning is then conditioned by all the considerations taken into account, that it is a lie, that it will save someone's life, etc. An overall practical conclusion in favor of one action a over another b, then, Davidson argues, is an *all-things-considered* judgment of the form, $pf(a$ is better than $b, r)$, that is, that r prima facie makes a better than b, where 'r' represents all the considerations.

How does this solve the problem of weakness of the will? An all-things-considered judgment is not an unconditional judgment that an action is best. But it is the unconditional judgment which Davidson holds is the commitment to action, and which reflects what it is that one most wants among the options one has considered. One's conditional all-things-considered judgment can then point in one direction, though one's unconditional judgment is made in favour of another.

What is the unconditional judgment? In 'Actions, Reasons and Causes', Davidson argued that in 'James did it with the intention of pleasing his mother' the phrase 'with the intention of' was syncategorematic, that is, that it was to be interpreted as a whole, and that in particular 'intention' was not to be taken any more seriously as a count noun than 'sake' in 'for the sake of'. It was rather a way of pointing to the reasons which James had without fully giving them. He retracts this view in 'Intending' (1978, reprinted as Essay 6, this volume) in large part because of the phenomenon of the prior intention which is never acted on. Someone may form an intention to write a novel without ever executing it. Davidson argues that intentions are a *sui generis* psychological state, a pro-attitude necessary for action, but distinct from action and belief and desire, and from the last in particular with respect to its consistency requirements. There is no incoherence in having desires that are mutually incompatible in the light of one's beliefs, but one is criticizably irrational in having intentions which are incompatible in the light of one's beliefs. This distinction between desire or want and intention Davidson links to the distinction drawn in 'How is Weakness of the Will Possible?' between conditional, prima facie judgments and unconditional, all-out judgments. Corresponding to pro-attitudes, Davidson argues, are evaluative judgments.

There is no short proof that evaluative sentences express desires and other pro-attitudes in the way that the sentence 'Snow is white' expresses the belief that snow is white. But the following consideration will perhaps help show what is involved. If someone who knows English says honestly 'snow is white', then he believes snow is white. If my thesis is correct, someone who says honestly 'It is desirable that I stop smoking' has some pro-attitude towards his stopping smoking. (p. 124)

Corresponding to desires then are conditional or prima facie evaluative judgments, and corresponding to intentions are unconditional evaluative judgments. Then weakness of the will, as Davidson explains it, is the interruption of the formation of an intention to do an act on the basis of an all-things-considered desire for it based on practical deliberation.

Actions on Davidson's view are an expression of our nature as agents, beings with interlocking propositional attitudes of different types: beliefs, desires, and intentions. Each is defined by its relations to the others and its mediated relations to actions. We identify a person's beliefs, desires, and intentions by projecting a rational pattern which makes sense of his or her behaviour. Rationality then is constitutive of the propositional attitudes. It is not just that every particular action can be seen as having something to be said for it in the light of the agent's beliefs and desires, but that to make sense of someone as an agent at all we must find his attitudes arranged in overall rational patterns. Yet perfect rationality is clearly at best an ideal for human beings, as the phenomenon of weakness of the will, among others, shows. How is the rational character of the attitudes compatible with this? Davidson's answer is to distinguish between irrationality and non-rationality (see 'Paradoxes of Irrationality', 1982, reprinted as Essay 7, this volume). Irrationality is a 'perturbation of rationality', a defect in the pattern of rational interplay among the attitudes that allows us to identify attitudes. Without a largely rational pattern that allows the identification of belief, desire, and intention, we would not be able to identify deviations from it. There is therefore no irrationality except against the background of a largely rational pattern of attitudes, just as to identify a plane as having broken formation, there must be a formation relative to which its proper position is identified. This picture of the attitudes as having a place constitutively in a pattern of matching attitudes and behaviour plays a central role in the project of radical interpretation, as we will see.

INDIVIDUATION OF EVENTS AND
ANOMALOUS MONISM

Davidson's work in the philosophy of action and on the logical form of action sentences led him to the view that events are part of our common sense ontology, the metaphysics of ordinary language. But what are events? Intuitively, they are changes, datable particulars, like the eruption of Krakatoa on 26 August 1883. A key question about events is how they are to be individuated. Davidson's account of the nature of actions requires that they be individuated so as to make sense of the possibility of actions being events that are redescribable in many different ways. In 'Individuation of Events' (1969, reprinted as Essay 4, this volume) Davidson argued that events could be individuated by their causes and effects, that is, that events x and y were the same just in case they had the same causes and effects. At the time of writing this article, Davidson rejected the idea of individuating events by their spatiotemporal location on the grounds that the rotation and warming of a sphere occurring in the same time interval constituted not one but two events. Davidson later revised his view (Davidson 1985) in response to a criticism from Quine (Quine 1985), who pointed out that Davidson's criterion of individuation presupposed the prior individuation of other events. He then adopted the view that events were individuated by their spatiotemporal locations, holding that the rotation and warming were identical with the same set of movements of molecules.

Many of the themes we have been reviewing come together in Davidson's seminal argument for Anomalous Monism in 'Mental Events'. Anomalous Monism holds that all token mental events are also token physical events, but at the same time denies that there are any strict psychological laws, which means there are no strict psycho-physical laws. If there are no strict psychological laws, then there is no reduction of mental properties or concepts to physical properties or concepts. Hence, Anomalous Monism is a form of nonreductive materialism. It holds that the mental is conceptually but not ontologically autonomous from the physical. The argument for anomalous monism rests on three main principles, each drawing on views we have already seen introduced (pp. 105–6).

1. The Principle of Causal Interaction: '. . . at least some mental events interact causally with physical events'.

2. The Principle of the Nomological Character of Causality: '. . . where there is causality, there must be a law: events related as cause and effect fall under strict deterministic laws'.

3. The Anomalism of the Mental: '. . . there are no strict deterministic laws on the basis of which mental events can be predicted and explained'.

Davidson later in the paper relaxes the requirement of 'deterministic laws' to just 'strict laws', a law 'there is no improving in point of precision and comprehensiveness' (p. 118). The first principle is drawn directly from Davidson's account of the nature of the propositional attitudes and their relation to action. The second principle (dropping 'deterministic') is widely accepted, and was evoked in Davidson's response to the logical-connection objection to action explanations being causal explanations, and depends as well on an account of the individuation of events that allows events to fall under different descriptions. The final principle rests on an assumption about the character of lawlike generalizations, and the constitutive role of the norms of rationality in attributions of propositional attitudes, that is, the fact that these attributions are guided by considerations of overall rationality. Lawlike generalizations are supported by their instances and projectible to future instances. 'Everyone who sits on this park bench is an Irishman' is not supported by its instances or projectible to future instances, but 'Copper expands when heated' is. Davidson argues that lawlikeness is a matter of degree, but that for a generalization to reach the highest degree of projectibility, to be a strict law, it must draw on concepts from the same family. Concepts are drawn from the same family if, and only if, they are governed by the same constitutive principles. For example, it is a constitutive principle of the attribution of lengths to rigid objects that the longer than relation is transitive; if *a* is longer than *b*, and *b* longer than *c*, then *a* is longer than *c*. But given this, and that it is a constraint on the attribution of propositional attitudes that they be attributed in largely rational patterns, but not a constraint on the attribution of physical properties, mental concepts (at least so far as they are tied to concepts of the propositional attitudes) and physical concepts are not members of the same family of concepts. It follows, if Davidson's assumptions are correct, that there can be no strict psycho-physical laws. If we assume that all mental events interact causally with physical events, then since the mental is not a closed system, there will be no strict psychological laws. If we assume then that the only remaining source of strict laws is the physical, then we can reach the conclusion that mental events stand in causal relations to physical events in virtue of being subsumed by strict physical laws. But that then requires that every mental event has a physical description that is suitable for subsumption by a strict law. Characterizing a physical event as one which has such a description we reach the conclusion that every token mental event is a token physical event, that is, token–token physicalism.

THEORY OF MEANING

In 'Theories of Meaning and Learnable Languages' Davidson introduced a requirement on a meaning theory for natural languages which we will call the compositionality requirement.

I propose what seems to me clearly to be a necessary feature of a learnable language: it must be possible to give a constructive account of the meaning of the sentences in the language. Such an account I call a theory of meaning for the language, and I suggest that a theory of meaning that conflicts with this condition, whether put forward by philosopher, linguist, or psychologist, cannot be a theory of a natural language; and if it ignores this condition, it fails to deal with something central to the concept of a language. (Davidson 2001*b*: 5)

Given that we are finite beings, and that it takes a finite amount of time to acquire each semantic primitive, unless natural languages, which contain an infinity of non-synonymous sentences, were understood on the basis of a finite number of primitives and rules for their combination, they would be unlearnable, contrary to fact. We will characterize a compositional meaning theory as follows (see Lepore and Ludwig 2005, chapter 2, for further discussion):

> [CM] A compositional meaning theory for a language *L* is a formal theory that enables anyone who understands the language in which the theory is stated to understand the primitive expressions of *L* and the complex expressions of *L* on the basis of understanding the primitive ones.

A compositional meaning theory must start with axioms for primitive expressions of the language and generate a specification of the meaning of any complex expression in the language. The axioms will be divided into base and recursive axioms. The recursive axioms tell us how to decompose complex expressions of our object language into simpler expressions, which may still be complex, until we arrive at primitive axioms to which the base axioms will apply.

In 'Truth and Meaning' (1967, reprinted as Essay 8, this volume) Davidson proposed using a truth theory to pursue the goals of a compositional meaning theory. The main alternative is to appeal to meanings, construed as entities, assigned to expressions, as, for example, on Frege's view. Davidson saw a number of difficulties with this view. He argued controversially in 'Truth and Meaning' that plausible assumptions lead to the view that any two sentences alike in truth value must have the same meaning, if sentences refer to their meanings. This is a difficulty for that view because sentences may be alike in truth value without being alike in meaning. 'George Bush is the President of the United States' and 'Tony Blair is the Prime Minister of England' are both true in 2005, but they are not synonymous (see Lepore and Ludwig 2005, chapter 3 §4, for detailed discussion). But Davidson also argued independently that the appeal to meanings does not actually do the real work in a theory of meaning, and that the utility of the appeal to meanings derives from their providing us with a way of matching expressions in the object language with expressions we already understand in the metalanguage (the language of the theory). In addition, these approaches do not make clear the connection between meaning and truth. What a sentence means determines under what conditions it is true. It is a plausible requirement on a theory that aims to show how we understand complex expressions on the basis of their parts that it make clear what this connection is. Davidson's brilliant suggestion was that a truth theory of the sort that Tarski had shown how to formulate for formal languages could be employed to produce the required matching of object-language sentences with metalanguage sentences already understood, and that appropriate knowledge about the truth theory would put us in a position to understand any object-language sentence on the basis of understanding its semantic primitives and rules for their combination.

The key to seeing how this is possible lies in the requirement, Convention T, which Tarski imposed on an adequate axiomatic truth definition ('truth theory' henceforth) for a language. Convention T requires that the truth theory be formally correct and that it have among its theorems all sentences of the form (T) in which 's' is replaced by a description of an object-language sentence as constructed out of its significant parts, and 'p' is replaced by a translation of s into the metalanguage, and 'is T' stands in for the truth predicate for the object language.

(T) s is T iff p

If we know that a truth theory meets Convention T, and that it is consistent, then we know that 'is T' has the extension of the truth predicate for the object language. But if we know that the theory meets Convention T, and we can pick out the appropriate theorems, those in virtue of which it meets this requirement described above, then we can replace 'is T iff' with 'means that' to arrive at an explicit statement of the meaning of s, as shown in (M).

(M) s means that p

This is because the condition for (M) being true is that 'p' translates s. (See Lepore and Ludwig 2005, Part I for further discussion.)

The essential features of a truth theory can be illustrated in a sample informal theory for a non-context-sensitive language, one without any expressions or devices (such as 'I' or 'now' or tense inflection) which contribute differently to the truth conditions of utterances of sentences containing them depending on the context of utterance. Let us call this language 'L'. The axioms attaching to semantically primitive expressions (those for which an understanding of the sentences in which they appear does not rest on understanding sentences in which they do not appear) are divided into reference axioms for proper names, predicate axioms, axioms for sentential connectives, and axioms for quantifiers. These illustrate the type of axioms for the most basic expressive devices of language. Here we invoke a technical term 'satisfies' which expresses a relation between assignments of objects to variables (functions from variables to objects) and formulas in assigning truth conditions. This is an extension of the intuitive notion of a predicate being true of an object, for example, 'est rouge' being true of a red ball. We may say then the ball satisfies 'est rouge'. Then to handle multiple argument places in a predicate $P(x, y, z, \ldots)$ we talk of a function from the variables to objects satisfying the predicate. The role of the function is to associate with each argument place in the predicate, by way of associating with the variable that occupies it, an object; we then ask essentially whether the resulting sentence, with the variables treated as if they were names with referents assigned by the function, is true. If so, then the function satisfies the predicate. This is required to handle quantification, which operates on us to build up complex formulas from formulas with free variables. The last axiom connects truth with satisfaction. For a sentence (i.e., a formula with no free variables), if one function satisfies it, all will do so. ('⌢' is the sign for concatenation, so that, for example, 'Russell'⌢'voit'⌢'Frege' = 'Russell voit Frege'.)

R1. Ref('Russell') = Russell.

R2. Ref('Frege') = Frege.

P1. For any function f, for any names N_1, N_2, f satisfies in L N_1⌢voit⌢N_2 iff ref(N_1) sees ref(N_2).

P2. For any function f, f satisfies in L 'x voit y' iff f('x') sees f('y').

C1. For any function f, for any sentences φ, ψ, f satisfies in L '(⌢φ⌢'et'⌢ψ⌢)' iff (f satisfies in L φ and f satisfies in L ψ).

C2. For any function f, for any sentence φ, f satisfies in L 'ce n'est pas le cas que'⌢φ iff it is not the case that f satisfies in L φ.

Q1. For any function f, for any variable v, f satisfies in L 'chaque'⌢v⌢':'⌢φ iff every f' that differs from f at most in what it assigns to v is such that f' satisfies in L φ.

T. For any sentence φ, φ is true in L iff for any function f, f satisfies in L φ.

From this theory, relative to an adequate logic in the metalanguage, we could prove, for example, (1). On the assumption that our axioms are using meta-language terms 'Russell', 'Frege', 'sees', 'and', 'it is not the case that', and 'every' alike in meaning with the object language terms they are used to give satisfaction conditions for, it is clear that in (1) the right-hand side translates the left. Thus, we can replace 'is true in L iff' with 'means that' to obtain (2) without loss of truth.

(1) 'Chaque x: x voit Russell' is true in L iff every x sees Russell;

(2) 'Chaque x: x voit Russell' means in L that every x sees Russell.

In fact, each 'minimal proof' of a sentence of the form of 's is true in L iff p' from the axioms will be one in which the right-hand side translates the sentence mentioned on the left. Knowledge of what the theory expresses and that it expresses it, together with the relevant knowledge about its axioms, puts us in a position to interpret any object-language sentence, on the basis of a proof that reveals how each term contributes to fixing the truth conditions of the sentence in which it appears. (See Lepore and Ludwig 2005, chapter 4; 2006, chapter 1, chapter 3, §7.)

RADICAL INTERPRETATION

At the same time that Davidson made his suggestion about how to pursue the goal of a compositional meaning theory by way of a truth theory, he suggested that it would suffice to know that a truth theory for a speaker was true to know that it met Convention *T*. While this is not plausible for a context-insensitive language, Davidson thought that modifying the form of the theory to accommodate context-sensitive elements would provide additional resolving power. The hope turned out to be misplaced (Lepore and Ludwig 2005, chapter 6), and he reformulated the requirement in 'Radical Interpretation' (1973, reprinted as Essay 10, this volume) as the truth theory's being confirmed from the standpoint of a radical interpreter (Lepore and Ludwig 2005, chapter 11).

This was inspired by Quine's approach to the philosophical study of language through the project of radical translation. The theme that links them is the idea that because language is by its nature an instrument for communication, meaning must be accessible from the public standpoint. However, there are some important differences between the two projects. Quine conceived of reflection on the project of radical translation as showing the way to constructing a scientifically respectable concept of meaning out of the concept of stimulus synonymy, which is characterized in terms of dispositions to verbal behaviour in response to patterns of physical stimulus. In contrast, Davidson conceived of the project of radical interpretation as aiming to illuminate the ordinary notion of meaning ('the task of a theory of meaning as I conceive it is not to change, improve, or reform a language, but to describe and understand it' ('Radical Interpretation', p. 184 below)), and keyed interpretation of another speaker not to proximal stimulus but to distal events in the environment that prompt a speaker to hold a sentence true. In addition, while the aim of the radical translator is to produce a translation manual, the aim of the radical interpreter is to produce an interpretation theory. For Davidson, this consists of a truth theory for the speaker's language. Davidson held that empirically confirming a truth theory for a speaker's language would give its theorems the status of natural laws, and that this together with the holistic constraints on theory confirmation and the requirement that we find the speaker to be largely rational would suffice for any confirmed theory to meet Convention *T*.

The interpreter aims to correlate when a speaker holds true an observation sentence with things going on in the speaker's environment, to arrive at sentences such as [HT].

[HT] *X* holds true *s* iff it is raining

To move beyond this correlation, the speaker must assume that the speaker is by and large right in his beliefs about his environment. Assuming that the condition we have identified is what his belief is about, and that he holds true *s* because he knows that it means that *p* and believes that *p*, we know that 'it is raining' translates *s*, and, thus, subject to correction in the light of further evidence, that [T1] is a target theorem of a truth theory that meets Convention *T*.

[T1] *s* is true in *X*'s language iff it is raining

The interpreter then formulates axioms for the constituents of *s* which have this as a consequence, and tests it against further observations, until theory and prediction coincide, compatibly with making the agent out to be as rational as possible. (We have ignored complications of tense here, see Lepore and Ludwig 2005, Chapter 5.)

The assumption that the speaker is largely rational and that most of his environmentally directed beliefs are true are two parts of the Principle of Charity. Davidson argues that Charity is not an option in interpretation but a constitutive feature of it. In later work he has called the first part of the Principle of Charity the Principle of Coherence and the second part the Principle of Correspondence (Davidson 1991; 2001*c*: 211c). The Principle of Coherence falls directly out of Davidson's work in the philosophy of action. We observed above that a central thesis of that work is that it is constitutive of the propositional attitudes that they present a largely rational pattern. The Principle of Correspondence is motivated directly by the assumption that

[t]he semantic features of language are public features. What no one can, in the nature of the case, figure out from the totality of the relevant evidence cannot be part of meaning. (Davidson 1979; 2001*b*: 235)

In this, we see the influence both of Quine and of Davidson's early work on experimental decision theory. The truth theory provides a formal structure which is interpreted in relation to the data to which it is applied. Quine's advocacy of the third-person standpoint as fundamental to understanding language motivates restricting the relevant data to that available to the radical interpreter. Given this, and that without the Principle of Correspondence, interpretation could not be possible, it must be treated, Davidson argues, as a constitutive principle of interpretation.

Conceptual Schemes, Knowledge of the World and Mind, the Reality of Language

The central role Davidson gives radical interpretation in understanding both language and thought is connected with a number of important theses Davidson has argued for, which are represented in this collection. These are (1) the view that there are no radically different conceptual schemes ('On the Very Idea of a Conceptual Scheme', 1974, reprinted as Essay 11, this volume); (2) the view that we cannot be massively mistaken about the external world because our beliefs are guaranteed to be largely true ('A Coherence Theory of Truth and Knowledge',

1983, reprinted as Essay 13, this volume); (3) the view that the source of our special authority about what we think is derived from constitutive principles of interpretation ('First Person Authority', 1984, reprinted as Essay 14, this volume); and (4) the view that a practice of using conventional meaning bearers is not essential to language ('A Nice Derangement of Epitaphs', 1986, reprinted as Essay 15, this volume). We provide a brief overview of these connections.

A conceptual scheme is a set of concepts with which a thinking being can operate. Davidson identifies different conceptual schemes with languages which cannot be intertranslated, or intertranslated to any significant extent. (This is motivated by Davidson's view that there is no genuine propositional thought without language; see Davidson 1975; 1982.) The question of whether there are radically different conceptual schemes is the question whether there can be languages which are not translatable into ours. The metaphors for conceptual relativism of this sort, which seek to make sense of different conceptual schemes, hold that conceptual schemes either organize or fit reality. The former metaphor fails because if different schemes organize the same thing differently, they must be capable of representing the same things organized, and so some translation between schemes is possible after all. The idea that conceptual schemes fit reality comes down to the idea that one can formulate true theories about the world in their terms. Thus, whether we can make sense of different conceptual schemes comes down to whether we can make sense of true theories not translatable into our language. However, Davidson argues that the best grip we have on truth derives from Tarski's Convention T, and that therefore there is no hope of making sense of truth in another language without finding translations into our own of its sentences. (See Lepore and Ludwig 2005, chapters 18 & 22 for further discussion.)

The argument against massive error can be seen as a byproduct of the Principle of Correspondence. For the Principle of Correspondence is supposed to be a principle constitutive of the interpreter's subject matter. For someone to be a speaker, he must be interpretable, and to be interpretable, he must be mostly right about his environment. Moreover, the interpreter in effect reads off from the conditions under which a speaker differentially holds true observation sentences what their contents are, and so what the contents of the beliefs are on which they are based. Thus, the contents of the speaker's beliefs are fixed by his pattern of causal interaction with his environment in such a way that the speaker must be largely right about it. This provides a transcendental argument then against an assumption of traditional skeptical arguments, namely, that it is logically possible for most of our beliefs about the world to be false. Given that most of our beliefs are true, to confirm any given one we may see how well it coheres with others. It is in this limited sense that we may say that Davidson offers a coherence theory of truth and knowledge: coherence is a *guide* to truth and a resource for justification, but it is not, on Davidson's view, what makes beliefs true, or justified. (See Lepore and Ludwig 2005, chapter 19 for further discussion.)

First person authority, understood as the presumption that when a speaker says what he thinks, he is right, derives likewise from the conditions on interpretation. Davidson argues that a necessary condition on success in interpretation is that the interpreter assume that the speaker knows what he means. His hold true attitudes are a vector of belief and knowledge of meaning. If the speaker did not know what he meant, even if his beliefs were true, what sentences he held true would not provide an entry into either his beliefs or his meanings. Thus, there is a presumption that derives from taking the stance of the interpreter toward another that the other is mostly right about what he means, though there is of course no such presumption about the interpreter. Therefore, other things being equal, the speaker is in a better position to infer what he believes from what he holds true. Since what the interpreter must assume as a condition on the possibility of success in interpretation is constitutive of his subject matter, first person authority is constitutive of speakers. There is perhaps a more straightforward argument to the same conclusion which avoids some questionable assumptions about Davidson's argument in 'First Person Authority'—for example the assumption that we should understand our knowledge of our psychological states as inferred from knowledge of the contents of hold true attitudes. The more straightforward argument is that it is a presumption of interpretation that the speaker knows what he believes because if he did not, then hold true attitudes could not function as evidence for target theorems of an interpretive truth theory.

In 'A Nice Derangement of Epitaphs' (1986, reprinted as Essay 15, this volume) Davidson argues for a thesis which has struck many philosophers as incompatible with his earlier views, namely, the thesis that 'there is no such thing as a language, not if a language is anything like what many philosophers and linguists have supposed' (p. 265). On the face of it, the goal of the radical interpreter is to confirm a truth theory for a speaker's language. But if there are no languages, he has no subject matter. However, the conflict is only apparent, for Davidson means something quite strong by a language in the above quotation, namely, a vocabulary and set of rules determined by conventions in a linguistic community which is mastered by members of the community and mastery of which is both necessary and sufficient for interpreting its speakers. His particular target is the idea that a speaker's meaning something by an expression depends on prior mastery of conventional rules in a community for the use of expressions. It is not that Davidson denies that there are conventional practices for the use of expressions which aid us in interpretation. He rather denies that these are essential for communication. What is essential for interpretation is that the speaker and interpreter arrive at a way of speaking and at a way of understanding that coincide. That prior learned conventions are not necessary for this falls out of taking the radical interpreter's stance as basic in understanding meaning and related matters. For what is essential for the interpreter is that he can impose on the entirety of a speaker's dispositions to verbal behavior a coherent interpretation, one that makes him out to be largely rational and a believer of the truth. Prior learned conventions are at best an epistemic aid to coming to a picture of what someone means and believes, dispensable in principle. (See Lepore and Ludwig 2005, chapter 17 for an extended discussion.)

Indirect Discourse and Metaphor

The two selections of the collection we have not discussed yet are 'On Saying That' and 'What Metaphors Mean.' The first is an investigation into the logical form of sentences of indirect discourse, such as (1).

(1) Galileo said that the earth moves.

The second is a particularly novel account of the way metaphors function. Both have been influential, and the first plays an important role in defense of Davidson's rejection of meanings—construed as entities—in the theory of meaning.

Indirect discourse presents a prima facie problem for an extensional truth theory of the sort that Davidson has sought to develop for natural languages, without the aid of appeal to propositions, properties, relations, or the like, because the truth of (1) is clearly sensitive not just to the referent of 'the earth' and the extension of 'moves', or the truth or falsity of 'the earth moves', but also to what 'the earth moves' means. Such sentences seem prima facie to be relational. A standard move is to treat them as relations to propositions, reified sentence meanings, which are denoted by expressions of the form 'that p'. Davidson argued, however, that this requires us to treat, as on Frege's view, the expressions in the complement as not having their customary meanings, and that this is intuitively incorrect.

If we could recover our pre-Fregean semantic innocence, I think it would seem to us plainly incredible that the words 'The Earth moves', uttered after the words 'Galileo said that', mean anything different, or refer to anything else, than is their wont when they come in other environments. . . . Language is the instrument it is because the same expression, with semantic features (meaning) unchanged, can serve countless purposes. (Davidson 1968: 2001, 108)

Davidson proposed an ingenious solution to the problem, namely, construing (1) as in effect two independent sentences, and 'that' as functioning like a demonstrative which refers in the context of utterance to the utterance of the second, which is not asserted. Since 'say' is an action verb, we can combine the analysis of action verbs with this suggestion and introduce a quantifier over an event of Galileo's uttering something: the truth of the first sentence in (2) below then requires that it be the same in content as the utterance of 'The earth moves', as in (3). (We press into different service than Davidson does a term he introduces as holding between speakers, namely, 'samesays', which we treat as holding between utterances when people may be said to have said the same thing in virtue of them.)

(2) Galileo said that. The earth moves.

(3) $(\exists u)$(uttered(Galileo, u) & samesays(u, that)). The earth moves.

In this way, we treat 'the earth moves' as having its usual meaning, and plausibly assign truth conditions to (1) that track the conditions under which we would judge it to be true or false.

Most theories of metaphor treat them as aiming to convey some information, either through a nonstandard meaning attaching to the metaphorical expressions, or through some propositions said to be pragmatically implied by the use of the metaphorical expressions in their contexts of use. What is novel about Davidson's account of metaphor is that it rejects both of these approaches. Davidson locates the function of metaphor instead in its ability to draw our attention to things the speaker wants us to see. When we attempt to paraphrase a metaphor, then, we are not giving its propositional content, but instead trying to say part of what it got us to see. When Melville says,

Bacon's brains were mere watch-maker's brains; but Christ was a chronometer; and the most exquisitely adjusted and exact one, and the least affected by all terrestrial jarrings, of any that have ever come to us.

he is not, on Davidson's view, attempting to convey some specific propositional content, but instead to get us to think about and compare the function of chronometers in navigation with the effect of Christ's teachings. A particular strength of Davidson's view is that it explains the openendedness of the best metaphors in a way its competitors cannot.

CONCLUDING REMARKS

This brings our introduction to this volume to a close. It is not meant to be a substitute for reading Davidson's essays, but an invitation to do so, and a guide and sort of map that helps to place them in relation to one another. Davidson's work is difficult. In breadth, influence, and interconnection of themes, Davidson's work has few rivals in the last 50 years in analytic philosophy. But this is remarkable because the essays that make up the bulk of his work are typically short and densely, if elegantly, written, and presuppose each other, as well as their technical and philosophical background. To gain an appreciation of his work one must read the essays as in effect a single work, seeing each in the light of the others. In the end, there emerges a systematic picture of man as a rational linguistic animal whose thoughts, though not reducible to the material, are part of the physical fabric of the world, and whose knowledge of his own mind, the minds of others, and of the world around him is as fundamental to his nature as the power of thought and speech itself.

BIBLIOGRAPHY

DAVIDSON, D. (1965). 'Theories of Meaning and Learnable Languages'. Reprinted in Davidson 2001*b*: 3–17.

—— (1971). 'Agency', in Binkley, Bronaugh, and Marras, eds, *Agent, Action, and Reason* (Toronto: University of Toronto Press, pp. 3–37). (Reprinted in Davidson 2001*a*: 43–61.)

—— (1975). 'Thought and Talk', in S. Guttenplan, ed., *Mind and Language* (Oxford: Oxford University Press). (Reprinted in Davidson 2001*b*: 155–70.)

—— (1979)). 'The Inscrutability of Reference', *The Southwest Journal of Philosophy* 10: 7–20. (Reprinted in Davidson 2001*b*: 227–41.)

—— (2001 (1982)). 'Rational Animals', *Dialectica*, 36: 317–28. (Reprinted in Davidson 2001*c*: 95–106.)

—— (1985). 'Reply to Quine on Events', in E. Lepore, ed., *Actions and Events: Perspectives on the Philosophy of Donald Davidson* (Oxford: Blackwell, pp. 173–6). (Reprinted in Davidson 2001*a*: 305–11.)

—— (1990). *Plato's Philebus*. New York: Garland.

—— (1991). 'Three Varieties of Knowledge', in A. P. Griffiths, ed., *A J Ayer: Memorial Essays* (New York: Cambridge University Press). (Reprinted in Davidson 2001*c*: 205–20).

—— (1999). 'Intellectual Autobiography of Donald Davidson', in L. E. Hahn, ed., *The Philosophy of Donald Davidson* (Chicago, IL: Open Court, pp. 3–70).

—— (2001*a*). *Essays on Actions and Events*, 2nd edn. (Oxford: Oxford University Press).

—— (2001*b*). *Inquiries into Truth and Interpretation*, 2nd edn. (Oxford: Oxford University Press Press).

—— (2001*c*). *Subjective, Intersubjective, Objective* (Oxford: Oxford University Press).

—— (2004). *Problems of Rationality* (Oxford: Oxford University Press).

—— (2005). *Truth, Language, and History* (Oxford: Oxford University Press).

—— and P. SUPPES (1957). *Decision Making: An Experimental Approach* (Stanford, CA: Stanford University Press).

LEPORE, E., and K. LUDWIG (2005). *Donald Davidson: Truth, Meaning, Language and Reality* (Oxford: Oxford University Press).

—— (2006). *Donald Davidson: Truth-Theoretic Semantics.* (Oxford: Oxford University Press).

QUINE, W. V. O. (1985). 'Events and Reification', in E. Lepore, ed., *Actions and Events: Perspectives on the Philosophy of Donald Davidson* (Oxford: Blackwell, pp. 162–71).

TARSKI, A. (1944). 'The Semantic Conception of Truth and the Foundations of Semantics', *Philosophy and Phenomenological Research*, 4: 341–76.

—— (1983 (1934)). 'The Concept of Truth in Formalized Languages', in *Logic, Semantics, Metamathematics*, 2nd edn. (Indianapolis: Hackett Publishing Company).

PHILOSOPHY OF ACTION AND PSYCHOLOGY

1

Actions, Reasons, and Causes

What is the relation between a reason and an action when the reason explains the action by giving the agent's reason for doing what he did? We may call such explanations *rationalizations*, and say that the reason *rationalizes* the action.

In this paper I want to defend the ancient—and commonsense—position that rationalization is a species of causal explanation. The defence no doubt requires some redeployment, but it does not seem necessary to abandon the position, as has been urged by many recent writers.[1]

I

A reason rationalizes an action only if it leads us to see something the agent saw, or thought he saw, in his action—some feature, consequence, or aspect of the action the agent wanted, desired, prized, held dear, thought dutiful, beneficial, obligatory, or agreeable. We cannot explain why someone did what he did simply by saying the particular action appealed to him; we must indicate what it was about the action that appealed. Whenever someone does something for a reason, therefore, he can be characterized as (*a*) having some sort of pro attitude toward actions of a certain kind, and (*b*) believing (or knowing, perceiving, noticing, remembering) that his action is of that kind. Under (*a*) are to be included desires, wantings, urges, promptings, and a great variety of moral views, aesthetic principles, economic prejudices, social conventions, and public and private goals and values in so far as these can be interpreted as attitudes of an agent directed toward actions of a certain kind. The word 'attitude' does yeoman service here, for it must cover not only permanent character traits that show themselves in a lifetime of behaviour, like love of children or a taste for loud company, but also the most passing fancy that prompts a unique action, like a sudden desire to touch a woman's elbow. In general, pro attitudes must not be taken for convictions,

---

[1] Some examples: Gilbert Ryle, *The Concept of Mind*, G. E. M. Anscombe, *Intention*, Stuart Hampshire, *Thought and Action*, H. L. A. Hart and A. M. Honoré, *Causation in the Law*, William Dray, *Laws and Explanation in History*, and most of the books in the series edited by R. F. Holland, *Studies in Philosophical Psychology*, including Anthony Kenny, *Action, Emotion and Will*, and A. I. Melden, *Free Action*. Page references in parentheses are to these works.

however temporary, that every action of a certain kind ought to be performed, is worth performing, or is, all things considered, desirable. On the contrary, a man may all his life have a yen, say, to drink a can of paint, without ever, even at the moment he yields, believing it would be worth doing.

Giving the reason why an agent did something is often a matter of naming the pro attitude (*a*) or the related belief (*b*) or both; let me call this pair the *primary reason* why the agent performed the action. Now it is possible both to reformulate the claim that rationalizations are causal explanations and to give structure to the argument by stating two theses about primary reasons:

1. In order to understand how a reason of any kind rationalizes an action it is necessary and sufficient that we see, at least in essential outline, how to construct a primary reason.
2. The primary reason for an action is its cause.

I shall argue for these points in turn.

II

I flip the switch, turn on the light, and illuminate the room. Unbeknownst to me I also alert a prowler to the fact that I am home. Here I need not have done four things, but only one, of which four descriptions have been given.[2] I flipped the switch because I wanted to turn on the light and by saying I wanted to turn on the light I explain (give my reason for, rationalize) the flipping. But I do not, by giving this reason, rationalize my alerting of the prowler nor my illuminating of the room. Since reasons may rationalize what someone does when it is described in one way and not when it is described in another, we cannot treat what was done simply as a term in sentences like 'My reason for flipping the switch was that I wanted to turn on the light'; otherwise we would be forced to conclude,

---

[2] We might not call my unintentional alerting of the prowler an action, but it should not be inferred from this that alerting the prowler is therefore something different from flipping the switch, say just its consequence. Actions, performances, and events not involving intention are alike in that they are often referred to or defined partly in terms of some terminal stage, outcome, or consequence.

The word 'action' does not very often occur in ordinary speech, and when it does it is usually reserved for fairly portentous occasions. I follow a useful philosophical practice in calling anything an agent does intentionally an action, including intentional omissions. What is really needed is some suitably generic term to bridge the following gap: suppose '*A*' is a description of an action, '*B*' is a description of something done voluntarily, though not intentionally, and '*C*' is a description of something done involuntarily and unintentionally; finally, suppose *A* = *B* = *C*. Then *A*, *B*, and *C* are the same—what? 'Action', 'event', 'thing done', each have, at least in some contexts, a strange ring when coupled with the wrong sort of description. Only the question, 'Why did you (he) do *A*?' has the true generality required. Obviously, the problem is greatly aggravated if we assume, as Melden does, that an action ('raising one's arm') can be identical with a bodily movement ('one's arm going up').

from the fact that flipping the switch was identical with alerting the prowler, that my reason for alerting the prowler was that I wanted to turn on the light. Let us mark this quasi-intensional[3] character of action descriptions in rationalizations by stating a bit more precisely a necessary condition for primary reasons:

C1. *R* is a primary reason why an agent performed the action *A* under the description *d* only if *R* consists of a pro attitude of the agent towards actions with a certain property, and a belief of the agent that *A*, under the description *d*, has that property.

How can my wanting to turn on the light be (part of) a primary reason, since it appears to lack the required element of generality? We may be taken in by the verbal parallel between 'I turned on the light' and 'I wanted to turn on the light'. The first clearly refers to a particular event, so we conclude that the second has this same event as its object. Of course it is obvious that the event of my turning on the light can't be referred to in the same way by both sentences since the existence of the event is required by the truth of 'I turned on the light' but not by the truth of 'I wanted to turn on the light'. If the reference were the same in both cases, the second sentence would entail the first; but in fact the sentences are logically independent. What is less obvious, at least until we attend to it, is that the event whose occurrence makes 'I turned on the light' true cannot be called the object, however intentional, of 'I wanted to turn on the light'. If I turned on the light, then I must have done it at a precise moment, in a particular way—every detail is fixed. But it makes no sense to demand that my want be directed to an action performed at any one moment or done in some unique manner. Any one of an indefinitely large number of actions would satisfy the want and can be considered equally eligible as its object. Wants and desires often are trained on physical objects. However, 'I want that gold watch in the window' is not a primary reason and explains why I went into the store only because it suggests a primary reason—for example, that I wanted to buy the watch.

Because 'I wanted to turn on the light' and 'I turned on the light' are logically independent, the first can be used to give a reason why the second is true. Such a reason gives minimal information: it implies that the action was intentional, and wanting tends to exclude some other pro attitudes, such as a sense of duty or obligation. But the exclusion depends very much on the action and the context of explanation. Wanting seems pallid beside lusting, but it would be odd to deny that someone who lusted after a woman or a cup of coffee wanted her or it. It is not unnatural, in fact, to treat wanting as a genus including all pro attitudes as species. When we do this and when we know some action is intentional, it is easy

---

[3] 'Quasi-intentional' because, besides its intentional aspect, the description of the action must also refer in rationalizations; otherwise it could be true that an action was done for a certain reason and yet the action not have been performed. Compare 'the author of *Waverley*' in 'George IV knew the author of Waverley wrote *Waverley*'. This semantical feature of action descriptions is discussed further in Essay 2.

to answer the question, 'Why did you do it?' with, 'For no reason', meaning not that there is no reason but that there is no *further* reason, no reason that cannot be inferred from the fact that the action was done intentionally; no reason, in other words, besides wanting to do it. This last point is not essential to the present argument, but it is of interest because it defends the possibility of defining an intentional action as one done for a reason.

A primary reason consists of a belief and an attitude, but it is generally otiose to mention both. If you tell me you are easing the jib because you think that will stop the main from backing, I don't need to be told that you want to stop the main from backing; and if you say you are biting your thumb at me because you want to insult me, there is no point in adding that you think that by biting your thumb at me you will insult me. Similarly, many explanations of actions in terms of reasons that are not primary do not require mention of the primary reason to complete the story. If I say I am pulling weeds because I want a beautiful lawn, it would be fatuous to eke out the account with, 'And so I see something desirable in any action that does, or has a good chance of, making the lawn beautiful'. Why insist that there is any *step*, logical or psychological, in the transfer of desire from an end that is not an action to the actions one conceives as means? It serves the argument as well that the desired end explains the action only if what are believed by the agent to be means are desired.

Fortunately, it is not necessary to classify and analyse the many varieties of emotions, sentiments, moods, motives, passions, and hungers whose mention may answer the question, 'Why did you do it?' in order to see how, when such mention rationalizes the action, a primary reason is involved. Claustrophobia gives a man's reason for leaving a cocktail party because we know people want to avoid, escape from, be safe from, put distance between themselves and what they fear. Jealousy is the motive in a poisoning because, among other things, the poisoner believes his action will harm his rival, remove the cause of his agony, or redress an injustice, and these are the sorts of things a jealous man wants to do. When we learn that a man cheated his son out of greed, we do not necessarily know what the primary reason was, but we know there was one, and its general nature. Ryle analyses 'he boasted from vanity' into 'he boasted on meeting the stranger and his doing so satisfies the lawlike proposition that whenever he finds a chance of securing the admiration and envy of others, he does whatever he thinks will produce this admiration and envy' (89). This analysis is often, and perhaps justly, criticized on the ground that a man may boast from vanity just once. But if Ryle's boaster did what he did from vanity, then something entailed by Ryle's analysis is true: the boaster wanted to secure the admiration and envy of others, and he believed that his action would produce this admiration and envy; true or false, Ryle's analysis does not dispense with primary reasons, but depends upon them.

To know a primary reason why someone acted as he did is to know an intention with which the action was done. If I turn left at the fork because I want to get to Katmandu, my intention in turning left is to get to Katmandu. But to know the intention is not necessarily to know the primary reason in full detail. If James goes to church with the intention of pleasing his mother, then he must have some pro attitude toward pleasing his mother, but it needs more information to tell whether his reason is that he enjoys pleasing his mother, or thinks it right, his duty, or an obligation. The expression 'the intention with which James went to church' has the outward form of a description, but in fact it is syncategorematic and cannot be taken to refer to an entity, state, disposition, or event. Its function in context is to generate new descriptions of actions in terms of their reasons; thus 'James went to church with the intention of pleasing his mother' yields a new, and fuller, description of the action described in 'James went to church'. Essentially the same process goes on when I answer the question, 'Why are you bobbing around that way?' with, 'I'm knitting, weaving, exercising, sculling, cuddling, training fleas'.

Straight description of an intended result often explains an action better than stating that the result was intended or desired. 'It will soothe your nerves' explains why I pour you a shot as efficiently as 'I want to do something to soothe your nerves', since the first in the context of explanation implies the second; but the first does better, because, if it is true, the facts will justify my choice of action. Because justifying and explaining an action so often go hand in hand, we frequently indicate the primary reason for an action by making a claim which, if true, would also verify, vindicate, or support the relevant belief or attitude of the agent. 'I knew I ought to return it', 'The paper said it was going to snow', 'You stepped on *my* toes', all, in appropriate reason-giving contexts, perform this familiar dual function.

The justifying role of a reason, given this interpretation, depends upon the explanatory role, but the converse does not hold. Your stepping on my toes neither explains nor justifies my stepping on your toes unless I believe you stepped on my toes, but the belief alone, true or false, explains my action.

III

In the light of a primary reason, an action is revealed as coherent with certain traits, long- or short-termed, characteristic or not, of the agent, and the agent is shown in his role of Rational Animal. Corresponding to the belief and attitude of a primary reason for an action, we can always construct (with a little ingenuity) the premises of a syllogism from which it follows that the action has some (as Anscombe calls it) 'desirability characteristic'.[4] Thus there is a certain

---

[4] Anscombe denies that the practical syllogism is deductive. This she does partly because she thinks of the practical syllogism, as Aristotle does, as corresponding to a piece of practical reasoning (whereas for me it is only part of the analysis of the concept of a reason with which someone acted),

irreducible—though somewhat anaemic—sense in which every rationalization justifies: from the agent's point of view there was, when he acted, something to be said for the action.

Noting that nonteleological causal explanations do not display the element of justification provided by reasons, some philosophers have concluded that the concept of cause that applies elsewhere cannot apply to the relation between reasons and actions, and that the pattern of justification provides, in the case of reasons, the required explanation. But suppose we grant that reasons alone justify actions in the course of explaining them; it does not follow that the explanation is not also—and necessarily—causal. Indeed our first condition for primary reasons (C1) is designed to help set rationalizations apart from other sorts of explanation. If rationalization is, as I want to argue, a species of causal explanation, then justification, in the sense given by C1, is at least one differentiating property. How about the other claim: that justifying is a kind of explaining, so that the ordinary notion of cause need not be brought in? Here it is necessary to decide what is being included under justification. It could be taken to cover only what is called for by C1: that the agent have certain beliefs and attitudes in the light of which the action is reasonable. But then something essential has certainly been left out, for a person can have a reason for an action, and perform the action, and yet this reason not be the reason why he did it. Central to the relation between a reason and an action it explains is the idea that the agent performed the action *because* he had the reason. Of course, we can include this idea too in justification; but then the notion of justification becomes as dark as the notion of reason until we can account for the force of that 'because'.

When we ask why someone acted as he did, we want to be provided with an interpretation. His behaviour seems strange, alien, outré, pointless, out of character, disconnected; or perhaps we cannot even recognize an action in it. When we learn his reason, we have an interpretation, a new description of what he did, which fits it into a familiar picture. The picture includes some of the agent's beliefs and attitudes; perhaps also goals, ends, principles, general character traits, virtues or vices. Beyond this, the redescription of an action afforded by a reason may place the action in a wider social, economic, linguistic, or evaluative context. To learn, through learning the reason, that the agent conceived his action as a lie, a repayment of a debt, an insult, the fulfilment of an avuncular obligation, or a knight's gambit is to grasp the point of the action in its setting of rules, practices, conventions, and expectations.

Remarks like these, inspired by the later Wittgenstein, have been elaborated with subtlety and insight by a number of philosophers. And there is no denying that this is true: when we explain an action, by giving the reason, we do redescribe

and therefore she is bound, again following Aristotle, to think of the conclusion of a practical syllogism as corresponding to a judgement, not merely that the action has a desirable characteristic, but that the action is desirable (reasonable, worth doing, etc.). Practical reasoning is discussed further in Essay 3.

the action; redescribing the action gives the action a place in a pattern, and in this way the action is explained. Here it is tempting to draw two conclusions that do not follow. First, we can't infer, from the fact that giving reasons merely redescribes the action and that causes are separate from effects, that therefore reasons are not causes. Reasons, being beliefs and attitudes, are certainly not identical with actions; but, more important, events are often redescribed in terms of their causes. (Suppose someone was injured. We could redescribe this event 'in terms of a cause' by saying he was burned.) Second, it is an error to think that, because placing the action in a larger pattern explains it, therefore we now understand the sort of explanation involved. Talk of patterns and contexts does not answer the question of how reasons explain actions, since the relevant pattern or context contains both reason and action. One way we can explain an event is by placing it in the context of its cause; cause and effect form the sort of pattern that explains the effect, in a sense of 'explain' that we understand as well as any. If reason and action illustrate a different pattern of explanation, that pattern must be identified.

Let me urge the point in connection with an example of Melden's. A man driving an automobile raises his arm in order to signal. His intention, to signal, explains his action, raising his arm, by redescribing it as signalling. What is the pattern that explains the action? Is it the familiar pattern of an action done for a reason? Then it does indeed explain the action, but only because it assumes the relation of reason and action that we want to analyse. Or is the pattern rather this: the man is driving, he is approaching a turn; he knows he ought to signal; he knows how to signal, by raising his arm. And now, in this context, he raises his arm. Perhaps, as Melden suggests, if all this happens, he does signal. And the explanation would then be this; if, under these conditions, a man raises his arm, then he signals. The difficulty is, of course, that this explanation does not touch the question of why he raised his arm. He had a reason to raise his arm, but this has not been shown to be the reason why he did it. If the description 'signalling' explains his action by giving his reason, then the signalling must be intentional; but, on the account just given, it may not be.

If, as Melden claims, causal explanations are 'wholly irrelevant to the understanding we seek' of human action (184) then we are without an analysis of the 'because' in 'He did it because . . .', where we go on to name a reason. Hampshire remarks, of the relation between reasons and action, 'In philosophy one ought surely to find this . . . connection altogether mysterious' (166). Hampshire rejects Aristotle's attempt to solve the mystery by introducing the concept of wanting as a causal factor, on the grounds that the resulting theory is too clear and definite to fit all cases and that, 'There is still no compelling ground for insisting that the word "want" *must* enter into every full statement of reasons for acting' (168). I agree that the concept of wanting is too narrow, but I have argued that, at least in a vast number of typical cases, some pro attitude must be assumed to be present if a statement of an agent's reasons in acting is to be intelligible. Hampshire does not see how Aristotle's scheme can be appraised as true or false, 'for it is not clear what could be the basis of assessment, or what kind of evidence could be decisive' (167). But I would urge that, failing a satisfactory alternative, the best argument for a scheme like Aristotle's is that it alone promises to give an account of the 'mysterious connection' between reasons and actions.

IV

In order to turn the first 'and' to 'because' in 'He exercised *and* he wanted to reduce and thought exercise would do it', we must, as the basic move,[5] augment condition C1 with:

>   C2. A primary reason for an action is its cause.

The considerations in favour of C2 are by now, I hope, obvious; in the remainder of this paper I wish to defend C2 against various lines of attack and, in the process, to clarify the notion of causal explanation involved.

A. The first line of attack is this. Primary reasons consist of attitudes and beliefs, which are states or dispositions, not events; therefore they cannot be causes.

It is easy to reply that states, dispositions, and conditions are frequently named as the causes of events: the bridge collapsed because of a structural defect; the plane crashed on takeoff because the air temperature was abnormally high; the plate broke because it had a crack. This reply does not, however, meet a closely related point. Mention of a causal condition for an event gives a cause only on the assumption that there was also a preceding event. But what is the preceding event that causes an action?

In many cases it is not difficult at all to find events very closely associated with the primary reason. States and dispositions are not events, but the onslaught of a state or disposition is. A desire to hurt your feelings may spring up at the moment you anger me; I may start wanting to eat a melon just when I see one; and beliefs may begin at the moment we notice, perceive, learn, or remember something. Those who have argued that there are no mental events to qualify as causes of actions have often missed the obvious because they have insisted that a mental event be observed or noticed (rather than an observing or a noticing) or that it be like a stab, a qualm, a prick or a quiver, a mysterious prod of conscience or act of the will. Melden, in discussing the driver who signals a turn by raising his arm, challenges those who want to explain actions causally to identify 'an event which is common and peculiar to all such cases' (87), perhaps a motive or an intention,

---

[5] I say 'as the basic move' to cancel any suggestion that C1 and C2 are jointly *sufficient* to define the relation of reasons to the actions they explain.

anyway 'some particular feeling or experience' (95). But of course there is a mental event; at some moment the driver noticed (or thought he noticed) his turn coming up, and that is the moment he signalled. During any continuing activity, like driving, or elaborate performance, like swimming the Hellespont, there are more or less fixed purposes, standards, desires, and habits that give direction and form to the entire enterprise, and there is the continuing input of information about what we are doing, about changes in the environment, in terms of which we regulate and adjust our actions. To dignify a driver's awareness that his turn has come by calling it an experience, or even a feeling, is no doubt exaggerated, but whether it deserves a name or not, it had better be the reason why he raises his arm. In this case, and typically, there may not be anything we would call a motive, but if we mention such a general purpose as wanting to get to one's destination safely, it is clear that the motive is not an event. The intention with which the driver raises his arm is also not an event, for it is no thing at all, neither event, attitude, disposition, nor object. Finally, Melden asks the causal theorist to find an event that is common and peculiar to all cases where a man intentionally raises his arm, and this, it must be admitted, cannot be produced. But then neither can a common and unique cause of bridge failures, plane crashes, or plate breakings be produced.

The signalling driver can answer the question, 'Why did you raise your arm when you did?', and from the answer we learn the event that caused the action. But can an actor always answer such a question? Sometimes the answer will mention a mental event that does not give a reason: 'Finally I made up my mind.' However, there also seem to be cases of intentional action where we cannot explain at all why we acted when we did. In such cases, explanation in terms of primary reasons parallels the explanation of the collapse of the bridge from a structural defect: we are ignorant of the event or sequence of events that led up to (caused) the collapse, but we are sure there was such an event or sequence of events.

B. According to Melden, a cause must be 'logically distinct from the alleged effect' (52); but a reason for an action is not logically distinct from the action; therefore, reasons are not causes of actions.[6]

One possible form of this argument has already been suggested. Since a reason makes an action intelligible by redescribing it, we do not have two events, but only one under different descriptions. Causal relations, however, demand distinct events.

Someone might be tempted into the mistake of thinking that my flipping of the switch caused my turning on of the light (in fact it caused the light to go on). But it does not follow that it is a mistake to take, 'My reason for flipping the switch was that I wanted to turn on the light' as entailing, in part, 'I flipped the switch, and

---

[6] This argument can be found in one or more versions, in Kenny, Hampshire, and Melden, as well as in P. Winch, *The Idea of a Social Science*, and R. S. Peters, *The Concept of Motivation*. In one of its forms, the argument was of course inspired by Ryle's treatment of motives in *The Concept of Mind*.

this action is further describable as having been caused by wanting to turn on the light'. To describe an event in terms of its cause is not to confuse the event with its cause, nor does explanation by redescription exclude causal explanation.

The example serves also to refute the claim that we cannot describe the action without using words that link it to the alleged cause. Here the action is to be explained under the description: 'my flipping the switch', and the alleged cause is 'my wanting to turn on the light'. What relevant logical relation is supposed to hold between these phrases? It seems more plausible to urge a logical link between 'my turning on the light' and 'my wanting to turn on the light', but even here the link turns out, on inspection, to be grammatical rather than logical.

In any case there is something very odd in the idea that causal relations are empirical rather than logical. What can this mean? Surely not that every true causal statement is empirical. For suppose 'A caused B' is true. Then the cause of $B = A$; so substituting, we have 'The cause of B caused B', which is analytic. The truth of a causal statement depends on *what* events are described; its status as analytic or synthetic depends on *how* the events are described. Still, it may be maintained that a reason rationalizes an action only when the descriptions are appropriately fixed, and the appropriate descriptions are not logically independent.

Suppose that to say a man wanted to turn on the light *meant* that he would perform any action he believed would accomplish his end. Then the statement of his primary reason for flipping the switch would entail that he flipped the switch—'straightway he acts', as Aristotle says. In this case there would certainly be a logical connection between reason and action, the same sort of connection as that between, 'It's water-soluble and was placed in water' and 'It dissolved'. Since the implication runs from description of cause to description of effect but not conversely, naming the cause still gives information. And, though the point is often overlooked, 'Placing it in water caused it to dissolve' does not entail 'It's water-soluble'; so the latter has additional explanatory force. Nevertheless, the explanation would be far more interesting if, in place of solubility, with its obvious definitional connection with the event to be explained, we could refer to some property, say a particular crystalline structure, whose connection with dissolution in water was known only through experiment. Now it is clear why primary reasons like desires and wants do not explain actions in the relatively trivial way solubility explains dissolvings. Solubility, we are assuming, is a pure disposition property: it is defined in terms of a single test. But desires cannot be defined in terms of the actions they may rationalize, even though the relation between desire and action is not simply empirical; there are other, equally essential criteria for desires—their expression in feelings and in actions that they do not rationalize, for example. The person who has a desire (or want or belief) does not normally need criteria at all—he generally knows, even in the absence of any clues available to others, what he wants, desires, and believes. These logical features of primary reasons show that it is not just lack of ingenuity that keeps us from defining them as dispositions to act for these reasons.

C. According to Hume, 'we may define a cause to be an object, followed by another, and where all the objects similar to the first are followed by objects similar to the second'. But, Hart and Honoré claim, 'The statement that one person did something because, for example, another threatened him, carries no implication or covert assertion that if the circumstances were repeated the same action would follow' (52). Hart and Honoré allow that Hume is right in saying that ordinary singular causal statements imply generalizations, but wrong for this very reason in supposing that motives and desires are ordinary causes of actions. In brief, laws are involved essentially in ordinary causal explanations, but not in rationalizations.

It is common to try to meet this argument by suggesting that we do have rough laws connecting reasons and actions, and these can, in theory, be improved. True, threatened people do not always respond in the same way; but we may distinguish between threats and also between agents, in terms of their beliefs and attitudes.

The suggestion is delusive, however, because generalizations connecting reasons and actions are not—and cannot be sharpened into—the kind of law on the basis of which accurate predictions can reliably be made. If we reflect on the way in which reasons determine choice, decision, and behaviour, it is easy to see why this is so. What emerges, in the *ex post facto* atmosphere of explanation and justification, as *the* reason frequently was, to the agent at the time of action, one consideration among many, *a* reason. Any serious theory for predicting action on the basis of reasons must find a way of evaluating the relative force of various desires and beliefs in the matrix of decision; it cannot take as its starting point the refinement of what is to be expected from a single desire. The practical syllogism exhausts its role in displaying an action as falling under one reason; so it cannot be subtilized into a reconstruction of practical reasoning, which involves the weighing of competing reasons. The practical syllogism provides a model neither for a predictive science of action nor for a normative account of evaluative reasoning.

Ignorance of competent predictive laws does not inhibit valid causal explanation, or few causal explanations could be made. I am certain the window broke because it was struck by a rock—I saw it all happen; but I am not (is anyone?) in command of laws on the basis of which I can predict what blows will break which windows. A generalization like, 'Windows are fragile, and fragile things tend to break when struck hard enough, other conditions being right' is not a predictive law in the rough—the predictive law, if we had it, would be quantitative and would use very different concepts. The generalization, like our generalizations about behaviour, serves a different function: it provides evidence for the existence of a causal law covering the case at hand.[7]

We are usually far more certain of a singular causal connection than we are of any causal law governing the case; does this show that Hume was wrong in

---

[7] Essay 5 discusses the issues of this paragraph and the one before it.

claiming that singular causal statements entail laws? Not necessarily, for Hume's claim, as quoted above, is ambiguous. It may mean that '*A* caused *B*' entails some particular law involving the predicates used in the descriptions '*A*' and '*B*', or it may mean that '*A* caused *B*' entails that there exists a causal law instantiated by some true descriptions of *A* and *B*.[8] Obviously, both versions of Hume's doctrine give a sense to the claim that singular causal statements entail laws, and both sustain the view that causal explanations 'involve laws'. But the second version is far weaker, in that no particular law is entailed by a singular causal claim, and a singular causal claim can be defended, if it needs defence, without defending any law. Only the second version of Hume's doctrine can be made to fit with most causal explanations; it suits rationalizations equally well.

The most primitive explanation of an event gives its cause; more elaborate explanations may tell more of the story, or defend the singular causal claim by producing a relevant law or by giving reasons for believing such exists. But it is an error to think no explanation has been given until a law has been produced. Linked with these errors is the idea that singular causal statements necessarily indicate, by the concepts they employ, the concepts that will occur in the entailed law. Suppose a hurricane, which is reported on page 5 of Tuesday's *Times*, causes a catastrophe, which is reported on page 13 of Wednesday's *Tribune*. Then the event reported on page 5 of Tuesday's *Times* caused the event reported on page 13 of Wednesday's *Tribune*. Should we look for a law relating events of these *kinds?* It is only slightly less ridiculous to look for a law relating hurricanes and catastrophes. The laws needed to predict the catastrophe with precision would, of course, have no use for concepts like hurricane and catastrophe. The trouble with predicting the weather is that the descriptions under which events interest us—'a cool, cloudy day with rain in the afternoon'—have only remote connections with the concepts employed by the more precise known laws.

The laws whose existence is required if reasons are causes of actions do not, we may be sure, deal in the concepts in which rationalizations must deal. If the causes of a class of events (actions) fall in a certain class (reasons) and there is a law to back each singular causal statement, it does not follow that there is any law connecting events classified as reasons with events classified as actions—the classifications may even be neurological, chemical, or physical.

D. It is said that the kind of knowledge one has of one's own reasons in acting is not compatible with the existence of a causal relation between reasons and actions: a person knows his own intentions in acting infallibly, without induction

---

[8] We could roughly characterize the analysis of singular causal statements hinted at here as follows: '*A* caused *B*' is true if and only if there are descriptions of *A* and *B* such that the sentence obtained by putting these descriptions for '*A*' and '*B*' in '*A* caused *B*' follows from a true causal law. This analysis is saved from triviality by the fact that not all true generalizations are causal laws; causal laws are distinguished (though of course this is no analysis) by the fact that they are inductively confirmed by their instances and by the fact that they support counterfactual and subjunctive singular causal statements.

or observation, and no ordinary causal relation can be known in this way. No doubt our knowledge of our own intentions in acting will show many of the oddities peculiar to first-person knowledge of one's own pains, beliefs, desires, and so on; the only question is whether these oddities prove that reasons do not cause, in any ordinary sense at least, the actions that they rationalize.

You may easily be wrong about the truth of a statement of the form 'I am poisoning Charles because I want to save him pain', because you may be wrong about whether you are poisoning Charles—you may yourself be drinking the poisoned cup by mistake. But it also seems that you may err about your reasons, particularly when you have two reasons for an action, one of which pleases you and one which does not. For example, you do want to save Charles pain; you also want him out of the way. You may be wrong about which motive made you do it.

The fact that you may be wrong does not show that in general it makes sense to ask you how you know what your reasons were or to ask for your evidence. Though you may, on rare occasions, accept public or private evidence as showing you are wrong about your reasons, you usually have no evidence and make no observations. Then your knowledge of your own reasons for your actions is not generally inductive, for where there is induction, there is evidence. Does this show the knowledge is not causal? I cannot see that it does.

Causal laws differ from true but nonlawlike generalizations in that their instances confirm them; induction is, therefore, certainly a good way to learn the truth of a law. It does not follow that it is the only way to learn the truth of a law. In any case, in order to know that a singular causal statement is true, it is not necessary to know the truth of a law; it is necessary only to know that some law covering the events at hand exists. And it is far from evident that induction, and induction alone, yields the knowledge that a causal law satisfying certain conditions exists. Or, to put it differently, one case is often enough, as Hume admitted, to persuade us that a law exists, and this amounts to saying that we are persuaded without direct inductive evidence, that a causal relation exists.

E. Finally I should like to say something about a certain uneasiness some philosophers feel in speaking of causes of actions at all. Melden, for example, says that actions are often identical with bodily movements, and that bodily movements have causes; yet he denies that the causes are causes of the actions. This is, I think, a contradiction. He is led to it by the following sort of consideration: 'It is futile to attempt to explain conduct through the causal efficacy of desire—all *that* can explain is further happenings, not actions performed by agents. The agent confronting the causal nexus in which such happenings occur is a helpless victim of all that occurs in and to him' (128, 129). Unless I am mistaken, this argument, if it were valid, would show that actions cannot have causes at all. I shall not point out the obvious difficulties in removing actions from the realm of causality entirely. But perhaps it is worth trying to uncover the source of the trouble. Why on earth should a cause turn an action into a mere happening and a person into a helpless victim? Is it because we tend to assume, at least in the arena of action, that a cause demands a causer, agency an agent? So we press the question; if my action is caused, what caused it? If I did, then there is the absurdity of infinite regress; if I did not, I am a victim. But of course the alternatives are not exhaustive. Some causes have no agents. Among these agentless causes are the states and changes of state in persons which, because they are reasons as well as causes, constitute certain events free and intentional actions.

2

The Logical Form of
Action Sentences

Strange goings on! Jones did it slowly, deliberately, in the bathroom, with a knife, at midnight. What he did was butter a piece of toast. We are too familiar with the language of action to notice at first an anomaly: the 'it' of 'Jones did it slowly, deliberately, . . .' seems to refer to some entity, presumably an action, that is then characterized in a number of ways. Asked for the logical form of this sentence, we might volunteer something like, 'There is an action x such that Jones did x slowly and Jones did x deliberately and Jones did x in the bathroom, . . .' and so on. But then we need an appropriate singular term to substitute for 'x'. In fact we know Jones buttered a piece of toast. And, allowing a little slack, we can substitute for 'x' and get 'Jones buttered a piece of toast slowly and Jones buttered a piece of toast deliberately and Jones buttered a piece of toast in the bathroom . . .' and so on. The trouble is that we have nothing here we would ordinarily recognize as a singular term. Another sign that we have not caught the logical form of the sentence is that in this last version there is no implication that any *one* action was slow, deliberate, and in the bathroom, though this is clearly part of what is meant by the original.

The present Essay is devoted to trying to get the logical form of simple sentences about actions straight. I would like to give an account of the logical or grammatical role of the parts or words of such sentences that is consistent with the entailment relations between such sentences and with what is known of the role of those same parts or words in other (non-action) sentences. I take this enterprise to be the same as showing how the meanings of action sentences depend on their structure. I am not concerned with the meaning analysis of logically simple expressions in so far as this goes beyond the question of logical form. Applied to the case at hand, for example, I am not concerned with the meaning of 'deliberately' as opposed, perhaps, to 'voluntary'; but I am interested in the logical role of both these words. To give another illustration of the distinction I have in mind: we need not view the difference between 'Joe believes that there is life on Mars' and 'Joe knows that there is life on Mars' as a difference in logical form. That the second, but not the first, entails 'There is life on Mars' is plausibly a logical truth; but it is a truth that emerges only when we consider the meaning analysis of 'believes' and 'knows'. Admittedly there is something arbitrary in how much of logic to pin on logical form. But limits are set if our interest is in giving a coherent and constructive account of meaning: we must uncover enough structure to make it possible to state, for an arbitrary sentence, how its meaning depends on that structure, and we must not attribute more structure than such a theory of meaning can accommodate.

Consider the sentence:

(1) Jones buttered the toast slowly, deliberately, in the bathroom, with a knife, at midnight.

Despite the superficial grammar we cannot, I shall argue later, treat the 'deliberately' on a par with the other modifying clauses. It alone imputes intention, for of course Jones may have buttered the toast slowly, in the bathroom, with a knife, at midnight, and quite unintentionally, having mistaken the toast for his hairbrush which was what he intended to butter. Let us, therefore, postpone discussion of the 'deliberately' and its intentional kindred.

'Slowly', unlike the other adverbial clauses, fails to introduce a new entity (a place, an instrument, a time), and also may involve a special difficulty. For suppose we take 'Jones buttered the toast slowly' as saying that Jones's buttering of the toast was slow; is it clear that we can equally well say of Jones's action, no matter how we describe it, that it was slow? A change in the example will help. Susan says, 'I crossed the Channel in fifteen hours.' 'Good grief, that was slow.' (Notice how much more naturally we say 'slow' here than 'slowly'. But *what* was slow, what does 'that' refer to? No appropriate singular term appears in 'I crossed the Channel in fifteen hours.') Now Susan adds, 'But I swam.' 'Good grief, that was fast.' We do not withdraw the claim that it was a slow crossing; this is consistent with its being a fast swimming. Here we have enough to show, I think, that we cannot construe 'It was a slow crossing' as 'It was slow and it was a crossing' since the crossing may also be a swimming that was not slow, in which case we would have 'It was slow and it was a crossing and it was a swimming and it was not slow.' The problem is not peculiar to talk of actions, however. It appears equally when we try to explain the logical role of the attributive adjectives in 'Grundy was a short basketball player, but a tall man', and 'This is a good memento of the murder, but a poor steak knife.' The problem of attributives is indeed a problem about logical form, but it may be put to one side here because it is not a problem for action sentences alone.

We have decided to ignore, for the moment at least, the first two adverbial modifiers in (1), and may now deal with the problem of the logical form of:

(2) Jones buttered the toast in the bathroom with a knife at midnight.

Anthony Kenny, who deserves the credit for calling explicit attention to this problem,[1] points out that most philosophers today would, as a start, analyse this

---

[1] Anthony Kenny, *Action, Emotion and Will*, Ch. VII.

sentence as containing a five-place predicate with the argument places filled in the obvious ways with singular terms or bound variables. If we go on to analyse 'Jones buttered the toast' as containing a two-place predicate, 'Jones buttered the toast in the bathroom' as containing a three-place predicate, and so forth, we obliterate the logical relations between these sentences, namely that (2) entails the others. Or, to put the objection another way, the original sentences contain a common syntactic element ('buttered') which we intuitively recognize as relevant to the meaning relations of the sentences. But the proposed analyses show no such common element.

Kenny rejects the suggestion that 'Jones buttered the toast' be considered as elliptical for 'Jones buttered the toast somewhere with something at some time', which would restore the wanted entailments, on the ground that we could never be sure how many standby positions to provide in each predicate of action. For example, couldn't we add to (2) the phrase 'by holding it between the toes of his left foot'? Still, this adds a place to the predicate only if it differs in meaning from, 'while holding it between the toes of his left foot', and it is not quite clear that this is so. I am inclined to agree with Kenny that we cannot view verbs of action as usually containing a large number of standby positions, but I do not have what I consider a knock-down argument. (A knock-down argument would consist in a method for increasing the number of places indefinitely.)[2]

Kenny proposes that we may exhibit the logical form of (2) in somewhat the following manner:

(3) Jones brought it about that the toast was buttered in the bathroom with a knife at midnight.

Whatever the other merits in this proposal (I shall consider some of them presently) it is clear that it does not solve the problem Kenny raises. For it is, if anything, even more obscure how (3) entails 'Jones brought it about that the toast was buttered' or 'The toast was buttered' then how (2) entails 'Jones buttered the toast.' Kenny seems to have confused two different problems. One is the problem of how to represent the idea of *agency*: it is this that prompts Kenny to assign 'Jones' a logically distinguished role in (3). The other is the problem of the 'variable polyadicity' (as Kenny calls it) of action verbs. And it is clear that this problem is independent of the first, since it arises with respect to the sentences that replace '*p*' in '*x* brings it about that *p*'.

If I say I bought a house downtown that has four bedrooms, two fireplaces, and a glass chandelier in the kitchen, it's obvious that I can go on forever adding details. Yet the logical form of the sentences I use presents no problem (in this

---

[2] Kenny seems to think there is such a method, for he writes, 'If we cast our net widely enough, we can make "Brutus killed Caesar" into a sentence which describes, with a certain lack of speci-fication, the whole history of the world (op. cit., 160). But he does not show how to make each addition to the sentence one that irreducibly modifies the killing as opposed, say, to Brutus or Caesar, or the place or the time.

respect). It is something like, 'There is a house such that I bought it, it is downtown, it has four bedrooms, . . .' and so forth. We can tack on a new clause at will because the iterated relative pronoun will carry the reference back to the same entity as often as desired. (Of course we know how to state this much more precisely.) Much of our talk of action suggests the same idea: that there are such *things* as actions, and that a sentence like (2) describes the action in a number of ways. 'Jones did it with a knife.' 'Please tell me more about it.' The 'it' here doesn't refer to Jones or the knife, but to what Jones did—or so it seems.

'. . . it is in principle always open to us, along various lines, to describe or refer to "what I did" in so many ways,' writes Austin.[3] Austin is obviously leery of the apparent singular term, which he puts in scare quotes; yet the grammar of his sentence requires a singular term. Austin would have had little sympathy, I imagine, for the investigation into logical form I am undertaking here, though the demand that underlies it, for an intuitively acceptable and constructive theory of meaning, is one that begins to appear in the closing chapters of *How to Do Things with Words*. But in any case, Austin's discussion of excuses illustrates over and over the fact that our common talk and reasoning about actions is most naturally analysed by supposing that there are such entities.

'I didn't know it was loaded' belongs to one standard pattern of excuse. I do not deny that I pointed the gun and pulled the trigger, nor that I shot the victim. My ignorance explains how it happened that I pointed the gun and pulled the trigger intentionally, but did not shoot the victim intentionally. That the bullet pierced the victim was a consequence of my pointing the gun and pulling the trigger. It is clear that these are two different events, since one began slightly after the other. But what is the relation between my pointing the gun and pulling the trigger, and my shooting the victim? The natural and, I think, correct answer is that the relation is that of identity. The logic of this sort of excuse includes, it seems, at least this much structure: I am accused of doing b, which is deplorable. I admit I did a, which is excusable. My excuse for doing b rests upon my claim that I did not know that $a = b$.

Another pattern of excuse would have me allow that I shot the victim intentionally, but in self-defence. Now the structure includes something more. I am still accused of b (my shooting the victim), which is deplorable. I admit I did c (my shooting the victim in self-defence), which is excusable. My excuse for doing b rests upon my claim that I knew or believed that $b = c$.

The story can be given another twist. Again I shoot the victim, again intentionally. What I am asked to explain is my shooting of the bank president (d), for the victim was that distinguished gentleman. My excuse is that I shot the escaping murderer (e), and surprising and unpleasant as it is, my shooting the escaping murderer and my shooting of the bank president were one and the same action ($e = d$), since the bank president and the escaping murderer were one and

---

[3] J. L. Austin, 'A Plea for Excuses', 148.

the same person. To justify the 'since' we must presumably think of 'my shooting of x' as a functional expression that names an action when the 'x' is replaced by an appropriate singular term. The relevant reasoning would then be an application of the principle $x = y \to fx = fy$.

Excuses provide endless examples of cases where we seem compelled to take talk of 'alternative descriptions of the same action' seriously, i.e., literally. But there are plenty of other contexts in which the same need presses. *Explaining* an action by giving an intention with which it was done provides new descriptions of the action: I am writing my name on a piece of paper with the intention of writing a cheque with the intention of paying my gambling debt. List all the different descriptions of my action. Here are a few for a start: I am writing my name. I am writing my name on a piece of paper. I am writing my name on a piece of paper with the intention of writing a cheque. I am writing a cheque. I am paying my gambling debt. It is hard to imagine how we can have a coherent theory of action unless we are allowed to say that each of these sentences is made true by the same action. Redescription may supply the motive ('I was getting my revenge'), place the action in the context of a rule ('I am castling'), give the outcome ('I killed him'), or provide evaluation ('I did the right thing').

According to Kenny, as we just noted, action sentences have the form 'Jones brought it about that p.' The sentence that replaces 'p' is to be in the present tense, and it describes the result that the agent has wrought: it is a sentence 'newly true of the patient'.[4] Thus, 'The doctor removed the patient's appendix' must be rendered, 'The doctor brought it about that the patient has no appendix.' By insisting that the sentence that replaces 'p' describe a terminal *state* rather than an *event*, it may be thought that Kenny can avoid the criticism made above that the problem of the logical form of action sentences turns up within the sentence that replaces 'p': we may allow that 'The patient has no appendix' presents no relevant problem. The difficulty is that neither will the analysis stand in its present form. The doctor may bring it about that the patient has no appendix by turning the patient over to another doctor who performs the operation; or by running the patient down with his Lincoln Continental. In neither case would we say the doctor removed the patient's appendix. Closer approximations to a correct analysis might be, 'The doctor brought it about that the doctor has removed the patient's appendix' or perhaps, 'The doctor brought it about that the patient has had his appendix removed by the doctor.' One may still have a few doubts, I think, as to whether these sentences have the same truth conditions as 'The doctor removed the patient's appendix.' But in any case it is plain that in these versions, the problem of the logical form of action sentences does turn up in the sentences that replace 'p': 'The patient has had his appendix removed by the doctor' or 'The doctor has removed the patient's appendix' are surely no *easier* to analyse than 'The doctor removed the patient's appendix.' By the same token,

---

[4] Kenny, op. cit., 181.

'Cass walked to the store' can't be given as 'Cass brought it about that Cass is at the store', since this drops the idea of walking. Nor is it clear that 'Cass brought it about that Cass is at the store and is there through having walked' will serve; but in any case, the contained sentence is again worse than what we started with.

It is not easy to decide what to do with 'Smith coughed.' Should we say 'Smith brought it about that Smith is in a state of just having coughed'? At best this would be correct only if Smith coughed on purpose.

The difficulty in Kenny's proposal that we have been discussing may perhaps be put this way: he wants to represent every (completed) action in terms only of the agent, the notion of bringing it about that a state of affairs obtains, and the state of affairs brought about by the agent. But many action sentences yield no description of the state of affairs brought about by the action except that it *is* the state of affairs brought about by that action. A natural move, then, is to allow that the sentence that replaces '*p*' in '*x* brings it about that *p*' may (or perhaps must) describe an event.

If I am not mistaken, Chisholm has suggested an analysis that at least permits the sentence that replaces '*p*' to describe (as we are allowing ourselves to say) an event.[5] His favoured locution is '*x* makes *p* happen', though he uses such variants as '*x* brings it about that *p*' or '*x* makes it true that *p*'. Chisholm speaks of the entities to which the expressions that replace '*p*' refer as 'states of affairs', and explicitly adds that states of affairs may be changes or events (as well as 'unchanges'). An example Chisholm provides is this: if a man raises his arm, then we may say he makes it happen that his arm goes up. I do not know whether Chisholm would propose 'Jones made it happen that Jones's arm went up' as an analysis of 'Jones raised his arm', but I think the proposal would be wrong because although the second of these sentences does perhaps entail the first, the first does not entail the second. The point is even clearer if we take as our example 'Jones made it happen that Jones batted an eyelash' (or some trivial variant), and this cannot be called progress in uncovering the logical form of 'Jones batted an eyelash.'

There is something else that may puzzle us about Chisholm's analysis of action sentences, and it is independent of the question what sentence we substitute for '*p*'. Whatever we put for '*p*', we are to interpret it as describing some event. It is natural to say, I think, that *whole* sentences of the form '*x* makes it happen that *p*' also describe events. Should we say that these events are the *same* event, or that they are different? If they are the same event, as many people would claim (perhaps including Chisholm), then no matter what we put for '*p*', we cannot have solved the *general* problem of the logical form of sentences about actions until we have dealt with the sentences that can replace '*p*'. If they are different events, we must ask how the element of agency has been introduced into the

---

[5] Roderick Chisholm, 'The Descriptive Element in the Concept of Action'. Also see Chisholm, 'The Ethics of Requirement'.

larger sentence though it is lacking in the sentence for which '*p*' stands; for each has the agent as its subject. The answer Chisholm gives, I think, is that the special notion of making it happen that he has in mind is intentional, and thus to be distinguished from simply causing something to happen. Suppose we want to say that Alice broke the mirror without implying that she did it intentionally. Then Chisholm's special idiom is not called for; but we could say, 'Alice caused it to happen that the mirror broke.' Suppose we now want to add that she did it intentionally. Then the Chisholm-sentence would be: 'Alice made it happen that Alice caused it to happen that the mirror broke.' And now we want to know, what is the event that the whole sentence reports, and that the contained sentence does not? It is, apparently, just what used to be called an act of the will. I will not dredge up the standard objections to the view that acts of the will are special events distinct from, say, our bodily movements, and perhaps the causes of them. But even if Chisholm is willing to accept such a view, the problem of the logical form of the sentences that can replace '*p*' remains, and these describe the things people do as we describe them when we do not impute intention.

A somewhat different view has been developed with care and precision by von Wright.[6] In effect, von Wright puts action sentences into the following form: '*x* brings it about that a state where *p* changes into a state where *q*'. Thus the important relevant difference between von Wright's analysis and the ones we have been considering is the more complex structure of the description of the change or event the agent brings about: where Kenny and Chisholm were content to describe the result of the change, von Wright includes also a description of the initial state.

Von Wright is interested in exploring the logic of change and action and not, at least primarily, in giving the logical form of our common sentences about acts or events. For the purposes of his study, it may be very fruitful to think of events as ordered pairs of states. But I think it is also fairly obvious that this does not give us a standard way of translating or representing the form of most sentences about acts and events. If I walk from San Francisco to Pittsburgh, for example, my initial state is that I am in San Francisco and my terminal state is that I am in Pittsburgh; but the same is more pleasantly true if I fly. Of course, we may describe the terminal state as my having walked to Pittsburgh from San Francisco, but then we no longer need the separate statement of the initial state. Indeed, viewed as an analysis of ordinary sentences about actions, von Wright's proposal seems subject to all the difficulties I have already outlined plus the extra one that most action sentences do not yield a non-trivial description of the initial state (try 'He circled the field', 'He recited the *Odyssey*', 'He flirted with Olga').

In two matters, however, it seems to me von Wright suggests important and valuable changes in the pattern of analysis we have been considering, or at least in our interpretation of it. First, he says that an action is not an event, but rather the

---

[6] Georg Henrik von Wright, *Norm and Action*.

bringing about of an event. I do not think this can be correct. If I fall down, this is an event whether I do it intentionally or not. If you thought my falling was an accident and later discovered I did it on purpose, you would not be tempted to withdraw your claim that you had witnessed an event. I take von Wright's refusal to call an action an event to reflect the embarrassment we found to follow if we say that an act is an event, taking agency to be introduced by a phrase like 'brings it about that'. The solution lies, however, not in distinguishing acts from events, but in finding a different logical form for action sentences. The second important idea von Wright introduces comes in the context of his distinction between *generic* and *individual* propositions about events.[7] The distinction, as von Wright makes it, is not quite clear, for he says both: that an individual proposition differs from a generic one in having a uniquely determined truth value, while a generic proposition has a truth value only when coupled with an occasion; and that, that Brutus killed Caesar is an individual proposition while that Brutus kissed Caesar is a generic proposition, because 'a person can be kissed by another on more than one occasion'. In fact the proposition that Brutus kissed Caesar seems to have a uniquely determined truth value in the same sense that the proposition that Brutus killed Caesar does. But it is, I believe, a very important observation that 'Brutus kissed Caesar' does not, by virtue of its meaning alone, describe a single act.

It is easy to see that the proposals we have been considering concerning the logical form of action sentences do not yield solutions to the problems with which we began. I have already pointed out that Kenny's problem, that verbs of action apparently have 'variable polyadicity', arises within the sentences that can replace 'p' in such formulas as 'x brought it about that p'. An analogous remark goes for von Wright's more elaborate formula. The other main problem may be put as that of assigning a logical form to action sentences that will justify claims that two sentences describe 'the same action'. Our study of some of the ways in which we excuse, or attempt to excuse, acts shows that we want to make inferences such as this: I flew my spaceship to the Morning Star, the Morning Star is identical with the Evening Star; so, I flew my spaceship to the Evening Star. (My leader told me not to go the Evening Star; I headed for the Morning Star not knowing.) But suppose we translate the action sentences along the lines suggested by Kenny or Chisholm or von Wright. Then we have something like, 'I brought it about that my spaceship is on the Morning Star.' How can we infer, given the well-known identity, 'I brought it about that my spaceship is on the Evening Star'? We know that if we replace 'the Morning Star' by 'the Evening Star' in, 'My spaceship is on the Morning Star' the truth-value will not be disturbed; and so if the occurrence of this sentence in, 'I brought it about that my spaceship is on the Morning Star' is truth-functional, the inference is justified. But of course the occurrence can't be truth-functional: otherwise, from the fact that

---

[7] von Wright, op. cit., 23.

I brought about one actual state of affairs it would follow that I brought about every actual state of affairs. It is no good saying that after the words 'bring it about that' sentences describe something *between* truth-values and propositions, say states of affairs. Such a claim must be backed by a semantic theory telling us how each sentence determines the state of affairs it does; otherwise the claim is empty.

Israel Scheffler has put forward an analysis of sentences about choice that can be applied without serious modification to sentences about intentional acts.[8] Scheffler makes no suggestion concerning action sentences that do not impute intention, and so has no solution to the chief problems I am discussing. Nevertheless, his analysis has a feature I should like to mention. Scheffler would have us render, 'Jones intentionally buttered the toast' as, 'Jones made-true a that Jones-buttered-the-toast inscription.' This cannot, for reasons I have urged in detail elsewhere,[9] be considered a finally satisfying form for such sentences because it contains the logically unstructured predicate 'is a that Jones-buttered-the-toast inscription', and there are an infinite number of such semantical primitives in the language. But in one respect, I believe Scheffler's analysis is clearly superior to the others, for it implies that introducing the element of intentionality does not call for a reduction in the content of the sentence that expresses *what* was done intentionally. This brings out a fact otherwise suppressed, that, to use our example, 'Jones' turns up twice, once inside and once outside the scope of the intensional operator. I shall return to this point.

A discussion of the logical form of action sentences in ordinary language is to be found in the justly famed Chapter VII of Reichenbach's *Elements of Symbolic Logic*.[10] According to Reichenbach's doctrine, we may transform a sentence like

(4) Amundsen flew to the North pole

into:

(5) $(\exists x)$ (x consists in the fact that Amundsen flew to the North Pole).

The expression 'is an event that consists in the fact that' is to be viewed as an operator which, when prefixed to a sentence, forms a predicate of events. Reichenbach does not think of (5) as showing or revealing the logical form of (4), for he thinks (4) is unproblematic. Rather he says (5) is logically equivalent to (4). (5) has its counterpart in a more ordinary idiom:

(6) A flight by Amundsen to the North Pole took place.

Thus Reichenbach seems to hold that we have two ways of expressing the same idea, (4) and (6); they have quite different logical forms, but they are logically equivalent; one speaks literally of events while the other does not. I believe this

[8] Israel Scheffler, *The Anatomy of Inquiry*, 104–5.
[9] Donald Davidson, 'Theories of Meaning and Learnable Languages', 390–1.
[10] Hans Reichenbach, *Elements of Symbolic Logic*, § 48.

view spoils much of the merit in Reichenbach's proposal, and that we must abandon the idea that (4) has an unproblematic logical form distinct from that of (5) or (6). Following Reichenbach's formula for putting any action sentence into the form of (5) we translate

(7) Amunsden flew to the North Pole in May 1926

into:

(8) $(\exists x)$ (x consists in the fact that Amundsen flew to the North Pole in May 1926).

The fact that (8) entails (5) is no more obvious than that (7) entails (4); what was obscure remains obscure. The correct way to render (7) is:

(9) $(\exists x)$ (x consists in the fact that Amundsen flew to the North Pole and x took place in May 1926).

But (9) does not bear the simple relation to the standard way of interpreting (7) that (8) does. We do not know of any logical operation on (7) as it would usually be formalised (with a three-place predicate) that would make it logically equivalent to (9). This is why I suggest that we treat (9) alone as giving the logical form of (7). If we follow this strategy, Kenny's problem of the 'variable polyadicity' of action verbs is on the way to solution; there is, of course, no variable polyadicity. The problem is solved in the natural way, by introducing events as entities about which an indefinite number of things can be said.

Reichenbach's proposal has another attractive feature: it eliminates a peculiar confusion that seemed to attach to the idea that sentences like (7) 'describe an event'. The difficulty was that one wavered between thinking of the sentence as describing or referring to that one flight Amundsen made in May 1926, or as describing a kind of event, or perhaps as describing (potentially?) several. As von Wright pointed out, any number of events might be described by a sentence like 'Brutus kissed Caesar.' This fog is dispelled in a way I find entirely persuasive by Reichenbach's proposal that ordinary action sentences have, in effect, an existential quantifier binding the action-variable. When we were tempted into thinking a sentence like (7) describes a single event we were misled: it does not describe any event at all. But if (7) is true, then there is an event that makes it true. (This unrecognized element of generality in action sentences is, I think, of the utmost importance in understanding the relation between actions and desires.)

There are two objections to Reichenbach's analysis of action sentences: The first may not be fatal. It is that as matters stand the analysis may be applied to any sentence whatsoever, whether it deals with actions, events, or anything else. Even '$2 + 3 = 5$' becomes '$(\exists x)$ (x consists in the fact that $2 + 3 = 5$)'. Why not say '$2 + 3 = 5$' does not show its true colours until put through the machine? For that matter, are we finished when we get to the first step? Shouldn't we go on to '$(\exists y)$

(y consists in the fact that ($\exists x$) (x consists in the fact that $2 + 3 = 5$))'? And so on. It isn't clear on what principle the decision to apply the analysis is based.

The second objection is worse. We have:

(10) ($\exists x$) (x consists in the fact that I flew my spaceship to the Morning Star)

and

(11) the Morning Star = the Evening Star

and we want to make the inference to

(12) ($\exists x$) (x consists in the fact that I flew my spaceship to the Evening Star).

The likely principle to justify the inference would be:

(13) (x) (x consists in the fact that $S \leftrightarrow x$ consists in the fact that S')

where 'S'' is obtained from 'S' by substituting, in one or more places, a co-referring singular term. It is plausible to add that (13) holds if 'S' and 'S'' are logically equivalent. But (13) and the last assumption lead to trouble. For observing that 'S' is logically equivalent to '$\hat{y}(y = y \ \& \ S) = \hat{y}(y = y)$' we get

(14) (x) (x consists in the fact that $S \leftrightarrow x$ consists in the fact that ($\hat{y}(y = y \ \& \ S) = \hat{y}(y = y)$)).

Now suppose 'R' is any sentence materially equivalent to 'S': then '$\hat{y}(y = y \ \& \ S)$' and '$\hat{y}(y = y \ \& \ R)$' will refer to the same thing. Substituting in (14) we obtain

(15) (x) (x consists in the fact that $S \leftrightarrow x$ consists in the fact that ($\hat{y}(y = y \ \& \ R) = \hat{y}(y = y)$),

which leads to

(16) (x) (x consists in the fact that $S \leftrightarrow x$ consists in the fact that R)

when we observe the logical equivalence of 'R' and '$\hat{y}(y = y \ \& \ R) = \hat{y}(y = y)$'. (16) may be interpreted as saying (considering that the sole assumption is that 'R' and 'S' are materially equivalent) that all events that occur (= all events) are identical. This demonstrates, I think, that Reichenbach's analysis is radically defective.

Now I would like to put forward an analysis of action sentences that seems to me to combine most of the merits of the alternatives already discussed, and to avoid the difficulties. The basic idea is that verbs of action—verbs that say 'what someone did'—should be construed as containing a place, for singular terms or variables, that they do not appear to. For example, we would normally suppose that 'Shem kicked Shaun' consisted in two names and a two-place predicate. I suggest, though, that we think of 'kicked' as a *three*-place predicate, and that the sentence to be given in this form:

(17) ($\exists x$) (Kicked(Shem, Shaun, x)).

If we try for an English sentence that directly reflects this form, we run into difficulties. 'There is an event x such that x is a kicking of Shaun by Shem' is about the best I can do, but we must remember 'a kicking' is not a singular term. Given this English reading, my proposal may sound very like Reichenbach's; but of course it has quite different logical properties. The *sentence* 'Shem kicked Shaun' nowhere appears inside my analytic sentence, and this makes it differ from all the theories we have considered.

The principles that license the Morning Star-Evening Star inference now make no trouble: they are the usual principles of extensionality. As a result, nothing now stands in the way of giving a standard theory of meaning for action sentences, in the form of a Tarski-type truth definition; nothing stands in the way, that is, of giving a coherent and constructive account of how the meanings (truth conditions) of these sentences depend upon their structure. To see how one of the troublesome inferences now goes through, consider (10) rewritten as

(18) $(\exists x)$ (Flew(I, my spaceship, x) & To(the Morning Star, x)).

which, along with (11), entails

(19) $(\exists x)$ (Flew(I, my spaceship, x) & To(the Evening Star, x)).

It is not necessary, in representing this argument, to separate off the To-relation; instead we could have taken, 'Flew' as a four-place predicate. But that would have obscured *another* inference, namely that from (19) to

(20) $(\exists x)$ (Flew(I, my spaceship, x)).

In general, we conceal logical structure when we treat prepositions as integral parts of verbs; it is a merit of the present proposal that it suggests a way of treating prepositions as contributing structure. Not only is it good to have the inference from (19) to (20); it is also good to be able to keep track of the common element in 'fly to' and 'fly away from' and this of course we cannot do if we treat these as unstructured predicates.

The problem that threatened in Reichenbach's analysis, that there seemed no clear principle on which to refrain from applying the analysis to every sentence, has a natural solution if my suggestion is accepted. Part of what we must learn when we learn the meaning of any predicate is how many places it has, and what sorts of entities the variables that hold these places range over. Some predicates have an event-place, some do not.

In general, what kinds of predicates do have event-places? Without pursuing this question very far, I think it is evident that if action predicates do, many predicates that have little relation to action do. Indeed, the problems we have been mainly concerned with are not at all unique to talk of actions: they are common to talk of events of any kind. An action of flying to the Morning Star is identical with an action of flying to the Evening Star; but equally, an eclipse of the Morning Star is an eclipse of the Evening Star. Our ordinary talk of events, of causes and effects, requires constant use of the idea of different descriptions of the same event. When it is pointed out that striking the match was not sufficient to light it, what is not sufficient is not the event, but the description of it—it was a *dry* match, and so on. And of course Kenny's problem of 'variable polyadicity', though he takes it to be a mark of verbs of action, is common to all verbs that describe events.

It may now appear that the apparent success of the analysis proposed here is due to the fact that it has simply omitted what is peculiar to action sentences as contrasted with other sentences about events. But I do not think so. The concept of agency contains two elements, and when we separate them clearly, I think we shall see that the present analysis has not left anything out. The first of these two elements we try, rather feebly, to elicit by saying that the agent acts, or does something, instead of being acted upon, or having something happen to him. Or we say that the agent is active rather than passive; and perhaps try to make use of the moods of the verb as a grammatical clue. And we may try to depend upon some fixed phrase like 'brings it about that' or 'makes it the case that'. But only a little thought will make it clear that there is no satisfactory grammatical test for verbs where we want to say there is agency. Perhaps it is a *necessary* condition of attributing agency that one argument-place in the verb is filled with a reference to the agent as a person; it will not do to refer to his body, or his members, or to anyone else. But beyond that it is hard to go. I sleep, I snore, I push buttons, I recite verses, I catch cold. Also others are insulted by me, struck by me, admired by me, and so on. No grammatical test I know of, in terms of the things we may be said to do, of active or passive mood, or of any other sort, will separate out the cases here where we want to speak of agency. Perhaps it is true that 'brings it about that' guarantees agency; but as we have seen, many sentences that do attribute agency cannot be cast in this grammatical form.

I believe the correct thing to say about *this* element in the concept of agency is that it is simply introduced by certain verbs and not by others; when we understand the verb we recognize whether or not it includes the idea of an agent. Thus, 'I fought' and 'I insulted him' do impute agency to the person referred to by the first singular term, 'I caught cold' and, 'I had my thirteenth birthday' do not. In these cases, we do seem to have the following test: we impute agency only where it makes sense to ask whether the agent acted intentionally. But there are other cases, or so it seems to me, where we impute agency only when the answer to the question whether the agent acted intentionally is 'yes'. If a man falls down by accident or because a truck knocks him down, we do not impute agency; but we do if he fell down on purpose.

This introduces the second element in the concept of agency, for we surely impute agency when we say or imply that the act is intentional. Instead of speaking of two elements in the concept of agency, perhaps it would be better to say there are two ways we can imply that a person acted as an agent: we may use a verb that implies it directly, or we may use a verb that is non-committal, and add that the act was intentional. But when we take the second course, it is important not to think of the intentionality as adding an extra doing of the agent; we must not make the expression that introduces intention a verb of action. In particular, we cannot use 'intentionally brings it about that' as the expression that introduces intention, for 'brings it about that' is in itself a verb of action, and imputes agency, but it is neutral with respect to the question whether the action was intentional as described.

This leaves the question what logical form the expression that introduces intention should have. It is obvious, I hope, that the adverbial form must be in some way deceptive; intentional actions are not a class of actions, or, to put the point a little differently, doing something intentionally is not a manner of doing it. To say someone did something intentionally is to describe the action in a way that bears a special relation to the beliefs and attitudes of the agent; and perhaps further to describe the action as having been caused by those beliefs and attitudes.[11] But of course to describe the action of the agent as having been caused in a certain way does not mean that the agent is described as performing any further action. From a logical point of view, there are thus these important conditions governing the expression that introduces intention: it must not be interpreted as a verb of action, it must be intensional, and the intention must be tied to a person. I propose then that we use some form of words like 'It was intentional of x that p' where 'x' names the agent, and 'p' is a sentence that says the agent did something. It is useful, perhaps necessary, that the agent be named twice when we try to make logical form explicit. It is useful, because it reminds us that to describe an action as intentional is to describe the action in the light of certain attitudes and beliefs of a particular person; it may be necessary in order to illuminate what goes on in those cases in which the agent makes a mistake about who he is. It was intentional of Oedipus, and hence of the slayer of Laius, that Oedipus sought the slayer of Laius, but it was not intentional of Oedipus (the slayer of Laius) that the slayer of Laius sought the slayer of Laius.

CRITICISM, COMMENT, AND DEFENCE

The above Essay brought in its wake a number of comments and criticisms from other philosophers, and in a few cases I responded. In this appendix to the Essay, I bring together some of my replies, for although they repeat much that can be found elsewhere in this volume, they often put a point in a new way or modify an old one. I have done some editing to make these replies intelligible without the comments to which they were replies, but of course some readers may want to look up the original work of the critic or commentator.

This Essay was first read at a three-day conference on *The Logic of Decision and Action* held at the University of Pittsburgh in March 1966; the proceedings were published

---

[11] See Essay 1.

the next year under the editorship of Nicholas Rescher. At the conference, E. J. Lemmon, H.-N. Castañeda, and R. M. Chisholm commented on my paper, and I replied. It is my replies (as rewritten for publication) that appear here (somewhat further edited).

In November of 1966 The University of Western Ontario held a colloquium on *Fact and Existence* at which I replied to a paper 'On Events and Event-Descriptions' by R. M. Martin. Both his paper and my reply were published by Blackwells in 1969 under the editorship of Joseph Margolis. Martin had not seen my Essay 6 when he wrote his paper, and in fairness to him it should be noted that his views on the semantics of sentences about events have been modified subsequently. I reprint my reply to him for the light it throws on my views, not on his.

Finally, the journal *Inquiry* devoted its Summer, 1970, issue to the subject of action, and it contained two criticisms of my work. One was by Carl G. Hedman, 'On the Individuation of Actions', the other was by James Cargile, 'Davidson's Notion of Logical Form'. My replies were printed under the title 'Action and Reaction', and are reprinted here.

A. *Reply to Lemmon on Tenses.* My goal was to get clear about the logical form of action sentences. By action sentences I mean sentences *in English* about actions. At the level of abstraction on which the discussion moved, little was said that would not apply to sentences about actions in many other languages if it applied to sentences in English. The ideal implicit in the paper is a theory that spells out every element of logical form in every English sentence about actions. I dream of a theory that makes the transition from the ordinary idiom to canonical notation purely mechanical, and a canonical notation rich enough to capture, in its dull and explicit way, every difference and connection legitimately considered the business of a theory of meaning. The point of canonical notation so conceived is not to improve on something left vague and defective in natural language, but to help elicit in a perspicuous and general form the understanding of logical grammar we all have that constitutes (part of) our grasp of our native tongue.

In exploring the logical form of sentences about actions and events, I concentrated on certain features of such sentences and neglected others. One feature I totally neglected was that of tense; Lemmon is absolutely right in pointing out that some of the inferences I consider valid depend (in a standard way we have become hardened to) on fudging with respect to time. The necessity for fudging shows that we have failed to bring out a feature of logical form.

I accept the implication that my own account was incomplete through neglect of the element of tense, and I welcome Lemmon's attempt to remedy the situation. I am very much in sympathy with the methods he apparently thinks appropriate. Logicians have almost always assumed that the demonstrative element in natural languages necessarily resists serious semantic treatment, and they have accordingly tried to show how to replace tensed expressions with others containing no demonstrative feature. What recommends this strategy to logicians (the elimination of sentences with variable truth-values) also serves to show that it is not a strategy for analysing the sentences of English. Lemmon makes no attempt to eliminate the demonstrative element from his canonical notation (substituting 'before now' for the past tense is a way of *articulating* the relation between the different tenses of the same verb, not of eliminating the demonstrative element). At the same time, he obviously has in mind that the structure he introduces must lend itself to formal semantic treatment. It is simply a mistake, Lemmon correctly assumes, to think that sentences with a demonstrative element resist the application of systematic semantic analysis.

B. *Reply to Lemmon on Identity Conditions for Events.* If we are going to quantify over events and interpret singular terms as referring to events, we need to say something about the conditions under which expressions of the form '$a = b$' are true where 'a' and 'b' refer, or purport to refer, to events. This is a difficult and complex subject, and I do not propose to do more here than comment briefly on some of Lemmon's remarks. But I think he is right to raise the issue; before we decide that our general approach to the analysis of event sentences is correct, there must be much more discussion of the criteria for individuating and identifying events.

Lemmon is surely right that a necessary condition for the identity of events is that they take place over exactly the same period of time. He suggests, very tentatively, that if we add that the events 'take the same place', then we have necessary and sufficient conditions for identity. I am not at all certain this suggestion is wrong, but before we accept it we shall need to remove two doubts. The first centres on the question whether we have adequate criteria for the location of an event. As Lemmon realizes, his principle that if $F(a,z)$ then a is a participant in z, cannot be true for every F (take 'F' as 'took place a thousand miles south of' and 'a' as 'New York'; we would not, presumably, say New York participated in every event that took place a thousand miles south of New York). And how do we deal with examples like this: if a man's arm goes up, the event takes place in the space-time zone occupied by the arm; but if a man raises his arm, doesn't the event fill the zone occupied by the whole man? Yet the events may be identical. If a man drives his car into his garage, how much of the garage does the event occupy? All of it, or only the zone occupied by the car? Finally, if events are to have a location in an interesting sense, we need to see what is wrong with the following argument: if an event is a change in a certain object, then the event occupies at least the zone occupied by the object during the time the event takes place. But if one object is part of another, a change in the first is a change in the second. Since an object is part of the universe, it follows that every event that is a change in an object takes place everywhere (throughout the universe). This argument is, I believe, faulty, but it must be shown to be so before we can talk intelligibly of the location of events.

The second doubt we must remove if we are to identify events with space-time zones is that there may be two different events in the same zone. Suppose that during exactly the same time interval Jones catches cold, swims the Hellespont, and counts his blessings. Are these all the same event? I suspect there may be a good argument to show they are; but until one is produced, we must suspend judgement on Lemmon's interesting proposal.[12]

C. *Reply to Castañeda on Agent and Patient.* Castañeda very usefully summarizes the main points in my paper, and raises some questions about the principles that are implicit in my examples. My lack of explicitness has perhaps misled him in one respect. It is not part of my programme to make all entailments matters of logical form. '$x > y$' entails '$y < x$', but not as a matter of form. 'x is a grandfather' entails 'x is a father', but not as a matter of form. And I think there are cases where, to use Castañeda's words, 'a larger polyadic action statement entails a shorter one which is a part of it' and yet this is not a matter of logical form. An example, perhaps, is this: 'I flew my spaceship' may entail, 'I flew', but if it does, it is not, I think, because of the logical form of the sentences. My reason for saying this is that I find no reason to believe the logical form of 'I flew my spaceship' differs from that of 'I sank the *Bismarck*', which does not entail 'I sank' though it does happen to entail 'The *Bismarck* sank'. A comparison of these examples ought to go a long way to persuade us that simple sentences containing transitive verbs do not, as a matter of logical form, entail sentences with intransitive verbs. Putting sentences in the passive will not radically change things. If I sank the *Bismarck*, the *Bismarck* was sunk and the *Bismarck* sank. But 'The *Bismarck* was sunk' and 'The *Bismarck* sank' are not equivalent, for the econd does not entail the first. Thus even if we were to accept Castañeda's view that 'The *Bismarck* was sunk' has a logically intransitive verb, the passivity of the subject remains a feature of this verb distinguishing it from the verb of 'The *Bismarck* sank'. Thus there is no obvious economy in Castañeda's idea of indicating the distinction between agent and patient by position in verbs of action. There would be real merit, however, in keeping track of the relation between 'The *Bismarck* was sunk' and 'The *Bismarck* sank', which is that the first entails the second; but Castañeda's notation does not help with this.

Castañeda would have us put 'The King insulted the Queen' in this form:

$$(\exists x) \,(\text{Insulted (the King, } x) \,\&\, \text{Insulted } (x, \text{ the Queen}))$$

What is this relation, that relates a person and an event or, *in the same way,* an event and a person? What logical feature is preserved by this form that is not as well preserved, and less misleadingly, by

$$(\exists x) \,(\text{Insulted (the King, } x) \,\&\, \text{Was insulted (the Queen, } x))$$

(i.e., 'There was an event that was an insulting by the King and of the Queen')? But I remain unconvinced of the advantages in splitting transitive verbs up in this way. The gain is the entailment of 'My spaceship was flown' by 'I flew my

---

[12] For more on the individuation of events, see Essay 4.

spaceship'; the loss becomes apparent when we realize that 'My spaceship was flown' has been interpreted so as not to entail 'Someone flew my spaceship'.[13]

D. *Reply to Castañeda on Prepositions.* My proposal to treat certain prepositions as verbs does seem odd, and perhaps it will turn out to be radically mistaken. But I am not quite convinced of this by what Castañeda says. My analysis of 'I flew my spaceship to the Morning Star' does entail '$(\exists x)$ (To (the Morning Star, x))', and Castañeda turns this into words as 'There was a to the Morning Star'. But I think we can do better: 'There was an event involving motion toward the Morning Star' or 'There was an event characterized by being to (toward) the Morning Star'. Castañeda himself proposes 'flying-to', which shows he understands the *sort* of verb I have in mind. But of course I don't like 'flying-to' as an unstructured predicate, since this breaks the connection with 'walking-to' and its kin. Castañeda complains, of my use of plain 'to', that there are many different senses of 'to', depending on the verb it is coupled with. Let us suppose we understand this difficulty, with its heavy dependence on the concept of sameness of relation. I shall meet Castañeda half-way by introducing a special form of 'to' which means, 'motion-toward-and-terminating-at'; this is more general than his 'flying-to' and less general than my former, plain, 'to'. And I assume that if Castañeda understands '$(\exists x)$ (flying-to (the Morning Star, x))' he will understand '$(\exists x)$ (Motion-towards-and-terminating-at (the Morning Star, x))', for this verb differs from his merely in degree of generality.

E. *Reply to Castañeda on Intention.* First Castañeda makes the point, also made by Lemmon, that I would have done well to make basic a notion of intention that does not imply that what is intended is done. I think they are right in this.

Castañeda then goes on to claim that my analysis of 'Oedipus intentionally sought the slayer of Laius' as 'It was intentional of Oedipus that Oedipus sought the slayer of Laius' is faulty because the first sentence might be true and the second false if Oedipus failed to know that he was Oedipus. Castañeda suggests that to correct the analysis, we should put 'he (himself)' for the second occurrence of 'Oedipus'. In my opinion, Castañeda is right both in his criticism and in his correction. There is, as he maintains, an irreducibly demonstrative element in the full analysis of sentences about intentions, and my proposal concealed it.

Perhaps I should remark here that I do not think it *solves* the problem of the analysis of sentences about intention to put them in the form of 'It was intentional of x that p'; such sentences are notoriously hard to bring under a semantical theory. I view putting such sentences in this form as a first step; the

---

[13] On the general point raised by Castañeda, whether transitive verbs entail their intransitive counterparts as a matter of logical form, and (a related matter) whether passive transformation is a matter of logical form, I would now side with Castañeda.

problem then looks, even with Castañeda's revision, much like the problem of analysing sentences about other propositional attitudes.

F. *Reply to Chisholm on Making Happen.* I am happy to have Chisholm's careful comments on the section of my paper that deals with his views; he has made me realize that I had not appreciated the subtlety of his analysis. It is not clear to me now whether, on the issues discussed in my paper, there is any disagreement between us. Let me formulate the questions that remain in my mind as I now understand them.

I assume that since he has not attempted an analysis of event sentences generally, and the '*p*' in, 'He made it happen that *p*' refers to an event, Chisholm does not dispute my claim that he has not solved the main problems with which I deal in my paper. The question is rather whether there are any special problems in his analysis of action and agency. The first difficulty I raised for Chisholm was whether he could produce, in a reasonably mechanical way, for every sentence of the form 'He raised his arm' or 'Alice broke the mirror', another sentence of the form 'He made it happen that *p*' or 'Alice made it happen that *p*' where '*p*' does not have the agent as subject. Chisholm shows, I think, that there is a chance he can handle 'He raised his arm' and 'Alice broke the mirror' except, perhaps, in the case where intention is not involved at all, and this is not under discussion. The cases I would now worry about are rather 'He walked to the corner', 'He carved the roast', 'He fell down', or 'The doctor removed the patient's appendix'. In each of these examples I find I am puzzled as to what the agent makes happen. My problem isn't that I can't imagine that there is some bodily movement that the agent might be said to make happen, but that I see no way *automatically* to produce the right description from the original sentence. No doubt each time a man walks to the corner there is some way he makes his body move; but of course it does not follow that there is some one way he makes his body move every time he walks to the corner.

The second difficulty I raised for Chisholm concerned the question whether his analysis committed him to 'acts of the will', perhaps contrary to his own intentions. It is clear that Chisholm does not *want* to be committed to acts of the will, and that his analysis does not *say* that there are acts of the will but I believe the question can still be raised. It can be raised by asking whether the event said to occur in 'Jones made it happen that his arm went up' is the same event or a different one from the event said to occur in 'Jones's arm went up'. It seems to me Chisholm can avoid acts of the will only by saying the events are the same. He is free to say this, of course, and then the only objection is terminological. And 'Jones's arm went up' would then be, when it was something Jones made happen, a description of an action.

At the end of his reply, Chisholm conjectures that I may not agree with him that agents may be causes. Actually I see no objection to saying that agents are causes, but I think we understand this only when we can reduce it to the case of an event being a cause; and here I do disagree with Chisholm. He asks how we are to render 'He made it happen that p' in terms merely of relations among events. If the problem is that of giving the logical form of action sentences, then I have made a suggestion in the present paper. If the problem is to give an *analysis* of the concept of agency using other concepts, then I am not sure it can be done. Why must it be possible?

G. *Reply to Martin*. There is a more or less innocent sense in which we say that a sentence refers to, describes, or is about, some entity when the sentence contains a singular term that refers to that entity. Speaking in this vein, we declare that, 'The cat has mange' refers to the cat, 'Caesar's death was brought on by a cold' describes Caesar and his death, and 'Jack fell down and broke his crown' is about Jack and Jack's crown. Observing how the reference of a complex singular term like 'Caesar's death' or 'Jack's crown' depends systematically on the reference of the contained singular term ('Caesar' or 'Jack') it is tempting to go on to ask what a sentence *as a whole* is about (or refers to, or describes), since it embraces singular terms like 'Caesar's death' in much the way 'Caesar's death' embraces 'Caesar'. There is now a danger of ambiguity in the phrases 'what a sentence refers to' or 'what a sentence is about'; let us resolve it by using only 'refers to' for the relation between patent singular terms and what they are about, and only 'corresponds to' for the relation between a sentence and what it is about.

Just as a complex singular term like 'Caesar's death' may fail of reference though contained singular terms do not, so a sentence may not correspond to anything, even though its contained singular terms refer; witness 'Caesar's death was brought on by a cold'. Clearly enough, it is just the true sentences that have a corresponding entity; 'The cat has mange' corresponds to the cat's having of mange, which alone can make it true; because there is no entity that is Caesar's death having been brought on by a cold, 'Caesar's death was brought on by a cold' is not true.[14]

These gerunds can get to be a bore, and we have a way around them in 'fact that' clauses. The entity to which 'The cat has mange' corresponds is the cat's having of mange; equivalently, it is the fact that the cat has mange. Quite generally we get a singular term for the entity to which a sentence corresponds by prefixing 'the fact that' to the sentence; assuming, of course, there are such entities.

Philosophical interest in facts springs partly from their promise for explaining truth. It's clear that most sentences would not have the truth value they do if the world were not the way it is, but *what* in the world makes a sentence true? Not just the objects to which a sentence refers (in the sense explained above), but

---

[14] For simplicity's sake I speak as if truth were a property of sentences: more properly it is a relation between a sentence, a person and a time. (We could equally think of truth as a property of utterances, of tokens, or of speech acts.) I assume here that when truth is attributed to a sentence, or reference to a singular term, the suppressed relativization to a speaker and a time could always be supplied; if so, the ellipsis is harmless.

rather the doings and havings of relations and properties of those objects; in two words, the facts. It seems that a fact contains, in appropriate array, just the objects any sentence it verifies is about. No wonder we may not be satisfied with the colourless 'corresponds to' for the relation between a true sentence and its fact; there is something, we may feel, to be said for 'is true to', 'is faithful to', or even 'pictures'.

To specify a fact is, then, a way of explaining what makes a sentence true. On the other hand, simply to say that a sentence is true is to say there is some fact or other to which it corresponds. On this account, *'s* is true to (or corresponds to) the facts' means more literally *'s* corresponds to a fact'. Just as we can say there is a fact to which a sentence corresponds when the sentence is true, we can also say there is a true sentence corresponding to a particular fact; this latter comes down to saying of the fact that it is one. English sentences that perhaps express this idea are 'That the cat has mange is a fact' and 'It is a fact that London is in Canada', and even 'London is in Canada, and that's a fact.' It is evident that we must distinguish here between idioms of at least two sorts, those that attribute fact-hood to an entity (a fact), and those that say of a sentence that it corresponds to a fact (or 'the facts'). Let us use the following sentences as our samples of the two sorts of idiom:

(1) That the cat has mange is a fact.
(2) The sentence, 'The cat has mange' corresponds to a fact.

Professor Martin says his analysis is intended to apply to sentences of the form 'So-and-so is a fact' where I suppose 'so-and-so' is to be replaced, typically, by a that-clause, and he suggests we interpret such sentences as saying of a sentence that it is true (non-analytically—but I shall ignore this twist). Which of the two idioms represented by (1) and (2) is Martin analysing? The sentences Martin says he wants to analyse apparently have the form of (1); his analysis, on the other hand, seems suited to sentences like (2).

Suppose we try the second tack. Then Martin's proposal comes to this: where we appear to say of a sentence that there is a fact to which it corresponds we might as well say simply that the sentence is true. There is nothing in this yet to offend the most devoted friend of facts. Martin has not explained away a singular term that ever purported to refer to a fact; on his analysis, as on the one the friend of facts would give, the only singular term in, 'The sentence "The cat has mange" corresponds to the facts' refers to a sentence. Nor would the friend of facts want to deny the equivalence of *'s* is true' and *'s* corresponds to a fact' when *'s'* is replaced by the name or description of a sentence. The friend of facts would, however, balk at the claim that this shows how, *in general*, to eliminate quantification over facts, or singular terms that refer to them. He would contend that it is only sentence (1) with its apparent singular term 'that the cat has mange' which clearly calls for an ontology of facts. Martin may reply that it is sentence (1) he had his eye on from the start. This reply leaves (2) out in the cold unless, of course, (1) and (2) can be given the same analysis. The partisan of facts will resist this idea, and plausibly, I think, on the ground that (2) is merely an existential generalization of the more interesting:

(3) The sentence, 'The cat has mange' corresponds to the fact that the cat has mange.

Here Martin's attempt to treat facts as sentences cannot be made to work without reducing (3) to the statement that the sentence, 'The cat has mange' corresponds to itself, and this cannot be right since (3), like (2), is clearly *semantical* in character; it relates a sentence to the world. Martin recognizes the semantic thrust in talk of facts, but does not notice that it cannot be reconciled with his analysis of (1).

Martin's thesis that we do not need an ontology of facts could still be saved by an argument to show that there is at most one fact, for the interest in taking sentences like (3) as containing singular terms referring to facts depends on the assumption that there is an indefinitely large number of different facts to be referred to: if there were only one, we could submerge reference to it into what might as well be considered a one-place predicate.[15] And an argument is handy, thanks to Frege, showing that if sentences refer at all, all true sentences must refer to the same thing.[16]

We may then with easy conscience side with Martin in viewing 'corresponds to a fact', when said of a sentence, as conveying no more than 'is true'. What should we say of the sentences like (1) that appear to attribute facthood to entities? As we have seen, such sentences cannot be analysed as being about sentences. Bearing in mind the unity of fact, we might say (1) affirms The Great Fact, or tells The Truth, by way of one of its infinity of tags, 'The cat has mange.' We could equally well accept the universe with 'That London is in Canada is a fact.' Equivalently, we could have simply said, 'London is in Canada.' So, on my account, 'The sentence "The cat has mange" corresponds to the facts' comes out 'The sentence "The cat has mange" is true', but 'That the cat has mange is a fact' comes out just 'The cat has mange'; not at all the same thing.[17]

It is often assumed or argued (though not by Martin) that events are a species of fact. Austin, for example, says, 'Phenomena, events, situations, states of affairs are commonly supposed to be genuinely-in-the-world. . . . Yet surely of all these we can say that they *are facts*. The collapse of the Germans is an event and is a fact—was an event and was a fact'.[18] Reichenbach even treats the words 'event'

[15] For a more general treatment of 'ontological reduction' by incorporation of a finite number of singular terms into predicates, see Quine's 'Existence and Quantification' and 'Ontological Reduction and the World of Numbers', 203.

[16] For the argument, see Essay 2. For the argument and discussion, see A. Church, *Introduction to Mathematical Logic*, 24–5.

[17] I think that failure to observe the distinction between these two cases is the cause of some of the endless debate whether attributions of truth are redundant.

[18] J. L. Austin, 'Unfair to Facts', 104.

and 'fact' as synonyms, or so he says.[19] The pressure to treat events as facts is easy, in a way, to understand: both offer themselves as what sentences—some sentence at least—refer to or are about. Causal laws, we are told, say that every event of a certain sort is followed by an event of another sort. According to Hempel, the sentence, 'The length of copper rod r increased between 9.00 and 9.01 a.m.' describes a particular event.[20] In philosophical discussion of action these days we very often learn such things as that 'Jones raised his arm' and 'Jones signalled' may describe the same action, or that an agent may perform an action intentionally under one description and not under another. It is obvious that most of the sentences usually said to be about events contain no singular terms that even appear to refer to events, nor are they normally shown to have variables that take events as values when put over into ordinary quantificational notation. The natural conclusion is that sentences as wholes describe or refer to events, just as they were said to correspond as wholes to facts, and this, as we have seen, must be wrong.

Martin does not fall into this common trap, for although he constructs singular terms for events from the material of a sentence, he does not have the sentence itself refer to an event. His procedure is to view an event as an ordered n-tuple made up of the extensions of the $n-1$ singular terms and the $n-1$-place predicate of a true sentence. So, 'Leopold met Stephen on Bloomsday' gives us the singular term, '$\langle M, l, s, b \rangle$' which refers to Leopold's meeting of Stephen on Bloomsday provided Leopold did meet Stephen on Bloomsday. I shall ignore the further step by which Martin eliminates ordered n-tuples in favour of virtual ordered n-tuples; the difficulties about to appear are independent of that idea.[21]

Given the premise that Bloomsday is 16 June 1904, we may infer from, 'Leopold met Stephen on Bloomsday' the sentence, 'Leopold met Stephen on 16 June 1904', and, events being the ordered n-tuples they are, Leopold's meeting of Stephen on Bloomsday is identical with Leopold's meeting of Stephen on 16 June 1904. This is surely as it should be so far; but not, I'm afraid, farther. Not every encounter is a meeting; according to the story, some encounters between Leopold and Stephen are meetings and some are not. But then by Martin's account no meeting is identical with an encounter, though between the same individuals and at the same time. The reason is that if any encounter is not a meeting, $\langle E, l, s, b \rangle$ is not identical with $\langle M, l, s, b \rangle$. Indeed, Leopold's first meeting with Stephen on Bloomsday in Dublin cannot be identical with Leopold's first meeting with Stephen on Bloomsday (since a fourplace predicate can't have the same extension as a three-place predicate); nor can a meeting between Stephen and Bloom be identical with a meeting between Bloom and Stephen (since entities will be ordered in a different way). No stabbing can be a

[19] Hans Reichenbach, *Elements of Symbolic Logic*, 269.
[20] Carl Hempel, *Aspects of Scientific Explanation*, 421.
[21] Substantially the same analysis of events as Martin's has been given by Jaegwon Kim, 'On the Psycho-Physical Identity Theory'. Kim does not take the extra step from real to virtual n-tuples.

killing and no killing can be a murder, no arm-raising a signalling, and no birthday party a celebration. I protest.

Martin's conditions on identity of events are clearly not necessary, but are they perhaps sufficient? Again I think the answer is no. Martin correctly remarks that on his analysis the expressions that are supposed to refer to events refer to one entity at most; but are these entities the events they should be? Suppose Leopold met Stephen more than once on Bloomsday; what unique meeting does Martin's ordered *n*-tuple pick out? 'Leopold's meeting with Stephen on Bloomsday', like Martin's '$\langle M, l, s, b \rangle$', is a true singular term. But there is this difference, that the first refers to a meeting if it refers to anything, while the second does not. Being more specific about time will not really mend matters: John's kissing of a girl at precisely noon is not a unique kissing if he kissed two girls simultaneously. Martin's method cannot be systematically applied to form singular terms guaranteed to pick out a particular kissing, marriage, or meeting if anything; but this is easy, with gerund phrases, in English.

Martin's mistake is natural, and it is connected with a basic confusion about the relation between a sentence like 'Leopold met Stephen on Bloomsday' or 'Caesar died' and particular events like Leopold's meeting with Stephen on Bloomsday or Caesar's death. The mistake may be encapsulated in the idea (common to Martin and many others) that 'Leopold met Stephen on Bloomsday' comes to the same as 'Leopold's meeting with Stephen on Bloomsday occurred' or that 'Caesar died' may be rendered 'Caesar's death took place'. 'Caesar's death', like 'Leopold's meeting with Stephen', is a true singular term, and so 'Caesar's death took place' and 'Leopold's meeting with Stephen occurred' are true only if there was just one such meeting or death. But 'Caesar died' is true even if Caesar died a thousand deaths, and Leopold and Stephen may meet as often as they please on Bloomsday without falsifying 'Leopold met Stephen on Bloomsday.'

A sentence such as 'Vesuvius erupted in A.D. 79' no more refers to an individual event than 'There's a fly in here' refers to an individual fly. Of course there may be just one eruption that verifies the first sentence and just one fly that verifies the second; but that is beside the point. The point is that neither sentence can properly be interpreted as referring or describing, or being about, a particular eruption or fly. No singular term for such is in the offing. 'There's a fly in here' is existential and general with respect to flies in here; 'Vesuvius erupted in A.D. 79' is existential and general with respect to eruptions of Vesuvius in A.D. 79—if there are such things as eruptions, of course.

Here I am going along with Ramsey who, in a passage quoted by Martin, wrote, ' "That Caesar died" is really an existential proposition, asserting the existence of an event of a certain sort, thus resembling "Italy has a King", which asserts the existence of a man of a certain sort. The event which is of that sort is called the death of Caesar, and should no more be confused with the fact that Caesar died than the King of Italy should be confused with the fact that Italy has a King.'[22] This seems to me nearly exactly right: facts, if such there are, correspond to whole sentences, while events, if such there are, correspond to singular terms like 'Caesar's death', and are quantified over in sentences such as 'Caesar died.'[23]

Martin says he doubts that 'Caesar died' must, or perhaps even can, be construed as asserting the existence of an event of a certain sort. I want to demonstrate briefly first that it can, and then, even more briefly, why I think it must.

It can be done by providing event-verbs with one more place than we generally think necessary, a place for events. I propose that 'died' in 'Caesar died' be taken as a two-place predicate, one place for 'Caesar' and another for a variable ranging over events. The sentence as a whole then becomes '$(\exists x)$ (Died (Caesar, x))', that is, there exists a Caesar-dying event, or there exists an event that is a dying of Caesar. There is no problem in forming a singular term like 'Caesar's death' from these materials: it is '$(\imath x)$ (Died (Caesar, x))'. We may then say truly, though this is not equivalent to 'Caesar died', that Caesar died just once: '$(\exists y)$ ($y = (\imath x)$ (Died (Caesar, x)))'; we may even say Caesar died Caesar's death: 'Died (Caesar, $(\imath x)$ (Died (Caesar, x)))'.

This gives us some idea what it would be like to treat events seriously as individuals, with variables ranging over them, and with corresponding singular terms. It is clear, I think, that none of the objections I have considered to Reichenbach's, Kim's, or Martin's analyses apply to the present suggestion. We *could* introduce an ontology of events in this way, but of course the question remains whether there is any good reason to do so. I have already mentioned some of the contexts, in the analysis of action, of explanation, and of causality in which we seem to need to talk of events; still, faced with a basic ontological decision, we might well try to explain the need as merely seeming. There remains however a clear problem that is solved by admitting events, and that has no other solution I know of.

The problem is simple, and ubiquitous. It can be illustrated by pointing out that 'Brutus stabbed Caesar in the back in the Forum with a knife' entails 'Brutus stabbed Caesar in the back in the Forum' and both these entail 'Brutus stabbed Caesar in the back' and all these entail 'Brutus stabbed Caesar'; and yet our common way of symbolizing these sentences reveals no logical connection. It may be thought the needed entailments could be supplied by interpreting 'Brutus stabbed Caesar' as elliptical for 'Brutus stabbed Caesar somewhere (in Caesar) somewhere (in the world) with something', but this is a general solution only if we know some fixed number of places for the predicate 'stabbed' large enough to

[22] Ramsey, F. P., *Foundations of Mathematics*, 138ff.

[23] Austin blundered when he thought a phrase like 'the collapse of the Germans' could unambiguously refer to a fact and to an event. Zeno Vendler very shrewdly uncovers the error, remarking that 'in as much as the collapse of the Germans is a fact, it can be mentioned or denied, it can be unlikely or probable, it can shock or surprise us; in as much as it is an event, however, and not a fact, it can be observed and followed, it can be sudden, violent, or prolonged, it can occur, begin, last and end.' This is from 'Comments' by Vendler (on a paper by Jerrold Katz).

accommodate all eventualities. It's unlikely we shall succeed, for a phrase like 'by' can introduce an indefinitely large number of modifications, as in 'He hung the picture by putting a nail in the wall, which in turn he did by hitting the nail with a hammer, which in turn he did by. . . .'[24] Intuitively, there is no end to what we can say about the causes and consequences of events; our theory of language has gone badly astray if we must treat each adverbial modification as introducing a new place into a predicate. The problem, you can easily persuade yourself, is not peculiar to verbs of action.

My proposed analysis of sentences with event-verbs solves this difficulty, for once we have events to talk about, we can say as much or as little as we please about them. Thus the troublesome sentence becomes (not in symbols, and not quite in English): 'There exists an event that is a stabbing of Caesar by Brutus event, it is an into the back of Caesar event, it took place in the Forum, and Brutus did it with a knife.' The wanted entailments now go through as a matter of form.

Before we enthusiastically embrace an ontology of events we will want to think long and hard about the criteria for individuating them. I am myself inclined to think we can do as well for events generally as we can for physical objects generally (which is not very well), and can do much better for sorts of events, like deaths and meetings, just as we can for sorts of physical objects, like tables and people. But all this must wait.[25] Meanwhile the situation seems to me to be this: there is a lot of language we can make systematic sense of if we suppose events exist, and we know no promising alternative. The presumption lies with events.

H. *Reply to Cargile.* I suggested that sentences about events and actions be construed as requiring an ontology of particular, unrepeatable, dated events. For example, I argued that a sentence like 'Lucifer fell' has the logical form of an existential quantification of an open sentence true of falls of Lucifer, the open sentence in turn consisting of a two-place predicate true of ordered pairs of things and their falls, and the predicate places filled with a proper name ('Lucifer') and a free variable (bound by the quantifier). I did not explain in detail what I meant by logical form, though I did devote some paragraphs to the subject. I suppose I thought the problems set, the examples and counter-examples offered, the arguments given and the answers entertained would, taken with the tradition and my hints, make the idea clear enough. I was wrong; and in retrospect I sympathize with my misunderstanders. I will try to do better.

Logical form was invented to contrast with something else that is held to be apparent but mere: the form we are led to assign to sentences by superficial analogy or traditional grammar. What meets the eye or ear in language has the

---

[24] I am indebted to Daniel Bennett for the example.   [25] See Essay 4.

charm, complexity, convenience, and deceit of other conventions of the market place, but underlying it is the solid currency of a plainer, duller structure, without wit but also without pretence. This true coin, the deep structure, need never feature directly in the transactions of real life. As long as we know how to redeem our paper we can enjoy the benefits of credit.

The image may help explain why the distinction between logical form and surface grammar can flourish without anyone ever quite explaining it. But what can we say to someone who wonders whether there is really any gold in the vaults? I think the concept of logical form can be clarified and thus defended; but the account I shall offer disclaims some of what is implied by the previous paragraph.

What do we mean when we say that 'Whales are mammals' is a quantified sentence? James Cargile suggests that the sentence is elliptical for 'All whales are mammals' (or 'Some whales are mammals') and once the ellipsis is mended we see that the sentence is quantified. Someone interested in logical form would, of course, go much further: he would maintain that 'All whales are mammals' is a universally quantified conditional whose antecedent is an open sentence true of whales and whose consequent is an open sentence true of mammals. The contrast with surface grammar is striking. The subject-predicate analysis goes by the board, 'all whales' is no longer treated as a unit, and the role of 'whales' and of 'mammals' is seen, or claimed, to be predicative.

What can justify this astonishing theory? Part of the answer—the part with which we are most familiar—is that inference is simplified and mechanized when we rewrite sentences in some standardized notation. If we want to deduce 'Moby Dick is a mammal' from 'All whales are mammals' and 'Moby Dick is a whale', we need to connect the predicate 'is a whale' in some systematic way with a suitable feature of 'All whales are mammals'. The theory of the logical form of this sentence tells us how.

Words for temporal precedence, like 'before' and 'after', provide another example. 'The inflation came after the war' is simple enough, at least if we accept events as entities, but how about 'Earwicker slept before Shem kicked Shaun'? Here 'before' connects expressions with the grammatical form of sentences. How is this 'before' related to the one that stands between descriptions of events? Is it a sentential connective, like 'and'? 'Earwicker slept before Shem kicked Shaun' does entail both 'Earwicker slept' and 'Shem kicked Shaun'. Yet clearly 'before' is not truth-functional, since reversing the order of the sentences does not preserve truth.

The solution proposed by Frege has been widely (if not universally) accepted; it is, as we all know, to think of our sentence as doubly quantified by existential quantifiers, to introduce extra places into the predicates to accommodate variables ranging over times, and to interpret 'before' as a two-place predicate. The result, roughly, is: 'There exist two times, t and u, such that Earwicker slept at t, Shem kicked Shaun at u, and t was before u.' This analysis relates the two uses of 'before', and it explains why 'Earwicker slept before Shem kicked Shaun' entails 'Shem kicked Shaun'. It does this, however, only by attributing to 'Shem kicked Shaun' the following form: 'There exists a *t* such that Shem kicked Shaun at *t*.' According to Cargile, not even Russell would have denied that '*x* kicked *y*' is a two-place relation form; but Russell had the same motive Frege did for holding that 'kicked' has the logical form of a three-place predicate.

The logical form that the problem of 'before' prompts us to assign to 'Shem kicked Shaun' and to its parts is the very form I suggested, though my reasons were somewhat different, and the ontology was different. So far as ontology is concerned, the two proposals may to advantage be merged, for we may think of 'before' and 'after' as relating events as easily as times. For most purposes, if not all, times are like lengths—convenient abstractions with which we can dispense in favour of the concreta that have them. A significant bonus from this analysis of sentences of temporal priority is that singular causal sentences can then be naturally related to them. According to Hume, if *x* caused *y*, then *x* preceded *y*. What are the entities these variables range over? Events, to be sure. But if this answer is to be taken seriously, then a sentence like 'Sandy's rocking the boat caused it to sink' must somehow refer to events. It does, if we analyse it along these lines: 'There exist two events, *e* and *f*, such that *e* is a rocking of the boat by Sandy, *f* is a sinking of the boat, and *e* caused *f*.'

Let us suppose, as Cargile seems willing to do, that I am right to this extent: by rewriting or rephrasing certain sentences into sentences that explicitly refer to or quantify over events, we can conveniently represent the entailment relations between the original sentences. The entailments we preanalytically recognize to hold between the original sentences become matters of quantificational logic applied to their rephrasals. And now Cargile asks: how can this project, assuming it to be successfully carried out, justify the claim that the original sentences have the logical form of their rewrites? Why not admit that the rewrites show, in many cases, a different form?

Here we have, I hope, the makings of a reconciliation, for I am happy to admit that much of the interest in logical form comes from an interest in logical geography: to give the logical form of a sentence is to give its logical location in the totality of sentences, to describe it in a way that explicitly determines what sentences it entails and what sentences it is entailed by. The location must be given relative to a specific deductive theory; so logical form itself is relative to a theory. The relatively does not stop here, either, since even given a theory of deduction there may be more than one total scheme for interpreting the sentences we are interested in and that preserves the pattern of entailments. The logical form of a particular sentence is, then, relative both to a theory of deduction and to some prior determinations as to how to render sentences in the language of the theory.

Seen in this light, to call the paraphrase of a sentence into some standard first-order quantificational form *the* logical form of the sentence seems arbitrary indeed. Quantification theory has its celebrated merits, to be sure: it is powerful, simple, consistent, and complete in its way. Not least, there are more or less standard techniques for paraphrasing many sentences of natural languages into quantificational languages, which helps excuse not making the relativity to a theory explicit. Still, the relativity remains.

Since there is no eliminating the relativity of logical form to a background theory, the only way to justify particular claims about logical form is by showing that they fit sentences into a *good* theory, at least a theory better than known alternatives. In calling quantificational form logical form I was assuming, like many others before me, that quantification theory is a good theory. What's so good about it?

Well, we should not sneeze at the virtues mentioned above, its known consistency and completeness (in the sense that all quantificational truths are provable). Cargile takes me to task for criticizing Reichenbach's analysis of sentences about events, which introduces an operator that, when prefixed to a sentence, results in a singular term referring to an event. I give a standard argument to show that on this analysis, if one keeps substitutivity of identity and a simple form of extensionality, all events collapse into one. I concluded, 'This demonstrates, I think, that Reichenbach's analysis is radically defective'. Cargile protests that Reichenbach gets in no trouble if the assumption of extensionality is abandoned; and the assumption is mine, not Reichenbach's. Fair enough; I ought not to have said the analysis was defective, but rather that on a natural assumption there was a calamitous consequence. Without the assumption there is no such consequence; but also no theory. Standard quantification theory plus Reichenbach's theory of event sentences plus substitutivity of identity in the new contexts leads to collapse of all events into one. Reichenbach indirectly commits himself to the principle of substitutivity, and Cargile goes along explicitly. So they are apparently committed to giving up standard quantification theory. Since neither offers a substitute, it is impossible to evaluate the position.[26]

Cargile has another idea, which is not to tamper with quantification theory, but simply to add some extra rules to it. If we give the quantificational form of 'Jones buttered the toast in the bathroom' as 'Buttered$_3$ (Jones, the toast, the bathroom)' and of 'Jones buttered the toast' as 'Buttered$_2$ (Jones, the toast)' then the inference from the first to the second is no longer a matter of quantificational logic; but why not interpret this as showing that quantificational form isn't logical form, and quantificational logic isn't all of logic? Cargile suggests that we might be able to give a purely formal (syntactical) rule that would systematize these inferences. I think Cargile underestimates the difficulties in doing this,

---

[26] For a discussion of the difficulties of combining substitutivity of identity and non-extensionality, see Dagfinn Føllesdal, 'Quine on Modality'.

particularly if, as I have argued, such an approach forces us to admit predicates with indefinitely large numbers of predicate places. I also think he slights the difference, in his remark that 'the standard symbolism of quantification theory is not good at keeping track of entailments between relational forms in English', between simple axioms (which are all that are needed to keep track of the entailments between relational forms in, say, a theory of measurement) and new rules of inference (or axiom schemata). But harping on the difficulties, unless they can be proven to be impossibilities, is inconclusive. It will be more instructive to assume that we are presented with a satisfactory deductive system that adds to quantification theory rules adequate to implement the entailments between event sentences of the sort under consideration. What could then be said in defence of my analysis?

What can be said comes down to this: it explains more, and it explains better. It explains more in the obvious sense of bringing more data under fewer rules. Given my account of the form of sentences about events and actions, certain entailments are a matter of quantificational logic; an account of the kind Cargile hopes to give requires quantificational logic, and then some. But there is a deeper difference.

We catch sight of the further difference if we ask ourselves why 'Jones buttered the toast in the bathroom' entails 'Jones buttered the toast'. So far, Cargile's only answer is, because 'buttered' and some other verbs (listed or characterized somehow) work that way; and my only answer is, because (given my paraphrases) it follows from the rules of quantification theory. But now suppose we ask, *why* do the rules endorse this inference? Surely it has something to do with the fact that 'buttered' turns up in both sentences? There must be a common conceptual element represented by this repeated syntactic feature; we would have a clue to it, and hence a better understanding of the meaning of the two sentences, if we could say what common role 'buttered' has in the two sentences. But here it is evident that Cargile's rules, if they were formulated, would be no help. These rules treat the fact that the word 'buttered' turns up in both sentences as an accident: the rule would work as well if unrelated words were used for the two- and for the three-place predicates. In the analysis I have proposed, the word 'buttered' is discovered to have a common role in the two sentences: in both cases it is a predicate satisfied by certain ordered triples of agents, things buttered, and events. So now we have the beginnings of a new sort of answer to the question why one of our sentences entails the other: it depends on the fact that the word 'buttered' is playing a certain common role in both sentences. By saying exactly what the role is, and what the roles of the other significant features of the sentences are, we will have a deep explanation of why one sentence entails the other, an explanation that draws on a systematic account of how the meaning of each sentence is a function of its structure.

To exhibit an entailment as a matter of quantificational form is to explain it better because we do not need to take the rules of quantificational logic on faith;

we can show that they are *valid*, i.e., truth-preserving, by giving an account of the conditions under which sentences in quantificational form are true. From such an account (a theory of truth satisfying Tarski's criteria) it can be seen that if certain sentences are true, others must be. The rules of quantificational logic are justified when we demonstrate that from truths they can lead only to truths.

Plenty of inferences that some might call logical cannot be shown to be valid in any interesting way by appeal to a theory of truth, for example the inference to '*a* is larger than *c*' from '*a* is larger than *b* and *b* is larger than *c*' or to 'Henry is not a man' from 'Henry is a frog'. Clearly a recursive account of truth can ignore these entailments simply by ignoring the logical features of the particular predicates involved. But if I am right, it may not be possible to give a coherent theory of truth that applies to sentences about events and that does not validate the adverbial inferences we have been discussing.

Let me state in more detail how I think our sample inference can be shown to be valid. On my view, a theory of truth would entail that 'Jones buttered the toast in the bathroom' is true if and only if there exists an event satisfying these two conditions: it is a buttering of the toast by Jones, and it occurred in the bathroom. But if these conditions are satisfied, then there is an event that is a buttering of the toast by Jones, and this is just what must be the case, according to the theory, if 'Jones buttered the toast' is true. I put the matter this way because it seems to me possible that Cargile may agree with what I say, then adding, 'But how does this show that "Jones buttered the toast" is a three-place predicate?' If this *is* his response, our troubles are over, or anyway are merely verbal, for all I *mean* by saying that 'Jones buttered the toast' has the logical form of an existentially quantified sentence, and that 'buttered' is a three-piece predicate, is that a theory of truth meeting Tarski's criteria would entail that this sentence is true if and only if there exists . . . etc. By my lights, we have given the logical form of a sentence when we have given the truth-conditions of the sentence in the context of a theory of truth that applies to the language as a whole. Such a theory must identify some finite stock of truth-relevant elements, and explicitly account for the truth-conditions of each sentence by how these elements feature in it; so to give the logical form of a sentence is to describe it as composed of the elements the theory isolates.

These remarks will help, I hope, to put talk of 'paraphrasing' or 'translating' in its place. A theory of truth entails, for each sentence *s* of the object language, a theorem of the form '*s* is true if and only if *p*'. Since the sentence that replaces '*p*' must be true (in the metalanguage) if and only if *s* is true (in the object language), there is a sense in which the sentence that replaces '*p*' may be called a translation of *s*; and if the metalanguage contains the object language, it may be called a paraphrase. (These claims must be modified in important ways in a theory of truth for a natural language.) But it should be emphasized that paraphrasis or translation serves no purpose here except that of giving a systematic account of truth-conditons. There is no further claim to synonymy, nor interest in regimentation or improvement. A theory of truth gives a point to such concepts as meaning, translation, and logical form; it does not depend on them.[27]

It should now be clear that my only reason for 'rendering' or 'paraphrasing' event sentences into quantificational form was as a way of giving the truth-conditions for those sentences within a going theory of truth. We have a clear semantics for first-order quantificational languages, and so if we can see how to paraphrase sentences in a natural language into quantificational form, we see how to extend a theory of truth to those sentences. Since the entailments that depend on quantificational form can be completely formalized, it is an easy test of our success in capturing logical form within a theory of truth to see whether our paraphrases articulate the entailments we independently recognize as due to form.

To give the logical form of a sentence is, then, for me, to describe it in terms that bring it within the scope of a semantic theory that meets clear requirements. Merely providing formal rules of inference, as Cargile suggests, thus fails to touch the question of logical form (except by generalizing some of the data a theory must explain); showing how to put sentences into quantificational form, on the other hand, does place them in the context of a semantic theory. The contrast is stark, for it is the contrast between having a theory, and hence a hypothesis about logical form, and having no theory, and hence no way of making sense of claims about form. But of course this does not show that a theory based on first-order quantificational structure and its semantics is all we need or can have. Many philosophers and logicians who have worked on the problem of event sentences (not to mention modalities, sentences about propositional attitudes, and so on) have come to the conclusion that a richer semantics is required, and can be provided. In Essay 2 above, I explicitly put to one side several obvious problems that invite appeal to such richer schemes. For various reasons I thought, or hoped, that the problem I isolated could be handled within a fairly austere scheme. But when other problems are also emphasized, it may well be that my simple proposal loses its initial appeal; at least the theory must be augmented, and perhaps it will have to be abandoned.

Cargile thinks that instead of suggesting that 'Shem kicked Shaun' has a logical form that is made more explicit by '$(\exists x)$ (Kicked (Shem, Shaun, x))' I ought (at most) to have said that the two sentences are logically equivalent (but have different logical forms). He makes an analogous point in defending Reichenbach against my strictures. I want to explain why I resist this adjustment.

Of course it can happen that two sentences are logically equivalent, yet have different logical forms; for example a sentence with the logical form of a conjunction is logically equivalent to the conjunction which takes the conjuncts in reverse order. Here we assume the theory gives the truth-conditions of each

---

[27] These claims and others made here are expanded and defended in my 'Truth and Meaning' (Essay 8, this volume).

sentence, and it will be possible to prove that one sentence is true if and only if the other is. But the theory doesn't independently supply truth-conditions for 'Shem kicked Shaun' and its canonical counterpart; rather the latter gives (or, in the present discussion, is used to suggest) the truth conditions of the former. If the theory were turned on itself, as well it might be, the sentence used to give the truth-conditions of '$(\exists x)$ (Kicked (Shem, Shaun, x))' would have the same form as this sentence; under some natural conditions, it would be this sentence. So there is no way within the theory of assigning different logical forms to 'Shem kicked Shaun' and its explicitly quantificational stand-in. Outside a theory, the notion of logical form has no clear application, as we have noted. That the two sentences have very different syntactical structures is evident; that is why the claim that the logical form is the same is interesting and, if correct, revealing.

Suppose that a rule of inference is added to our logic, making each of the two sentences deducible from the other. (Reichenbach may have had this in mind: see *Elements of Symbolic Logic*, § 48.) Will this then make it possible to hold that the sentences have different logical forms? The answer is as before: rules of inference that are not backed by a semantic theory are irrelevant to logical form.

I would like to mention very briefly another point on which Cargile may have misunderstood me. He says that, 'The idea that philosophical "analysis" consists in this revealing of logical form is a popular one . . .' and he may think I share this notion. I don't, and I said that I didn't on the first page of the article he discusses. Even if philosophical analysis were concerned only with language (which I do not believe), revealing logical form would be only part of the enterprise. To know the logical form of a sentence is to know, in the context of a comprehensive theory, the semantic roles of the significant features of the sentence. Aside from the logical constants, this knowledge leaves us ignorant of the relations between predicates, and of their logical properties. To know the logical form of 'The rain caused the flood' is to know whether 'caused' is a sentential connective or a two-place predicate (or something else), but it hardly begins to be knowledge of an analysis of the concept of causality (or the word 'caused'). Or perhaps it is the beginning; but that is all.

On the score of ontology, too, the study of logical form can carry us only a certain distance. If I am right, we cannot give a satisfactory account of the semantics of certain sentences without recognizing that if any of those sentences are true, there must exist such things as events and actions. Given this much, a study of event sentences will show a great deal about what we assume to be true concerning events. But deep metaphysical problems will remain as to the nature of these entities, their mode of individuation, their relations to other categories. Perhaps we will find a way of reducing events to entities of other kinds, for example, sets of points in space-time, or ordered n-tuples of times, physical objects, and classes of ordered n-tuples of such. Successful reductions along these lines may, in an honoured tradition, be advertised as showing that there are no such things as events. As long as the quantifiers and variables remain in the same places, however, the analysis of logical form will stick.

I. *Reply to Hedman.* If we are committed to events, we are committed to making sense of identity-sentences, like '$a = b$', where the terms flanking the identity sign refer to events. I think in fact we use sentences in this form constantly: 'The third round of the fight was (identical with) the one in which he took a dive', 'Our worst accident was (identical with) the one where we hit four other cars', 'Falling off the tower was (identical with) the cause of his death'. The problem of individuation for events is the problem of giving criteria saying when such sentences are true. Carl Hedman raises a tricky question about these criteria as applied to actions.

In Essay 2 above, I asserted, as Hedman says, that 'intentional actions are not a class of actions'. I said this to protect my theory against an obvious objection. If 'intentional' modifies actions the way 'in the kitchen' does, then intentional actions *are* a class of actions. Does Oedipus's striking of the rude old man belong in this class or not? Oedipus struck the rude old man intentionally, but he did not strike his father intentionally. But on my theory, these strikings were one, since the rude old man was Oedipus's father. The obvious solution, which I endorsed, is to take 'intentionally' as creating a semantically opaque context in which one would expect substitutivity of identity to seem to fail.

I did not argue for this view in the article Hedman discusses; in the long passage he quotes I say only that it is 'the natural and, I think, correct answer'. In that passage I was surveying a number of topics, such as causality, theory of action, explanations, and the identity theory of mind, where philosophers tend to say things which take for granted an ontology of events and actions. My point was that if they do make this assumption, they ought to come up with a serious theory about how reference to events occurs; my intention was to soften up potential opposition to the analysis which (I argued) is forced on us anyway when we try to give a systematic semantics for natural language.

Elsewhere I have argued for the view that one and the same action may be correctly said to be intentional (when described in one way) and not intentional (when described in another). The position is hardly new with me; it was expounded at length by Anscombe,[28] and has been accepted by many other writers on action. It is harder to avoid taking this position than one might think. I suppose no one wants to deny that if the rude old man was Oedipus's father, then 'Oedipus struck the rude old man' and 'Oedipus struck his father' entail one another. If one accepts, as Hedman apparently does, an ontology of events, one will also presumably want to infer 'The striking of the rude old man by Oedipus occurred at the crossroads' from 'The striking of Oedipus's father by Oedipus occurred at the crossroads' and vice versa. But how can these entailments be

---

[28] G. E. M. Anscombe, *Intention.*

shown (by a semantical theory) to be valid without also proving the following to be true: 'The striking of the rude old man by Oedipus was identical with the striking of Oedipus's father by Oedipus'? Yet one of these actions was intentional and the other not. I don't say no theory could be contrived to validate the wanted inferences while not endorsing the identity; but we don't now have such a theory.

3

How is Weakness of the Will Possible?

An agent's will is weak if he acts, and acts intentionally, counter to his own best judgement; in such cases we sometimes say he lacks the willpower to do what he knows, or at any rate believes, would, everything considered, be better. It will be convenient to call actions of this kind incontinent actions, or to say that in doing them the agent acts incontinently. In using this terminology I depart from tradition, at least in making the class of incontinent actions larger than usual. But it is the larger class I want to discuss, and I believe it includes all of the actions some philosophers have called incontinent, and some of the actions many philosophers have called incontinent.

Let me explain how my conception of incontinence is more general than some others. It is often made a condition of an incontinent action that it be performed despite the agent's knowledge that another course of action is better. I count such actions incontinent, but the puzzle I shall discuss depends only on the attitude or belief of the agent, so it would restrict the field to no purpose to insist on knowledge. Knowledge also has an unneeded, and hence unwanted, flavour of the cognitive; my subject concerns evaluative judgements, whether they are analysed cognitively, prescriptively, or otherwise. So even the concept of belief is perhaps too special, and I shall speak of what the agent judges or holds.

If a man holds some course of action to be the best one, everything considered, or the right one, or the thing he ought to do, and yet does something else, he acts incontinently. But I would also say he acts incontinently provided he holds some available course of action to be better on the whole than the one he takes; or that, as between some other course of action which he believes open to him and the action he performs, he judges that he ought to perform the other. In other words, comparative judgements suffice for incontinence. We may now characterize an action that reveals weakness of the will or incontinence:

> D. In doing x an agent acts incontinently if and only if: (a) the agent does x intentionally; (b) the agent believes there is an alternative action y open to him; and (c) the agent judges that, all things considered, it would be better to do y than to do x.[1]

---

[1] In a useful article, G. Santas gives this account of incontinence: 'In a case of weakness a man does something that he knows or believes he should (ought) not do, or fails to do something that he

There seem to be incontinent actions in this sense. The difficulty is that their existence challenges another doctrine that has an air of self-evidence: that, in so far as a person acts intentionally he acts, as Aquinas puts it, in the light of some imagined good. This view does not, as it stands, directly contradict the claim that there are incontinent actions. But it is hard to deny that the considerations that recommend this view recommend also a relativized version: in so far as a person acts intentionally he acts in the light of what he imagines (judges) to be the better.

It will be useful to spell out this claim in the form of two principles. The first expresses the natural assumption about the relation between wanting or desiring something, and action. 'The primitive sign of wanting is trying to get', says Anscombe in *Intention*.[2] Hampshire comes closer to exactly what I need when he writes, in *Freedom of the Individual*,[3] that 'A wants to do X' is equivalent to 'other things being equal, he would do X, if he could'. Here I take (possibly contrary to Hampshire's intent) 'other things being equal' to mean, or anyway to allow, the interpretation, 'provided there is not something he wants more'. Given this interpretation, Hampshire's principle could perhaps be put:

P1. If an agent wants to do *x* more than he wants to do *y* and he believes himself free to do either *x* or *y*, then he will intentionally do *x* if he does either *x* or *y* intentionally.

The second principle connects judgements of what it is better to do with motivation or wanting:

P2. If an agent judges that it would be better to do *x* than to do *y*, then he wants to do *x* more than he wants to do *y*.

P1 and P2 together obviously entail that if an agent judges that it would be better for him to do *x* than to do *y*, and he believes himself to be free to do either *x* or *y*, then he will intentionally do *x* if he does either *x* or *y* intentionally. This conclusion, I suggest, appears to show that it is false that:

P3. There are incontinent actions.

Someone who is convinced that P1–P3 form an inconsistent triad, but who finds only one or two of the principles really persuasive, will have no difficulty deciding

---

knows or believes he should do, when the occasion and the opportunity for acting or refraining is present, and when it is in his power, in some significant sense, to act in accordance with his knowledge or belief.' ('Plato's *Protagoras* and Explanations of Weakness', 3.) Most of the differences between this description and mine are due to my deliberate deviation from the tradition. But there seem to me to be the two minor errors in Santas's account. First, weakness of the will does not require that the alternative action actually be available, only that the agent think it is. What Santas is after, and correctly, is that the agent acts freely; but for this it is not necessary that the alternative the agent thinks better (or that he ought to do) be open to him. On the other hand (and this is the second point), Santas's criteria are not sufficient to guarantee that the agent acts intentionally, and this is, I think, essential to incontinence.

² G. E. M. Anscombe, *Intention*, 67.   ³ S. Hampshire, *Freedom of the Individual*, 36.

what to say. But for someone (like myself) to whom the principles expressed by P1–P3 seem self-evident, the problem posed by the apparent contradiction is acute enough to be called a paradox. I cannot agree with Lemmon when he writes, in an otherwise admirable article, 'Perhaps akrasia is one of the best examples of a pseudo-problem in philosophical literature: in view of its existence, if you find it a problem you have already made a philosophical mistake.'[4] If your assumptions lead to a contradiction, no doubt you have made a mistake, but since you can know you have made a mistake without knowing what the mistake is, your problem may be real.

The attempted solutions with which I am familiar to the problem created by the initial plausibility of P1–P3 assume that P1–P3 do really contradict one another. These attempts naturally end by giving up one or another of the principles. I am not very happy about P1–P3 as I have stated them: perhaps it is easy to doubt whether they are true in just their present form (particularly P1 and P2). And reflecting on the ambiguities, or plurality of uses, of various critical words or phrases ('judge better', 'want', 'intentional') it is not surprising that philosophers have tried interpreting some key phrase as meaning one thing in one principle and meaning something else in another. But I am convinced that no amount of tinkering with P1–P3 will eliminate the underlying problem: the problem will survive new wording, refinement, and elimination of ambiguity. I shall mention a few of the standard moves, and try to discredit them, but endless ways of dealing with the problem will remain. My basic strategy is therefore not that of trying to make an airtight case for P1–P3, perhaps by working them into less exceptionable form. What I hope rather is to show that P1–P3 do not contradict one another, and therefore we do not have to give up any of them. At the same time I shall offer an explanation of why we are inclined to think P1–P3 lead to a contradiction; for if I am right, a common and important mistake explains our confusion, a mistake about the nature of practical reason.

I

Here are some of the ways in which philosophers have sought, or might seek, to cope with the problem of incontinence as I have stated it.

The sins of the leopard—lust, gluttony, avarice, and wrath—are the least serious sins for which we may be eternally damned, according to Dante. Dante has these sins, which he calls the sins of incontinence, punished in the second, third, fourth, and fifth circles of Hell. In a famous example, Dante describes the adulterous sin of Francesca da Rimini and Paolo Malatesta. Commentators show their cleverness by pointing out that even in telling her story Francesca reveals her weakness of character. Thus Charles Williams says, 'Dante so manages the

---

[4] E. J. Lemmon, 'Moral Dilemmas', 144–5.

description, he so heightens the excuse, that the excuse reveals itself as precisely the sin . . . the persistent parleying with the occasion of sin, the sweet prolonged laziness of love . . .'⁵ Perhaps all this is true of Francesca, but it is not essential to incontinence, for the 'weakness' may be momentary, not a character trait: when we speak of 'weakness' we may merely express, without explaining, the fact that the agent did what he knew to be wrong. ('It was one page did it.') Aristotle even seems to imply that it is impossible to be habitually incontinent, on the grounds that habitual action involves a principle in accord with which one acts, while the incontinent man acts against his principle. I suppose, then, that it is at least possible to perform isolated incontinent actions, and I shall discuss incontinence as a habit or vice only as the vice is construed as the vice of often or habitually performing incontinent actions.⁶

A man might hold it to be wrong, everything considered, for him to send a valentine to Marjorie Morningstar. Yet he might send a valentine to Marjorie Eveningstar, and do it intentionally, not knowing that Marjorie Eveningstar was identical with Marjorie Morningstar. We might want to say he did something he held to be wrong, but it would be misleading to say he intentionally did something he held to be wrong; and the case I illustrate is certainly not an example of an incontinent action. We must not, I hope it is clear, think that actions can be simply sorted into the incontinent and others. 'Incontinent', like 'intentional', 'voluntary', and 'deliberate', characterizes actions only as conceived in one way rather than another. In any serious analysis of the logical form of action sentences, such words must be construed, I think, as non-truth-functional sentential operators: 'It was incontinent of Francesca that . . .' and 'It was intentional of the agent that . . .' But for present purposes it is enough to avoid the mistake of overlooking the intentionality of these expressions.

Incontinence is often characterized in one of the following ways: the agent *intends* to do *y*, which he holds to be the best course, or a better course than doing *x*; nevertheless he does *x*. Or, the agent *decides* to do *y*, which he holds to be the best course, or a better course than doing *x*, and yet he does *x*. Or, the agent *chooses y* as the result of deliberation,⁷ and yet does *x*, which he deems inferior to *y*.

---

⁵ C. Williams, *The Figure of Beatrice*, 118.

⁶ 'Incontinence is not strictly a vice . . . for incontinence acts against choice, vice in accord with it' (*Nic. Eth.* 1151a); 'vice is like dropsy and consumption, while incontinence is like epilepsy, vice being chronic, incontinence intermittent' (1150b). But Donne apparently describes the vice of incontinence in one of the Holy Sonnets:

> Oh, to vex me, contraries meet in one;
> Inconstancy unnaturally hath begot
> A constant habit; that when I would not
> I change in vows, and in devotion.

⁷ Aristotle sometimes characterizes the incontinent man (the akrates) as 'abandoning his choice' (*Nic. Eth.*, 1151a) or 'abandoning the conclusion he has reached' (1145b); but also often along the lines suggested here: 'he does the thing he knows to be evil' (1134b) or 'he is convinced that he ought to do one thing and nevertheless does another thing' (1146b).

Each of these forms of behaviour is interesting, and given some provisos may be characterized as inconsistent, weak, vacillating, or irrational. Any of them might be a case of incontinence, as I have defined it. But as they stand, they are not necessarily cases of incontinence because none of them entails that at the time he acts the agent holds that another course of action would, all things considered, be better. And on the other hand, an action can be incontinent without the agent's ever having decided, chosen, or intended to do what he judges best.

Principle 2 states a mild form of internalism. It says that a judgement of value must be reflected in wants (or desires or motives). This is not as strong as many forms of internalism: it does not, for example, say anything at all about the connection between the actual value of things (or the obligatory character of actions) and desires or motives. Nor does it, so far as I can see, involve us in any doctrine about what evaluative judgements mean. According to Hare, 'to draw attention to the close logical relations, on the one hand between wanting and thinking good, and on the other between wanting and doing something about getting what one wants, is to play into the hands of the prescriptivist; for it's to provide yet another link between thinking good and action'.[8] I confess I do not see how these 'close logical relations', which are given in one form by P1 and P2, support any particular theory about the meaning of evaluative sentences or terms. A possible source of confusion is revealed when Hare says '. . . if moral judgements were not prescriptive, there would be no problem about moral weakness; but there is a problem; therefore they are prescriptive' (p. 68). The confusion is between making a judgement, and the content of the judgement. It is P2 (or its ilk) that creates the problem, and P2 connects *making* a judgement with wanting and hence, *via* P1, with acting. But prescriptivism is a doctrine about the *content or meaning* of what is judged, and P2 says nothing about this. One could hold, for example, that to say one course of action is better than another is just to say that it will create more pleasure and yet maintain, as Mill perhaps did, that anyone who believes a certain course of action will create more pleasure than another (necessarily) wants it more. So I should like to deny that there is a simple connection between the problem of incontinence as I have posed it and any particular ethical theory.

Perhaps the most common way of dealing with the problem of incontinence is to reject P2. It seems obvious enough, after all, that we may think *x* better, yet want *y* more. P2 is even easier to question if it is stated in the form: if an agent thinks he ought (or is obligated) to do *x*, then he wants to do *x*; for of course we often don't want to do what we think we ought. Hare, if I understand him, accounts for some cases of incontinence in such a way; so, according to Santas, did Plato.[9]

It is easy to interpret P2 in a way that makes it false, but it is harder to believe there is not a natural reading that makes it true. For against our tendency to agree

---

[8] R. M. Hare, *Freedom and Reason*, 71.   [9] G. Santas, 'The Socratic Paradoxes'.

that we often believe we ought to do something and yet don't want to, there is also the opposite tendency to say that if someone really (sincerely) believes he ought, then his belief must show itself in his behaviour (and hence, of course, in his inclination to act, or his desire). When we make a point of contrasting thinking we ought with wanting, this line continues, either we are using the phrase 'thinking we ought' to mean something like 'thinking it is what is required by the usual standards of the community' or we are restricting wanting to what is attractive on a purely selfish or personal basis. Such ways of defending P2, though I find them attractive, are hard to make conclusive without begging the present question. So I am inclined, in order to move ahead, to point out that a problem about incontinence will occur in some form as long as there is any word or phrase we can convincingly substitute for 'wants' in both P1 and P2.

Another common line to take with incontinence is to depict the akrates as overcome by passion or unstrung by emotion. 'I know indeed what evil I intend to do. But stronger than all my afterthoughts is my fury', rants Medea. Hare makes this the paradigm of all cases of weakness of the will where we cannot simply separate moral judgement and desire, and he adds that in such cases the agent is psychologically unable to do what he thinks he ought (*Freedom and Reason*, p. 77). Hare continues to quote Euripides' Medea when she says '. . . an unknown compulsion bears me, all reluctant, down', and St. Paul when he writes, 'The good which I want to do, I fail to do; but what I do is the wrong which is against my will; and if what I do is against my will, clearly it is no longer I who am the agent . . .' (*Romans* 7). This line leads to the view that one never acts intentionally contrary to one's best judgement, and so denies P3; there are no incontinent actions in the sense we have defined.[10]

A related, but different, view is Aristotle's, that passion, lust, or pleasure distort judgement and so prevent an agent from forming a full-fledged judgement that his action is wrong. Though there is plenty of room for doubt as to precisely what Aristotle's view was, it is safe to say that he tried to solve our problem by distinguishing two senses in which a man may be said to know (or believe) that one thing is better than another; one sense makes P2 true, while the other sense is needed in the definition of incontinence. The flavour of this second sense is given by Aristotle's remark that the incontinent man has knowledge 'in the sense in which having knowledge does not mean knowing but only talking, as a drunken man may mutter the verses of Empedocles' (*Nic. Eth.*, 1147b).

Perhaps it is evident that there is a considerable range of actions, similar to incontinent actions in one respect or another, where we may speak of self-deception, insincerity, *mauvaise foi*, hypocrisy, unconscious desires, motives and

---

[10] Aquinas is excellent on this point. He clearly distinguishes between actions performed from a strong emotion, such as fear, which he allows are involuntary to a certain extent and hence not truly incontinent, and actions performed from concupiscence, for example: here, he says 'concupiscence inclines the will to desire the object of concupiscence. Therefore the effect of concupiscence is to make something to be voluntary.' (*Summa Theologica*, Part II, Q.6.)

intentions, and so on.[11] There is in fact a very great temptation, in working on this subject, to play the amateur psychologist. We are dying to say: remember the enormous variety of ways a man can believe or hold something, or know it, or want something, or be afraid of it, or do something. We can act as if we knew something, and yet profoundly doubt it; we can act at the limit of our capacity and at the same time stand off like an observer and say to ourselves, 'What an odd thing to do.' We can desire things and tell ourselves we hate them. These half-states and contradictory states are common, and full of interest to the philosopher. No doubt they explain, or at least point to a way of describing without contradiction, many cases where we find ourselves talking of weakness of the will or of incontinence. But we ourselves show a certain weakness as philosophers if we do not go on to ask: does every case of incontinence involve one of the shadow-zones where we want both to apply, and to withhold, some mental predicate? Does it never happen that I have an unclouded, unwavering judgement that my action is not for the best, all things considered, and yet where the action I do perform has no hint of compulsion or of the compulsive? There is no proving such actions exist; but it seems to me absolutely certain that they do. And if this is so, no amount of attention to the subtle borderline bits of behaviour will resolve the central problem.[12]

Austin complains that in discussing the present topic, we are prone to '... collapse succumbing to temptation into losing control of ourselves...' He elaborates:

Plato, I suppose, and after him Aristotle, fastened this confusion upon us, as bad in its day and way as the later, grotesque, confusion of moral weakness with weakness of will. I am very partial to ice cream, and a bombe is served divided into segments corresponding one to one with persons at High Table: I am tempted to help myself to two segments and do, thus succumbing to temptation and even conceivably (but why necessarily?) going against my principles. But do I lose control of myself? Do I raven, do I snatch the morsels from the dish and wolf them down, impervious to the consternation of my colleagues? Not a bit of it. We often succumb to temptation with calm and even with finesse.[13]

We succumb to temptation with calm; there are also plenty of cases where we act against our better judgement and which cannot be described as succumbing to temptation.

In the usual accounts of incontinence there are, it begins to appear, two quite different themes that interweave and tend to get confused. One is, that desire

---

[11] 'It is but a shallow haste which concludeth insincerity from what outsiders call inconsistency.' (George Eliot, *Middlemarch*.)

[12] 'Oh, tell me, who first declared, who first proclaimed, that man only does nasty things because he does not know his own real interests...? What is to be done with the millions of facts that bear witness that men, knowingly, that is fully understanding their real interests, have left them in the background and have rushed headlong on another path... compelled to this course by nobody and by nothing...' (Dostoevsky, *Notes from the Underground*.)

[13] J. L. Austin, 'A Plea for Excuses', 146.

distracts us from the good, or forces us to the bad; the other is that incontinent action always favours the beastly, selfish passion over the call of duty and morality. That these two themes can be separated was emphasized by Plato both in the *Protagoras* and the *Philebus* when he showed that the hedonist, on nothing but his own pleasure bent, could go against his own best judgement as easily as anyone else. Mill makes the same point, though presumably from a position more sympathetic to the hedonist: 'Men often, from infirmity of character, make their election for the nearer good, though they know it to be the less valuable; and this no less when the choice is between two bodily pleasures than when it is between bodily and mental' (*Utilitarianism*, chapter 11.) Unfortunately, Mill goes on to spoil the effect of his point by adding, 'They pursue sensual indulgences to the injury of health, though perfectly aware that health is the greater good.'

As a first positive step in dealing with the problem of incontinence, I propose to divorce that problem entirely from the moralist's concern that our sense of the conventionally right may be lulled, dulled, or duped by a lively pleasure. I have just relaxed in bed after a hard day when it occurs to me that I have not brushed my teeth. Concern for my health bids me rise and brush; sensual indulgence suggests I forget my teeth for once. I weigh the alternatives in the light of the reasons: on the one hand, my teeth are strong, and at my age decay is slow. It won't matter much if I don't brush them. On the other hand, if I get up, it will spoil my calm and may result in a bad night's sleep. Everything considered I judge I would do better to stay in bed. Yet my feeling that I ought to brush my teeth is too strong for me: wearily I leave my bed and brush my teeth. My act is clearly intentional, although against my better judgement, and so is incontinent.

There are numerous occasions when immediate pleasure yields to principle, politeness, or sense of duty and yet we judge (or know) that all things considered we should opt for pleasure. In approaching the problem of incontinence it is a good idea to dwell on the cases where morality simply doesn't enter the picture as one of the contestants for our favour—or if it does, it is on the wrong side. Then we shall not succumb to the temptation to reduce incontinence to such special cases as being overcome by the beast in us, or of failing to heed the call of duty, or of succumbing to temptation.[14]

[14] I know no clear case of a philosopher who recognizes that incontinence is not essentially a problem in moral philosophy, but a problem in the philosophy of action. Samuel Butler, in the *Sermons* (Paragraph 39, Preface to 'The Fifteen Sermons Preached at the Rolls Chapel'), points out that 'Benevolence towards particular persons may be to a degree of weakness, and so be blamable', but here the note of self-indulgence sounds too loud. And P. H. Nowell-Smith, *Ethics*, 243ff., describes many cases of incontinence where we are overcome by conscience or duty: 'We might paradoxically, but not unfairly, say that in such a case it is difficult to resist the temptation to tell the truth. We are the slaves of our own consciences.' Slaves don't act freely; the case is again not clear.

Aristotle discusses the case of the man who, contrary to his own principle (and best judgement) pursues (too strongly) something noble and good (he cares too much for honour or his children), but he refuses to call this incontinence (*Nic. Eth.*, 1148).

II

Under sceptical scrutiny, P1 and P2 appear vulnerable enough, and yet tinkering with them yields no satisfactory account of how incontinence is possible. Part of the reason at least lies in the fact that P1 and P2 derive their force from a very persuasive view of the nature of intentional action and practical reasoning. When a person acts with an intention, the following seems to be a true, if rough and incomplete, description of what goes on: he sets a positive value on some state of affairs (an end, or the performance by himself of an action satisfying certain conditions); he believes (or knows or perceives) that an action, of a kind open to him to perform, will promote or produce or realize the valued state of affairs; and so he acts (that is, he acts *because* of his value or desire and his belief). Generalized and refined, this description has seemed to many philosophers, from Aristotle on, to promise to give an analysis of what it is to act with an intention; to illuminate how we explain an action by giving the reasons the agent had in acting; and to provide the beginning of an account of practical reasoning, i.e., reasoning about what to do, reasoning that leads to action.

In the simplest case, we imagine that the agent has a desire, for example, to know the time. He realizes that by looking at his watch he will satisfy his desire; so he looks at his watch. We can answer the question why he looked at his watch; we know the intention with which he did it. Following Aristotle, the desire may be conceived as a principle of action, and its natural propositional expression would here be something like 'It would be good for me to know the time' or, even more stiffly, 'Any act of mine that results in my knowing the time is desirable.' Such a principle Aristotle compares to the major premise in a syllogism. The propositional expression of the agent's belief would in this case be, 'Looking at my watch will result in my knowing the time': this corresponds to the minor premise. Subsuming the case under the rule, the agent performs the desirable action: he looks at his watch.

It seems that, given this desire and this belief, the agent is in a position to infer that looking at his watch is desirable, and in fact the making of such an inference is something it would be natural to describe as subsuming the case under the rule. But given the desire and this belief, the conditions are also satisfied that lead to (and hence explain) an intentional action, so Aristotle says that once a person has the desire and believes some action will satisfy it, *straightway he acts*. Since there is no distinguishing the conditions under which an agent is in a position to infer that an action he is free to perform is desirable from the conditions under which he acts, Aristotle apparently identifies drawing the inference and acting: he says, 'the conclusion is an action'. But of course this account of intentional action and practical reason contradicts the assumption that there are incontinent actions.

As long as we keep the general outline of Aristotle's theory before us, I think we cannot fail to realize that he can offer no satisfactory analysis of incontinent action. No doubt he can explain why, in borderline cases, we are tempted both to say an agent acted intentionally and thát he knew better. But if we postulate a strong desire from which he acted, then on the theory, we also attribute to the agent a strong judgement that the action is desirable; and if we emphasize that the agent's ability to reason to the wrongness of his action was weakened or distorted, to that extent we show that he did not fully appreciate that what he was doing was undesirable.

It should not be supposed we can escape Aristotle's difficulty simply by giving up the doctrine that having the reasons for action always results in action. We might allow, for example, that a man can have a desire and believe an action will satisfy it, and yet fail to act, and add that it is only if the desire and belief cause him to act that we can speak of an intentional action.[15] On such a modified version of Aristotle's theory (if it really is a modification) we would still have to explain why in some cases the desire and belief caused an action, while in other cases they merely led to the judgement that a course of action was desirable.

The incontinent man believes it would be better on the whole to do something else, but he has a reason for what he does, for his action is intentional. We must therefore be able to abstract from his behaviour and state of mind a piece of practical reasoning the conclusion of which is, or would be if the conclusion were drawn from the premises, that the action actually performed is desirable. Aristotle tends to obscure this point by concentrating on cases where the incontinent man behaves 'under the influence of rule and an opinion' (*Nic. Eth.*, 1147b; cf. 1102b).

Aquinas is far clearer on this important point than Aristotle. He says:

He that has knowledge of the universal is hindered, because of a passion, from reasoning in the light of that universal, so as to draw the conclusion; but he reasons in the light of another universal proposition suggested by the inclination of the passion, and draws his conclusion accordingly . . . Hence passion fetters the reason, and hinders it from thinking and concluding under the first proposition; so that while passion lasts, the reason argues and concludes under the second.[16]

An example, given by Aquinas, shows the plight of the incontinent man:

THE SIDE OF REASON	THE SIDE OF LUST
(M_1) No fornication is lawful	(M_2) Pleasure is to be pursued
(m_1) This is an act of fornication	(m_2) This act is pleasant
(C_1) This act is not lawful	(C_2) This act is to be pursued

We can make the point more poignantly, though here we go beyond Aristotle and Aquinas, if we construe principles and conclusions as comparative judgements concerning the merits of committing, or not committing, the act in

[15] For a version of this theory, see Essay 1.

[16] *Summa Theologica*, Part II, Q. 77, Art. 2, reply to objection 4. Aquinas quotes the apostle: 'I see another law in my members fighting against the law of my mind.'

question. The two conclusions (C_1) and (C_2) will then be (given some natural assumptions): It is better not to perform this act than to perform it, and, It is better to perform this act than not to perform it. And these are in flat contradiction on the assumption that better-than is asymmetric.

And now we must observe that *this picture of moral reasoning is not merely inadequate to account for incontinence; it cannot give a correct account of simple cases of moral conflict.* By a case of moral conflict I mean a case where there are good reasons both for performing an action and for performing one that rules it out (perhaps refraining from the action). There is conflict in this minimal sense whenever the agent is aware of considerations that, taken alone, would lead to mutually incompatible actions; feelings of strife and anxiety are inessential embellishments. Clearly enough, incontinence can exist only when there is conflict in this sense, for the incontinent man holds one course to be better (for a reason) and yet does something else (also for a reason). So we may set aside what is special to incontinence for the moment, and consider conflict generally. The twin arguments of the previous paragraph depict not only the plight of the incontinent man, but also of the righteous man in the toils of temptation; one of them does the wrong thing and the other the right, but both act in the face of competing claims.

The situation is common; life is crowded with examples: I ought to do it because it will save a life, I ought not because it will be a lie; if I do it, I will break my word to Lavinia, if I don't, I will break my word to Lolita; and so on. Anyone may find himself in this fix, whether he be upright or temporizing, weak-willed or strong. But then unless we take the line that moral principles cannot conflict in application to a case, we must give up the concept of the nature of practical reason we have so far been assuming. For how can premises, all of which are true (or acceptable), entail a contradiction?

It is astonishing that in contemporary moral philosophy this problem has received little attention, and no satisfactory treatment. Those who recognize the difficulty seem ready to accept one of two solutions: in effect they allow only a single ultimate moral principle; or they rest happy with the notion of a distinction between the prima facie desirable (good, obligatory, etc.) and the absolutely desirable (good, obligatory, etc).[17] I shall not argue the point here, but I do not believe any version of the 'single principle' solution, once its implications are understood, can be accepted: principles, or reasons for acting, are

---

[17] Examples of views that in effect allow only one ultimate moral principle: Kurt Baier, in *The Moral Point of View*, holds that in cases of conflict between principles there are higher-order principles that tell which principles take precedence; M. Singer, 'Moral Rules and Principles', claims that moral principles cannot conflict; Hare, in *The Language of Morals*, argues that there are no exceptions to acceptable moral principles. If ultimate principles never conflict or have counter-examples, we may accept the conjunction of ultimate principles as our single principle, while if there is a higher-order principle that resolves conflicts, we can obviously construct a single, exceptionless principle. And of course all outright utilitarians, rule or otherwise, believe there is a single exceptionless moral principle.

irreducibly multiple. On the other hand, it is not easy to see how to take advantage of the purported distinction between prima facie and absolute value. Suppose first that we try to think of 'prima facie' as an attributive adverb, helping to form such predicates as '*x* is prima facie good, right, obligatory' or '*x* is better, prima facie, than *y*'. To avoid our recent trouble, we must suppose that '*x* is better, prima facie, than *y*' does not contradict '*y* is better, prima facie, than *x*', and that '*x* is prima facie right' does not contradict '*x* is prima facie wrong'. But then the conclusion we can draw, in every case of conflict (and hence of incontinence) will be '*x* is better, prima facie, than *y*, and *y* is better, prima facie, than *x*'. This comes down, as is clear from the structure practical reasoning would have on this assumption, to saying 'There is something to be said for, and something to be said against, doing so and so—and also for and against not doing it.' Probably this can be said about any action whatsoever; in any case it is hard to accept the idea that the sum of our moral wisdom concerning what to do in a given situation has this form. The situation I describe is not altered in any interesting way if 'prima facie' or 'prima facie obligatory' is treated as a (non-truth-functional) sentential operator rather than as a predicate. I shall return shortly to this problem; now let us reconsider incontinence.

The image we get of incontinence from Aristotle, Aquinas, and Hare is of a battle or struggle between two contestants. Each contestant is armed with his argument or principle. One side may be labelled 'passion' and the other 'reason'; they fight; one side wins, the wrong side, the side called 'passion' (or 'lust' or 'pleasure'). There is, however, a competing image (to be found in Plato, as well as in Butler and many others). It is adumbrated perhaps by Dante (who thinks he is following Aquinas and Aristotle) when he speaks of the incontinent man as one who 'lets desire pull reason from her throne' (*Inferno*, Canto v). Here there are three actors on the stage: reason, desire, and the one who lets desire get the upper hand. The third actor is perhaps named 'The Will' (or 'Conscience'). It is up to The Will to decide who wins the battle. If The Will is strong, he gives the palm to reason; if he is weak, he may allow pleasure or passion the upper hand.

This second image is, I suggest, superior to the first, absurd as we may find both. On the first story, not only can we not account for incontinence; it is not clear how we can ever blame the agent for what he does: his action merely reflects the outcome of a struggle within him. What could he do about it? And more important, the first image does not allow us to make sense of a conflict in one person's soul, for it leaves no room for the all-important process of weighing considerations.[18] In the second image, the agent's representative, The Will, can judge the strength of the arguments on both sides, can execute the decision, and take the rap. The only trouble is that we seem back where we started. For how can The Will judge one course of action better and yet choose the other?

---

[18] A more sophisticated account of conflict that seems to raise the same problem is Ryle's account in *The Concept of Mind*, 93–5.

It would be a mistake to think we have made no progress. For what these colourful gladiatorial and judicial metaphors ought now to suggest is that there is a piece of practical reasoning present in moral conflict, and hence in incontinence, which we have so far entirely neglected. What must be added to the picture is a new argument:

THE WILL (CONSCIENCE)
(M_3) M_1 and M_2
(m_3) m_1 and m_2
(C_3) This action is wrong

Clearly something like this third argument is necessary if an agent is to act either rightly or incontinently in the face of conflict. It is not enough to know the reasons on each side: he must know how they add up.[19] The incontinent man goes against his better judgement, and this surely is (C_3), which is based on all the considerations, and not (C_1) which fails to bring in the reasons on the other side. You could say we have discovered two quite different meanings of the phrase 'his better judgement'. It might mean, any judgement for the right side (reason, morality, family, country); or, the judgement based on all relevant considerations known to the actor. The first notion, I have argued, is really irrelevant to the analysis of incontinence.

But now we are brought up against our other problem, the form or nature of practical reasoning. For nothing could be more obvious than that our third 'practical syllogism' is no syllogism at all; the conclusion simply doesn't follow by logic from the premises. And introducing the third piece of reasoning doesn't solve the problem we had before anyway: we still have contradictory 'conclusions'. We could at this point try once more introducing 'prima facie' in suitable places: for example, in (M_1), (M_2), (C_1), and (C_2). We might then try to relate prima facie desirability to desirability sans phrase by making (C_1) and (C_2), thus interpreted, the data for (C_3). But this is an unpromising line. We can hardly expect to learn whether an action ought to be performed simply from the fact that it is both prima facie right and prima facie wrong.

The real source of difficulty is now apparent: if we are to have a coherent theory of practical reason, we must give up the idea that we can *detach* conclusions about what is desirable (or better) or obligatory from the principles that lend those conclusions colour. The trouble lies in the tacit assumption that moral principles have the form of universalized conditionals; once this assumption is made, nothing we can do with a prima facie operator in the conclusion will save things. The situation is, in this respect, like reasoning from probabilistic evidence. As Hempel has emphasized with great clarity,[20] we

---

[19] My authority for how they do add up in this case is Aquinas: see the reference in footnote 16.
[20] Carl Hempel, *Aspects of Scientific Explanation*, 394–403.

cannot reason from:

(M₄) If the barometer falls, it almost certainly will rain
(m₄) The barometer is falling

to the conclusion:

(C₄) It almost certainly will rain

since we may at the same time be equally justified in arguing:

(M₅) Red skies at night, it almost certainly won't rain
(m₅) The sky is red tonight
∴ (C₅) It almost certainly won't rain

The crucial blunder is interpreting (M₄) and (M₅) to allow detachment of the modal conclusion. A way to mend matters is to view the 'almost certainly' of (M₄) and (M₅) as modifying, not the conclusion, but the connective. Thus we might render (M₄), 'That the barometer falls probabilizes that it will rain'; in symbols, '$pr(Rx, Fx)$', where the variable ranges over areas of space-time that may be characterized by falling barometers or rain. If we let 'a' name the space and time of here and now, and 'Sx' mean that the early part of x is characterized by a red sky of evening, we may attempt to reconstruct the thought bungled above thus:

$pr(Rx,Fx)$ $pr(-Rx,Sx)$
Fa Sa
∴ $pr(Ra,pr(Rx,Fx)$ and $Fa)$ ∴ $pr(-Ra,pr(-Rx,Sx)$ and $Sa)$

If we want to predict the weather, we will take a special interest in:

$pr(-Ra,e)$ or $pr(Ra,e)$

where e is all the relevant evidence we have. But it is clear that we can infer neither of these from the two arguments that went before, even if e is simply the conjunction of their premises (and even if for our qualitative 'pr' we substitute a numerical measure of degree of support).

I propose to apply the pattern to practical reasoning in the obvious way. The central idea is that a moral principle, like 'Lying is (prima facie) wrong', cannot coherently be treated as a universally quantified conditional, but should be recognized to mean something like, 'That an act is a lie prima facie makes it wrong'; in symbols, '$pf(Wx,Lx)$'. The concept of the prima facie, as it is needed in moral philosophy, relates propositions. In logical grammar, 'prima facie' is not an operator on single sentences, much less on predicates of actions, but on pairs of sentences related as (expressing) moral judgement and ground. Here is how the piece of practical reasoning misrepresented by (M₁), (m₁) and (C₁) might look when reconstituted:

(M₆) pf (x is better than y, x is a refraining from fornication and y is an act of fornication)

(m_6) a is a refraining from fornication and b is an act of fornication

$\therefore$ (C_6) pf (a is better than b, (M_6) and (m_6))

Similarly, (M_2) and (m_2), when rewritten in the new mode, and labelled (M7) and (m_7), will yield:

(C_7) pf (b is better than a, (M_7) and (m_7))

A judgement in which we will take particular interest is:

(C_8) pf (a is better than b, e)

where e is all the relevant considerations known to us, including at least (M_6), (m_6), (M_7), and (m_7).

Of course (C_8) does not follow logically from anything that went before, but in this respect moral reasoning seems no worse off than predicting the weather. In neither case do we know a general formula for computing how far or whether a conjunction of evidence statements supports a conclusion from how far or whether each conjunct supports it. There is no loss either, in this respect, in our strategy of relativizing moral judgements: we have no clue how to arrive at (C_8) from the reasons, but its faulty prototype (C_3) was in no better shape. There has, however, been a loss of relevance, for the conditionalization that keeps (C_6) from clashing with (C_7), and (C_8) from clashing with either, also insulates all three from action. Intentional action, I have argued in defending P1 and P2, is geared directly to unconditional judgements like 'It would be better to do a than to do b.' Reasoning that stops at conditional judgements such as (C_8) is practical only in its subject, not in its issue.[21]

Practical reasoning does however often arrive at unconditional judgements that one action is better than another—otherwise there would be no such thing as acting on a reason. The minimal elements of such reasoning are these: the agent accepts some reason (or set of reasons) r, and holds that pf (a is better than b, r), and these constitute the reason why he judges that a is better than b. Under these conditions, the agent will do a if he does either a or b intentionally, and his reason for doing a rather than b will be identical with the reason why he judges a better than b.

This modified account of acting on a reason leaves P1 and P2 untouched, and Aristotle's remark that the conclusion (of a piece of practical reasoning) is an action remains cogent. But now there is no (logical) difficulty in the fact of incontinence, for the akrates is characterized as holding that, all things considered, it would be better to do b than to do a, even though he does a rather than b and with a reason. The logical difficulty has vanished because a judgement that a is better than b, all things considered, is a relational, or pf, judgement, and so cannot conflict logically with any unconditional judgement.

---

[21] This claim is further pursued in Essay 6.

Possibly it will be granted that P1–P3, as interpreted here, do not yield a contradiction. But at the same time, a doubt may arise whether P3 is plausible, given this interpretation. For how is it possible for a man to judge that *a* is better than *b*, all things considered, and not judge that *a* is better than *b*?

One potential confusion is quickly set aside. '*a* is better than *b*, all things (viz. all truths, moral and otherwise) considered' surely does entail '*a* is better than *b*', and we do not want to explain incontinence as a simple logical blunder. The phrase 'all things considered' must, of course, refer only to things known, believed, or held by the agent, the sum of his relevant principles, opinions, attitudes, and desires. Setting this straight may, however, seem only to emphasize the real difficulty. We want now to ask: how is it possible for a man to judge that *a* is better than *b* on the grounds that *r*, and yet not judge that *a* is better than *b*, when *r* is the sum of all that seems relevant to him? When we say that *r* contains all that seems relevant to the agent, don't we just mean that nothing has been omitted that influences his judgement that *a* is better than *b*?

Since what is central to the solution of the problem of incontinence proposed in this paper is the contrast between conditional (prima facie) evaluative judgements and evaluative judgements sans phrase, perhaps we can give a characterization of incontinence that avoids the troublesome 'all things considered'. A plausible modification of our original definition (D) of incontinence might label an action, *x*, as incontinent provided simply that the agent has a better reason for doing something else: he does *x* for a reason *r*, but he has a reason *r'* that includes *r* and more, on the basis of which he judges some alternative *y* to be better than *x*.[22] Of course it might also have been incontinent of him to have done *y*, since he may have had a better reason still for performing some third action *z*. Following this line, we might say that an action *x* is continent if *x* is done for a reason *r*, and there is no reason *r'* (that includes *r*,) on the basis of which the agent judges some action better than *x*.

This shows we can make sense of incontinence without appeal to the idea of an agent's total wisdom, and the new formulation might in any case be considered an improvement on (D) since it allows (correctly, I think) that there are incontinent actions even when no judgement is made in the light of all the reasons. Still, we cannot rule out the case where a judgement is made in the light of all the reasons, so the underlying difficulty may be thought to remain.

In fact, however, the difficulty is not real. Every judgement is made in the light of all the reasons in this sense, that it is made in the presence of, and is conditioned by, that totality. But this does not mean that every judgement is reasonable, or thought to be so by the agent, on the basis of those reasons, nor that the judgement was reached from that basis by a process of reasoning. There is no paradox in supposing a person sometimes holds that all that he believes and

---

[22] We might want to rule out the case, allowed by this formulation, where the agent does what he has the best reason for doing, but does not do it for that reason.

values supports a certain course of action, when at the same time those same beliefs and values cause him to reject that course of action.[23] If r is someone's reason for holding that p, then his holding that r must be, I think, a cause of his holding that p. But, and this is what is crucial here, his holding that r may cause his holding that p without r being his reason; indeed, the agent may even think that r is a reason to reject p.

It is possible, then, to be incontinent, even if P1 and P2 are true. But what, on this analysis, is the fault in incontinence? The akrates does not, as is now clear, hold logically contradictory beliefs, nor is his failure necessarily a moral failure. What is wrong is that the incontinent man acts, and judges, irrationally, for this is surely what we must say of a man who goes against his own best judgement. Carnap and Hempel have argued that there is a principle which is no part of the logic of inductive (or statistical) reasoning, but is a directive the rational man will accept. It is the *requirement of total evidence for inductive reasoning*: give your credence to the hypothesis supported by all available relevant evidence.[24] There is, I suggest, an analogous principle the rational man will accept in applying practical reasoning: perform the action judged best on the basis of all available relevant reasons. It would be appropriate to call this the *principle of continence*. There may seem something queer in making the requirement of total evidence an imperative (can one tailor one's beliefs to order?), but there is no such awkwardness about the principle of continence. It exhorts us to actions we can perform if we want; it leaves the motives to us. What is hard is to acquire the virtue of continence, to make the principle of continence our own. But there is no reason in principle why it is any more difficult to become continent than to become chaste or brave. One gets a lively sense of the difficulties in St. Augustine's extraordinary prayer: 'Give me chastity and continence, only not yet' (*Confessions*, VIII, vii).

Why would anyone ever perform an action when he thought that, everything considered, another action would be better? If this is a request for a psychological explanation, then the answers will no doubt refer to the interesting phenomena familiar from most discussions of incontinence: self-deception, overpowering desires, lack of imagination, and the rest. But if the question is read, what is the agent's reason for doing a when he believes it would be better, all things considered, to do another thing, then the answer must be: for this, the agent has no reason.[25] We perceive a creature as rational in so far as we are able to view his movements as part of a rational pattern comprising also thoughts, desires, emotions, and volitions. (In this we are much aided by the actions we conceive to be utterances.) Through faulty inference, incomplete evidence, lack of diligence,

---

[23] At this point my account of incontinence seems to me very close to Aristotle's. See G. E. M. Anscombe, 'Thought and Action in Aristotle'.

[24] See Hempel, op. cit., 397–403, for important modifications, and further references.

[25] Of course he has a reason for doing a; what he lacks is a reason for not letting his better reason for not doing a prevail.

or flagging sympathy, we often enough fail to detect a pattern that is there. But in the case of incontinence, the attempt to read reason into behaviour is necessarily subject to a degree of frustration.

What is special in incontinence is that the actor cannot understand himself: he recognizes, in his own intentional behaviour, something essentially surd.

4

The Individuation of Events

When are events identical, when distinct? What criteria are there for deciding one way or the other in particular cases?

There is a familiar embarrassment in asking identity questions of this sort that comes out clearly if we rephrase the question slightly: when are two events identical? Or, when is one event identical with another? It seems only one answer is possible: no *two* events are identical, no event is ever identical with *another*. It is hopeless to try to improve matters by asking instead, when is an event identical with itself? For again, only one answer is possible: always.

The difficulty obviously has nothing special to do with events, it arises in relation to all identity questions. The only move I know for circumventing this conundrum is to substitute for questions about identities questions about sentences about identities. Then instead of asking when events are identical, we may ask when sentences of the form '$a = b$' are true, where we suppose 'a' and 'b' supplanted by singular terms referring to events.

We have no sooner to restate our problem in this standard way, however, than to realize something scandalous about events. Events, even in the best philosophical circles, lead a double life. On the one hand, we talk confidently of sentences that 'describe' or 'refer to' events, and of cases where two sentences refer to the same event; we have grown used to speaking of actions (presumably a species of event) 'under a description'. We characterize causal laws as asserting that every event of one sort is followed by an event of another sort, and it is said that explanation in history and science is often of particular events, though perhaps only as those events are described in one way rather than another. But— and this is the other hand—when we turn to the sentences, formalized in standard ways or in our native dialect, that are so familiarly interpreted as describing or referring to events, or as making universal claims about events, we generally find nothing commonly counted as singular terms that could be taken to refer to events. We are told, for example, that on occasion 'He raised his arm' and 'He signalled' describe the same action; yet where are the singular terms in these sentences that could do the describing? 'Whenever a piece of metal is heated it expands' is normally taken as quantifying over physical objects and perhaps times; how could we analyse it so as to justify the claim that it literally speaks of events?

Quine has quipped: 'No entity without identity' in support of the Fregean thesis that we ought not to countenance entities unless we are prepared to make sense of sentences affirming and denying identity of such entities. But then more obvious still is the motto: 'No identity without an entity', and its linguistic counterpart: 'No statements of identity without singular terms'.

Our problem was to determine when sentences formed by flanking an identity sign with singular terms referring to events are true; at this point the problem seems to invite the response that there are no such sentences because there are no such singular terms. But of course this is too strong; there are singular terms that apparently name events: 'Sally's third birthday party', 'the eruption of Vesuvius in A.D. 1906', 'my eating breakfast this morning', 'the first performance of *Lulu* in Chicago'. Still, the existence of these singular terms is of uncertain relevance until we can firmly connect such singular terms with sentences like 'Vesuvius erupted in A.D. 1906' or 'I ate breakfast this morning', for most of our interest in identity sentences about events depends upon the assumption that the singular terms that appear in them refer to entities that are needed for the analysis of more ordinary sentences. If the only pressure for adopting an ontology of events comes from such phrases as 'Sally's third birthday party', we would probably do better to try and paraphrase these away in context than meddle with the logical form of sentences like 'Brutus killed Caesar' or 'Bread nourishes' so as to show singular terms referring to events or variables ranging over them.

Are there good reasons for taking events seriously as entities? There are indeed. First, it is hard to imagine a satisfactory theory of action if we cannot talk literally of the same action under different descriptions. Jones managed to apologize by saying 'I apologize'; but only because, under the circumstances, saying 'I apologize' *was* apologizing. Cedric intentionally burned the scrap of paper; this serves to excuse his burning a valuable document only because he did not know the scrap was the document and because his burning the scrap was (identical with) his burning the document. Explanation, as already hinted, also seems to call for events. Last week there was a catastrophe in the village. In the course of explaining why it happened, we need to redescribe it, perhaps as an avalanche. There are rough statistical laws about avalanches: avalanches tend to occur when a heavy snow falls after a period of melting and freezing, so that the new snow does not bind to the old. But we could go further in explaining this avalanche— why it came just when it did, why it covered the area it did, and so forth—if we described it in still a different and more precise vocabulary. And when we mention, in one way or another, the cause of the avalanche, we apparently claim that though we may not know such a description or such a law, there must *be* descriptions of cause and avalanche such that those descriptions instantiate a true causal law. All this talk of descriptions and redescriptions makes sense, it would seem, only on the assumption that there are *bona fide* entities to be described and redescribed. A further need for events springs from the fact that the most perspicuous forms of the identity theory of mind require that we identify mental events with certain physiological events; if such theories or their denials are intelligible, events must be individuals. And for such theories to be interesting, there must be ways of telling when statements of event-identity are true.[1]

The reasons just canvassed for accepting an explicit ontology of events rest upon the assumption that one or another currently accepted or debated philosophical position or doctrine is intelligible when taken at face value; so it remains possible to resist the conclusion by rejecting the relevant doctrines as unintelligible, or by attempting to reinterpret them without appeal to events. The prospects for successful resistance are, in my opinion, dim: I do not believe we can give a cogent account of action, of explanation, of causality, or of the relation between the mental and the physical, unless we accept events as individuals. Each of these claims needs detailed defence.[2]

There remains, however, a more direct consideration (of which the others are symptoms) in favour of an ontology of events, which is that without events it does not seem possible to give a natural and acceptable account of the logical form of certain sentences of the most common sorts; it does not seem possible, that is, to show how the meanings of such sentences depend upon their composition. The situation may be sketched as follows. It is clear that the sentence 'Sebastian strolled through the streets of Bologna at 2 a.m.' entails 'Sebastian strolled through the streets of Bologna', and does so by virtue of its logical form. This requires, it would seem, that the patent syntactical fact that the entailed sentence is contained in the entailing sentence be reflected in the logical form we assign to each sentence. Yet the usual way of formalizing these sentences does not show any such feature: it directs us to consider the first sentence as containing an irreducibly three-place predicate 'x strolled through y at t' while the second contains the unrelated predicate 'x strolled through y'. It is sometimes proposed that we can mend matters by treating 'Sebastian strolled through the streets of Bologna' as elliptical for 'There exists a time t such that Sebastian strolled through the streets of Bologna at t'. This suggestion contains the seed of a general solution, however, only if we can form a clear idea of how many places predicates of action or change involve. But it is unlikely that we can do this since there appear to be ways of adding indefinitely to the number of places that would be required. Consider, for example, 'The shark devoured Danny by chewing up his left foot, then his left ankle, then his left knee, then . . . ', or, 'The fall of the first domino caused the fall of the last by causing the fall of the second, which caused the fall of the third, which caused . . . .'.[3]

Ingenuity may conceive more than one way of coping with these and associated puzzles, but it is impressive how well everything comes out if we accept the obvious idea that there are things like falls, devourings, and strolls for sentences

---

[1] This point is well stated by Jaegwon Kim, 'On the Psycho-Physical Identity Theory'.

[2] See Essays 1, 2, and 5.

[3] The difficulty discussed here is raised by Anthony Kenny in *Action, Emotion and Will*, Ch. VII. In Essay 2, I devote more space to these matters and to the solution about to be outlined.

such as these to be about. In short, I propose to legitimize our intuition that events are true particulars by recognizing explicit reference to them, or quantification over them, in much of our ordinary talk. Take as an example, 'Sebastian strolled': this may be construed along lines suggested by 'Sebastian took a stroll.' 'There is an x such that x is a stroll and Sebastian took x' is more ornate than necessary, since there is nothing an agent can do with a stroll except take it; thus we may capture all there is with 'There is an x such that Sebastian strolled x.'

In this way we provide each verb of action or change with an event-place; we may say of such verbs that they take an *event-object*. Adverbial modification is thus seen to be logically on a par with adjectival modification: what adverbial clauses modify is not verbs, but the events that certain verbs introduce. 'Sebastian strolled through the streets of Bologna at 2 a.m.' then has this form: 'There is an event x such that Sebastian strolled x, x took place in the streets of Bologna, and x was going on at 2 a.m.' Clearly, the entailments that worried us before go through directly on this analysis.

We recognize that there is no singular term referring to a mosquito in 'There is a mosquito in here' when we realize that the truth of this sentence is not impugned if there are two mosquitos in the room. It would not be appropriate if, noticing that there are two mosquitos in the room, I were to ask the person who says, 'There is a mosquito in the room', 'Which one are you referring to?' On the present analysis, ordinary sentences about events, like 'Doris capsized the canoe yesterday', are related to particular events in just the same way that 'There is a mosquito in here' is related to particular mosquitos. It is no less true that Doris capsized the canoe yesterday if she capsized it a dozen times than if she capsized it once; nor, if she capsized it a dozen times, does it make sense to ask, 'Which time are you referring to?' as if this were needed to *clarify* 'Doris capsized the canoe yesterday'. We learned some time ago, and it is a very important lesson, that phrases like 'a mosquito' are not singular terms, and hence do not refer as names or descriptions do. The temptation to treat a sentence like 'Doris capsized the canoe yesterday' as if it contained a singular term referring to an action comes from other sources, but we should be equally steadfast in resisting it.

Some actions are difficult or unusual to perform more than once in a short or specified time, and this may provide a specious reason in some cases for holding that action sentences refer to unique actions. Thus with 'Jones got married last Saturday', 'Doris wrote a cheque at noon', 'Mary kissed an admirer at the stroke of midnight'. It is merely illegal to get married twice on the same day, merely unusual to write cheques simultaneously, and merely good fortune to get to kiss two admirers at once. Similarly, if I say, 'There is an elephant in the bathtub', you are no doubt justified in supposing that one elephant at most is in the bathtub, but you are confused if you think my sentence contains a singular term that refers to a particular elephant if any. A special case arises when we characterize actions in ways that logically entail that at most one action so characterized exists: perhaps you can break a certain piece of news to a particular audience only once;

a man can assassinate his enemy only once; a woman can lose her virtue only once. 'Brutus killed Caesar' is then arguably equivalent to 'Brutus killed Caesar exactly once' which is arguably equivalent (by way of Russell's theory of descriptions) to 'The killing of Caesar by Brutus occurred.' This last certainly does contain a description, in the technical sense, of an action, and so we could say that 'Brutus killed Caesar' refers to or describes the killing of Caesar by Brutus in that it is logically equivalent to a sentence that overtly refers to or describes the killing of Caesar by Brutus. By parity of reasoning we should, of course, maintain that 'There exists a prime between 20 and 28' refers to the number 23. There is a good reason against taking this line, however, which is that on this view someone could be uniquely referring without knowing he was using words that imputed singularity.

Confusion over the relation between ordinary sentences about actions, and particular actions, has led some philosophers to suppose or to suggest that these sentences are about *generic* actions, or *kinds* of actions. Von Wright, for example, says that 'Brutus killed Caesar' is about a particular action, while 'Brutus kissed Caesar' is about a generic action.[4] It is true that we can paraphrase 'Brutus kissed Caesar' as 'There is at least one event belonging to the genus, a kissing of Caesar by Brutus'; but we can equally well paraphrase 'Brutus killed Caesar' as 'There is at least one event belonging to the genus, a killing of Caesar by Brutus.' In neither case does the sentence refer to a generic action. Analogous remarks apply to the idea that 'Lying is wrong' is about a kind of action. 'Lying is wrong' may be rendered, 'For all x if x is a lie then x is wrong' or even, 'The class of lies is included in the class of wrong actions', but neither of these says that a kind of action is wrong, but rather that each action of a kind is wrong.

Failure to find an ordinary singular term referring to an event in a sentence like 'Caesar died' is properly explained by the fact that such sentences are existential and general with respect to events: we do not find a singular term referring to an event because there is none. But many philosophers, not doubting that 'Caesar died' refers to or describes an event, have confusedly concluded that the sentence *as a whole* refers to (or perhaps 'corresponds to') an event. As long ago as 1927, Frank Ramsey pointed out this error, and how to correct it; he described it as the error of conflating facts (which in his view are what sentences or propositions correspond to) and events.[5] And certainly there are difficulties, of a kind more general than we have indicated, with the idea that whole sentences refer to events. For suppose we agree, as I think we must, that the death of Scott is the same event as the death of the author of *Waverley*: then if sentences refer to events, the sentence 'Scott died' must refer to the same event as 'The author of *Waverley* died.' If we allow that substitution of singular terms in this way does not change the event referred to, then a short and persuasive argument will lead to the

---

[4] Georg Henrik von Wright, *Norm and Action*, 23.
[5] 'Facts and Propositions', 140, 141. Also see the reply to Martin in Essay 2.

conclusion that all true sentences refer to the same event. And presumably only true sentences refer to an event; the conclusion may therefore be put: there is exactly one event. Since the argument is essentially the argument used by Frege to show that all sentences alike in truth-value must name the same thing, I spare you the details.[6]

The mistaken view that a sentence like 'Doris capsized the canoe yesterday' refers to a particular event, whether or not tied to the idea that it is the sentence as a whole that does the referring, is pretty sure to obliterate the difference between 'Doris capsized the canoe yesterday' and 'Doris' capsizing of the canoe occurred yesterday.' Yet without this distinction firm in our minds I do not believe we can make good sense of questions about the individuation of events and actions, for while the second sentence does indeed contain a singular description (the sentence as a whole meaning 'There is an event identical with the capsizing of the canoe yesterday by Doris'), the first sentence merely asserts the existence of at least one capsizing. If we are not alert to the difference, we are apt to ask wrongheaded questions like: if Jones apologized by saying 'I apologize', do 'Jones apologized' and 'Jones said "I apologize" ' describes the same action? The right response is, I have urged, that neither sentence describes an action. We may then add, if we please, that at least one, or perhaps exactly one, action accounts for the truth of both sentences; but both sentences could be true although no apology by Jones was made by his saying, 'I apologize.'[7]

To see how not appreciating the generality in 'Jones apologized' can lead to mistakes about the individuation of events, consider a suggestion of Kim's.[8] Kim assumes that sentences such as 'Brutus killed Caesar' and 'Brutus stabbed Caesar' refer to events, and he asks under what conditions two such sentences describe or refer to the same event. He proposes the following criterion: two sentences are about the same event if they assert truly of the same particulars (i.e., substances) that the same properties (or relations) hold of them. Kim has a rather complicated doctrine of property identity, but it need not delay us since the point to be made depends only on a simple principle to which Kim agrees: properties differ if their extensions do. The effect is to substitute for what I think of as particular, dated events classes of such, and thus to make identities harder to come by. Where I would say the same event may make 'Jones apologized' and 'Jones said "I apologize" ' true, Kim is committed to holding that these sentences describe different events. Nor can Kim allow that a stabbing is ever a killing, or the signing of a cheque the paying of a bill. He must also hold that if psychological predicates

---

[6] See Essay 2.

[7] F. I. Dretske in 'Can Events Move?' correctly says that sentences do not refer to or describe events, and proposes that the expressions that do refer to events are the ones that can properly fill the blank in 'When did—occur (happen, take place)?' This criterion includes (as it should) such phrases as 'the immersion of the paper' and 'the death of Socrates' but also includes (as it should not) 'a discoloration of the fluid'.

[8] In 'On the Psycho-Physical Identity Theory'. Essentially the same suggestion is made by Richard Martin in 'On Events and Event-Descriptions'.

have no coextensive physical predicates, then no psychological event is identical with a physical event.

Kim recognizes these consequences of his criterion, and accepts them; but for reasons I find weak. He writes:

Brutus' killing Caesar and Brutus' stabbing Caesar turn out, on the proposed criterion of event identity, to be different events, and similarly, 'Brutus killed Caesar' and 'Brutus stabbed Caesar' describe different events. Notice, however, that it is not at all absurd to say that Brutus' killing Caesar is *not the same as* Brutus' stabbing Caesar. Further, to explain Brutus' killing Caesar (why Brutus killed Caesar) is not the same as to explain Brutus' stabbing Caesar (why Brutus stabbed Caesar)....[9]

Certainly Brutus had different reasons for stabbing Caesar than for killing him; we may suppose he went through a little piece of practical reasoning the upshot of which was that stabbing Caesar was a good way to do him in. But this reasoning was futile if, having stabbed Caesar, Brutus has a different action yet to perform (killing him). And explanation, like giving reasons, is geared to sentences or propositions rather than directly to what sentences are about: thus an explanation of why Scott died is not necessarily an explanation of why the author of *Waverley* died. Yet not even Kim wants to say the death of Scott is a different event from the death of the author of *Waverley*. I turn last to Kim's remark that it is not absurd to say that Brutus's killing Caesar is not the same as Brutus's stabbing Caesar. The plausibility in this is due, I think, to the undisputed fact that not all stabbings are killings. We are inclined to say: *this* stabbing might not have resulted in a death, so how can it be identical with the killing? Of course the death is not identical with the stabbing; it occurred later. But neither this nor the fact that some stabbings are not killings shows that this particular stabbing was not a killing. Brutus's stabbing of Caesar did result in Caesar's death; so it was in fact, though of course not necessarily, identical with Brutus's killing of Caesar.

Discussions of explanation may also suffer from confusion about how sentences are related to events. It is sometimes said, for example, that when we explain the occurrence of an event, we can do so only under one or another of its sentential descriptions. In so far as this remark reminds us of the essential intensionality of explanation, it is unexceptionable. But a mistake may lurk. If what we are to explain is why an avalanche fell on the village last week, we need to show that conditions were present adequate to produce *an* avalanche. It would be confused to say we have explained only an aspect of 'the real avalanche' if the reason for saying this lies in the fact that what was to be explained was itself general (for the explanandum contained no mention of a particular avalanche). We might instead have asked for an explanation of why *the* avalanche fell on the village last week. This is, of course, a harder task, for we are now asking not only why there was at least one avalanche, but also why there was not more than one. In

---

[9] Kim, op. cit., 232 (footnote).

a perfectly good sense the second explanation can be said to explain a particular event; the first cannot.

An associated point may be made about causal relations. Suppose it claimed that the lighting of this match was caused by the striking of the match. The inevitable comment (since the time of Mill anyway) is that the striking may have been *part* of the cause, but it was hardly sufficient for the lighting since it was also necessary for the match to be dry, that there be enough oxygen, etc. This comment is, in my opinion, confused. For since this match was dry, and was struck in enough oxygen, etc., the striking of this match was identical with the striking of a dry match in enough oxygen. How can one and the same event both be, and not be, sufficient for the lighting? In fact, it is not *events* that are necessary or sufficient as causes, but events as *described* in one way or another. It is true that we cannot infer, from the fact that the match was struck, and plausible causal laws, that the match lit; we can do better if we start with the fact that a dry match was struck in enough oxygen. It does not follow that more than the striking of this match was required to cause it to light.

Now that we have a clearer idea what it is like to have singular terms, say '*a*' and '*b*', that refer to events we may return to our original question when a sentence of the form '$a = b$' is true. Of course we cannot expect a general method for *telling* when such sentences are true. For suppose '$(ix)(Fx)$' describes some event. Letting '*S*' abbreviate any sentence,

$$(ix)(Fx) = (ix)(Fx \ \& S)$$

is true just in case '*S*' is true. Since '*S*' is an arbitrary sentence, a general method for telling when identity sentences were true would have to include a method for telling when any sentence was true. What we want, rather, is a statement of necessary and sufficient conditions for identity of events, a satisfactory filling for the blank in:

If x and y are events, then $x = y$ if and only if——.

Samples of answers (true or false) for other sorts of entities are: classes are identical if and only if they have exactly the same members; times are identical if and only if they are overlapped by exactly the same events; places are identical if and only if they are overlapped by exactly the same objects; material objects are identical if and only if they occupy exactly the same places at the same times. Can we do as well as this for events? Here follows a series of remarks that culminate in what I hope is a satisfactory positive answer.

(1) Many events are changes in a substance. If an event a is a change in some substance, then $a = b$ only if b is also a change in the same substance. Indeed, if $a = b$, every substance in which a is a change is identical with a substance in which b is a change. To touch on such necessary conditions of event-identity is to do little more than reflect on what follows if events really do exist; but that is to the present point. And of course we will not alter the event, if any, to which a

description refers if in that description we substitute for the name or description of a substance another name or description of the same substance: witness the fact that the death of Scott is identical with the death of the author of *Waverley*. This is an example of a sufficient condition of identity.

We very often describe and identify events in terms of the objects to which they are in one way or another related. But it would be a mistake to suppose that, even for events that are naturally described as changes in an object, we *must* describe them (i.e., produce unique descriptions of them) by referring to the object. For in fact any predicate of any event may provide a unique description: if an event *a* is *F*, *a* may turn out also to be the only event that is *F*, in which case 'the event that is *F*' uniquely refers to *a*. One important way to identify events without explicit reference to a substance is by demonstrative reference: 'that shriek', 'that dripping sound', 'the next sonic boom'.

These last points are well made by Strawson.[10] Strawson also remarks that the possibilities for identifying events without reference to objects are limited, because, as he puts it, events do not provide 'a single, comprehensive and continuously usable framework' of reference of the kind provided by physical objects.[11] This claim is made by Strawson in support of a grander thesis, that events are conceptually dependent on objects. According to Strawson we could not have the idea of a birth or a death or a blow without the idea of an animal that is born or dies, or of an agent who strikes the blow.

I do not doubt that Strawson is right in this: most events are understood as changes in a more or less permanent object or substance. It even seems likely to me that the concept of an event depends in every case on the idea of a change in a substance, despite the fact that for some events it is not easy to say what substance it is that undergoes the change.

What does seem doubtful to me is Strawson's contention that while there is a conceptual dependence of the category of events on the category of objects, there is not a symmetrical dependence of the category of objects on the category of events. His principle argument may, I think, be not unfairly stated as follows: in a sentence like 'There is an event that is the birth of this animal' we refer to, or quantify over, events and objects alike. But we can, if we please, express exactly the same idea by saying, 'This animal was born' and here there is no reference to, or quantification over, events. We cannot in the same way eliminate the reference to the object.[12] This is supposed to show that objects are more fundamental than events.

A closely related argument of Strawson's is this: the sentence 'The blow which blinded John was struck by Peter' presupposes, for its truth, that John exists, that Peter exists, and that there is a striking of John by Peter. But the last

---

[10] *Individuals*, 46ff. I am not sure, however, that Strawson distinguishes clearly among: pointing out an entity to someone; producing a unique description of an entity; producing a description guaranteed to be unique.   [11] Ibid., 53.
[12] Ibid., 51ff.

presupposition may also be expressed simply by saying that Peter struck John, which does not treat the blow as an entity on a par with Peter and John. Strawson again concludes that events are dispensable in a sense in which objects are not.[13] It is hard to see how the evidence supports the conclusion.

If 'Peter struck John' and 'There was a striking of John by Peter' express the same presupposition, how can they require different ontologies? If 'This animal was born' and 'There is an event that is the birth of this animal' are genuine paraphrases one of the other, how can one of them be about a birth and the other not? The argument proves either too much or too little. If every context that seems to refer to, or to presuppose, events may be systematically rephrased so as not to refer to events, then this shows we do not need an ontology of events at all. On the other hand if some categories of sentence resist transformation into an eventless idiom, then the fact that we can apparently banish events from other areas cannot suffice to relegate events to a secondary status; indeed it does not even serve to show that the sentences we know how to parse in superficially event-free terms are not about events. It was in fact in just this vein that I have been urging that we cannot give acceptable analyses of 'This animal was born' and 'Peter struck John' without supposing that there are such things as births and blows. In Strawson's view, if I understand him, 'The blow which blinded John was struck by Peter' entails 'Peter struck John.' But a theory about what these sentences mean that justifies the entailment must, or so I have argued, acknowledge an ontology of events. Thus if my interpretation of the evidence is correct, there is no reason to assign second rank to events; while if, contrary to what I have maintained, total reducibility is possible, then again events do not take a back seat, for there are no events.

In my view, a sentence like 'John struck the blow' is about two particulars, John and the blow. The distinction between singular terms and predicates is not abolished: rather, striking is predicated alike of John and of the blow. This symmetry in the treatment of substances and their changes reflects, I think, an underlying symmetry of conceptual dependence. Substances owe their special importance in the enterprise of identification to the fact that they survive through time. But the idea of survival is inseparable from the idea of surviving certain sorts of change—of position, size, shape, colour, and so forth. As we might expect, events often play an essential role in identifying a substance. Thus if we track down the author of Waverley or the father of Annette, it is by identifying an event, of writing, or of fathering. Neither the category of substance nor the category of change is conceivable apart from the other.[14]

(2) Should we say that events are identical only if they are in the same place? Of course if events have a location, same events have same locations; but here is a puzzle that may seem to cast a doubt on the project of assigning a clear location to

---

[13] Ibid., 200.
[14] The same conclusion is reached by J. Moravscik, 'Strawson and Ontological Priority'.

events. Perhaps those events are easiest to locate that are obviously changes in some substance: we locate the event by locating the substance. But if one substance is part of another, a change in the first is a change in the second. Every substance is a part of the universe: hence every change is a change in the universe. It seems to follow that all simultaneous events have the same location. The error lies in the assumption that if an event is a change in a substance, the location of the event is the entire space occupied by the substance. Rather, the location of the event at a moment is the location of the smallest part of the substance a change in which is identical with the event.

Does it make sense to assign a location to a mental event such as remembering that one has left a zipper open, deciding to schuss the headwall, or solving an equation? I think we do assign a location to such an event when we identify the person who remembered, decided, or solved: the event took place where the person was. Questions about the location of mental events are generally otiose because in identifying the event we have usually identified the person in whom the event was a change, so no interesting question about the location of the event remains that is not answered by knowing where the person was when the event occurred. When we do not know who the relevant person is, queries about the location of mental events are perfectly in order: 'Where was the infinitesimal calculus invented?'

Mental events (by which I mean events described in the mental vocabulary, whatever exactly that may be) are like many other sorts of events, and like material objects, in that we give their locations with no more accuracy than easy individuation (within the relevant vocabulary) demands. Aside from a few dubious cases, like pains, itches, pricks, and twitches, we have no reason to locate mental events more precisely than by identifying a person, for more than this would normally be irrelevant to individuation. Similarly, we uniquely identify a mountain by giving the latitude and longitude of its highest summit, and in one good sense this gives the location of the mountain. But a mountain is a material object, and so occupies more than a point; nevertheless convention decrees no formula for defining its boundaries.

An explosion is an event to which we find no difficulty in assigning a location, although again we may be baffled by a request to describe the total area. The following quotation from an article on locating earthquakes and underground explosions illustrates how smoothly we operate with the concept of the place of an event:

Information on the accuracy with which a seismic event can be located is not as complete as could be wished . . . . If data from stations distant from the event are used, it seems realistic to estimate that the site can be located within a circular area whose radius is about eight kilometers. Stations that are 500–2,000 kilometers from the event may give much larger errors . . . .[15]

[15] E. C. Bullard, 'The Detection of Underground Explosions', 24.

(3) No principle for the individuation of events is clearer or more certain than this, that if events are identical, they consume identical stretches of time. Yet even this principle seems to lead to a paradox.

Suppose I pour poison in the water tank of a spaceship while it stands on earth. My purpose is to kill the space traveller, and I succeed: when he reaches Mars he takes a drink and dies. Two events are easy to distinguish: my pouring of the poison, and the death of the traveller. One precedes the other, and causes it. But where does the event of my killing the traveller come in? The most usual answer is that my killing the traveller is identical with my pouring the poison. In that case, the killing is over when the pouring is. We are driven to the conclusion that I have killed the traveller long before he dies.

The conclusion to which we are driven is, I think, true, so coping with the paradox should take the form of reconciling us to the conclusion. First, we should observe that we may easily know that an event is a pouring of poison without knowing it is a killing, just as we may know that an event is the death of Scott with knowing it is the death of the author of *Waverley*. To describe an event as a killing is to describe it as an event (here an action) that caused a death, and we are not apt to describe an action as one that caused a death until the death occurs; yet it may be such an action before the death occurs. (And as it becomes more certain that a death will result from an action, we feel less paradox in saying, 'You have killed him'.)[16]

Directness of causal connection may also play a role. To describe the pouring as a killing is to describe it as the causing of a death; such a description loses cogency as the causal relation is attenuated. In general, the longer it takes for the effect to be registered, the more room there is for a slip, which is another way of saying, the less justification there is for calling the action alone the cause.

Finally, there may be a tendency to confuse events described (partly or wholly) in terms of terminal states and events described (partly or wholly) in terms of what they cause. Examples of the first sort are 'the rolling of the stone to the bottom of the hill' (which is not over until the stone is at the bottom of the hill) or 'his painting the barn red' (not over until he has finished painting the barn red); examples of the second sort are 'the destruction of the crops by the flood' (over when the flood is, which may be finished before the crops are) and 'Jones' inviting Smith to the party' (which Jones does only if Smith gets invited, but has finished doing when he drops the card in the mail).

It is a matter of the first importance that we may, and often do, describe actions and events in terms of their causal relations—their causes, their effects, or both. My poisoning of the victim must be an action that results in the victim being

---

[16] Harry Levin, *The Question of Hamlet*, 35, says in effect that the poisoned Hamlet, in killing the King, avenges, among other murders, his own. This he could not do if he had not already been murdered.

poisoned; my killing of the victim must be an action that results in the death of the victim; my murdering of the victim must be an action that results in the death of the victim and also an action that was caused, in part, by my desire for the victim's death. If I see that the cat is on the mat, my seeing must be caused, in part, by the cat's being on the mat. If I contract Favism, I must contract haemolytic anaemia as a consequence of eating, or otherwise coming in contact with, the Fava bean. And so forth. This tendency to identify events in terms of their causal relations has deep roots, as I shall suggest in a moment. But it should not lead to a serious difficulty about the dates of events.

(4) Do place and time together uniquely determine an event; that is, is it sufficient as well as necessary, if events are to be identical, that they occupy exactly the same time and the same place? This proposal was made (somewhat tentatively) by John Lemmon;[17] of course the same proposal has often been made for physical objects. I am uncertain both in the case of substances and in the case of events whether or not sameness of time and place is enough to insure identity. Doubt comes easily in the case of events, for it seems natural to say that two different changes can come over the whole of a substance at the same time. For example, if a metal ball becomes warmer during a certain minute, and during the same minute rotates through 35 degrees, must we say these are the same event? It would seem not; but there may be arguments the other way. Thus in the present instance it might be maintained that the warming of the ball during m is identical with the sum of the motions of the particles that constitute the ball during m; and so is the rotation. In the case of material objects it is perhaps possible to imagine two objects that in fact occupy just the same places at all times but are different because, though never separated, they are separable.

(5) We have not yet found a clearly acceptable criterion for the identity of events. Does one exist? I believe it does, and it is this: events are identical if and only if they have exactly the same causes and effects. Events have a unique position in the framework of causal relations between events in somewhat the way objects have a unique position in the spatial framework of objects. This criterion may seem to have an air of circularity about it, but if there is circularity it certainly is not formal. For the criterion is simply this: where x and y are events,

$(x = y$ if and only if $((z)$ $(z$ caused $x \leftrightarrow z$ caused $y)$ and (z) $(x$ caused $z \leftrightarrow y$ caused $z))$.

No identities appear on the right of the biconditional.

If this proposal is correct, then it is easy to appreciate why we so often identify or describe events in terms of their causes and effects. Not only are these the

---

[17] E. J. Lemmon, 'Comments on D. Davidson's "The Logical Form of Action Sentences"'. Lemmon goes further, suggesting that '. . . we may invoke a version of the identity of indiscernibles and identify events with *space-time zones*'. But even if there can be only one event that fully occupies a space-time zone, it would be wrong to say a space-time zone *is* a change or a cause (unless we want to alter the language).

features that often interest us about events, but they are features guaranteed to individuate them in the sense not only of telling them apart but also of telling them together. It is one thing for a criterion to be correct, another for it to be useful. But there are certainly important classes of cases at least where the causal criterion appears to be the best we have. If we claim, for example, that someone's having a pain on a specific occasion is identical with a certain complex physiological event, the best evidence for the identity is apt to be whatever evidence we have that the pain had the same causes and the same effects as the physiological change. Sameness of cause and effect seems, in cases like this one, a far more useful criterion than sameness of place and time.[18]

Perhaps sameness of causal relations is the only condition always sufficient to establish sameness of events (sameness of location in space and time may be another). But this should not be taken to mean that the only way of establishing, or supporting, a claim that two events are identical is by giving causal evidence. On the contrary, logic alone, or logic plus physics, or almost anything else, may help do the job, depending on the descriptions provided. What I do want to propose is that the causal nexus provides for events a 'comprehensive and continuously usable framework' for the identification and description of events analogous in many ways to the space-time coordinate system for material objects.

This paper may be viewed as an indirect defence of events as constituting a fundamental ontological category. A defence, because unless we can make sense of assertions and denials of identity we cannot claim to have made sense of the idea that events are particulars. Indirect, because it might be possible to make such needed sense, and to provide clear criteria for identity, and yet to have made no case at all for the need to posit events as an independent category. In other places I have tried to make good on the question of need; here I have not much more than summarized the arguments. But I have found that even those who are impressed with the arguments often have a residual doubt that centres on the apparent intractability of the question when events are identical.

I have tried to banish this doubt as far as I could. The results are not, it must be allowed, overwhelming. But how much should one expect? Can we do any better when it comes to giving criteria for individuating material objects? It should be noticed that the subject has been the individuation of events quite generally, not kinds of events. The analogous problem for material objects would be to ask for conditions of identity of equal generality. At this level, there is individuation without counting. We cannot answer the question, 'How many events occurred (since midnight, between Easter and Christmas)?', but neither can we answer the question, 'How many material objects are there (in the world, in this room)?' We do equally badly on counting classes, points, and intervals of time. Nor are there

---

[18] Thomas Nagel suggests the same criterion of the identity of events in 'Physicalism', 346.

very good *formulas* for individuating in some of these cases, though we make good enough sense of assertions and denials of identity.

Individuation at its best requires sorts or kinds that give a principle for counting. But here again, events come out well enough: rings of the bell, major wars, eclipses of the moon, and performances of *Lulu* can be counted as easily as pencils, pots, and people. Problems can arise in either domain. The conclusion to be drawn, I think, is that the individuation of events poses no problems worse in principle than the problems posed by individuation of material objects; and there is as good reason to believe events exist.

5

Mental Events

Mental events such as perceivings, rememberings, decisions, and actions resist capture in the nomological net of physical theory. How can this fact be reconciled with the causal role of mental events in the physical world? Reconciling freedom with causal determinism is a special case of the problem if we suppose that causal determinism entails capture in, and freedom requires escape from, the nomological net. But the broader issue can remain alive even for someone who believes a correct analysis of free action reveals no conflict with determinism. *Autonomy* (freedom, self-rule) may or may not clash with determinism; *anomaly* (failure to fall under a law) is, it would seem, another matter.

I start from the assumption that both the causal dependence, and the anomalousness, of mental events are undeniable facts. My aim is therefore to explain, in the face of apparent difficulties, how this can be. I am in sympathy with Kant when he says,

it is as impossible for the subtlest philosophy as for the commonest reasoning to argue freedom away. Philosophy must therefore assume that no true contradiction will be found between freedom and natural necessity in the same human actions, for it cannot give up the idea of nature any more than that of freedom. Hence even if we should never be able to conceive how freedom is possible, at least this apparent contradiction must be convincingly eradicated. For if the thought of freedom contradicts itself or nature . . . it would have to be surrendered in competition with natural necessity.[1]

Generalize human actions to mental events, substitute anomaly for freedom, and this is a description of my problem. And of course the connection is closer, since Kant believed freedom entails anomaly.

Now let me try to formulate a little more carefully the 'apparent contradiction' about mental events that I want to discuss and finally dissipate. It may be seen as stemming from three principles.

The first principle asserts that at least some mental events interact causally with physical events. (We could call this the Principle of Causal Interaction.) Thus for example if someone sank the *Bismarck*, then various mental events such as perceivings, notings, calculations, judgements, decisions, intentional actions, and

[1] *Fundamental Principles of the Metaphysics of Morals*, 75–6.

changes of belief played a causal role in the sinking of the *Bismarck*. In particular, I would urge that the fact that someone sank the *Bismarck* entails that he moved his body in a way that was caused by mental events of certain sorts, and that this bodily movement in turn caused the *Bismarck* to sink.[2] Perception illustrates how causality may run from the physical to the mental: if a man perceives that a ship is approaching, then a ship approaching must have caused him to come to believe that a ship is approaching. (Nothing depends on accepting these as examples of causal interaction.)

Though perception and action provide the most obvious cases where mental and physical events interact causally, I think reasons could be given for the view that all mental events ultimately, perhaps through causal relations with other mental events, have causal intercourse with physical events. But if there are mental events that have no physical events as causes or effects, the argument will not touch them.

The second principle is that where there is causality, there must be a law: events related as cause and effect fall under strict deterministic laws. (We may term this the Principle of the Nomological Character of Causality.) This principle, like the first, will be treated here as an assumption, though I shall say something by way of interpretation.[3]

The third principle is that there are no strict deterministic laws on the basis of which mental events can be predicted and explained (the Anomalism of the Mental).

The paradox I wish to discuss arises for someone who is inclined to accept these three assumptions or principles, and who thinks they are inconsistent with one another. The inconsistency is not, of course, formal unless more premises are added. Nevertheless it is natural to reason that the first two principles, that of causal interaction and that of the nomological character of causality, together imply that at least some mental events can be predicted and explained on the basis of laws, while the principle of the anomalism of the mental denies this. Many philosophers have accepted, with or without argument, the view that the three principles do lead to a contradiction. It seems to me, however, that all three principles are true, so that what must be done is to explain away the appearance of contradiction; essentially the Kantian line.

The rest of this paper falls into three parts. The first part describes a version of the identity theory of the mental and the physical that shows how the three principles may be reconciled. The second part argues that there cannot be strict psychophysical laws; this is not quite the principle of the anomalism of the mental, but on reasonable assumptions entails it. The last part tries to show that from the fact that there can be no strict psychophysical laws, and our other two

---

[2] These claims are defended in Essay 1.

[3] The stipulation that the laws be deterministic is stronger than required by the reasoning, and will be relaxed.

principles, we can infer the truth of a version of the identity theory, that is, a theory that identifies at least some mental events with physical events. It is clear that this 'proof' of the identity theory will be at best conditional, since two of its premises are unsupported, and the argument for the third may be found less than conclusive. But even someone unpersuaded of the truth of the premises may be interested to learn how they can be reconciled and that they serve to establish a version of the identity theory of the mental. Finally, if the argument is a good one, it should lay to rest the view, common to many friends and some foes of identity theories, that support for such theories can come only from the discovery of psychophysical laws.

I

The three principles will be shown consistent with one another by describing a view of the mental and the physical that contains no inner contradiction and that entails the three principles. According to this view, mental events are identical with physical events. Events are taken to be unrepeatable, dated individuals such as the particular eruption of a volcano, the (first) birth or death of a person, the playing of the 1968 World Series, or the historic utterance of the words, 'You may fire when ready, Gridley.' We can easily frame identity statements about individual events; examples (true or false) might be:

The death of Scott = the death of the author of *Waverley*;
The assassination of the Archduke Ferdinand = the event that started the First World War;
The eruption of Vesuvius in A.D. 79 = the cause of the destruction of Pompeii.

The theory under discussion is silent about processes, states, and attributes if these differ from individual events.

What does it mean to say that an event is mental or physical? One natural answer is that an event is physical if it is describable in a purely physical vocabulary, mental if describable in mental terms. But if this is taken to suggest that an event is physical, say, if some physical predicate is true of it, then there is the following difficulty. Assume that the predicate 'x took place at Noosa Heads' belongs to the physical vocabulary; then so also must the predicate 'x did not take place at Noosa Heads' belong to the physical vocabulary. But the predicate 'x did or did not take place at Noosa Heads' is true of every event, whether mental or physical.[4] We might rule out predicates that are tautologically true of every event,

---

[4] The point depends on assuming that mental events may intelligibly be said to have a location; but it is an assumption that must be true if an identity theory is, and here I am not trying to prove the theory but to formulate it.

but this will not help since every event is truly describable either by '*x* took place at Noosa Heads' or by '*x* did not take place at Noosa Heads.' A different approach is needed.[5]

We may call those verbs mental that express propositional attitudes like believing, intending, desiring, hoping, knowing, perceiving, noticing, remembering, and so on. Such verbs are characterized by the fact that they sometimes feature in sentences with subjects that refer to persons, and are completed by embedded sentences in which the usual rules of substitution appear to break down. This criterion is not precise, since I do not want to include these verbs when they occur in contexts that are fully extensional ('He knows Paris,' 'He perceives the moon' may be cases), nor exclude them whenever they are not followed by embedded sentences. An alternative characterization of the desired class of mental verbs might be that they are psychological verbs as used when they create apparently nonextensional contexts.

Let us call a description of the form 'the event that is *M*' or an open sentence of the form 'event *x* is *M*' a *mental description* or a *mental open sentence* if and only if the expression that replaces '*M*' contains at least one mental verb essentially. (Essentially, so as to rule out cases where the description or open sentence is logically equivalent to one or not containing mental vocabulary.) Now we may say that an event is mental if and only if it has a mental description, or (the description operator not being primitive) if there is a mental open sentence true of that event alone. Physical events are those picked out by descriptions or open sentences that contain only the physical vocabulary essentially. It is less important to characterize a physical vocabulary because relative to the mental it is, so to speak, recessive in determining whether a description is mental or physical. (There will be some comments presently on the nature of a physical vocabulary, but these comments will fall far short of providing a criterion.)

On the proposed test of the mental, the distinguishing feature of the mental is not that it is private, subjective, or immaterial, but that it exhibits what Brentano called intentionality. Thus intentional actions are clearly included in the realm of the mental along with thoughts, hopes, and regrets (or the events tied to these). What may seem doubtful is whether the criterion will include events that have often been considered paradigmatic of the mental. Is it obvious, for example, that feeling a pain or seeing an after-image will count as mental? Sentences that report such events seem free from taint of nonextensionality, and the same should be true of reports of raw feels, sense data, and other uninterpreted sensations, if there are any.

However, the criterion actually covers not only the havings of pains and after-images, but much more besides. Take some event one would intuitively accept as physical, let's say the collision of two stars in distant space. There must be a purely physical predicate '*Px*' true of this collision, and of others, but true of only

---

[5] I am indebted to Lee Bowie for emphasizing this difficulty.

this one at the time it occurred. This particular time, though, may be pinpointed as the same time that Jones notices that a pencil starts to roll across his desk. The distant stellar collision is thus *the* event *x* such that *Px* and *x* is simultaneous with Jones's noticing that a pencil starts to roll across his desk. The collision has now been picked out by a mental description and must be counted as a mental event.

This strategy will probably work to show every event to be mental; we have obviously failed to capture the intuitive concept of the mental. It would be instructive to try to mend this trouble, but it is not necessary for present purposes. We can afford Spinozistic extravagance with the mental since accidental inclusions can only strengthen the hypothesis that all mental events are identical with physical events. What would matter would be failure to include bona fide mental events, but of this there seems to be no danger.

I want to describe, and presently to argue for, a version of the identity theory that denies that there can be strict laws connecting the mental and the physical. The very possibility of such a theory is easily obscured by the way in which identity theories are commonly defended and attacked. Charles Taylor, for example, agrees with protagonists of identity theories that the sole 'ground' for accepting such theories is the supposition that correlations or laws can be established linking events described as mental with events described as physical. He says, 'It is easy to see why this is so: unless a given mental event is invariably accompanied by a given, say, brain process, there is no ground for even mooting a general identity between the two.'[6] Taylor goes on (correctly, I think) to allow that there may be identity without correlating laws, but my present interest is in noticing the invitation to confusion in the statement just quoted. What can 'a given mental event' mean here? Not a particular, dated, event, for it would not make sense to speak of an individual event being 'invariably accompanied' by another. Taylor is evidently thinking of events of a given *kind*. But if the only identities are of kinds of events, the identity theory presupposes correlating laws.

One finds the same tendency to build laws into the statements of the identity theory in these typical remarks:

When I say that a sensation is a brain process or that lightning is an electrical discharge, I am using 'is' in the sense of strict identity... there are not two things: a flash of lightning and an electrical discharge. There is one thing, a flash of lightning, which is described scientifically as an electrical discharge to the earth from a cloud of ionized water molecules.[7]

---

[6] Charles Taylor, 'Mind-Body Identity, a Side Issue?', 202.

[7] J. J. C. Smart, 'Sensations and Brain Processes'. The quoted passages are on pages 163–5 of the reprinted version in *The Philosophy of Mind*, ed. V. C. Chappell (Englewood Cliffs, NJ, 1962). For another example, see David K. Lewis, 'An Argument for the Identity Theory'. Here the assumption is made explicit when Lewis takes events as universals (p. 17, footnotes 1 and 2). I do not suggest that Smart and Lewis are confused, only that their way of stating the identity theory tends to obscure the distinction between particular events and kinds of events on which the formulations of my theory depends.

The last sentence of this quotation is perhaps to be understood as saying that for every lightning flash there exists an electrical discharge to the earth from a cloud of ionized water molecules with which it is identical. Here we have an honest ontology of individual events and can make literal sense of identity. We can also see how there could be identities without correlating laws. It is possible, however, to have an ontology of events with the conditions of individuation specified in such a way that any identity implies a correlating law. Kim, for example, suggests that Fa and Gb 'describe or refer to the same event' if and only if $a = b$ and the property of being $F =$ the property of being G. The identity of the properties in turn entails that (x) $(Fx \leftrightarrow Gx)$.[8] No wonder Kim says:

> If pain is identical with brain state B, there must be a concomitance between occurrences of pain and occurrences of brain state B. . . . Thus, a necessary condition of the pain-brain state B identity is that the two expressions 'being in pain' and 'being in brain state B' have the same extension. . . . There is no conceivable observation that would confirm or refute the identity but not the associated correlation.[9]

It may make the situation clearer to give a fourfold classification of theories of the relation between mental and physical events that emphasizes the independence of claims about laws and claims of identity. On the one hand there are those who assert, and those who deny, the existence of psychophysical laws; on the other hand there are those who say mental events are identical with physical and those who deny this. Theories are thus divided into four sorts: *nomological monism*, which affirms that there are correlating laws and that the events correlated are one (materialists belong in this category); *nomological dualism*, which comprises various forms of parallelism, interactionism, and epiphenomenalism; *anomalous dualism*, which combines ontological dualism with the general failure of laws correlating the mental and the physical (Cartesianism). And finally there is *anomalous monism*, which classifies the position I wish to occupy.[10]

Anomalous monism resembles materialism in its claim that all events are physical, but rejects the thesis, usually considered essential to materialism, that mental phenomena can be given purely physical explanations. Anomalous monism shows an ontological bias only in that it allows the possibility that not all events are mental, while insisting that all events are physical. Such a bland

---

[8] Jaegwon Kim, 'On the Psycho-Physical Identity Theory', 231.

[9] Ibid., 227–8. Richard Brandt and Jaegwon Kim propose roughly the same criterion in 'The Logic of the Identity Theory'. They remark that on their conception of event identity, the identity theory 'makes a stronger claim than merely that there is a pervasive phenomenal-physical correlation', 518. I do not discuss the stronger claim.

[10] Anomalous monism is more or less explicitly recognized as a possible position by Herbert Feigl, 'The "Mental" and the "Physical"'; Sydney Shoemaker, 'Ziff's Other Minds'; David Randall Luce, 'Mind–Body Identity and Psycho-Physical Correlation'; Charles Taylor, op. cit., 207. Something like my position is tentatively accepted by Thomas Nagel, 'Physicalism', and endorsed by P. F. Strawson in *Freedom and the Will*, 63–7.

monism, unbuttressed by correlating laws or conceptual economies, does not seem to merit the term 'reductionism'; in any case it is not apt to inspire the nothing-but reflex ('Conceiving the *Art of the Fugue* was nothing but a complex neural event', and so forth).

Although the position I describe denies there are psychophysical laws, it is consistent with the view that mental characteristics are in some sense dependent, or supervenient, on physical characteristics. Such supervenience might be taken to mean that there cannot be two events alike in all physical respects but differing in some mental respect, or that an object cannot alter in some mental respect without altering in some physical respect. Dependence or supervenience of this kind does not entail reducibility through law or definition: if it did, we could reduce moral properties to descriptive, and this there is good reason to *believe* cannot be done; and we might be able to reduce truth in a formal system to syntactical properties, and this we *know* cannot in general be done.

This last example is in useful analogy with the sort of lawless monism under consideration. Think of the physical vocabulary as the entire vocabulary of some language L with resources adequate to express a certain amount of mathematics, and its own syntax. L' is L augmented with the truth predicate 'true-in-L', which is 'mental'. In L (and hence L') it is possible to pick out, with a definite description or open sentence, each sentence in the extension of the truth predicate, but if L is consistent there exists no predicate of syntax (of the 'physical' vocabulary), no matter how complex, that applies to all and only the true sentence of L. There can be no 'psychophysical law' in the form of a biconditional, '(x) (x is true-in-L if and only if x is φ)' where 'φ' is replaced by a 'physical' predicate (a predicate of L). Similarly, we can pick out each mental event using the physical vocabulary alone, but no purely physical predicate, no matter how complex, has, as a matter of law, the same extension as a mental predicate.

It should now be evident how anomalous monism reconciles the three original principles. Causality and identity are relations between individual events no matter how described. But laws are linguistic; and so events can instantiate laws, and hence be explained or predicted in the light of laws, only as those events are described in one or another way. The principle of causal interaction deals with events in extension and is therefore blind to the mental-physical dichotomy. The principle of the anomalism of the mental concerns events described as mental, for events are mental only as described. The principle of the nomological character of causality must be read carefully: it says that when events are related as cause and effect, they have descriptions that instantiate a law. It does not say that every true singular statement of causality instantiates a law.[11]

---

[11] The point that substitutivity of identity fails in the context of explanation is made in connection with the present subject by Norman Malcolm, 'Scientific Materialism and the Identity Theory', 123–4. Also see Essays 1 and 4.

II

The analogy just bruited, between the place of the mental amid the physical, and the place of the semantical in a world of syntax, should not be strained. Tarski proved that a consistent language cannot (under some natural assumptions) contain an open sentence '*Fx*' true of all and only the true sentences of that language. If our analogy were pressed, then we would expect a proof that there can be no physical open sentence '*Px*' true of all and only the events having some mental property. In fact, however, nothing I can say about the irreducibility of the mental deserves to be called a proof; and the kind of irreducibility is different. For if anomalous monism is correct, not only can every mental event be uniquely singled out using only physical concepts, but since the number of events that falls under each mental predicate may, for all we know, be finite, there may well exist a physical open sentence coextensive with each mental predicate, though to construct it might involve the tedium of a lengthy and uninstructive alternation. Indeed, even if finitude is not assumed, there seems no compelling reason to deny that there could be coextensive predicates, one mental and one physical.

The thesis is rather that the mental is nomologically irreducible: there may be *true* general statements relating the mental and the physical, statements that have the logical form of a law; but they are not *lawlike* (in a strong sense to be described). If by absurdly remote chance we were to stumble on a nonstochastic true psychophysical generalization, we would have no reason to believe it more than roughly true.

Do we, by declaring that there are no (strict) psychophysical laws, poach on the empirical preserves of science—a form of *hubris* against which philosophers are often warned? Of course, to judge a statement lawlike or illegal is not to decide its truth outright; relative to the acceptance of a general statement on the basis of instances, ruling it lawlike must be a priori. But such relative apriorism does not in itself justify philosophy, for in general the grounds for deciding to trust a statement on the basis of its instances will in turn be governed by theoretical and empirical concerns not to be distinguished from those of science. If the case of supposed laws linking the mental and the physical is different, it can only be because to allow the possibility of such laws would amount to changing the subject. By changing the subject I mean here: deciding not to accept the criterion of the mental in terms of the vocabulary of the propositional attitudes. This short answer cannot prevent further ramifications of the problem, however, for there is no clear line between changing the subject and changing what one says on an old subject, which is to admit, in the present context at least, that there is no clear line between philosophy and science. Where there are no fixed boundaries only the timid never risk trespass.

It will sharpen our appreciation of the anomological character of mental–physical generalizations to consider a related matter, the failure of definitional behaviourism. Why are we willing (as I assume we are) to abandon the attempt to give explicit definitions of mental concepts in terms of behavioural ones? Not, surely, just because all actual tries are conspicuously inadequate. Rather it is because we are persuaded, as we are in the case of so many other forms of definitional reductionism (naturalism in ethics, instrumentalism and operationalism in the sciences, the causal theory of meaning, phenomenalism, and so on—the catalogue of philosophy's defeats), that there is system in the failures. Suppose we try to say, not using any mental concepts, what it is for a man to believe there is life on Mars. One line we could take is this: when a certain sound is produced in the man's presence ('Is there life on Mars?') he produces another ('Yes'). But of course this shows he believes there is life on Mars only if he understands English, his production of the sound was intentional, and was a response to the sounds as meaning something in English; and so on. For each discovered deficiency, we add a new proviso. Yet no matter how we patch and fit the nonmental conditions, we always find the need for an additional condition (provided he *notices, understands*, etc.) that is mental in character.[12]

A striking feature of attempts at definitional reduction is how little seems to hinge on the question of synonymy between definiens and definiendum. Of course, by imagining counterexamples we do discredit claims of synonymy. But the pattern of failure prompts a stronger conclusion: if we were to find an open sentence couched in behavioural terms and exactly coextensive with some mental predicate, nothing could reasonably persuade us that we had found it. We know too much about thought and behaviour to trust exact and universal statements linking them. Beliefs and desires issue in behaviour only as modified and mediated by further beliefs and desires, attitudes and attendings, without limit. Clearly this holism of the mental realm is a clue both to the autonomy and to the anomalous character of the mental.

These remarks apropos definitional behaviourism provide at best hints of why we should not expect nomological connections between the mental and the physical. The central case invites further consideration.

Lawlike statements are general statements that support counterfactual and subjunctive claims, and are supported by their instances. There is (in my view) no non-question-begging criterion of the lawlike, which is not to say there are no reasons in particular cases for a judgement. Lawlikeness is a matter of degree, which is not to deny that there may be cases beyond debate. And within limits set by the conditions of communication, there is room for much variation between individuals in the pattern of statements to which various degrees of nomologicality are assigned. In all these respects nomologicality is much like analyticity, as one might expect since both are linked to meaning.

'All emeralds are green' is lawlike in that its instances confirm it, but 'all emeralds are grue' is not, for 'grue' means 'observed before time *t* and green,

---

[12] The theme is developed in Roderick Chisholm, *Perceiving*, Ch. 2.

otherwise blue', and if our observations were all made before *t* and uniformly revealed green emeralds, this would not be a reason to expect other emeralds to be blue. Nelson Goodman has suggested that this shows that some predicates, 'grue' for example, are unsuited to laws (and thus a criterion of suitable predicates could lead to a criterion of the lawlike). But it seems to me the anomalous character of 'All emeralds are grue' shows only that the predicates 'is an emerald' and 'is grue' are not suited to one another: grueness is not an inductive property of emeralds. Grueness *is* however an inductive property of entities of other sorts, for instance of emerires. (Something is an emerire if it is examined before *t* and is an emerald, and otherwise is a sapphire.) Not only is 'All emerires are grue' entailed by the conjunction of a lawlike statements 'All emeralds are green' and 'All sapphires are blue,' but there is no reason, as far as I can see, to reject the deliverance of intuition, that it is itself lawlike.[13] Nomological statements bring together predicates that we know a priori are made for each other—know, that is, independently of knowing whether the evidence supports a connection between them. 'Blue', 'red', and 'green' are made for emeralds, sapphires, and roses; 'grue', 'bleen', and 'gred' are made for sapphalds, emerires, and emeroses.

The direction in which the discussion seems headed is this: mental and physical predicates are not made for one another. In point of lawlikeness, psychophysical statements are more like 'All emeralds are grue' than like 'All emeralds are green.'

Before this claim is plausible, it must be seriously modified. The fact that emeralds examined before *t* are grue not only is no reason to believe all emeralds are grue; it is not even a reason (if we know the time) to believe *any* unobserved emeralds are grue. But if an event of a certain mental sort has usually been accompanied by an event of a certain physical sort, this often is a good reason to expect other cases to follow suit roughly in proportion. The generalizations that embody such practical wisdom are assumed to be only roughly true, or they are explicitly stated in probabilistic terms, or they are insulated from counterexample by generous escape clauses. Their importance lies mainly in the support they lend singular causal claims and related explanations of particular events. The support derives from the fact that such a generalization, however crude and vague, may provide good reason to believe that underlying the particular case there is a regularity that could be formulated sharply and without caveat.

In our daily traffic with events and actions that must be foreseen or understood, we perforce make use of the sketchy summary generalization, for we do not know a more accurate law, or if we do, we lack a description of the particular events in which we are interested that would show the relevance of the law. But

---

[13] The view is accepted by Richard C. Jeffrey, 'Goodman's Query', John R. Wallace, 'Goodman, Logic, Induction', and John M. Vickers, 'Characteristics of Projectible Predicates'. Goodman, in 'Comments', disputes the lawlikeness of statements like 'All emerires are grue.' I cannot see, however, that he meets the point of my 'Emeroses by Other Names'. This short paper is printed as an appendix to the present essay.

there is an important distinction to be made within the category of the rude rule of thumb. On the one hand, there are generalizations whose positive instances give us reason to believe the generalization itself could be improved by adding further provisos and conditions stated in the same general vocabulary as the original generalization. Such a generalization points to the form and vocabulary of the finished law: we may say that it is a *homonomic* generalization. On the other hand there are generalizations which when instantiated may give us reason to believe there is a precise law at work, but one that can be stated only by shifting to a different vocabulary. We may call such generalizations *heteronomic*.

I suppose most of our practical lore (and science) is heteronomic. This is because a law can hope to be precise, explicit, and as exceptionless as possible only if it draws its concepts from a comprehensive closed theory. This ideal theory may or may not be deterministic, but it is if any true theory is. Within the physical sciences we do find homonomic generalizations, generalizations such that if the evidence supports them, we then have reason to believe they may be sharpened indefinitely by drawing upon further physical concepts: there is a theoretical asymptote of perfect coherence with all the evidence, perfect predictability (under the terms of the system), total explanation (again under the terms of the system). Or perhaps the ultimate theory is probabilistic, and the asymptote is less than perfection; but in that case there will be no better to be had.

Confidence that a statement is homonomic, correctible within its own conceptual domain, demands that it draw its concepts from a theory with strong constitutive elements. Here is the simplest possible illustration; if the lesson carries, it will be obvious that the simplification could be mended.

The measurement of length, weight, temperature, or time depends (among many other things, of course) on the existence in each case of a two-place relation that is transitive and asymmetric: warmer than, later than, heavier than, and so forth. Let us take the relation *longer than* as our example. The law or postulate of transitivity is this:

(L) $L(x,y)$ and $L(y,z) \rightarrow L(x,z)$

Unless this law (or some sophisticated variant) holds, we cannot easily make sense of the concept of length. There will be no way of assigning numbers to register even so much as ranking in length, let alone the more powerful demands of measurement on a ratio scale. And this remark goes not only for any three items directly involved in an intransitivity: it is easy to show (given a few more assumptions essential to measurement of length) that there is no consistent assignment of a ranking to any item unless (L) holds in full generality.

Clearly (L) alone cannot exhaust the import of 'longer than'—otherwise it would not differ from 'warmer than' or 'later than'. We must suppose there is some empirical content, however difficult to formulate in the available vocabulary, that distinguishes 'longer than' from the other two-place transitive predicates of measurement and on the basis of which we may assert that one thing is longer than another. Imagine this empirical content to be partly given by the predicate '$O(x,y)$'. So we have this 'meaning postulate':

(M) $O(x,y) \rightarrow L(x,y)$

that partly interprets (L). But now (L) and (M) together yield an empirical theory of great strength, for together they entail that there do not exist three objects a, b, and c such that $O(a,b)$, $O(b,c)$, and $O(c,a)$. Yet what is to prevent this happening if '$O(x,y)$' is a predicate we can ever, with confidence, apply? Suppose we *think* we observe an intransitive triad; what do we say? We could count (L) false, but then we would have no application for the concept of length. We could say (M) gives a wrong test for length; but then it is unclear what we thought was the *content* of the idea of one thing being longer than another. Or we could say that the objects under observation are not, as the theory requires, *rigid* objects. It is a mistake to think we are forced to accept some one of these answers. Concepts such as that of length are sustained in equilibrium by a number of conceptual pressures, and theories of fundamental measurement are distorted if we force the decision, among such principles as (L) and (M): analytic or synthetic. It is better to say the whole set of axioms, laws, or postulates for the measurement of length is partly constitutive of the idea of a system of macroscopic, rigid, physical objects. I suggest that the existence of lawlike statements in physical science depends upon the existence of constitutive (or synthetic a priori) laws like those of the measurement of length within the same conceptual domain.

Just as we cannot intelligibly assign a length to any object unless a comprehensive theory holds of objects of that sort, we cannot intelligibly attribute any propositional attitude to an agent except within the framework of a viable theory of his beliefs, desires, intentions, and decisions.

There is no assigning beliefs to a person one by one on the basis of his verbal behaviour, his choices, or other local signs no matter how plain and evident, for we make sense of particular beliefs only as they cohere with other beliefs, with preferences, with intentions, hopes, fears, expectations, and the rest. It is not merely, as with the measurement of length, that each case tests a theory and depends upon it, but that the content of a propositional attitude derives from its place in the pattern.

Crediting people with a large degree of consistency cannot be counted mere charity: it is unavoidable if we are to be in a position to accuse them meaningfully of error and some degree of irrationality. Global confusion, like universal mistake, is unthinkable, not because imagination boggles, but because too much confusion leaves nothing to be confused about and massive error erodes the background of true belief against which alone failure can be construed. To appreciate the limits to the kind and amount of blunder and bad thinking we can intelligibly pin on others is to see once more the inseparability of the question what concepts a person commands and the question what he does with those concepts in the way of belief, desire, and intention. To the extent that we fail to discover a coherent and plausible pattern in the attitudes and actions of others we simply forego the chance of treating them as persons.

The problem is not bypassed but given centre stage by appeal to explicit speech behaviour. For we could not begin to decode a man's sayings if we could not make out his attitudes towards his sentences, such as holding, wishing, or wanting them to be true. Beginning from these attitudes, we must work out a theory of what he means, thus simultaneously giving content to his attitudes and to his words. In our need to make him make sense, we will try for a theory that finds him consistent, a believer of truths, and a lover of the good (all by our own lights, it goes without saying). Life being what it is, there will be no simple theory that fully meets these demands. Many theories will effect a more or less acceptable compromise, and between these theories there may be no objective grounds for choice.

The heteronomic character of general statements linking the mental and the physical traces back to this central role of translation in the description of all propositional attitudes, and to the indeterminacy of translation.[14] There are no strict psychophysical laws because of the disparate commitments of the mental and physical schemes. It is a feature of physical reality that physical change can be explained by laws that connect it with other changes and conditions physically described. It is a feature of the mental that the attribution of mental phenomena must be responsible to the background of reasons, beliefs, and intentions of the individual. There cannot be tight connections between the realms if each is to retain allegiance to its proper source of evidence. The nomological irreducibility of the mental does not derive merely from the seamless nature of the world of thought, preference, and intention, for such interdependence is common to physical theory, and is compatible with there being a single right way of inter-preting a man's attitudes without relativization to a scheme of translation. Nor is the irreducibility due simply to the possibility of many equally eligible schemes, for this is compatible with an arbitrary choice of one scheme relative to which assignments of mental traits are made. The point is rather that when we use the concepts of belief, desire, and the rest, we must stand prepared, as the evidence accumulates, to adjust our theory in the light of considerations of overall cogency: the constitutive ideal of rationality partly controls each phase in the evolution of what must be an evolving theory. An arbitrary choice of translation scheme would preclude such opportunistic tempering of theory; put differently, a right arbitrary choice of a translation manual would be of a manual acceptable in the light of all possible evidence, and this is a choice we cannot make. We must conclude, I think, that nomological slack between the mental and the physical is essential as long as we conceive of man as a rational animal.

[14] The influence of W. V. Quine's doctrine of the indeterminacy of translation, as in Ch. 2 of *Word and Object*, is, I hope, obvious. In sect. 45 Quine develops the connection between translation and the propositional attitudes, and remarks that 'Brentano's thesis of the irreducibility of inten-tional idioms is of a piece with the thesis of indeterminacy of translation', 221.

III

The gist of the foregoing discussion, as well as its conclusion, will be familiar. That there is a categorial difference between the mental and the physical is a commonplace. It may seem odd that I say nothing of the supposed privacy of the mental, or the special authority an agent has with respect to his own propositional attitudes, but this appearance of novelty would fade if we were to investigate in more detail the grounds for accepting a scheme of translation. The step from the categorial difference between the mental and the physical to the impossibility of strict laws relating them is less common, but certainly not new. If there is a surprise, then, it will be to find the lawlessness of the mental serving to help establish the identity of the mental with that paradigm of the lawlike, the physical.

The reasoning is this. We are assuming, under the Principle of the Causal Dependence of the Mental, that some mental events at least are causes or effects of physical events; the argument applies only to these. A second Principle (of the Nomological Character of Causality) says that each true singular causal statement is backed by a strict law connecting events of kinds to which events mentioned as cause and effect belong. Where there are rough, but homonomic, laws, there are laws drawing on concepts from the same conceptual domain and upon which there is no improving in point of precision and comprehensiveness. We urged in the last section that such laws occur in the physical sciences. Physical theory promises to provide a comprehensive closed system guaranteed to yield a standardized, unique description of every physical event couched in a vocabulary amenable to law.

It is not plausible that mental concepts alone can provide such a framework, simply because the mental does not, by our first principle, constitute a closed system. Too much happens to affect the mental that is not itself a systematic part of the mental. But if we combine this observation with the conclusion that no psycho-physical statement is, or can be built into, a strict law, we have the Principle of the Anomalism of the Mental: there are no strict laws at all on the basis of which we can predict and explain mental phenomena.

The demonstration of identity follows easily. Suppose m, a mental event, caused p, a physical event; then, under some description m and p instantiate a strict law. This law can only be physical, according to the previous paragraph. But if m falls under a physical law, it has a physical description; which is to say it is a physical event. An analogous argument works when a physical event causes a mental event. So every mental event that is causally related to a physical event is a physical event. In order to establish anomalous monism in full generality it would be sufficient to show that every mental event is cause or effect of some physical event; I shall not attempt this.

If one event causes another, there is a strict law which those events instantiate when properly described. But it is possible (and typical) to know of the singular causal relation without knowing the law or the relevant descriptions. Knowledge requires reasons, but these are available in the form of rough heteronomic generalizations, which are lawlike in that instances make it reasonable to expect other instances to follow suit without being lawlike in the sense of being indefinitely refinable. Applying these facts to knowledge of identities, we see that it is possible to know that a mental event is identical with some physical event without knowing which one (in the sense of being able to give it a unique physical description that brings it under a relevant law). Even if someone knew the entire physical history of the world, and every mental event were identical with a physical, it would not follow that he could predict or explain a single mental event (so described, of course).

Two features of mental events in their relation to the physical—causal dependence and nomological independence—combine, then, to dissolve what has often seemed a paradox, the efficacy of thought and purpose in the material world, and their freedom from law. When we portray events as perceivings, rememberings, decisions and actions, we necessarily locate them amid physical happenings through the relation of cause and effect; but as long as we do not change the idiom that same mode of portrayal insulates mental events from the strict laws that can in principle be called upon to explain and predict physical phenomena.

Mental events as a class cannot be explained by physical science; particular mental events can when we know particular identities. But the explanations of mental events in which we are typically interested relate them to other mental events and conditions. We explain a man's free actions, for example, by appeal to his desires, habits, knowledge and perceptions. Such accounts of intentional behaviour operate in a conceptual framework removed from the direct reach of physical law by describing both cause and effect, reason and action, as aspects of a portrait of a human agent. The anomalism of the mental is thus a necessary condition for viewing action as autonomous. I conclude with a second passage from Kant:

It is an indispensable problem of speculative philosophy to show that its illusion respecting the contradiction rests on this, that we think of man in a different sense and relation when we call him free, and when we regard him as subject to the laws of nature.... It must therefore show that not only can both of these very well co-exist, but that both must be thought *as necessarily united* in the same subject.... [15]

APPENDIX: EMEROSES BY OTHER NAMES

Consider a hypothesis saying that everything that is examined before t and is an emerald (or else is a rose) is green if examined before t (or else is red); briefly:

H_1 All emeroses are gred

[15] Kant, op. cit., 76.

If H_1 is lawlike, it is a counterexample to Goodman's analysis in *Fact, Fiction and Forecast*, and one that would seem to cut pretty deep. Goodman's tests for deciding whether a statement is lawlike depend primarily on how well behaved its predicates are, taken one by one; thus for Goodman H_1 comes out doubly illegal. What H_1 suggests, however, is that it is a relation between the predicates that makes a statement lawlike, and it is not evident that this relation can be defined on the basis of the entrenchment of individual predicates.

But is H_1 lawlike? Recently Goodman has claimed it is not.[16] Here I consider whether he is right.

Let us pretend the following are true and lawlike:

H_2 All emeralds are green
H_3 All roses are red

Then H_1 is true, and we have good reason to believe it. Still, as Goodman points out, it does not follow that H_1 is lawlike, for it does not follow, from the fact that H_1 is entailed by hypotheses that are confirmed by their positive instances, that H_1 is confirmed by its positive instances.

Unless I am mistaken, the only reason Goodman gives for saying H_1 is not lawlike is contained in this remark: '... however true H_1 may be, it is unprojectible in that positive instances do not in general increase its credibility; emeralds found before t to be green do not confirm H_1' (328). Here the conclusion falls between comma and semicolon; what follows presumably gives the reason. The problem is to see how the reason supports the conclusion.

If positive instances were objects in the world, then the argument might be this: The positive instances of H_1 are gred emeroses, and if they are examined before t they are also green emeralds examined before t. But green emeralds examined before t do not tell us anything about the colour of roses examined after t. Unfortunately, if this were a good argument, it would also show that H_2 is not lawlike, for the positive instances of H_2 examined before t would be nothing but gred emeroses examined before t; and what can they tell us about the colour of emeralds after t?

In any case the assumption of the argument just examined is flatly at odds with clear indications in *Fact, Fiction and Forecast* (see p. 91, first edition, for example) that the positive instances of a hypothesis are sentences (or 'statements') immediately derivable from the hypothesis by instantiation. The question whether H_1 is lawlike is then the question whether H_1 is confirmed by statements to the effect that this or that object is a gred emerose. Given this reading of 'positive instance', Goodman's remark quoted above seems to be a *non sequitur*: for how can the fact that H_1 is not confirmed by emeralds found before t to be

---

[16] Richard Jeffrey in 'Goodman's Query' and John Wallace in 'Goodman, Logic, Induction' generously mention me in connection with the difficulty apparently raised for Goodman by hypotheses like H_1, and Goodman responds in the first two pages of 'Comments'.

green show that H_1 is not confirmed by statements that this or that object is a gred emerose?

The positive instances of H_1 do not mention time t any more than H_1 itself does. Nevertheless, an assumption of the discussion is that the objects described in the positive instances are actually observed before t, and perhaps a further assumption is that this fact is part of the background evidence against which the lawlike character of H_1 is to be judged. Given these assumptions, it is natural to suppose that the observer determines that an instance is positive by noting the time and observing that the object is a green emerald. But this supposition is adventitious, and may be false. I may know that at t a change will take place in the chemistry of my eye so that after t things that are red look green in normal light (before t green things look green); so, whether I know the time or not, I can tell by just looking that something is gred. Similarly I may be able to tell whether something is an emerose without knowing the time. Under these circumstances, it is hard to see why we would want to deny that H_1 is confirmed by its positive instances, i.e., that it is lawlike.

6

Intending

Someone may intend to build a squirrel house without having decided to do it, deliberated about it, formed an intention to do it, or reasoned about it. And despite his intention, he may never build a squirrel house, try to build a squirrel house, or do anything whatever with the intention of getting a squirrel house built. Pure intending of this kind, intending that may occur without practical reasoning, action, or consequence, poses a problem if we want to give an account of the concept of intention that does not invoke unanalysed episodes or attitudes like willing, mysterious acts of the will, or kinds of causation foreign to science.

When action is added to intention, for example when someone nails two boards together with the intention of building a squirrel house, then it may at first seem that the same problem does not necessarily arise. We are able to explain what goes on in such a case without assuming or postulating any odd or special events, episodes, attitudes or acts. Here is how we may explain it. Someone who acts with a certain intention acts for a reason; he has something in mind that he wants to promote or accomplish. A man who nails boards together with the intention of building a squirrel house must want to build a squirrel house, or think that he ought to (no doubt for further reasons), and he must believe that by nailing the boards together he will advance his project. Reference to other attitudes besides wanting, or thinking he ought, may help specify the agent's reasons, but it seems that some positive, or pro-, attitude must be involved. When we talk of reasons in this way, we do not require that the reasons be good ones. We learn something about a man's reasons for starting a war when we learn that he did it with the intention of ending all wars, even if we know that his belief that starting a war would end all wars was false. Similarly, a desire to humiliate an acquaintance may be someone's reason for cutting him at a party though an observer might, in a more normative vein, think that that was no reason. The falsity of a belief, or the patent wrongness of a value or desire, does not disqualify the belief or desire from providing an explanatory reason. On the other hand, beliefs and desires tell us an agent's reasons for acting only if those attitudes are appropriately related to the action as viewed by the actor. To serve as reasons for an action, beliefs and desires need not be reasonable, but a normative element nevertheless enters, since the action must be reasonable in the light of the beliefs and desires (naturally it may not be reasonable in the light of further considerations).

What does it mean to say that an action, as viewed by the agent, is reasonable in the light of his beliefs and desires? Suppose that a man boards an aeroplane marked 'London' with the intention of boarding an aeroplane headed for London, England. His reasons for boarding the plane marked 'London' are given by his desire to board a plane headed for London, England, and his belief that the plane marked 'London' is headed for London, England. His reasons explain why he intentionally boarded the plane marked 'London'. As it happens, the plane marked 'London' was headed for London, Ontario, not London, England, and so his reasons cannot explain why he boarded a plane headed for London, England. They can explain why he boarded a plane headed for London, Ontario, but only when the reasons are conjoined to the fact that the plane marked 'London' was headed for London, Ontario; and of course his reasons cannot explain why he intentionally boarded a plane headed for London, Ontario, since he had no such intention.[1]

The relation between reasons and intentions may be appreciated by comparing these statements:

(1) His reason for boarding the plane marked 'London' was that he wanted to board a plane headed for London, England, and he believed the plane marked 'London' was headed for London, England.

(2) His intention in boarding the plane marked 'London' was to board a plane headed for London, England.

The first of these sentences entails the second, but not conversely. The failure of the converse is due to two differences between (1) and (2). First, from (2) it is not possible to reconstruct the specific pro attitude mentioned in (1). Given (2), there must be some appropriate pro attitude, but it does not have to be wanting. And second, the description of the action ('boarding the plane marked "London"') occupies an opaque context in (1), but a transparent context in (2). Thus 'boarding the plane headed for London, Ontario' describes the same action as 'boarding the plane marked "London"', since the plane marked 'London' *was* the plane headed for London, Ontario. But substitution of 'boarding the plane headed for London, Ontario' for 'boarding the plane marked "London"' will turn (1) false, while leaving (2) true. Of course the description of the intention in (2), like the description of the contents of the belief and pro attitude in (1), occupies an opaque context.

Finally, there is this relation between statements with the forms of (1) and (2): although (2) does not entail (1), if (2) is true, *some* statements with the form of (1) is true (with perhaps another description of the action, and with an appropriate pro attitude and belief filled in). Statement (1), unlike (2), must describe the agent's action in a way that makes clear a sense in which the action was

---

[1] I take the 'intentionally' to govern the entire phrase 'boarded a plane headed for London, Ontario'. On an alternative reading, only the boarding would be intentional. Similarly, in (1) below his reason extends to the marking on the plane.

reasonable in the light of the agent's reasons. So we can say, if an agent does *A* with the intention of doing *B*, there is some description of *A* which reveals the action as reasonable in the light of reasons the agent had in performing it.

When is an action (described in a particular way) reasonable in the light of specific beliefs and pro attitudes? One way to approach the matter is through a rather abstract account of practical reasoning. We cannot suppose that whenever an agent acts intentionally he goes through a process of deliberation or reasoning, marshals evidence and principles, and draws conclusions. Nevertheless, if someone acts with an intention, he must have attitudes and beliefs from which, had he been aware of them and had the time, he *could* have reasoned that his action was desirable (or had some other positive attribute). If we can characterize the reasoning that would serve, we will in effect have described the logical relations between descriptions of beliefs and desires, and the description of an action, when the former give the reasons with which the latter was performed. We are to imagine, then, that the agent's beliefs and desires provide him with the premises of an argument. In the case of belief, it is clear at once what the premise is. Take an example: someone adds sage to the stew with the intention of improving the taste. So his corresponding premise is: Adding sage to the stew will improve its taste.

The agent's pro attitude is perhaps a desire or want; let us suppose he wants to improve the taste of the stew. But what is the corresponding premise? If we were to look for the proposition toward which his desire is directed, the proposition he wants true, it would be something like: He does something that improves the taste of the stew (more briefly: He improves the taste of the stew). This cannot be his premise, however, for nothing interesting follows from the two premises: Adding sage to the stew will improve its taste, and the agent improves the taste of the stew. The trouble is that the attitude of *approval* which the agent has toward the second proposition has been left out. It cannot be put back in by making the premise 'The agent wants to improve the taste of the stew': we do not want a *description* of his desire, but an *expression* of it in a form in which he might use it to arrive at an action. The natural expression of his desire is, it seems to me, evaluative in form; for example, 'It is desirable to improve the taste of the stew,' or, 'I ought to improve the taste of the stew'. We may suppose different pro attitudes are expressed with other evaluative words in place of 'desirable'.

There is no short proof that evaluative sentences express desires and other pro attitudes in the way that the sentence 'Snow is white' expresses the belief that snow is white. But the following consideration will perhaps help show what is involved. If someone who knows English says honestly 'Snow is white', then he believes snow is white. If my thesis is correct, someone who says honestly 'It is desirable that I stop smoking' has some pro attitude towards his stopping smoking. He feels some inclination to do it; in fact he will do it if nothing stands in the way, he knows how, and he has no contrary values or desires. Given this assumption, it is reasonable to generalize: if explicit value judgements represent pro attitudes, all pro attitudes may be expressed by value judgements that are at least implicit.

This last stipulation allows us to give a uniform account of acting with an intention. If someone performs an action of type *A* with the intention of performing an action of type *B*, then he must have a pro attitude toward actions of type *B* (which may be expressed in the form: an action of type *B* is good (or has some other positive attribute)) and a belief that in performing an action of type *A* he will be (or probably will be) performing an action of type *B* (the belief may be expressed in the obvious way). The expressions of the belief and desire entail that actions of type *A* are, or probably will be, good (or desirable, just, dutiful, etc.). The description of the action provided by the phrase substituted for '*A*' gives the description under which the desire and the belief rationalize the action. So to bring things back to our example, the desire to improve the taste of the stew and the belief that adding sage to the stew will improve its taste serve to rationalize an action described as 'adding sage to the stew'. (This more or less standard account of practical reasoning will be radically modified presently.)

There must be such rationalizing beliefs and desires if an action is done for a reason, but of course the presence of such beliefs and desires when the action is done does not suffice to ensure that what is done is done with the appropriate intention, or even with any intention at all. Someone might want tasty stew and believe sage would do the trick and put in sage thinking it was parsley; or put in sage because his hand was joggled. So we must add that the agent put in the sage because of his reasons. This 'because' is a source of trouble; it implies, so I believe, and have argued at length, the notion of cause. But not any causal relation will do, since an agent might have attitudes and beliefs that would rationalize an action, and they might cause him to perform it, and yet because of some anomaly in the causal chain, the action would not be intentional in the expected sense, or perhaps in any sense.

We end up, then, with this incomplete and unsatisfactory account of acting with an intention: an action is performed with a certain intention if it is caused in the right way by attitudes and beliefs that rationalize it.[2]

If this account is correct, then acting with an intention does not require that there be any mysterious act of the will or special attitude or episode of willing. For the account needs only desires (or other pro attitudes), beliefs, and the actions themselves. There is indeed the relation between these, causal or otherwise, to be analysed, but that is not an embarrassing entity that has to be added to the world's furniture. We would not, it is true, have shown how to *define* the concept of acting with an intention; the reduction is not definitional but ontological. But the ontological reduction, if it succeeds, is enough to answer

---

[2] This is where Essay 1 left things. At the time I wrote it I believed it would be possible to characterize 'the right way' in non-circular terms.

many puzzles about the relation between the mind and the body, and to explain the possibility of autonomous action in a world of causality.

This brings me back to the problem I mentioned at the start, for the strategy that appears to work for acting with an intention has no obvious application to pure intending, that is, intending that is not necessarily accompanied by action. If someone digs a pit with the intention of trapping a tiger, it is perhaps plausible that no entity at all, act, event, or disposition, corresponds to the noun phrase, 'the intention of trapping a tiger'—this is what our survey has led us to hope. But it is not likely that if a man has the intention of trapping a tiger, his intention is not a state, disposition, or attitude of some sort. Yet if this is so, it is quite incredible that this state or attitude (and the connected event or act of *forming an intention*) should play no role in acting with an intention. Our inability to give a satisfactory account of pure intending on the basis of our account of intentional action thus reflects back on the account of intentional action itself. And I believe the account I have outlined will be seen to be incomplete when we have an adequate analysis of pure intending.

Of course, we perform many intentional actions without forming an intention to perform them, and often intentional action is not preceded by an intention. So it would not be surprising if something were present in pure intending that is not always present in intentional action. But it would be astonishing if that extra element were foreign to our understanding of intentional action. For consider some simple action, like writing the word 'action'. Some temporal segments of this action are themselves actions: for example, first I write the letter 'a'. This I do with the intention of initiating an action that will not be complete until I have written the rest of the word. It is hard to see how the attitude towards the complete act which I have as I write the letter 'a' differs from the pure intention I may have had a moment before. To be sure, my intention has now begun to be realized, but why should that necessarily change my attitude? It seems that in any intentional action that takes much time, or involves preparatory steps, something like pure intending must be present.

We began with pure intending—intending without conscious deliberation or overt consequence—because it left no room for doubt that intending is a state or event separate from the intended action or the reasons that prompted the action. Once the existence of pure intending is recognized, there is no reason not to allow that intention of exactly the same kind is also present when the intended action eventuates. So though I may, in what follows, seem sometimes to concentrate on the rather special case of unfulfilled intentions, the subject is, in fact, all intending—intending abstracted from a context which may include any degree of deliberation and any degree of success in execution. Pure intending merely shows that there is something there to be abstracted.

What success we had in coping with the concept of intentional action came from treating talk of the intention with which an action is done as talk of beliefs, desires, and action. This suggests that we try treating pure intentions—intendings abstracted from normal outcomes—as actions, beliefs or pro-attitudes of some sort. The rest of this, Essay is concerned with these possibilities.

Is pure intending an action? It may be objected that intending to do something is not a change or event of any kind, and so cannot be something the agent does. But this objection is met by an adjustment in the thesis; we should say that the action is forming an intention, while pure intending is the state of an agent who has formed an intention (and has not changed his mind). Thus all the weight is put on the idea of forming an intention. It will be said that most intentions are not formed, at least if forming an intention requires conscious deliberation or decision. What we need then is the broader and more neutral concept of coming to have an intention—a change that may take place so slowly or unnoticed that the agent cannot say when it happens. Still, it is an event, and we could decide to call it an action, or at least something the agent does.

I see no reason to reject this proposal; the worst that can be said of it is that it provides so little illumination. The state of intention just is what results from coming to have an intention—but what sort of a state is it? The coming to have an intention we might try connecting with desires and beliefs as we did other intentional actions (again with a causal chain that works 'in the right way'). But the story does not have the substantial quality of the account of intentional action because the purported action is not familiar or observable, even to the agent himself.

Another approach focuses on overt speech acts. *Saying* that one intends to do something, or that one will do it, is undeniably an action and it has some of the characteristics of forming an intention. Saying, under appropriate circumstances, that one intends to do something, or that one will do it, can commit one to doing it; if the deed does not follow, it is appropriate to ask for an explanation. Actually to identify saying one intends to do something with forming an intention would be to endorse a sort of performative theory of intention; just as saying one promises to do something may be promising to do it, saying one intends to do it may be intending (or forming the intention) to do it. Of course one may form an intention without saying anything aloud, but this gap may be filled with the notion of speaking to oneself, 'saying in one's heart'.[3] A variant theory would make forming an intention like (or identical with) addressing a command to oneself.

I think it is easy to see that forming an intention is quite different from saying something, even to oneself, and that intending to do something is quite different from having said something. For one thing, the performative character of commands and promises which makes certain speech acts surprisingly momentous depends on highly specific conventions, and there are no such conventions governing the formation of intentions. Promising involves assuming

---

[3] See P. T. Geach, *Mental Acts*.

an obligation, but even if there are obligations to oneself, intending does not normally create one. If an agent does not do what he intended to do, he does not normally owe himself an explanation or apology, especially if he simply changed his mind; yet this is just the case that calls for explanation or apology when a promise has been made to another and broken. A command may be disobeyed, but only while it is in force. But if an agent does not do what he intended because he has changed his mind, the original intention is no longer in force. Perhaps it is enough to discredit these theories to point out that promising and commanding, as we usually understand them, are necessarily public performances, while forming an intention is not. Forming an intention may be an action but it is not a performance, and having an intention is not generally the aftermath of one.

None of this is to deny that saying 'I intend to do it' or 'I will do it' is much like, or on occasion identical with, promising to do it. If I say any of these things in the right context, I entitle a hearer to believe I believe I will do it. Perhaps a simpler way to put it is this: if I say 'I intend to do it' or 'I will do it' or 'I promise to do it' under certain conditions, then I *represent myself* as believing that I will. I may not believe I will, I may not intend that my hearer believe I will, but I have given him ground for complaint if I do not. These facts suggest that if I not only say 'I intend' or 'I will' in such a way as to represent myself as believing I will, but I am sincere as well, then my sincerity guarantees both that I intend to do it and that I believe I will. Some such line of argument has led many philosophers to hold that intending to do something entails believing one will, and has led a few philosophers to the more extreme view that to intend to do something is identical with a sort of belief that one will.

Is intending to act a belief that one will? The argument just sketched does not even show that intending implies belief. The argument proves that a man who sincerely says 'I intend to do it' or 'I will do it' under certain conditions must believe he will do it. But it may be the saying, not the intention, that implies the belief. And I think we can see this is the case. The trouble is that we have asked the notion of sincerity to do two different pieces of work. We began by considering cases where, by saying 'I intend to' or 'I will', I entitle a hearer to believe I will. And here it is obvious that if I am sincere, if things are as I represent them, then I must believe I will. But it is an assumption unsupported by the argument that any time I sincerely say I intend to do something I must believe I will do it, for sincerity in this case merely requires that I know I intend to do it. We are agreed that there are cases where sincerity in the utterer of 'I intend to' requires him to believe he will, but the argument requires that these cases include all those in which the speaker knows or believes he intends to do it.

Once we have distinguished the question how belief is involved in avowals of intention from the question how belief is involved in intention, we ought to be struck with how dubious the latter connection is.

It is a mistake to suppose that if an agent is doing something intentionally, he must know that he is doing it. For suppose a man is writing his will with the intention of providing for the welfare of his children. He may be in doubt about his success and remain so to his death; yet in writing his will he may in fact be providing for the welfare of his children, and if so he is certainly doing it intentionally. Some sceptics may think this example fails because they refuse to allow that a man may *now* be providing for the welfare of his children if that welfare includes events yet to happen. So here is another example: in writing heavily on this page I may be intending to produce ten legible carbon copies. I do not know, or believe with any confidence, that I am succeeding. But if I am producing ten legible carbon copies, I am certainly doing it intentionally. These examples do not prove that pure intending may not imply belief, for the examples involve acting with an intention. Nevertheless, it is hard to imagine that the point does not carry over to pure intending. As he writes his will, the man not only is acting with the intention of securing the welfare of his children, but he also intends to secure the welfare of his children. If he can be in doubt whether he is now doing what he intends, surely he can be in doubt whether he will do what he intends.

The thesis that intending implies believing is sometimes defended by claiming that expressions of intention are generally incomplete or elliptical. Thus the man writing his will should be described as intending to try to secure the welfare of his children, not as intending to secure it, and the man with the carbon paper is merely intending to try to produce his copies. The phrases sound wrong: we should be much more apt to say he *is* trying, and intends to do it. But where the action is entirely in the future, we do sometimes allow that we intend to try, and we see this as more accurate than the bald statement of intention when the outcome is sufficiently in doubt. Nevertheless, I do not think the claim of ellipsis can be used to defend the general thesis.

Without doubt many intentions are conditional in form—one intends to do something only if certain conditions are satisfied—and without doubt we often suppress mention of the conditions for one reason or another. So elliptical statements of intention are common. Grice gives us this exchange:

X. I intend to go to that concert on Tuesday.
Y. You will enjoy that.
X. I may not be there.
Y. I am afraid I don't understand.
X. The police are going to ask me some awkward questions on Tuesday afternoon, and I may be in prison by Tuesday evening.
Y. Then you should have said to begin with, 'I intend to go to the concert if I am not in prison', or, if you wished to be more reticent, something like, 'I should probably be going', or 'I hope to go', or, 'I aim to go', or, 'I intend to go if I can'.[4]

---

[4] H. P. Grice, 'Intention and Uncertainty', 4–5.

Grice does not speak of ellipsis here but he does think that this example, and others like it, make a strong case for the view that 'X intends to do *A*' is true, when 'intends' is used in the *strict* sense, only if X is sure that he will do *A*. The man in the example must intend *something*, and so if we knew what it was, we could say that his remark 'I intend to go to the concert' was elliptical for what he would have said if he had used 'intend' in the strict sense. What would he have said? 'I hope to go' is not more accurate about the intention, since it declares no intention at all; similarly for 'I aim to go' and 'I should probably be going', 'I intend to go if I can' is vague and general given the particularity of X's doubts, but there seems something worse wrong with it. For if an agent cannot intend what he believes to be impossible, then he asserts neither more nor less by saying 'I intend to do it if I can' than he would by saying 'I intend to do it.' How about 'I intend to go to the concert if I am not in prison'? Intuitively, this comes closest to conveying the truth about the situation as X sees it. But is it *literally* more accurate? It is hard to see how. On the view Grice is arguing for, if X said in the strict sense, and honestly, 'I intend to be at the concert', he would imply that he believed he would be there. If X said in the strict sense, and honestly, 'I intend to be at the concert if I am not in jail', he would imply that he believed he would be at the concert if he were not in jail. Now obviously the first belief implies the second but is not implied by it, and so an expression of the second belief makes a lesser claim and may be thought to be more accurate. Of course, the stronger claim cannot, by its contents, lead Y into error about what X will do, for whether X says he will be at the concert, or only that he will be there if he is not in jail, both X and Y know X will not be at the concert if he is in jail. Where Y might be misled, if the thesis we are examining is true, is with respect to what X believes he will do, and hence what he intends. For on the thesis, 'I intend to be at the concert if I am not in jail' implies a weaker belief than 'I intend to be at the concert'. If this is right, then greater accuracy still would result from further provisos, since X also does not believe he will be at the concert if he changes his mind, or if something besides imprisonment prevents him. We are thus led further and further toward the nearly empty, 'I intend to do it if nothing prevents me, if I don't change my mind, if nothing untoward happens'. This tells us almost nothing about what the agent believes about the future, or what he will in fact do.

I think X spoke correctly and accurately, but misleadingly, when he said, 'I intend to go to the concert'. He could have corrected the impression while still being accurate by saying, 'I now intend to go to the concert, but since I may be put in jail, I may not be there'. A man who says, 'I intend to be there, but I may not be' does not contradict himself, he is at worst inscrutable until he says more. We should realize there is something wrong with the idea that most statements of intention are elliptical until tempered by our doubts about what we shall in fact do when we notice that there is no satisfactory *general* method for supplying the more accurate statement for which the original statement went proxy. And the reason is clear: there can be no finite list of things we think might prevent us from doing what we intend, or of circumstances that might cause us to stay our hand. If we are reasonably sure something will prevent us from acting, this does, perhaps, baffle intention, but if we are simply uncertain, as is often the case, intention is not necessarily dulled. We can be clear what it is we intend to do while being in the dark as to the details, and therefore the pitfalls. If this is so, being more accurate about what we intend cannot be a matter of being more accurate about what we believe we will bring off.

There are genuine conditional intentions, but I do not think they come in the form, 'I intend to do it if I can' or, 'if I don't change my mind'. Genuine conditional intentions are appropriate when we explicitly consider what to do in various contingencies; for example, someone may intend to go home early from a party if the music is too loud. If we ask for the difference between conditions that really do make the statement of an intention more accurate and bogus conditions like 'if I can' or 'if nothing comes up' or 'if I don't change my mind', it seems to me clear that the difference is this: bona fide conditions are ones that are reasons for acting that are contemporary with the intention. Someone may not like loud music now, and that may be why he now intends to go home early from the party if the music is too loud. His not being able to go home early is not a reason for or against his going home early, and so it is not a relevant condition for an intention, though if he believes he cannot do it, that may prevent his having the intention. Changing his mind is a tricky case, but in general someone is not apt to view a possible future change of intention as a reason to modify his present intention unless he thinks the future change will itself be brought about by something he would now consider a reason.

The contrast that has emerged, between the circumstances we do sometimes allow to condition our intentions and the circumstances we would allow if intentions implied the belief that we will do what we intend, seems to me to indicate pretty conclusively that we do not necessarily believe we will do what we intend to do, and that we do not state our intentions more accurately by making them conditional on all the circumstances in whose presence we think we would act.

These last considerations point to the strongest argument against identifying pure intending with belief one will do what one intends. This is that reasons for intending to do something are in general quite different from reasons for believing one will do it. Here is why I intend to reef the main: I see a squall coming, I want to prevent the boat from capsizing, and I believe that reefing the main will prevent the boat from capsizing. I would put my reasons for intending to reef the main this way: a squall is coming, it would be a shame to capsize the boat, and reefing the main will prevent the boat from capsizing. But these reasons for intending to reef the main in themselves give me no reason to believe I will reef the main. Given additional assumptions, for example, that the approach of a squall is a reason to believe I believe a squall is coming, and that the shamefulness of capsizing the boat may be a reason to believe I want to prevent the boat from capsizing; and given that I have these beliefs and desires, it may be reasonable to suppose I intend to reef the main, and will in fact do so. So there may be a loose connection between reasons of the two kinds, but they are not at all identical (individual reasons may be the same, but a smallest natural set of reasons that supports the intention to act cannot be a set that supports the belief that the act will take place).

It is often maintained that an intention is a belief not arrived at by reasoning from evidence, or that an intention is a belief about one's future action that differs in some other way in its origin from an ordinary prediction. But such claims do not help the thesis. How someone arrived at a belief, what reasons he would give in support of it, what sustains his faith, these are matters that are simply irrelevant to the question what constitute reasons for the belief; the former events are accidents that befall a belief and cannot change its logical status without making it a new belief.

Is intending to do something the same as wanting to do it? Clearly reasons for intending to do something are very much like reasons for action, indeed one might hold that they are exactly the same except for time. As John Donne says, 'To will implies delay', but we may reduce the delay to a moment. I am writing the letter 'a' of 'action', and I intend to write the letter 'c' as soon as I finish the 'a'. The reason I intend to write the letter 'c' as soon as I finish the 'a' is that I want to write the word 'action', and I know that to do this I must, after writing the letter 'a', write the letter 'c'. Now I have finished the 'a' and have begun 'c'! What is my reason for writing the 'c'? It is that I want to write the word 'action', and I know that to this I must . . . So far the reasons sound identical, but if we look closer a difference will emerge. When I am writing the 'a' I intend to write the 'c' in just a moment, and part of my reason is that I believe this moment looms in the immediate future; when I am writing the 'c', my reasons include the belief that *now* is the time to write the 'c' if I am to write 'action', as I wish to. Aristotle sometimes neglects this difference and as a result says things that sound fatuous. He is apt to give as an example of practical reasoning something of this sort: I want to be warm, I believe a house will keep me warm, straightway I build a house. It is an important doctrine that the conclusion of a piece of practical reasoning may be an action; it is also important that the conclusion may be the formation of an intention to do something in the future.

Now I would like to draw attention to an aspect of this picture of what it is like to form an intention that seems to make for a difficulty. Consider again a case of intentional action. I want to eat something sweet, that is, I hold that my eating something sweet is desirable. I believe this candy is sweet, and so my eating this candy will be a case of my eating something sweet, and I conclude that my eating this candy is desirable. Since nothing stands in the way, I eat the candy—the conclusion is the action. But this also means I could express the conclusion by using a demonstrative reference to the action: 'This action of mine, this eating by me of this candy now, is desirable'. What seems so important about the possibility of a demonstrative reference to the action is that it is a case where it makes sense to couple a value judgement directly to action. My evaluative reason for acting was, 'My eating something sweet is desirable'. But of course this cannot mean that any action of mine whatsoever that is an eating of something sweet is something it makes sense to do—my judgement merely deals with actions in so far as they are sweet-consuming. Some such actions, even all of them, may have plenty else wrong with them. It is only when I come to an actual action that it makes sense to judge it as a whole as desirable or not; up until that moment there was no object with which I was acquainted to judge. Of course I can still say of the completed action that it is desirable in so far as it is this or that, but in choosing to perform it I went beyond this; my choice represented, or perhaps was, a judgement that the action itself was desirable.

And now the trouble about pure intending is that there is no action to judge simply good or desirable. All we can judge at the stage of pure intending is the desirability of actions of a sort, and actions of a sort are generally judged on the basis of the aspect that defines the sort. Such judgements, however, do not always lead to reasonable action, or we would be eating everything sweet we could lay our hands on (as Anscombe pointed out).[5]

The major step in clearing up these matters is to make a firm distinction between the kind of judgement that corresponds to a desire like wanting to eat something sweet and the kind of judgement that can be the conclusion of a piece of practical reasoning—that can correspond to an intentional action.[6] The first sort of judgement is often thought to have the form of a law: any action that is an eating of something sweet is desirable. If practical reasoning is deductive, this is what we should expect (and it seems to be how Aristotle and Hume, for example, thought of practical reasoning). But there is a fundamental objection to this idea, as can be seen when we consider an action that has both a desirable and an undesirable aspect. For suppose the propositional expression of a desire to eat something sweet were a universally quantified conditional. While holding it desirable to eat something sweet, we may also hold that it is undesirable to eat something poisonous. But one and the same object may be sweet and poisonous, and so one and the same action may be the eating of something sweet and of something poisonous. Our evaluative principles, which seem consistent, can then lead us to conclude that the same action is both desirable and undesirable. If undesirable actions are not desirable, we have derived a contradiction from

---

[5] G. E. M. Anscombe, *Intention*, 59.

[6] No weight should be given the word 'judgement'. I am considering here the *form* of propositions that express desires and other attitudes. I do not suppose that someone who wants to eat something sweet necessarily *judges* that it would be good to eat something sweet; perhaps we can say he *holds* that his eating something sweet has some positive characteristic. By distinguishing among the propositional expressions of attitudes I hope to mark differences among the attitudes.

premises all of which are plausible. The cure is to recognize that we have assigned the wrong form to evaluative principles. If they are judgements to the effect that *in so far as* an action has a certain characteristic it is good (or desirable, etc.), then they must not be construed in such a way that detachment works, or we will find ourselves concluding that the action is simply desirable when all that is warranted is the conclusion that it is desirable in a certain respect. Let us call judgements that actions are desirable in so far as they have a certain attribute, prima facie judgements.

Prima facie judgements cannot be directly associated with actions, for it is not reasonable to perform an action merely because it has a desirable characteristic. It is a reason for acting that the action is believed to have some desirable characteristic, but the fact that the action is performed represents a further judgement that the desirable characteristic was enough to act on—that other considerations did not outweigh it. The judgement that corresponds to, or perhaps is identical with, the action cannot, therefore, be a prima facie judgement; it must be an all-out or unconditional judgement which, if we were to express it in words, would have a form like 'This action is desirable'.

It can now be seen that our earlier account of acting with an intention was misleading or at least incomplete in an important respect. The reasons that determine the description under which an action is intended do not allow us to *deduce* that the action is simply worth performing; all we can deduce is that the action has a feature that argues in its favour. This is enough, however, to allow us to give the intention with which the action was performed. What is misleading is that the reasons that enter this account do not generally constitute all the reasons the agent considered in acting, and so knowing the intention with which someone acted does not allow us to reconstruct his actual reasoning. For we may not know how the agent got from his desires and other attitudes—his prima facie reasons—to the conclusion that a certain action was desirable.[7]

In the case of intentional action, at least when the action is of brief duration, nothing seems to stand in the way of an Aristotelian identification of the action with a judgement of a certain kind—an all-out, unconditional judgement that the action is desirable (or has some other positive characteristic). The identification of the action with the conclusion of a piece of practical reasoning is not essential to the view I am endorsing, but the fact that it can be made explains why, in our original account of intentional action, what was needed to relate it to pure intending remained hidden.

In the case of pure intending, I now suggest that the intention simply is an all-out judgement. Forming an intention, deciding, choosing, and deliberating are various modes of arriving at the judgement, but it is possible to come to have such a judgement or attitude without any of these modes applying.

---

[7] I have said more about the form of prima facie evaluative judgements, and the importance of distinguishing them from unconditional judgements, in Essay 3.

Let me elaborate on this suggestion and try to defend it against some objections. A few pages ago I remarked that an all-out judgement makes sense only when there is an action present (or past) that is known by acquaintance. Otherwise (I argued) the judgement must be general, that is, it must cover all actions of a certain sort, and among these there are bound to be actions some of which are desirable and some not. Yet an intention cannot single out a particular action in an intelligible sense, since it is directed to the future. The puzzle arises, I think, because we have overlooked an important distinction. It would be mad to hold that any action of mine in the immediate future that is the eating of something sweet would be desirable. But there is nothing absurd in my judging that any action of mine in the immediate future that is the eating of something sweet would be desirable *given the rest of what I believe about the immediate future*. I do not believe I will eat a poisonous candy, and so that is not one of the actions of eating something sweet that my all-out judgement includes. It would be a mistake to try to improve the statement of my intention by saying, 'I intend to eat something sweet, provided it isn't poisonous'. As we saw, this is a mistake because if this is the road I must travel, I will never get my intentions right. There are *endless* circumstances under which I would not eat something sweet, and I cannot begin to foresee them all. The point is, I do not believe anything will come up to make my eating undesirable or impossible. That belief is not part of what I intend, but an assumption without which I would not have the intention. The intention is not conditional in form; rather, the existence of the intention is conditioned by my beliefs.

I intend to eat a hearty breakfast tomorrow. You know, and I know, that I will not eat a hearty breakfast tomorrow if I am not hungry. And I am not certain I will be hungry, I just think I will be. Under these conditions it is not only not more accurate to say, 'I intend to eat a hearty breakfast if I'm hungry', it is *less* accurate. I have the second intention as well as the first, but the first implies the second, and not vice versa, and so the first is a more complete account of my intentions. If you knew only that I intended to eat a hearty breakfast if I was hungry, you would not know that I believe I will be hungry, which is actually the case. But you might figure this out if you knew I intend to eat a hearty breakfast tomorrow.

I think this view of the matter explains the trouble we had about the relation between intending to do something and believing one will—why, on the one hand, it is so strange to say, 'I intend to do it but perhaps I won't', and yet, on the other hand, it is so impossible to increase the accuracy of statements of intention by making the content of the intention conditional on how things turn out. The explanation is that the intention assumes, but does not contain a reference to, a certain view of the future. A present intention with respect to the future is in itself like an interim report: given what I now know and believe, here is my judgement of what kind of action is desirable. Since the intention is based on one's best estimate of the situation, it merely distorts matters to say the agent intends to act in the way he does only if his estimate turns out to be right. A present intention does not need to be anything like a resolve or a commitment (though *saying* one intends to do something may sometimes have this character). My intention is based on my present view of the situation; there is no reason in general why I should act as I now intend if my present view turns out to be wrong.

We can now see why adding, 'if I can' never makes the statement of an intention more accurate, although it may serve to cancel an unwanted natural suggestion of the act of saying one intends to do something. To intend to perform an action is, on my account, to hold that it is desirable to perform an action of a certain sort in the light of what one believes is and will be the case. But if one believes no such action is possible, then there can be no judgement that such an action consistent with one's beliefs is desirable. There can be no such intention.

If an intention is just a judgement that an action of a certain sort is desirable, what is there to distinguish an intention from a mere wish? We may put aside wishes for things that are not consistent with what one believes, for these are ruled out by our conception of an intention. And we may put aside wishes that do not correspond to all-out judgements. ('I wish I could go to London next week': my going to London next week may be consistent with all I believe, but not with all I want. This wish is idle because it is based on only some of my prima facie reasons.) But once we put these cases aside, there is no need to distinguish intentions from wishes. For a judgement that something I think I can do, and that I think I see my way clear to doing, a judgement that such an action is desirable not only for one or another reason but in the light of all my reasons; a judgement like this is not a mere wish. It *is* an intention. (This is not to deny that there are borderline cases.)

How well have we coped with the problem with which we began? That problem was, in effect, to give an account of intending (and of forming an intention) that would mesh in a satisfactory way with our account of acting with an intention and would not sacrifice the merits of that account. With respect to the first point, finding an account of intending that would mesh with our account of intentional action, we devised a satisfactory way of relating the two concepts, but only by introducing a new element, an all-out judgement, into the analysis of intentional action. Given this sort of judgement and the idea of such a judgement made in the light of what is believed about the future course of affairs, we were able, I think, to arrive at a plausible view of intending.

There remains the question whether the sort of judgement to which I have referred, an all-out judgement, can be understood without appeal to the notions of intention or will. I asked at the beginning of this last section of my paper whether intending to do something is wanting to do it; if it were, we might consider that our aim had been achieved. What we intend to do we want, in some very broad sense of want, to do. But this does not mean that intending is a form of wanting. For consider the actions that I want to perform and that are consistent with what I believe. Among them are the actions I intend to perform, and many more. I want to go to London next week, but I do not intend to, not because I think I cannot, but because it would interfere with other things I want more. This suggests strongly that wanting and desiring are best viewed as corresponding to, or constituting, prima facie judgements.

If this is correct, we cannot claim that we have made out a case for viewing intentions as something familiar, a kind of wanting, where we can distinguish the kind without having to use the concept of intention or will. What we can say, however, is that intending and wanting belong to the same genus of pro attitudes expressed by value judgements. Wants, desires, principles, prejudices, felt duties, and obligations provide reasons for actions and intentions, and are expressed by prima facie judgements; intentions and the judgements that go with intentional actions are distinguished by their all-out or unconditional form. Pure intendings constitute a subclass of the all-out judgements, those directed to future actions of the agent, and made in the light of his beliefs.

7

Paradoxes of Irrationality

The idea of an irrational action, belief, intention, inference, or emotion is paradoxical. For the irrational is not merely the non-rational, which lies outside the ambit of the rational; irrationality is a failure within the house of reason. When Hobbes says only man has 'the privilege of absurdity' he suggests that only a rational creature can be irrational. Irrationality is a mental process or state—a rational process or state—gone wrong. How can this be?

The paradox of irrationality is not as simple as the seeming paradox in the concept of an unsuccessful joke, or of a bad piece of art. The paradox of irrationality springs from what is involved in our most basic ways of describing, understanding, and explaining psychological states and events. Sophia is pleased that she can tie a bowline. Then her pleasure must be due to her belief that she can tie a bowline and her positive assessment of that accomplishment. Further, and doubtless more searching, explanations may be available, but they cannot displace this one, since this one flows from what it is to be pleased that something is the case. Or take Roger, who intends to pass an examination by memorizing the Koran. This intention must be explained by his desire to pass the examination and his belief that by memorizing the Koran he will enhance his chances of passing the examination. The existence of reason explanations of this sort is a built-in aspect of intentions, intentional actions, and many other attitudes and emotions. Such explanations explain by rationalizing: they enable us to see the events or attitudes as reasonable from the point of view of the agent. An aura of rationality, of fitting into a rational pattern, is thus inseparable from these phenomena, at least as long as they are described in psychological terms. How then can we explain, or even tolerate as possible, irrational thoughts, actions, or emotions?

Psychoanalytic theory as developed by Freud claims to provide a conceptual framework within which to describe and understand irrationality. But many philosophers think there are fundamental errors or confusions in Freud's thought. So I consider here some elements in that thought that have often come

A precursor of this paper was delivered as the Ernest Jones Lecture before the British Psycho-analytical Association on 26 April 1978. Dr Edna O'Shaughnessy commented, and I have profited from her informative remarks. I am also indebted for further useful suggestions to Dagfinn Føllesdal, Sue Larson, and Richard Wollheim.

under attack, elements that consist of a few very general doctrines central to all stages of Freud's mature writings. After analysing the underlying problem of explaining irrationality, I conclude that any satisfactory view must embrace some of Freud's most important theses, and when these theses are stated in a sufficiently broad way, they are free from conceptual confusion. It perhaps needs to be emphasized that my 'defence' of Freud is directed to some only of Freud's ideas, and these are ideas at the conceptual, in contrast to the empirical, end of that vague spectrum.

Much that is called irrational does not make for paradox. Many might hold that it is irrational, given the dangers, discomforts, and meagre rewards to be expected on success, for any person to attempt to climb Mt Everest without oxygen (or even with it). But there is no puzzle in explaining the attempt if it is undertaken by someone who has assembled all the facts he can, given full consideration to all his desires, ambitions, and attitudes, and has acted in the light of his knowledge and values. Perhaps it is in some sense irrational to believe in astrology, flying saucers, or witches, but such beliefs may have standard explanations if they are based on what their holders take to be the evidence. It is sensible to try to square the circle if you don't know it can't be done. The sort of irrationality that makes conceptual trouble is not the failure of someone else to believe or feel or do what we deem reasonable, but rather the failure, within a single person, of coherence or consistency in the pattern of beliefs, attitudes, emotions, intentions, and actions. Examples are wishful thinking, acting contrary to one's own best judgement, self-deception, believing something that one holds to be discredited by the weight of the evidence.

In attempting to explain such phenomena (along with much more, of course) Freudians have made the following claims:

First, the mind contains a number of semi-independent structures, these structures being characterized by mental attributes like thoughts, desires, and memories.

Second, parts of the mind are in important respects like people, not only in having (or consisting of) beliefs, wants, and other psychological traits, but in that these factors can combine, as in intentional action, to cause further events in the mind or outside it.

Third, some of the dispositions, attitudes, and events that characterize the various substructures in the mind must be viewed on the model of physical dispositions and forces when they affect, or are affected by, other substructures in the mind.

A further doctrine about which I shall say only a little is that some mental phenomena that we normally assume to be conscious, or at least available to consciousness, are not conscious, and can become accessible only with difficulty, if at all. In most functional respects, these unconscious mental states and events are like conscious beliefs, memories, desires, wishes, and fears.

I hope it will be agreed that these doctrines are all to be found in Freud, and that they are central to his theories. They are, as I have said, far less strong and detailed than Freud's views. Yet even in reduced form, they require more defence than is possible, in the view of many philosophers. The criticisms I shall be attempting to meet are related in various ways, but they are essentially of two sorts.

First, the idea that the mind can be partitioned at all has often been held to be unintelligible, since it seems to require that thoughts and desires and even actions be attributed to something less than, and therefore distinct from, the whole person. But can we make sense of acts and attitudes that are not those of an agent? Also, as Sartre suggests, the notion of responsibility would lose its essential point if acts and intentions were pried loose from people and attached instead to semi-autonomous parts of the mind. The parts would then stand proxy for the person: each part would become a little woman, man, or child. What was once a single mind is turned into a battlefield where opposed forces contend, deceive one another, conceal information, devise strategies. As Irving Thalberg and others point out, sometimes it even happens that one segment protects itself from its own forces (thoughts).[1] The prime agent may appear as a sort of chairman of the board, arbiter, or dictator. It is not surprising that doubts have arisen as to whether these metaphors can be traded for a consistent theory.

A second, though related, set of worries concerns the underlying explanatory methodology. On the one hand, psychoanalytic theory extends the reach of teleological or reason explanation by discovering motives, wishes, and intentions that were not recognized before. In this respect, as has often been noted, Freud greatly increased the number and variety of phenomena that can be viewed as rational: it turns out that we have reasons for our forgettings, slips of the tongue, and exaggerated fears. But on the other side, Freud wants his explanations to yield what explanations in natural science often promise: causal accounts that permit control. In this vein, he applies to mental events and states terms drawn from hydraulics, electromagnetism, neurology, and mechanics. Toulmin, Flew, MacIntyre, and Peters among philosophers have at one time or another suggested that psychoanalytic theories attempt the impossible by trying to bring psychological phenomena (which require explanations in terms of reasons) under causal laws: they think this accounts for, but does not justify, Freud's constant use, when talking of the mind, of metaphors drawn from other sciences.[2]

It seems then, that there are two irreconcilable tendencies in Freud's methodology. On the one hand he wanted to extend the range of phenomena subject

---

[1] See Irving Thalberg, 'Freud's Anatomies of the Self', in *Philosophical Essays on Freud*, ed. R. Wollheim and J. Hopkins (Cambridge University Press, 1982).

[2] See, for examples, Antony Flew, 'Motives and the Unconscious', in *Minnesota Studies in the Philosophy of Science*, vol. 1, ed. H. Feigl and M. Scriven (University of Minnesota Press, Minneapolis, 1956); Alasdair MacIntyre, *The Unconscious* (Routledge, London, 1958); R. S. Peters, *The Concept of Motivation* (Routledge, London, 1958); Charles Taylor, *The Explanation of Behaviour* (Routledge, London, 1965).

to reason explanations, and on the other to treat these same phenomena as forces and states are treated in the natural sciences. But in the natural sciences, reasons and propositional attitudes are out of place, and blind causality rules.

In order to evaluate these charges against psychoanalytic theory, I want first to rehearse part of what I think is a correct analysis of normal intentional action. Then we can consider irrationality.

A man walking in a park stumbles on a branch in the path.[3] Thinking the branch may endanger others, he picks it up and throws it in a hedge beside the path. On his way home it occurs to him that the branch may be projecting from the hedge and so still be a threat to unwary walkers. He gets off the tram he is on, returns to the park, and restores the branch to its original position. Here everything the agent does (except stumble on the branch) is done for a reason, a reason in the light of which the corresponding action was reasonable. Given that the man believed the stick was a danger if left on the path, and a desire to eliminate the danger, it was reasonable to remove the stick. Given that, on second thought, he believed the stick was a danger in the hedge, it was reasonable to extract the stick from the hedge and replace it on the path. Given that the man wanted to take the stick from the hedge, it was reasonable to dismount from the tram and return to the park. In each case the reasons for the action tell us what the agent saw in his action, they give the intention with which he acted, and they thereby give an explanation of the action. Such an explanation, as I have said, must exist if something a person does is to count as an action at all.

The pattern of reason explanations has been noted by many philosophers. Hume puts it pithily: 'Ask a man why he uses exercise: he will answer, because he desires to keep his health. If you then enquire why he desires health, he will readily reply, because sickness is painful.'[4] The pattern is so familiar that we may miss its subtlety. What is to be explained is the action, say taking exercise. At the minimum, the explanation calls on two factors: a value, goal, want, or attitude of the agent, and a belief that by acting in the way to be explained he can promote the relevant value or goal, or will be acting in accord with his attitude. The action on the one hand, and the belief–desire pair which give the reason on the other, must be related in two very different ways to yield an explanation. First, there must be a logical relation. Beliefs and desires have a content, and these contents must be such as to imply that there is something valuable or desirable about the action. Thus a man who finds something desirable in health, and believes that exercise will make him healthy can conclude that there is something desirable in exercise, which may explain why he takes exercise. Second, the reasons an agent has for acting must, if they are to explain the action, be the reasons on which he acted; the reasons must have played a *causal* role in the occurrence of

---

[3] The example, though not the use I make of it, comes from Sigmund Freud, 'Notes upon a Case of Obsessional Neurosis', *Standard Edition*, x, 23.

[4] David Hume, *An Inquiry Concerning the Principle of Morals*, ed. L. A. Selby Bigge (The Clarendon Press, Oxford, 1957), Appendix I, p. 293.

the action. These two conditions on reason explanations are both necessary, but they are not sufficient, since some causal relations between belief–desire pairs and actions do not give reason explanations. (This complication will not concern us here, though there are no doubt irrational actions that hinge on the complication.)

This much of the analysis of action makes clear why all intentional actions, whether or not they are in some further sense irrational, have a rational element at the core; it is this that makes for one of the paradoxes of irrationality. But we also see that Freud can be defended on one important point: there is no inherent conflict between reason explanations and causal explanations. Since beliefs and desires are causes of the actions for which they are reasons, reason explanations include an essential causal element.

What can be said of intentional action can be extended to many other psychological phenomena. If a person intends to steal some Brussels sprouts, then whether or not he executes his intention, the intention itself must be caused by a desire to possess some Brussels sprouts and a belief that by stealing them he will come into possession of them. (Once again, the logical, or rational, aspect of the intention is obvious.) Similarly, most of our wishes, hopes, desires, emotions, beliefs, and fears depend upon a simple inference (usually, no doubt, unnoticed) from other beliefs and attitudes. We fear poverty because we believe it will bring what we hold to be evils; we hope it will rain because we believe rain will help the crops, and we want the crops to prosper; we believe rain will help the crops on the basis of induction or hearsay or reading; and so on. In each of these cases, there is the logical connection between the contents of various attitudes and beliefs, and what they cause.

The conclusion up to this point is that merely to label a psychological state or event as being or entailing what is loosely called a propositional attitude is to guarantee the relevance of a reason explanation, and hence an element of rationality. But of course if such states and events can be irrational, the element of rationality cannot prevent their being at the same time less than rational. Consider the case of an action where the agent acts counter to what he believes, everything considered, is better. (Aristotle called such behaviour a case of akrasia; other terms are 'incontinence' or 'weakness of the will'.) It is easy to imagine that the man who returned to the park to restore the branch to its original position in the path realizes that his action is not sensible. He has a motive for moving the stick, namely, that it may endanger a passer-by. But he also has a motive for not returning, which is the time and trouble it costs. In his own judgement, the latter consideration outweighs the former; yet he acts on the former. In short, he goes against his own best judgement.

The problem of explaining such behaviour has puzzled philosophers and moralists at least since Plato. According to Plato, Socrates argued that since no one willingly acts counter to what he knows to be best, only ignorance can explain foolish or evil acts. This is often called a paradox, but Socrates' view is paradoxical only because it denies what we all believe, that there are akratic acts.

If Socrates is right—if such actions are ruled out by the logic of the concepts—then there is nothing puzzling about the facts to be explained. Nevertheless, Socrates (or Plato) has brought our problem to a head: there is a conflict between the standard way of explaining intentional action and the idea that such an action can be irrational. Since the view that no intentional action can be internally irrational stands at one extreme in the continuum of possible views, let me give it a name: the *Plato Principle*. It is the doctrine of pure rationality.

At an opposite extreme is the *Medea Principle*. According to this doctrine, a person can act against his better judgement, but only when an alien force overwhelms his or her will. This is what happens when Medea begs her own hand not to murder her children. Her hand, or the passion of revenge behind it, overcomes her will. Some such treatment of weakness of the will is popular.[5] And given the thesis, the term is suitable, for the will of the agent is weaker than the alien passion. Moralists particularly have been attracted to this view, since it suggests that no more is needed to overcome temptation than greater resolve to do the right. Just the same, it is a strange doctrine, since it implies that akratic acts are not intentional, and so not in themselves actions for which the agent can be held responsible. If the agent is to blame, it is not for what he did, but because he did not resist with enough vigour. What the agent found himself doing had a reason—the passion or impulse that overcame his better judgement—but the reason was not *his*. From the agent's point of view, what he did was the effect of a cause that came from outside, as if another person had moved him.

Aristotle suggested that weakness of the will is due to a kind of forgetting. The akrates has two desires; in our example, he wants to save his time and effort, and also wants to move the branch. He can't act on both desires, but Aristotle will not let him get so far as to appreciate his problem, for according to Aristotle the agent loses active touch with his knowledge that by not returning to the park he can save time and effort. It is not quite a case of a conscious and an unconscious desire in conflict; rather there is a conscious and an unconscious piece of knowledge, where action depends on which piece of knowledge is conscious.

There are situations in which Aristotle's analysis is appropriate, and other situations ruled by the Medea Principle. But such situations are not the only ones, and they are not the defining cases of akrasia, where the agent acts intentionally while aware that everything considered a better course of action is open to him. For when the Medea Principle is at work, intention is not present; and in Aristotle's analysis, the agent is not aware of an alternative.

On reflection it is obvious that neither the Medea Principle nor Aristotle's analysis allows for straightforward cases of conflict, cases in which an agent has good reasons both for doing, and for refraining from, a course of action; or, what comes to the same thing, good reasons for doing each of two mutually exclusive

---

[5] For further discussion of these issues, and references, see Essay 3, this volume.

things. Such situations are too familiar to require special explanation: we are not normally paralysed when competing claims are laid on us, nor do we usually suppress part of the relevant information, or drive one of our desires under-ground. Usually we can face situations where a decision must be made, and we decide best when we manage to keep all the considerations, the pros and the cons, before us.

What requires explaining is the action of an agent who, having weighed up the reasons on both sides, and having judged that the preponderance of reasons is on one side, then acts against this judgement. We should not say he has no reason for his action, since he has reasons both for and against. It is because he has a reason for what he does that we can give the intention with which he acted. And like all intentional actions, his action can be explained, by referring to the beliefs and desires that caused it and gave it point.

But although the agent has a reason for doing what he did, he had better reasons, by his own reckoning, for acting otherwise. What needs explaining is not why the agent acted as he did, but why he *didn't* act otherwise, given his judgement that all things considered it would be better.

A person who appreciates the fact that he has good reasons both for and against an action should not be thought to be entertaining a contradiction. It follows that moral principles, or the judgements that correspond to desires, cannot be expressed by sentences like 'It is wrong to lie' or 'It is good to give pleasure'. Not, that is, if these sentences are taken in the natural way to express universal statements like 'All lies are wrong' or 'All acts that give pleasure are good'. For one and the same act may be a lie and an act that gives pleasure, and so be both wrong and good. On many moral theories, this is a contradiction. Or to take an even simpler case, if it is right to keep promises and wrong to break them, then someone who through no fault of his own has made incompatible promises will do something wrong if he does something right.

The solution to this puzzle about the logic of practical reasoning is to recognize that evaluative principles are not correctly stated in the form 'It is wrong to lie'. For not all lies are wrong; there are cases when one ought to lie for the sake of some more important consideration. The fact that an action is a lie, or the breaking of a promise, or a consumer of time is a count against the action, to be weighed along with other reasons for the action. Every action we perform, or consider performing, has something to be said for it and something against; but we speak of conflict only when the pros and cons are weighty and close to being in balance. Simple deduction can tell me that if I wish to keep promise A I must be in Addis Ababa on a certain date, and if I wish to keep promise B I must be in Bora Bora at that same time; but logic cannot tell me which to do.

Since logic cannot tell me which to do, it is unclear in what respect either action would be irrational. Nor is the irrationality evident if we add that I judge that all things considered I ought to keep promise A, and yet I keep promise B. For the first judgement is merely conditional: in the light of all my evidence,

I ought to do *A*; and this cannot contradict the unconditional judgement that I ought to do *B*. Pure internal inconsistency enters only if I also hold—as in fact I do—that I ought to act on my own best judgement, what I judge best or obligatory, everything considered.

A purely formal description of what is irrational in an akratic act is, then, that the agent goes against his own second-order principle that he ought to act on what he holds to be best, everything considered. It is only when we can describe his action in just this way that there is a puzzle about explaining it. If the agent does not have the principle that he ought to act on what he holds to be best, everything considered, then though his action may be irrational from *our* point of view, it need not be irrational from his point of view—at least not in a way that poses a problem for explanation. For to explain his behaviour we need only say that his desire to do what he held to be best, all things considered, was not as strong as his desire to do something else.

But someone who knowingly and intentionally acts contrary to his own principle; how can we explain that? The explanation must, it is evident, contain some feature that goes beyond the Plato Principle; otherwise the action is perfectly rational. On the other hand, the explanation must retain the core of the Plato Principle; otherwise the action is not intentional. An account like this seems to satisfy both requirements: there is, we have agreed, a normal reason explanation for an akratic action. Thus the man who returns to the park to replace the branch has a reason: to remove a danger. But in doing this he ignores his principle of acting on what he thinks is best, all things considered. And there is no denying that he has a motive for ignoring his principle, namely that he wants, perhaps very strongly, to return the branch to its original position. Let us say this motive does explain the fact that he fails to act on his principle. This is the point at which irrationality enters. For the desire to replace the branch has entered into the decision to do it twice over. First it was a consideration in favour of replacing the branch, a consideration that, in the agent's opinion, was less important than the reasons against returning to the park. The agent then held that everything considered he ought not to return to the park. Given his principle that one ought to act on such a conclusion, the rational thing for him to do was, of course, not to return to the park. Irrationality entered when his desire to return made him ignore or override his principle. For though his motive for ignoring his principle was a reason for ignoring the principle, it was not a reason against the principle itself, and so when it entered in this second way, it was irrelevant as a reason, to the principle and to the action. The irrationality depends on the distinction between a reason for having, or acting on, a principle, and a reason for the principle.

Another, and simpler, example will make the point clear. Suppose a young man very much wishes he had a well-turned calf and this leads him to believe he has a well-turned calf. He has a normal reason for wanting to have this belief—it gives him pleasure. But if the entire explanation of his holding the belief is that he wanted to believe it, then his holding the belief is irrational. For the wish to have a belief is not evidence for the truth of the belief, nor does it give it rational support in any other way. What his wish to have this belief makes rational is that this proposition should be true: He believes that he has a well-turned calf. This does not rationalize his believing: I have a well-turned calf. This is a case of wishful thinking, which is a model for the simplest kind of irrationality. Simple as it is, however, the model has a complexity which is obscured by the ambiguity of the phrase 'reason for believing'.

In some cases of irrationality it is unlikely, and perhaps impossible, for the agent to be fully aware of all that is going on in his mind. If someone 'forgets' that today is Thursday because he does not want to keep a disagreeable social commitment, it is perhaps ruled out that he should be aware of this. But in many cases there is no logical difficulty in supposing the agent knows what is going on. The young man may know he believes he has a well-turned calf only because he wants to believe it, just as the man who returns to the park to replace the branch may realize both the absurdity and the explanation of his action.

In standard reason explanations, as we have seen, not only do the propositional contents of various beliefs and desires bear appropriate logical relations to one another and to the contents of the belief, attitude, or intention they help explain; the actual states of belief and desire cause the explained state or event. In the case of irrationality, the causal relation remains, while the logical relation is missing or distorted. In the cases of irrationality we have been discussing, there is a mental cause that is not a reason for what it causes. So in wishful thinking, a desire causes a belief. But the judgement that a state of affairs is, or would be, desirable, is not a reason to believe that it exists.

It is clear that the cause must be mental in this sense: it is a state or event with a propositional content. If a bird flying by causes a belief that a bird is flying by (or that an airplane is flying by) the issue of rationality does not arise; these are causes that are not reasons for what they cause, but the cause has no logical properties, and so cannot of itself explain or engender irrationality (of the kind I have described). Can there be other forms of irrationality? The issue is not clear, and I make no claims concerning it. So far my thesis is only that many common examples of irrationality may be characterized by the fact that there is a mental cause that is not a reason. This characterization points the way to one kind of explanation of irrationality.

Irrationality of this kind may turn up wherever rationality operates. Just as incontinent actions are irrational, there can be irrational intentions to act, whether or not they are acted out. Beliefs may be irrational, as may courses of reasoning. Many desires and emotions are shown to be irrational if they are explained by mental causes that are not reasons for them. The general concept applies also to unchanges. A person is irrational if he is not open to reason—if, on accepting a belief or attitude on the basis of which he ought to make accommodating changes in his other beliefs, desires, or intentions, he fails to make those changes. He has a reason which does not cause what it is a sufficient reason for.

We now see how it is possible to reconcile an explanation that shows an action, belief, or emotion to be irrational with the element of rationality inherent in the description and explanation of all such phenomena. Thus we have dealt, at least in a preliminary way, with one paradox of irrationality. But now a second source of paradox emerges which cannot be so easily dissipated.

If events are related as cause and effect, they remain so no matter in what vocabulary we choose to describe them. Mental or psychological events are such only under a manner of description, for these very events surely are at the same time neurophysiological, and ultimately physical, events, though recognizable and identifiable within these realms only when given neurophysiological or physical descriptions. As we have seen, there is no difficulty in general in explaining mental events by appeal to neurophysiological or physical causes: this is central to the analysis of perception or memory, for example. But when the cause is described in non-mental terms, we necessarily lose touch with what is needed to explain the element of irrationality. For irrationality appears only when rationality is evidently appropriate: where both cause and effect have contents that have the sort of logical relations that make for reason or its failure. Events conceived solely in terms of their physical or physiological properties cannot be judged as reasons, or as in conflict, or as concerned with a subject matter. So we face the following dilemma: if we think of the cause in a neutral mode, disregarding its mental status as a belief or other attitude—if we think of it merely as a force that works on the mind without being identified as part of it—then we fail to explain, or even describe, irrationality. Blind forces are in the category of the non-rational, not the irrational. So, we introduce a mental description of the cause, which thus makes it a candidate for being a reason. But we still remain outside the only clear pattern of explanation that applies to the mental, for that pattern demands that the cause be more than a candidate for being a reason; it must *be* a reason, which in the present case it cannot be. For an explanation of a mental effect we need a mental cause that is also a reason for this effect, but, if we have it, the effect cannot be a case of irrationality. Or so it seems.

There is, however, a way one mental event can cause another mental event without being a reason for it, and where there is no puzzle and not necessarily any irrationality. This can happen when cause and effect occur in different minds. For example, wishing to have you enter my garden, I grow a beautiful flower there. You crave a look at my flower and enter my garden. My desire caused your craving and action, but my desire was not a reason for your craving, nor a reason on which you acted. (Perhaps you did not even know about my wish.) Mental phenomena may cause other mental phenomena without being reasons for them, then, and still keep their character as mental, provided cause and effect are adequately segregated. The obvious and clear cases are those of social interaction. But I suggest that the idea can be applied to a single mind and person. Indeed, if we are going to explain irrationality at all, it seems we must assume that the mind can be partitioned into quasi-independent structures that interact in ways the Plato Principle cannot accept or explain.

To constitute a structure of the required sort, a part of the mind must show a larger degree of consistency or rationality than is attributed to the whole.[6] Unless this is the case, the point of the analogy with social interaction is destroyed. The idea is that if parts of the mind are to some degree independent, we can understand how they are able to harbour inconsistencies, and to interact on a causal level. Recall the analysis of akrasia. There I mentioned no partitioning of the mind because the analysis was at that point more descriptive than explanatory. But the way could be cleared for explanation if we were to suppose two semi-autonomous departments of the mind, one that finds a certain course of action to be, all things considered, best, and another that prompts another course of action. On each side, the side of sober judgement and the side of incontinent intent and action, there is a supporting structure of reasons, of interlocking beliefs, expectations, assumptions, attitudes, and desires. To set the scene in this way still leaves much unexplained, for we want to know why this double structure developed, how it accounts for the action taken, and also, no doubt, its psychic consequences and cure. What I stress here is that the partitioned mind leaves the field open to such further explanations, and helps resolve the conceptual tension between the Plato Principle and the problem of accounting for irrationality.

The partitioning I propose does not correspond in nature or function to the ancient metaphor of a battle between Virtue and Temptation or Reason and Passion. For the competing desires or values which akrasia demands do not, on my account, in themselves suggest irrationality. Indeed, a judgement that, all things considered, one ought to act in a certain way presupposes that the competing factors have been brought within the same division of the mind. Nor is it a matter of the bald intervention of a fey and alien emotion, as in the Medea Principle. What is called for is organized elements, within each of which there is a fair degree of consistency, and where one element can operate on another in the modality of non-rational causality.

Allowing a degree of autonomy to provinces of the mind dissipates to a degree the problems we have discussed, but it generates others. For to the extent that the Plato Principle fails to explain the workings of the mind, mere causal relations replace it, and these explain best, or make most progress toward science, as they can be summarized in laws. But there is a question how far the workings of the mind can be reduced to strict, deterministic laws as long as the phenomena are

---

[6] Here as elsewhere my highly abstract account of the partitioning of the mind deviates from Freud's. In particular, I have nothing to say about the number or nature of divisions of the mind, their permanence or aetiology. I am solely concerned to defend the idea of mental compartmentalization, and to argue that it is necessary if we are to explain a common form of irrationality. I should perhaps emphasize that phrases like 'partition of the mind', 'part of the mind', 'segment', etc. are misleading if they suggest that what belongs to one division of the mind cannot belong to another. The picture I want is of overlapping territories.

identified in mental terms. For one thing, the realm of the mental cannot form a closed system; much that happens in it is perforce caused by events with no mental description. And for another, once we contemplate causal relations between mental events in partial disregard of the logical relations between the descriptions of those events, we enter a realm without a unified and coherent set of constitutive principles: the concepts employed must be treated as mixed, owing allegiance partly to their connections with the world of non-mental forces, and partly to their character as mental and directed to a propositional content. These matters bear directly on the important question what kind of laws or generalizations will be found to hold in this area, and therefore on the question how scientific a science of the mental can be: that is, however, a subject I have put to one side.

There is one other problem that springs from recognizing semi-independent departments within the same mind. We attribute beliefs, purposes, motives, and desires to people in an endeavour to organize, explain, and predict their behaviour, verbal and otherwise. We describe their intentions, their actions, and their feelings in the light of the most unified and intelligible scheme we can contrive. Speech yields no more direct access into this scheme than any other behaviour, since speech itself must be interpreted; indeed speech requires at least two levels of interpretation, there being both the question what the speaker's words mean, and the question what the speaker means in speaking them. Not that an agent knows directly what he believes, wants, and intends in some way that reduces observers to mere detectives. For though he can often say what is on his mind, an agent's words have meaning in the public domain; what his words mean is up to the interpreter as well as to him. How he is to be understood is a problem for him as it is for others.

What makes interpretation difficult is the multiplicity of mental factors that produce behaviour and speech. To take an instance, if we know that in speaking certain words a man meant to assert that the price of plutonium is rising, then generally we must know a great deal more about his intentions, his beliefs, and the meaning of his words. If we imagine ourselves starting out from scratch to construct a theory that would unify and explain what we observe—a theory of the man's thoughts and emotions and language—we should be overwhelmed by the difficulty. There are too many unknowns for the number of equations. We necessarily cope with this problem by a strategy that is simple to state, though vastly complex in application: the strategy is to assume that the person to be understood is much like ourselves. That is perforce the opening strategy, from which we deviate as the evidence piles up. We start out assuming that others have, in the basic and largest matters, beliefs and values similar to ours. We are bound to suppose someone we want to understand inhabits our world of macroscopic, more or less enduring, physical objects with familiar causal dispositions; that his world, like ours, contains people with minds and motives; and that he shares with us the desire to find warmth, love, security, and success, and the desire to avoid pain and distress. As we get to matters of detail, or to matters in one way or another less central to our thinking, we can more and more easily allow for differences between ourselves and others. But unless we can interpret others as sharing a vast amount of what makes up our common sense we will not be able to identify any of their beliefs and desires and intentions, any of their propositional attitudes.

The reason is the holistic character of the mental. The meaning of a sentence, the content of a belief or desire, is not an item that can be attached to it in isolation from its fellows. We cannot intelligibly attribute the thought that a piece of ice is melting to someone who does not have many true beliefs about the nature of ice, its physical properties connected with water, cold, solidity, and so forth. The one attribution rests on the supposition of many more—endlessly more. And among the beliefs we suppose a man to have, many must be true (in our view) if any are to be understood by us. The clarity and cogency of our attributions of attitude, motive, and belief are proportionate, then, to the extent to which we find others consistent and correct. We often, and justifiably, find others irrational and wrong; but such judgements are most firmly based when there is the most agreement. We understand someone best when we hold him to be rational and sage, and this understanding is what gives our disputes with him a keen edge.

There is no question but that the precept of unavoidable charity in interpretation is opposed to the partitioning of the mind. For the point of partitioning was to allow inconsistent or conflicting beliefs and desires and feelings to exist in the same mind, while the basic methodology of all interpretation tells us that inconsistency breeds unintelligibility.

It is a matter of degree. We have no trouble understanding small perturbations against a background with which we are largely in sympathy, but large deviations from reality or consistency begin to undermine our ability to describe and explain what is going on in mental terms. What sets a limit to the amount of irrationality we can make psychological sense of is a purely conceptual or theoretical matter—the fact that mental states and events are the states and events they are by their location in a logical space. On the other hand, what constrains the amount and kind of consistency and correspondence with reality we find in our fellow men and women is the frailty of human nature: the failure of imagination or sympathy on the part of the interpreter, and the stubborn imperfection of the interpreted. The underlying paradox of irrationality, from which no theory can entirely escape, is this: if we explain it too well, we turn it into a concealed form of rationality; while if we assign incoherence too glibly, we merely compromise our ability to diagnose irrationality by withdrawing the background of rationality needed to justify any diagnosis at all.

What I have tried to show, then, is that the very general features of psychoanalytic theory that I listed as having puzzled philosophers and others are, if I am right, features that will be found in any theory that sets itself to explain irrationality.

The first feature was that the mind is to be regarded as having two or more semi-autonomous structures. This feature we found to be necessary to account for mental causes that are not reasons for the mental states they cause. Only by partitioning the mind does it seem possible to explain how a thought or impulse can cause another to which it bears no rational relation.

The second feature assigned a particular kind of structure to one or more subdivisions of the mind: a structure similar to that needed to explain ordinary actions. This calls for a constellation of beliefs, purposes, and affects of the sort that, through the application of the Plato Principle, allow us to characterize certain events as having a goal or intention. The analogy does not have to be carried so far as to demand that we speak of parts of the mind as independent agents. What is essential is that certain thoughts and feelings of the person be conceived as interacting to produce consequences on the principles of intentional actions, these consequences then serving as causes, but not reasons, for further mental events. The breakdown of reason relations defines the boundary of a subdivision. Though I talk here, with Freud, of parts and agencies, there does not seem to be anything that demands a metaphor. The parts are defined in terms of function; ultimately, in terms of the concepts of reason and of cause. The idea of a quasi-autonomous division is not one that demands a little agent in the division; again, the operative concepts are those of cause and reason.

The third feature on which we remarked was that certain mental events take on the character of mere causes relative to some other mental events in the same mind. This feature also we found to be required by any account of irrationality. It is a feature that can be accommodated, I argued, but in order to accommodate it we must allow a degree of autonomy to parts of the mind.

The three elements of psychoanalytic theory on which I have concentrated, the partitioning of the mind, the existence of a considerable structure in each quasi-autonomous part, and non-logical causal relations between the parts; these elements combine to provide the basis for a coherent way of describing and explaining important kinds of irrationality. They also account for, and justify, Freud's mixture of standard reason explanations with causal interactions more like those of the natural sciences, interactions in which reason does not play its usual normative and rationalizing role.

Finally, I must mention the claim that many mental phenomena which normally are accessible to consciousness are sometimes neither conscious nor easily accessible to consciousness. The reason I have said nothing about this claim is that I think the relevant objections to unconscious mental states and events are answered by showing that the theory is acceptable without them. It is striking, for example, that nothing in the description of akrasia requires that any thought or motive be unconscious—indeed, I criticized Aristotle for introducing something like an unconscious piece of knowledge when this was not necessary. The standard case of akrasia is one in which the agent knows what he is doing, and why, and knows that it is not for the best, and knows why. He acknowledges his own irrationality. If all this is possible, then the description cannot be made untenable by supposing that sometimes some of the thoughts or desires involved are unconscious.

If to an otherwise unobjectionable theory we add the assumption of unconscious elements, the theory can only be made more acceptable, that is, capable of explaining more. For suppose we are led to realize by a genius like Freud that if we posit certain mental states and events we can explain much behaviour that otherwise goes unexplained; but we also discover that the associated verbal behaviour does not fit the normal pattern. The agent denies he has the attitudes and feelings we would attribute to him. We can reconcile observation and theory by stipulating the existence of unconscious events and states that, aside from awareness, are like conscious beliefs, desires, and emotions. There are, to be sure, further puzzles lurking here. But these seem to be puzzles that result from other problems; unconscious mental events do not add to the other problems but are natural companions of them.

I have urged that a certain scheme of analysis applies to important cases of irrationality. Possibly some version of this scheme will be found in every case of 'internal' inconsistency or irrationality. But does the scheme give a sufficient condition for irrationality? It would seem not. For simple cases of association do not count as irrational. If I manage to remember a name by humming a certain tune, there is a mental cause of something for which it is not a reason; and similarly for a host of further cases. But far more interesting, and more important, is a form of self-criticism and reform that we tend to hold in high esteem, and that has even been thought to be the very essence of rationality and the source of freedom. Yet it is clearly a case of mental causality that transcends reason (in the somewhat technical sense in which I have been using the concept).

What I have in mind is a special kind of second-order desire or value, and the actions it can touch off. This happens when a person forms a positive or negative judgement of some of his own desires, and he acts to change these desires. From the point of view of the changed desire, there is no reason for the change—the reason comes from an independent source, and is based on further, and partly contrary, considerations. The agent has reasons for changing his own habits and character, but those reasons come from a domain of values necessarily extrinsic to the contents of the views or values to undergo change. The cause of the change, if it comes, can therefore not be a reason for what it causes. A theory that could not explain irrationality would be one that also could not explain our salutary efforts, and occasional successes, at self-criticism and self-improvement.

TRUTH, MEANING, AND INTERPRETATION

8

Truth and Meaning

It is conceded by most philosophers of language, and recently by some linguists, that a satisfactory theory of meaning must give an account of how the meanings of sentences depend upon the meanings of words. Unless such an account could be supplied for a particular language, it is argued, there would be no explaining the fact that we can learn the language: no explaining the fact that, on mastering a finite vocabulary and a finitely stated set of rules, we are prepared to produce and to understand any of a potential infinitude of sentences. I do not dispute these vague claims, in which I sense more than a kernel of truth.[1] Instead I want to ask what it is for a theory to give an account of the kind adumbrated.

One proposal is to begin by assigning some entity as meaning to each word (or other significant syntactical feature) of the sentence; thus we might assign Theaetetus to 'Theaetetus' and the property of flying to 'flies' in the sentence 'Theaetetus flies'. The problem then arises how the meaning of the sentence is generated from these meanings. Viewing concatenation as a significant piece of syntax, we may assign to it the relation of participating in or instantiating; however, it is obvious that we have here the start of an infinite regress. Frege sought to avoid the regress by saying that the entities corresponding to predicates (for example) are 'unsaturated' or 'incomplete' in contrast to the entities that correspond to names, but this doctrine seems to label a difficulty rather than solve it.

The point will emerge if we think for a moment of complex singular terms, to which Frege's theory applies along with sentences. Consider the expression 'the father of Annette'; how does the meaning of the whole depend on the meaning of the parts? The answer would seem to be that the meaning of 'the father of' is such that when this expression is prefixed to a singular term the result refers to the father of the person to whom the singular term refers. What part is played, in this account, by the unsaturated or incomplete entity for which 'the father of' stands? All we can think to say is that this entity 'yields' or 'gives' the father of x as value when the argument is x, or perhaps that this entity maps people on to their fathers. It may not be clear whether the entity for which 'the father of' is said to stand performs any genuine explanatory function as long as we stick to individual expressions; so think instead of the infinite class of expressions formed by writing

---

[1] See Donald Davidson (1965), 'Theories of Meaning and Learnable Languages'.

'the father of' zero or more times in front of 'Annette'. It is easy to supply a theory that tells, for an arbitrary one of these singular terms, what it refers to: if the term is 'Annette' it refers to Annette, while if the term is complex, consisting of 'the father of' prefixed to a singular term *t*, then it refers to the father of the person to whom *t* refers. It is obvious that no entity corresponding to 'the father of' is, or needs to be, mentioned in stating this theory.

It would be inappropriate to complain that this little theory *uses* the words 'the father of' in giving the reference of expressions containing those words. For the task was to give the meaning of all expressions in a certain infinite set on the basis of the meaning of the parts; it was not in the bargain also to give the meanings of the atomic parts. On the other hand, it is now evident that a satisfactory theory of the meanings of complex expressions may not require entities as meanings of all the parts. It behoves us then to rephrase our demand on a satisfactory theory of meaning so as not to suggest that individual words must have meanings at all, in any sense that transcends the fact that they have a systematic effect on the meanings of the sentences in which they occur. Actually, for the case at hand we can do better still in stating the criterion of success: what we wanted, and what we got, is a theory that entails every sentence of the form '*t* refers to *x*' where '*t*' is replaced by a structural description[2] of a singular term, and '*x*' is replaced by that term itself. Further, our theory accomplishes this without appeal to any semantical concepts beyond the basic 'refers to'. Finally, the theory clearly suggests an effective procedure for determining, for any singular term in its universe, what that term refers to.

A theory with such evident merits deserves wider application. The device proposed by Frege to this end has a brilliant simplicity: count predicates as a special case of functional expressions, and sentences as a special case of complex singular terms. Now, however, a difficulty looms if we want to continue in our present (implicit) course of identifying the meaning of a singular term with its reference. The difficulty follows upon making two reasonable assumptions: that logically equivalent singular terms have the same reference, and that a singular term does not change its reference if a contained singular term is replaced by another with the same reference. But now suppose that '*R*' and '*S*' abbreviate any two sentences alike in truth value. Then the following four sentences have the same reference:

(1) R

(2) $\hat{x}(x = x . R) = \hat{x}(x = x)$

(3) $\hat{x}(x = x . S) = \hat{x}(x = x)$

(4) S

---

[2] A 'structural description' of an expression describes the expression as a concatenation of elements drawn from a fixed finite list (for example of words or letters).

For (1) and (2) are logically equivalent, as are (3) and (4), while (3) differs from (2) only in containing the singular term '$\hat{x}(x = x . S)$' where (2) contains '$\hat{x}(x = x . R)$' and these refer to the same thing if S and R are alike in truth value. Hence any two sentences have the same reference if they have the same truth value.[3] And if the meaning of a sentence is what it refers to, all sentences alike in truth value must be synonymous—an intolerable result.

Apparently we must abandon the present approach as leading to a theory of meaning. This is the natural point at which to turn for help to the distinction between meaning and reference. The trouble, we are told, is that questions of reference are, in general, settled by extra-linguistic facts, questions of meaning not, and the facts can conflate the references of expressions that are not synonymous. If we want a theory that gives the meaning (as distinct from reference) of each sentence, we must start with the meaning (as distinct from reference) of the parts.

Up to here we have been following in Frege's footsteps; thanks to him, the path is well known and even well worn. But now, I would like to suggest, we have reached an impasse: the switch from reference to meaning leads to no useful account of how the meanings of sentences depend upon the meanings of the words (or other structural features) that compose them. Ask, for example, for the meaning of 'Theaetetus flies'. A Fregean answer might go something like this: given the meaning of 'Theaetetus' as argument, the meaning of 'flies' yields the meaning of 'Theaetetus flies' as value. The vacuity of this answer is obvious. We wanted to know what the meaning of 'Theaetetus flies' is; it is no progress to be told that it is the meaning of 'Theaetetus flies'. This much we knew before any theory was in sight. In the bogus account just given, talk of the structure of the sentence and of the meanings of words was idle, for it played no role in producing the given description of the meaning of the sentence.

The contrast here between a real and pretended account will be plainer still if we ask for a theory, analogous to the miniature theory of reference of singular terms just sketched, but different in dealing with meanings in place of references. What analogy demands is a theory that has as consequences all sentences of the form 's means m' where 's' is replaced by a structural description of a sentence and 'm' is replaced by a singular term that refers to the meaning of that sentence; a theory, moreover, that provides an effective method for arriving at the meaning of an arbitrary sentence structurally described. Clearly some more articulate way of referring to meanings than any we have seen is essential if these criteria are to be met.[4] Meanings as entities, or the related concept of synonymy, allow us to

---

[3] The argument derives from Frege. See A. Church, *Introduction to Mathematical Logic*, 24–5. It is perhaps worth mentioning that the argument does not depend on any particular identification of the entities to which sentences are supposed to refer.

[4] It may be thought that Church, in 'A Formulation of the Logic of Sense and Denotation', has given a theory of meaning that makes essential use of meanings as entities. But this is not the case: Church's logics of sense and denotation are interpreted as being about meanings, but they do not

formulate the following rule relating sentences and their parts: sentences are synonymous whose corresponding parts are synonymous ('corresponding' here needs spelling out of course). And meanings as entities may, in theories such as Frege's, do duty, on occasion, as references, thus losing their status as entities distinct from references. Paradoxically, the one thing meanings do not seem to do is oil the wheels of a theory of meaning—at least as long as we require of such a theory that it non-trivially give the meaning of every sentence in the language. My objection to meanings in the theory of meaning is not that they are abstract or that their identity conditions are obscure, but that they have no demonstrated use.

This is the place to scotch another hopeful thought. Suppose we have a satisfactory theory of syntax for our language, consisting of an effective method of telling, for an arbitrary expression, whether or not it is independently meaningful (i.e., a sentence), and assume as usual that this involves viewing each sentence as composed, in allowable ways, out of elements drawn from a fixed finite stock of atomic syntactical elements (roughly, words). The hopeful thought is that syntax, so conceived, will yield semantics when a dictionary giving the meaning of each syntactic atom is added. Hopes will be dashed, however, if semantics is to comprise a theory of meaning in our sense, for knowledge of the structural characteristics that make for meaningfulness in a sentence, plus knowledge of the meanings of the ultimate parts, does not add up to knowledge of what a sentence means. The point is easily illustrated by belief sentences. Their syntax is relatively unproblematic. Yet, adding a dictionary does not touch the standard semantic problem, which is that we cannot account for even as much as the truth conditions of such sentences on the basis of what we know of the meanings of the words in them. The situation is not radically altered by refining the dictionary to indicate which meaning or meanings an ambiguous expression bears in each of its possible contexts; the problem of belief sentences persists after ambiguities are resolved.

The fact that recursive syntax with dictionary added is not necessarily recursive semantics has been obscured in some recent writing on linguistics by the intrusion of semantic criteria into the discussion of purportedly syntactic theories. The matter would boil down to a harmless difference over terminology if the semantic criteria were clear; but they are not. While there is agreement that it is the central task of semantics to give the semantic interpretation (the meaning) of every sentence in the language, nowhere in the linguistic literature will one find, so far as I know, a straightforward account of how a theory performs this task, or how to tell when it has been accomplished. The contrast with syntax is striking. The main job of a modest syntax is to characterize *meaningfulness* (or sentencehood). We may have as much confidence in the correctness of such a

mention expressions and so cannot of course be theories of meaning in the sense now under discussion.

characterization as we have in the representativeness of our sample and our ability to say when particular expressions are meaningful (sentences). What clear and analogous task and test exist for semantics?[5]

We decided a while back not to assume that parts of sentences have meanings except in the ontologically neutral sense of making a systematic contribution to the meaning of the sentences in which they occur. Since postulating meanings has netted nothing, let us return to that insight. One direction in which it points is a certain holistic view of meaning. If sentences depend for their meaning on their structure, and we understand the meaning of each item in the structure only as an abstraction from the totality of sentences in which it features, then we can give the meaning of any sentence (or word) only by giving the meaning of every sentence (and word) in the language. Frege said that only in the context of a sentence does a word have meaning; in the same vein he might have added that only in the context of the language does a sentence (and therefore a word) have meaning.

This degree of holism was already implicit in the suggestion that an adequate theory of meaning must entail *all* sentences of the form '*s* means *m*'. But now, having found no more help in meanings of sentences than in meanings of words, let us ask whether we can get rid of the troublesome singular terms supposed to replace '*m*' and to refer to meanings. In a way, nothing could be easier: just write '*s* means that *p*', and imagine '*p*' replaced by a sentence. Sentences, as we have seen, cannot name meanings, and sentences with 'that' prefixed are not names at all, unless we decide so. It looks as though we are in trouble on another count, however, for it is reasonable to expect that in wrestling with the logic of the apparently non-extensional 'means that' we will encounter problems as hard as, or perhaps identical with, the problems our theory is out to solve.

The only way I know to deal with this difficulty is simple, and radical. Anxiety that we are enmeshed in the intensional springs from using the words 'means that' as filling between description of sentence and sentence, but it may be that the success of our venture depends not on the filling but on what it fills. The theory will have done its work if it provides, for every sentence *s* in the language under study, a matching sentence (to replace '*p*') that, in some way yet to be made clear, 'gives the meaning' of *s*. One obvious candidate for matching sentence is just *s* itself, if the object language is contained in the metalanguage; otherwise a translation of *s* in the metalanguage. As a final bold step, let us try treating the position occupied by '*p*' extensionally: to implement this, sweep away the obscure 'means that', provide the sentence that replaces '*p*' with a

---

[5] For a recent statement of the role of semantics in linguistics, see Noam Chomsky, 'Topics in the Theory of Generative Grammar'. In this article, Chomsky (1) emphasizes the central importance of semantics in linguistic theory, (2) argues for the superiority of transformational grammars over phrase-structure grammars largely on the grounds that, although phrase-structure grammars may be adequate to define sentencehood for (at least) some natural languages, they are inadequate as a foundation for semantics, and (3) comments repeatedly on the 'rather primitive state' of the concepts of semantics and remarks that the notion of semantic interpretation 'still resists any deep analysis'.

proper sentential connective, and supply the description that replaces 's' with its own predicate. The plausible result is

(T) s is T if and only if p.

What we require of a theory of meaning for a language L is that without appeal to any (further) semantical notions it place enough restrictions on the predicate 'is T' to entail all sentences got from schema T when 's' is replaced by a structural description of a sentence of L and 'p' by that sentence.

Any two predicates satisfying this condition have the same extension,[6] so if the metalanguage is rich enough, nothing stands in the way of putting what I am calling a theory of meaning into the form of an explicit definition of a predicate 'is T'. But whether explicitly defined or recursively characterized, it is clear that the sentences to which the predicate 'is T' applies will be just the true sentences of L, for the condition we have placed on satisfactory theories of meaning is in essence Tarski's Convention T that tests the adequacy of a formal semantical definition of truth.[7]

The path to this point has been tortuous, but the conclusion may be stated simply: a theory of meaning for a language L shows 'how the meanings of sentences depend upon the meanings of words' if it contains a (recursive) definition of truth-in-L. And, so far at least, we have no other idea how to turn the trick. It is worth emphasizing that the concept of truth played no ostensible role in stating our original problem. That problem, upon refinement, led to the view that an adequate theory of meaning must characterize a predicate meeting certain conditions. It was in the nature of a discovery that such a predicate would apply exactly to the true sentences. I hope that what I am saying may be described in part as defending the philosophical importance of Tarski's semantical concept of truth. But my defence is only distantly related, if at all, to the question whether the concept Tarski has shown how to define is the (or a) philosophically interesting conception of truth, or the question whether Tarski has cast any light on the ordinary use of such words as 'true' and 'truth'. It is a misfortune that dust from futile and confused battles over these questions has prevented those with a theoretical interest in language—philosophers, logicians, psychologists, and linguists alike—from seeing in the semantical concept of truth (under whatever name) the sophisticated and powerful foundation of a competent theory of meaning.

There is no need to suppress, of course, the obvious connection between a definition of truth of the kind Tarski has shown how to construct, and the concept of meaning. It is this: the definition works by giving necessary and sufficient conditions for the truth of every sentence, and to give truth conditions is a way of giving the meaning of a sentence. To know the semantic concept of

---

[6] Assuming, of course, that the extension of these predicates is limited to the sentences of L.

[7] A. Tarski, 'The Concept of Truth in Formalized Languages'.

truth for a language is to know what it is for a sentence—any sentence—to be true, and this amounts, in one good sense we can give to the phrase, to understanding the language. This at any rate is my excuse for a feature of the present discussion that is apt to shock old hands; my freewheeling use of the word 'meaning', for what I call a theory of meaning has after all turned out to make no use of meanings, whether of sentences or of words. Indeed, since a Tarski-type truth definition supplies all we have asked so far of a theory of meaning, it is clear that such a theory falls comfortably within what Quine terms the 'theory of reference' as distinguished from what he terms the 'theory of meaning'. So much to the good for what I call a theory of meaning, and so much, perhaps, against my so calling it.[8]

A theory of meaning (in my mildly perverse sense) is an empirical theory, and its ambition is to account for the workings of a natural language. Like any theory, it may be tested by comparing some of its consequences with the facts. In the present case this is easy, for the theory has been characterized as issuing in an infinite flood of sentences each giving the truth conditions of a sentence; we only need to ask, in sample cases, whether what the theory avers to be the truth conditions for a sentence really are. A typical test case might involve deciding whether the sentence 'Snow is white' *is true* if and only if snow is white. Not all cases will be so simple (for reasons to be sketched), but it is evident that this sort of test does not invite counting noses. A sharp conception of what constitutes a theory in this domain furnishes an exciting context for raising deep questions about when a theory of language is correct and how it is to be tried. But the difficulties are theoretical, not practical. In application, the trouble is to get a theory that comes close to working; anyone can tell whether it is right.[9] One can see why this is so. The theory reveals nothing new about the conditions under which an individual sentence is true; it does not make those conditions any clearer than the sentence itself does. The work of the theory is in relating the known truth conditions of each sentence to those aspects ('words') of the sentence that recur in other sentences, and can be assigned identical roles in other sentences. Empirical power in such a theory depends on success in recovering the structure of a very complicated ability—the ability to speak and understand a language. We can tell easily enough when particular pronouncements of the theory comport with our understanding of the language; this is consistent with a feeble insight into the design of the machinery of our linguistic accomplishments.

---

[8] But Quine may be quoted in support of my usage: '. . . in point of *meaning* . . . a word may be said to be determined to whatever extent the truth or falsehood of its contexts is determined.' ('Truth by Convention', 82.) Since a truth definition determines the truth value of every sentence in the object language (relative to a sentence in the metalanguage), it determines the meaning of every word and sentence. This would seem to justify the title Theory of Meaning.

[9] To give a single example: it is clearly a count in favour of a theory that it entails ' "Snow is white" is true if and only if snow is white'. But to contrive a theory that entails this (and works for all related sentences) is not trivial. I do not know a wholly satisfactory theory that succeeds with this very case (the problem of 'mass terms').

The remarks of the last paragraph apply directly only to the special case where it is assumed that the language for which truth is being characterized is part of the language used and understood by the characterizer. Under these circumstances, the framer of a theory will as a matter of course avail himself when he can of the built-in convenience of a metalanguage with a sentence guaranteed equivalent to each sentence in the object language. Still, this fact ought not to con us into thinking a theory any more correct that entails ' "Snow is white" is true if and only if snow is white' than one that entails instead:

(S) 'Snow is white' is true if and only if grass is green,

provided, of course, we are as sure of the truth of (S) as we are of that of its more celebrated predecessor. Yet (S) may not encourage the same confidence that a theory that entails it deserves to be called a theory of meaning.

The threatened failure of nerve may be counteracted as follows. The grotesqueness of (S) is in itself nothing against a theory of which it is a consequence, provided the theory gives the correct results for every sentence (on the basis of its structure, there being no other way). It is not easy to see how (S) could be party to such an enterprise, but if it were—if, that is, (S) followed from a characterization of the predicate 'is true' that led to the invariable pairing of truths with truths and falsehoods with falsehoods—then there would not, I think, be anything essential to the idea of meaning that remained to be captured.[10]

What appears to the right of the biconditional in sentences of the form 's is true if and only if p' when such sentences are consequences of a theory of truth plays its role in determining the meaning of s not by pretending synonymy but by adding one more brush-stroke to the picture which, taken as a whole, tells what there is to know of the meaning of s; this stroke is added by virtue of the fact that the sentence that replaces 'p' is true if and only if s is.

It may help to reflect that (S) is acceptable, if it is, because we are independently sure of the truth of 'Snow is white' and 'Grass is green'; but in cases where we are unsure of the truth of a sentence, we can have confidence in a characterization of the truth predicate only if it pairs that sentence with one we have good reason to believe equivalent. It would be ill advised for someone who had any doubts about the colour of snow or grass to accept a theory that yielded (S), even if his doubts were of equal degree, unless he thought the colour of the one was tied to the colour of the other.[11] Omniscience can obviously afford more

---

[10] Critics have often failed to notice the essential proviso mentioned in this paragraph. The point is that (S) could not belong to any reasonably simple theory that also gave the right truth conditions for 'That is snow' and 'This is white'. (See the discussion of indexical expressions below.) [Footnote added in 1982.]

[11] This paragraph is confused. What it should say is that sentences of the theory are empirical generalizations about speakers, and so must not only be true but also lawlike. (S) presumably is not a law, since it does not support appropriate counter-factuals. It's also important that the evidence for accepting the (time and speaker relativized) truth conditions for 'That is snow' is based on the causal connection between a speaker's assent to the sentence and the demonstrative presentation of snow.

bizzare theories of meaning than ignorance; but then, omniscience has less need of communication.

It must be possible, of course, for the speaker of one language to construct a theory of meaning for the speaker of another, though in this case the empirical test of the correctness of the theory will no longer be trivial. As before, the aim of theory will be an infinite correlation of sentences alike in truth. But this time the theory-builder must not be assumed to have direct insight into likely equivalences between his own tongue and the alien. What he must do is find out, however he can, what sentences the alien holds true in his own tongue (or better, to what degree he holds them true). The linguist then will attempt to construct a characterization of truth-for-the-alien which yields, so far as possible, a mapping of sentences held true (or false) by the alien on to sentences held true (or false) by the linguist. Supposing no perfect fit is found, the residue of sentences held true translated by sentences held false (and vice versa) is the margin for error (foreign or domestic). Charity in interpreting the words and thoughts of others is unavoidable in another direction as well: just as we must maximize agreement, or risk not making sense of what the alien is talking about, so we must maximize the self-consistency we attribute to him, on pain of not understanding *him*. No single principle of optimum charity emerges; the constraints therefore determine no single theory. In a theory of radical translation (as Quine calls it) there is no completely disentangling questions of what the alien means from questions of what he believes. We do not know what someone means unless we know what he believes; we do not know what someone believes unless we know what he means. In radical interpretation we are able to break into this circle, if only incompletely, because we can sometimes tell that a person accedes to a sentence we do not understand.[12]

In the past few pages I have been asking how a theory of meaning that takes the form of a truth definition can be empirically tested, and have blithely ignored the prior question whether there is any serious chance such a theory can be given for a natural language. What are the prospects for a formal semantical theory of a natural language? Very poor, according to Tarski; and I believe most logicians, philosophers of language, and linguists agree.[13] Let me do what I can to dispel the pessimism. What I can in a general and programmatic way, of course, for here the proof of the pudding will certainly be in the proof of the right theorems.

---

[12] This sketch of how a theory of meaning for an alien tongue can be tested obviously owes its inspiration to Quine's account of radical translation in Chapter II of *Word and Object*. In suggesting that an acceptable theory of radical translation take the form of a recursive characterization of truth, I go beyond Quine. Toward the end of this paper, in the discussion of demonstratives, another strong point of agreement will turn up.

[13] So far as I am aware, there has been very little discussion of whether a formal truth definition can be given for a natural language. But in a more general vein, several people have urged that the concepts of formal semantics be applied to natural language. See, for example, the contributions of Yehoshua Bar-Hillel and Evert Beth to *The Philosophy of Rudolph Carnap*, and Bar-Hillel's 'Logical Syntax and Semantics'.

Tarski concludes the first section of his classic essay on the concept of truth in formalized languages with the following remarks, which he italicizes:

... The very possibility of a consistent use of the expression 'true sentence' which is in harmony with the laws of logic and the spirit of everyday language seems to be very questionable, and consequently the same doubt attaches to the possibility of constructing a correct definition of this expression. (165)

Late in the same essay, he returns to the subject:

... the concept of truth (as well as other semantical concepts) when applied to colloquial language in conjunction with the normal laws of logic leads inevitably to confusions and contradictions. Whoever wishes, in spite of all difficulties, to pursue the semantics of colloquial language with the help of exact methods will be driven first to undertake the thankless task of a reform of this language. He will find it necessary to define its structure, to overcome the ambiguity of the terms which occur in it, and finally to split the language into a series of languages of greater and greater extent, each of which stands in the same relation to the next in which a formalized language stands to its metalanguage. It may, however be doubted whether the language of everyday life, after being 'rationalized' in this way, would still preserve its naturalness and whether it would not rather take on the characteristic features of the formalized languages. (267)

Two themes emerge: that the universal character of natural languages leads to contradiction (the semantic paradoxes), and that natural languages are too confused and amorphous to permit the direct application of formal methods. The first point deserves a serious answer, and I wish I had one. As it is, I will say only why I think we are justified in carrying on without having disinfected this particular source of conceptual anxiety. The semantic paradoxes arise when the range of the quantifiers in the object language is too generous in certain ways. But it is not really clear how unfair to Urdu or to Wendish it would be to view the range of their quantifiers as insufficient to yield an explicit definition of 'true-in-Urdu' or 'true-in-Wendish'. Or, to put the matter in another, if not more serious way, there may in the nature of the case always be something we grasp in understanding the language of another (the concept of truth) that we cannot communicate to him. In any case, most of the problems of general philosophical interest arise within a fragment of the relevant natural language that may be conceived as containing very little set theory. Of course these comments do not meet the claim that natural languages are universal. But it seems to me that this claim, now that we know such universality leads to paradox, is suspect.

Tarski's second point is that we would have to reform a natural language out of all recognition before we could apply formal semantical methods. If this is true, it is fatal to my project, for the task of a theory of meaning as I conceive it is not to change, improve, or reform a language, but to describe and understand it. Let us look at the positive side. Tarski has shown the way to giving a theory for interpreted formal languages of various kinds; pick one as much like English as possible. Since this new language has been explained in English and contains much English we not only may, but I think must, view it as part of English for those who understand it. For this fragment of English we have, *ex hypothesi*, a theory of the required sort. Not only that, but in interpreting this adjunct of English in old English we necessarily gave hints connecting old and new. Wherever there are sentences of old English with the same truth conditions as sentences in the adjunct we may extend the theory to cover them. Much of what is called for is to mechanize as far as possible what we now do by art when we put ordinary English into one or another canonical notation. The point is not that canonical notation is better than the rough original idiom, but rather that if we know what idiom the canonical notation is canonical *for*, we have as good a theory for the idiom as for its kept companion.

Philosophers have long been at the hard work of applying theory to ordinary language by the device of matching sentences in the vernacular with sentences for which they have a theory. Frege's massive contribution was to show how 'all', 'some', 'every', 'each', 'none', and associated pronouns, in some of their uses, could be tamed; for the first time, it was possible to dream of a formal semantics for a significant part of a natural language. This dream came true in a sharp way with the work of Tarski. It would be a shame to miss the fact that as a result of these two magnificent achievements, Frege's and Tarski's, we have gained a deep insight into the structure of our mother tongues. Philosophers of a logical bent have tended to start where the theory was and work out towards the complications of natural language. Contemporary linguists, with an aim that cannot easily be seen to be different, start with the ordinary and work toward a general theory. If either party is successful, there must be a meeting. Recent work by Chomsky and others is doing much to bring the complexities of natural languages within the scope of serious theory. To give an example: suppose success in giving the truth conditions for some significant range of sentences in the active voice. Then with a formal procedure for transforming each such sentence into a corresponding sentence in the passive voice, the theory of truth could be extended in an obvious way to this new set of sentences.[14]

One problem touched on in passing by Tarski does not, at least in all its manifestations, have to be solved to get ahead with theory: the existence in natural languages of 'ambiguous terms'. As long as ambiguity does not affect

---

[14] The *rapprochement* I prospectively imagine between transformational grammar and a sound theory of meaning has been much advanced by a recent change in the conception of transformational grammar described by Chomsky in the article referred to above (footnote 5). The structures generated by the phrase-structure part of the grammar, it has been realized for some time, are those suited to semantic interpretation; but this view is inconsistent with the idea, held by Chomsky until recently, that recursive operations are introduced only by the transformation rules. Chomsky now believes the phrase-structure rules are recursive. Since languages to which formal semantic methods directly and naturally apply are ones for which a (recursive) phrase-structure grammar is appropriate, it is clear that Chomsky's present picture of the relation between the structures generated by the phrase-structure part of the grammar, and the sentences of the language, is very much like the picture many logicians and philosophers have had of the relation between the richer formalized languages and ordinary language. (In these remarks I am indebted to Bruce Vermazen.)

grammatical form, and can be translated, ambiguity for ambiguity, into the metalanguage, a truth definition will not tell us any lies. The chief trouble, for systematic semantics, with the phrase 'believes that' in English lies not in its vagueness, ambiguity, or unsuitability for incorporation in a serious science: let our metalanguage be English, and all *these* problems will be carried without loss or gain into the metalanguage. But the central problem of the logical grammar of 'believes that' will remain to haunt us.

The example is suited to illustrating another, and related, point, for the discussion of belief sentences has been plagued by failure to observe a fundamental distinction between tasks: uncovering the logical grammar or form of sentences (which is in the province of a theory of meaning as I construe it), and the analysis of individual words or expressions (which are treated as primitive by the theory). Thus Carnap, in the first edition of *Meaning and Necessity*, suggested we render 'John believes that the earth is round' as 'John responds affirmatively to "the earth is round" as an English sentence'. He gave this up when Mates pointed out that John might respond affirmatively to one sentence and not to another no matter how close in meaning.[15] But there is a confusion here from the start. The semantic structure of a belief sentence, according to this idea of Carnap's, is given by a three-place predicate with places reserved for expressions referring to a person, a sentence, and a language. It is a different sort of problem entirely to attempt an analysis of this predicate, perhaps along behaviouristic lines. Not least among the merits of Tarski's conception of a theory of truth is that the purity of method it demands of us follows from the formulation of the problem itself, not from the self-imposed restraint of some adventitious philosophical puritanism.

I think it is hard to exaggerate the advantages to philosophy of language of bearing in mind this distinction between questions of logical form or grammar, and the analysis of individual concepts. Another example may help advertise the point.

If we suppose questions of logical grammar settled, sentences like 'Bardot is good' raise no special problems for a truth definition. The deep differences between descriptive and evaluative (emotive, expressive, etc.) terms do not show here. Even if we hold there is some important sense in which moral or evaluative sentences do not have a truth value (for example, because they cannot be verified), we ought not to boggle at ' "Bardot is good" is true if and only if Bardot is good'; in a theory of truth, this consequence should, follow with the rest, keeping track, as must be done, of the semantic location of such sentences in the language as a whole—of their relation to generalizations, their role in such compound sentences as 'Bardot is good and Bardot is foolish', and so on. What is special to evaluative words is simply not touched: the mystery is transferred from the word 'good' in the object language to its translation in the metalanguage.

---

[15] B. Mates, 'Synonymity'.

But 'good' as it features in 'Bardot is a good actress' is another matter. The problem is not that the translation of this sentence is not in the metalanguage—let us suppose it is. The problem is to frame a truth definition such that ' "Bardot is a good actress" is true if and only if Bardot is a good actress' —and all other sentences like it—are consequences. Obviously 'good actress' does not mean 'good and an actress'. We might think of taking 'is a good actress' as an unanalysed predicate. This would obliterate all connection between 'is a good actress' and 'is a good mother', and it would give us no excuse to think of 'good', in these uses, as a word or semantic element. But worse, it would bar us from framing a truth definition at all, for there is no end to the predicates we would have to treat as logically simple (and hence accommodate in separate clauses in the definition of satisfaction): 'is a good companion to dogs', 'is a good 28-years old conversationalist', and so forth. The problem is not peculiar to the case: it is the problem of attributive adjectives generally.

It is consistent with the attitude taken here to deem it usually a strategic error to undertake philosophical analysis of words or expressions which is not preceded by or at any rate accompanied by the attempt to get the logical grammar straight. For how can we have any confidence in our analyses of words like 'right', 'ought', 'can', and 'obliged', or the phrases we use to talk of actions, events, and causes, when we do not know what (logical, semantical) parts of speech we have to deal with? I would say much the same about studies of the 'logic' of these and other words, and the sentences containing them. Whether the effort and ingenuity that have gone into the study of deontic logics, modal logics, imperative and erotetic logics have been largely futile or not cannot be known until we have acceptable semantic analyses of the sentences such systems purport to treat. Philosophers and logicians sometimes talk or work as if they were free to choose between, say, the truth-functional conditional and others, or free to introduce non-truth-functional sentential operators like 'Let it be the case that' or 'It ought to be the case that'. But in fact the decision is crucial. When we depart from idioms we can accommodate in a truth definition, we lapse into (or create) language for which we have no coherent semantical account—that is, no account at all of how such talk can be integrated into the language as a whole.

To return to our main theme: we have recognized that a theory of the kind proposed leaves the whole matter of what individual words mean exactly where it was. Even when the metalanguage is different from the object language, the theory exerts no pressure for improvement, clarification, or analysis of individual words, except when, by accident of vocabulary, straightforward translation fails. Just as synonymy, as between expressions, goes generally untreated, so also synonymy of sentences, and analyticity. Even such sentences as 'A vixen is a female fox' bear no special tag unless it is our pleasure to provide it. A truth definition does not distinguish between analytic sentences and others, except for sentences that owe their truth to the presence alone of the constants that give the theory its grip on structure: the theory entails not only that these sentences are true but that they will remain true under all significant rewritings of their non-logical parts. A notion of logical truth thus given limited application, related notions of logical equivalence and entailment will tag along. It is hard to imagine how a theory of meaning could fail to read a logic into its object language to this degree; and to the extent that it does, our intuitions of logical truth, equivalence, and entailment may be called upon in constructing and testing the theory.

I turn now to one more, and very large, fly in the ointment: the fact that the same sentence may at one time or in one mouth be true and at another time or in another mouth be false. Both logicians and those critical of formal methods here seem largely (though by no means universally) agreed that formal semantics and logic are incompetent to deal with the disturbances caused by demonstratives. Logicians have often reacted by downgrading natural language and trying to show how to get along without demonstratives; their critics react by down-grading logic and formal semantics. None of this can make me happy: clearly demonstratives cannot be eliminated from a natural language without loss or radical change, so there is no choice but to accommodate theory to them.

No logical errors result if we simply treat demonstratives as constants;[16] nei-ther do any problems arise for giving a semantic truth definition. ' "I am wise" is true if and only if I am wise', with its bland ignoring of the demonstrative element in 'I' comes off the assembly line along with ' "Socrates is wise" is true if and only if Socrates is wise' with *its* bland indifference to the demonstrative element in 'is wise' (the tense).

What suffers in this treatment of demonstratives is not the definition of a truth predicate, but the plausibility of the claim that what has been defined is truth. For this claim is acceptable only if the speaker and circumstances of utterance of each sentence mentioned in the definition is matched by the speaker and cir-cumstances of utterance of the truth definition itself. It could also be fairly pointed out that part of understanding demonstratives is knowing the rules by which they adjust their reference to circumstance; assimilating demonstratives to constant terms obliterates this feature. These complaints can be met, I think, though only by a fairly far-reaching revision in the theory of truth. I shall barely suggest how this could be done, but bare suggestion is all that is needed: the idea is technically trivial, and in line with work being done on the logic of the tenses.[17]

We could take truth to be a property, not of sentences, but of utterances, or speech acts, or ordered triples of sentences, times, and persons; but it is simplest just to view truth as a relation between a sentence, a person, and a time. Under such treatment, ordinary logic as now read applies as usual, but only to sets of sentences relativized to the same speaker and time; further logical relations between sentences spoken at different times and by different speakers may be

---

[16] See W. V. Quine, *Methods of Logic*, 8.
[17] This claim has turned out to be naïvely optimistic. For some serious work on the subject, see S. Weinstein, 'Truth and Demonstratives'. [Note added in 1982.]

articulated by new axioms. Such is not my concern. The theory of meaning undergoes a systematic but not puzzling change; corresponding to each expression with a demonstrative element there must in the theory be a phrase that relates the truth conditions of sentences in which the expression occurs to changing times and speakers. Thus the theory will entail sentences like the following:

'I am tired' is true as (potentially) spoken by p at t if and only if p is tired at t.
'That book was stolen' is true as (potentially) spoken by p at t if and only if the book demonstrated by p at t is stolen prior to t.[18]

Plainly, this course does not show how to eliminate demonstratives; for example, there is no suggestion that 'the book demonstrated by the speaker' can be substituted ubiquitously for 'that book' *salva veritate*. The fact that demonstratives are amenable to formal treatment ought greatly to improve hopes for a serious semantics of natural language, for it is likely that many outstanding puzzles, such as the analysis of quotations or sentences about propositional attitudes, can be solved if we recognize a concealed demonstrative construction.

Now that we have relativized truth to times and speakers, it is appropriate to glance back at the problem of empirically testing a theory of meaning for an alien tongue. The essence of the method was, it will be remembered, to correlate held-true sentences with held-true sentences by way of a truth definition, and within the bounds of intelligible error. Now the picture must be elaborated to allow for the fact that sentences are true, and held true, only relative to a speaker and a time. Sentences with demonstratives obviously yield a very sensitive test of the correctness of a theory of meaning, and constitute the most direct link between language and the recurrent macroscopic objects of human interest and attention.[19]

In this paper I have assumed that the speakers of a language can effectively determine the meaning or meanings of an arbitrary expression (if it has a meaning), and that it is the central task of a theory of meaning to show how this is possible. I have argued that a characterization of a truth predicate describes the required kind of structure, and provides a clear and testable criterion of an adequate semantics for a natural language. No doubt there are other reasonable demands that may be put on a theory of meaning. But a theory that does no more than define truth for a language comes far closer to constituting a complete theory of meaning than superficial analysis might suggest; so, at least, I have urged.

Since I think there is no alternative, I have taken an optimistic and programmatic view of the possibilities for a formal characterization of a truth

[18] There is more than an intimation of this approach to demonstratives and truth in J. L. Austin, 'Truth'.
[19] These remarks derive from Quine's idea that 'occasion sentences' (those with a demonstrative element) must play a central role in constructing a translation manual.

predicate for a natural language. But it must be allowed that a staggering list of difficulties and conundrums remains. To name a few: we do not know the logical form of counterfactual or subjunctive sentences; nor of sentences about probabilities and about causal relations; we have no good idea what the logical role of adverbs is, nor the role of attributive adjectives; we have no theory for mass terms like 'fire', 'water', and 'snow', nor for sentences about belief, perception, and intention, nor for verbs of action that imply purpose. And finally, there are all the sentences that seem not to have truth values at all: the imperatives, optatives, interrogatives, and a host more. A comprehensive theory of meaning for a natural language must cope successfully with each of these problems.[20]

---

[20] For attempted solutions to some of these problems see Essays 9 and 10 in this book, with special reference to section 1 of Essay 10. See also Essays 6–10 of Davidson, *Essays on Actions and Events* (1980, 2nd edn. 2001), and Essays 6, 8, and 10 in Davidson, *Inquiries into Truth and Interpretation* (1984, 2nd edn. 2001).

9

On Saying That

'I wish I had said that', said Oscar Wilde in applauding one of Whistler's witticisms. Whistler, who took a dim view of Wilde's originality, retorted, 'You will, Oscar; you will'.[1] This tale reminds us that an expression like 'Whistler said that' may on occasion serve as a grammatically complete sentence. Here we have, I suggest, the key to a correct analysis of indirect discourse, an analysis that opens a lead to an analysis of psychological sentences generally (sentences about propositional attitudes, so-called), and even, though this looks beyond anything to be discussed in the present paper, a clue to what distinguishes psychological concepts from others.

But let us begin with sentences usually deemed more representative of *oratio obliqua*, for example 'Galileo said that the earth moves' or 'Scott said that Venus is an inferior planet'. One trouble with such sentences is that we do not know their logical form. And to admit this is to admit that, whatever else we may know about them, we do not know the first thing. If we accept surface grammar as guide to logical form, we will see 'Galileo said that the earth moves' as containing the sentence 'the earth moves', and this sentence in turn as consisting of the singular term 'the earth', and a predicate, 'moves'. But if 'the earth' is, in this context, a singular term, it can be replaced, so far as the truth or falsity of the containing sentence is concerned, by any other singular term that refers to the same thing. Yet what seem like appropriate replacements can alter the truth of the original sentence.

The notorious apparent invalidity of this move can only be apparent, for the rule on which it is based no more than spells out what is involved in the idea of a (logically) singular term. Only two lines of explanation, then, are open: we are wrong about the logical form, or we are wrong about the reference of the singular term.

What seems anomalous behaviour on the part of what seem singular terms dramatizes the problem of giving an orderly account of indirect discourse, but the problem is more pervasive. For what touches singular terms touches what they touch, and that is everything: quantifiers, variables, predicates, connectives. Singular terms refer, or pretend to refer, to the entities over which the variables of

---

[1] From H. Jackson, *The Eighteen-Nineties*, 73.

quantification range, and it is these entities of which the predicates are or are not true. So it should not surprise us that if we can make trouble for the sentence 'Scott said that Venus is an inferior planet' by substituting 'the Evening Star' for 'Venus', we can equally make trouble by substituting 'is identical with Venus or with Mercury' for the coextensive 'is an inferior planet'. The difficulties with indirect discourse cannot be solved simply by abolishing singular terms.

What should we ask of an adequate account of the logical form of a sentence? Above all, I would say, such an account must lead us to see the semantic character of the sentence—its truth or falsity—as owed to how it is composed, by a finite number of applications of some of a finite number of devices that suffice for the language as a whole, out of elements drawn from a finite stock (the vocabulary) that suffices for the language as a whole. To see a sentence in this light is to see it in the light of a theory for its language, a theory that gives the form of every sentence in that language. A way to provide such a theory is by recursively characterizing a truth predicate, along the lines suggested by Tarski.[2]

Two closely linked considerations support the idea that the structure with which a sentence is endowed by a theory of truth in Tarski's style deserves to be called the logical form of the sentence. By giving such a theory, we demonstrate in a persuasive way that the language, though it consists in an indefinitely large number of sentences, can be comprehended by a creature with finite powers. A theory of truth may be said to supply an effective explanation of the semantic role of each significant expression in any of its appearances. Armed with the theory, we can always answer the question, 'What are these familiar words doing here?' by saying how they contribute to the truth conditions of the sentence. (This is not to assign a 'meaning', much less a reference, to every significant expression.)

The study of the logical form of sentences is often seen in the light of another interest, that of expediting inference. From this point of view, to give the logical form of a sentence is to catalogue the features relevant to its place on the logical scene, the features that determine what sentences it is a logical consequence of, and what sentences it has as logical consequences. A canonical notation graphically encodes the relevant information, making theory of inference simple, and practice mechanical where possible.

Obviously the two approaches to logical form cannot yield wholly independent results, for logical consequence is defined in terms of truth. To say a second sentence is a logical consequence of a first is to say, roughly, that the second is true if the first is no matter how the non-logical constants are interpreted. Since what we count as a logical constant can vary independently of the set of truths, it is clear that the two versions of logical form, though related, need not be identical. The relation, in brief, seems this. Any theory of truth that satisfies Tarski's criteria must take account of all truth-affecting iterative devices in the language. In the familiar languages for which we know how to define truth

---

[2] A. Tarski, 'The Concept of Truth in Formalized Languages'. See Essay 2.

the basic iterative devices are reducible to the sentential connectives, the apparatus of quantification, and the description operator if it is primitive. Where one sentence is a logical consequence of another on the basis of quantificational structure alone, a theory of truth will therefore entail that if the first sentence is true, the second is. There is no point, then, in not including the expressions that determine quantificational structure among the logical constants, for when we have characterized truth, on which any account of logical consequence depends, we have already committed ourselves to all that calling such expressions logical constants could commit us. Adding to this list of logical constants will increase the inventory of logical truths and consequence-relations beyond anything a truth definition demands, and will therefore yield richer versions of logical form. For the purposes of the present paper, however, we can cleave to the most austere interpretations of logical consequence and logical form, those that are forced on us when we give a theory of truth.[3]

We are now in a position to explain our aporia over indirect discourse: what happens is that the relation between truth and consequence just sketched appears to break down. In a sentence like 'Galileo said that the earth moves' the eye and mind perceive familiar structure in the words 'the earth moves'. And structure there must be if we are to have a theory of truth at all, for an infinite number of sentences (all sentences in the indicative, apart from some trouble over tense) yield sense when plugged into the slot in 'Galileo said that _____'. So if we are to give conditions of truth for all the sentences so generated, we cannot do it sentence by sentence, but only by discovering an articulate structure that permits us to treat each sentence as composed of a finite number of devices that make a stated contribution to its truth conditions. As soon as we assign familiar structure, however, we must allow the consequences of that assignment to flow, and these, as we know, are in the case of indirect discourse consequences we refuse to buy. In a way, the matter is even stranger than that. Not only do familiar consequences fail to flow from what looks to be familiar structure, but our common sense of language feels little assurance in any inferences based on the words that follow the 'said that' of indirect discourse (there are exceptions).

So the paradox is this: on the one hand, intuition suggests, and theory demands, that we discover semantically significant structure in the 'content-sentences' of indirect discourse (as I shall call sentences following 'said that'). On the other hand, the failure of consequence-relations invites us to treat contained sentences as semantically inert. Yet logical form and consequence relations cannot be divorced in this way.

One proposal at this point is to view the words that succeed the 'said that' as operating within concealed quotation marks, their sole function being to help refer to a sentence, and their semantic inertness explained by an account of

---

[3] For further defence of a concept of logical form based on a theory of truth, see *Essays on Actions and Events*, 137–46.

quotation. One drawback of this proposal is that no usual account of quotation is acceptable, even by the minimal standards we have set for an account of logical form. For according to most stories, quotations are singular terms without significant semantic structure, and since there must be an infinite number of different quotations, no language that contains them can have a recursively defined truth predicate. This may be taken to show that the received accounts of quotation must be mistaken—I think it does. But then we can hardly pretend that we have solved the problem of indirect discourse by appeal to quotation.[4]

Perhaps it is not hard to invent a theory of quotation that will serve: the following theory is all but explicit in Quine. Simply view quotations as abbreviations for what you get if you follow these instructions: to the right of the first letter that has opening quotation marks on its left write right-hand quotation marks, then the sign for concatenation, and then left-hand quotation marks, in that order; do this after each letter (treating punctuation signs as letters) until you reach the terminating right-hand quotation marks. What you now have is a complex singular term that gives what Tarski calls a structural description of an expression. There is a modest addition to vocabulary: names of letters and of punctuation signs, and the sign for concatenation. There is a corresponding addition to ontology: letters and punctuation signs. And finally, if we carry out the application to sentences in indirect discourse, there will be the logical consequences that the new structure dictates. For two examples, each of the following will be entailed by 'Galileo said that the earth moves':

$(\exists x)$ (Galileo said that 'the ea'$^\cap$x$^\cap$'th moves')

and (with the premise 'r = the 18th letter in the alphabet'):

Galileo said that 'the ea'$^\cap$the 18th letter of the alphabet$^\cap$'th moves'

(I have clung to abbreviations as far as possible.) These inferences are not meant in themselves as criticism of the theory of quotation; they merely illuminate it.

Quine discusses the quotational approach to indirect discourse in *Word and Object*,[5] and abandons it for what seems, to me, a wrong reason. Not that there is not a good reason; but to appreciate *it* is to be next door to a solution, as I shall try to show.

Let us follow Quine through the steps that lead him to reject the quotational approach. The version of the theory he considers is not the one once proposed by Carnap to the effect that 'said that' is a two-place predicate true of ordered pairs of people and sentences.[6] The trouble with this idea is not that it forces us to assimilate indirect discourse to direct, for it does not. The 'said that' of indirect

---

[4] See Essays 1 and 6 in Davidson, *Inquiries into Truth and Interpretation*.

[5] W. V. Quine, *Word and Object*, Ch. 6. Hereafter numerals in parentheses refer to pages of this book.

[6] R. Carnap, *The Logical Syntax of Language*, 248. The same was in effect proposed by P. T. Geach in *Mental Acts*.

discourse, like the 'said' of direct, may relate persons and sentences, but be a different relation; the former, unlike the latter, may be true of a person, and a sentence he never spoke in a language he never knew. The trouble lies rather in the chance that the same sentence may have different meanings in different languages—not too long a chance either if we count ideolects as languages. To give an example, the sounds 'Empedokles liebt' do fairly well as a German or an English sentence, in one case saying that Empedokles loved and in the other telling us what he did from the top of Etna. If we analyse 'Galileo said that the earth moves' as asserting a relation between Galileo and the sentence 'The earth moves', we do not have to assume that Galileo spoke English, but we cannot avoid the assumption that the words of the content-sentence are to be understood as an English sentence.[7]

Calling the relativity to English an assumption may be misleading; perhaps the reference to English is explicit, as follows. A long-winded version of our favourite sentence might be 'Galileo spoke a sentence that meant in his language what "The earth moves" means in English'. Since in this version it needs all the words except 'Galileo' and 'The earth moves' to do the work of 'said that', we must count the reference to English as explicit in the 'said that'. To see how odd this is, however, it is only necessary to reflect that the English words 'said that', with their built-in reference to English, would no longer translate (by even the roughest extensional standards) the French 'dit que'.

We can shift the difficulty over translation away from the 'said that' or 'dit que' by taking these expressions as three-place predicates relating a speaker, a sentence, and a language, the reference to a language to be supplied either by our (in practice nearly infallible) knowledge of the language to which the quoted material is to be taken as belonging, or by a demonstrative reference to the language of the entire sentence. Each of these suggestions has its own appeal, but neither leads to an analysis that will pass the translation test. To take the demonstrative proposal, translation into French will carry 'said that' into 'dit que', the demonstrative reference will automatically, and hence perhaps still within the bounds of strict translation, shift from English to French. But when we translate the final singular term, which names an English sentence, we produce a palpably false result.

These exercises help bring out important features of the quotational approach. But now it is time to remark that there would be an anomaly in a position, like the one under consideration, that abjured reference to propositions in favour of reference to languages. For languages (as Quine remarks in a similar context in *Word and Object*) are at least as badly individuated, and for much the same reasons, as propositions. Indeed, an obvious proposal linking them is this: languages are identical when identical sentences express identical propositions. We see, then, that quotational theories of indirect discourse, those we have discussed

---

[7] The point is due to A. Church, 'On Carnap's Analysis of Statements of Assertion and Belief'.

anyway, cannot claim an advantage over theories that frankly introduce intensional entities from the start; so let us briefly consider theories of the latter sort.

It might be thought, and perhaps often is, that if we are willing to welcome
intensional entities without stint—properties, propositions, individual concepts,
and whatever else—then no further difficulties stand in the way of giving an
account of the logical form of sentences in *oratio obliqua*. This is not so. Neither
the languages Frege suggests as models for natural languages nor the languages
described by Church are amenable to theory in the sense of a truth definition
meeting Tarski's standards.[8] What stands in the way in Frege's case is that every
referring expression has an infinite number of entities it may refer to, depending
on the context, and there is no rule that gives the reference in more complex
contexts on the basis of the reference in simpler ones. In Church's languages,
there is an infinite number of primitive expressions; this directly blocks the
possibility of recursively characterizing a truth predicate satisfying Tarski's
requirements.

Things might be patched up by following a leading idea of Carnap's *Meaning
and Necessity* and limiting the semantic levels to two: extensions and (first-level)
intensions.[9] An attractive strategy might then be to turn Frege, thus simplified,
upside down by letting each singular term refer to its sense or intension, and
providing a reality function (similar to Church's delta function) to map intensions on to extensions. Under such treatment our sample sentence would emerge
like this: 'The reality of Galileo said that the earth moves.' Here we must suppose
that 'the earth' names an individual concept which the function referred to by
'moves' maps on to the proposition that the earth moves; the function referred to
by 'said that' in turn maps Galileo and the proposition that the earth moves on to
a truth value. Finally, the name 'Galileo' refers to an individual concept which is
mapped, by the function referred to by 'the reality of' on to Galileo. With
ingenuity, this theory can perhaps be made to accommodate quantifiers that bind
variables both inside and outside contexts created by verbs like 'said' and
'believes'. There is no special problem about defining truth for such a language:
everything is on the up and up, purely extensional save in ontology. This seems to
be a theory that might do all we have asked. Apart from nominalistic qualms,
why not accept it?

My reasons against this course are essentially Quine's. Finding right words of
my own to communicate another's saying is a problem in translation (216–17).
The words I use in the particular case may be viewed as products of my total
theory (however vague and subject to correction) of what the originating speaker
means by anything he says: such a theory is indistinguishable from a characterization of a truth predicate, with his language as object language and mine as

[8] G. Frege, 'On Sense and Reference'; A. Church, 'A Formulation of the Logic of Sense and
Denotation'.
[9] The idea of an essentially Fregean approach limited to two semantic levels has been suggested
by M. Dummett in *Frege: Philosophy of Language*, Ch. 9.

metalanguage. The crucial point is that there will be equally acceptable alternative theories which differ in assigning clearly non-synonymous sentences of mine as translations of his same utterance. This is Quine's thesis of the indeterminacy of translation (218–21).[10] An example will help bring out the fact that the thesis applies not only to translation between speakers of conspicuously different languages, but also to cases nearer home.

Let someone say (and now discourse is direct), 'There's a hippopotamus in the refrigerator'; am I necessarily right in reporting him as having said that there is a hippopotamus in the refrigerator? Perhaps; but under questioning he goes on, 'It's roundish, has a wrinkled skin, does not mind being touched. It has a pleasant taste, at least the juice, and it costs a dime. I squeeze two or three for breakfast.' After some finite amount of such talk we slip over the line where it is plausible or even possible to say correctly that he said there was a hippopotamus in the refrigerator, for it becomes clear he means something else by at least some of his words than I do. The simplest hypothesis so far is that my word 'hippopotamus' no longer translates his word 'hippopotamus'; my word 'orange' might do better. But in any case, long before we reach the point where homophonic translation must be abandoned, charity invites departures. Hesitation over whether to translate a saying of another by one or another of various non-synonymous sentences of mine does not necessarily reflect a lack of information: it is just that beyond a point there is no deciding, even in principle, between the view that the Other has used words as we do but has more or less weird beliefs, and the view that we have translated him wrong. Torn between the need to make sense of a speaker's words and the need to make sense of the pattern of his beliefs, the best we can do is choose a theory of translation that maximizes agreement. Surely there is no future in supposing that in earnestly uttering the words 'There's a hippopotamus in the refrigerator' the Other has disagreed with us about what can be in the refrigerator if we also must then find ourselves disagreeing with him about the size, shape, colour, manufacturer, horsepower, and wheelbase of hippopotami.

None of this shows there is no such thing as correctly reporting, through indirect discourse, what another has said. All that the indeterminacy shows is that if there is one way of getting it right there are other ways that differ substantially in that non-synonymous sentences are used after 'said that'. And this is enough to justify our feeling that there is something bogus about the sharpness questions of meaning must in principle have if meanings are entities.

The lesson was implicit in a discussion started some years ago by Benson Mates. Mates claimed that the sentence 'Nobody doubts that whoever believes that the seventh consulate of Marius lasted less than a fortnight believes that the seventh consulate of Marius lasted less than a fortnight' is true and yet might well become false if the last word were replaced by the (supposed synonymous) words

---

[10] My assimilation of a translation manual to a theory of truth is not in Quine. For more on this and related matters, see Essay 8 in this volume and Essays 11 and 16 in Davidson, *Inquiries into Truth and Interpretation*.

'period of fourteen days', and that this could happen no matter what standards of synonymy we adopt short of the question-begging 'substitutable everywhere *salva veritate*'.[11] Church and Sellars responded by saying the difficulty could be resolved by firmly distinguishing between substitutions based on the speaker's use of language and substitutions coloured by the use attributed to others.[12] But this is a solution only if we think there is some way of telling, in what another says, what is owed to the meanings he gives his words and what to his beliefs about the world. According to Quine, this is a distinction that cannot be drawn.

The detour has been lengthy; I return now to Quine's discussion of the quotational approach in *Word and Object*. As reported above, Quine rejects relativization to a language on the grounds that the principle of the individuation of languages is obscure, and the issue when languages are identical irrelevant to indirect discourse (214). He now suggests that instead of interpreting the content-sentence of indirect discourse as occurring in a language, we interpret it as voiced by a speaker at a time. The speaker and time relative to which the content-sentence needs understanding is, of course, the speaker of that sentence, who is thereby indirectly attributing a saying to another. So now 'Galileo said that the earth moves' comes to mean something like 'Galileo spoke a sentence that in his mouth meant what "The earth moves" now means in mine'. Quine makes no objection to this proposal because he thinks he has something simpler and at least as good in reserve. But in my opinion the present proposal deserves more serious consideration, for I think it is nearly right, while Quine's preferred alternatives are seriously defective.

The first of these alternatives is Scheffler's inscriptional theory.[13] Scheffler suggests that sentences in indirect discourse relate a speaker and an utterance: the role of the content-sentence is to help convey what sort of utterance it was. What we get this way is, 'Galileo spoke a that-the-earth-moves utterance'. The predicate 'x is-a-that-the-earth-moves-utterance' has, so far as theory of truth and of inference are concerned, the form of an unstructured one-place predicate. Quine does not put the matter quite this way, and he may resist my appropriation of the terms 'logical form' and 'structure' for purposes that exclude application to Scheffler's predicate. Quine calls the predicate 'compound' and describes it as composed of an operator and a sentence (214, 215). These are matters of terminology; the substance, about which there may be no disagreement, is that on Scheffler's theory sentences in *oratio obliqua* have no logical relations that depend on structure in the predicate, and a truth predicate that applies to all such sentences cannot be characterized in Tarski's style. The reason is plain: there is an infinite number of predicates with the syntax 'x is-a-_____-utterance' each of which is, in the eyes of semantic theory, unrelated to the rest.

[11] B. Mates, 'Synonymity'. The example is Church's.
[12] A. Church, 'Intensional Isomorphism and Identity of Belief'; W. Sellars, 'Putnam on Synonymity and Belief'.
[13] I. Scheffler, 'An Inscriptional Approach to Indirect Quotation'.

Quine has seized one horn of the dilemma. Since attributing semantic structure to content-sentences in indirect discourse apparently forces us to endorse logical relations we do not want, Quine gives up the structure. The result is that another desideratum of theory is neglected, that truth be defined.

Consistent with his policy of renouncing structure that supports no inferences worth their keep, Quine contemplates one further step; he says, '. . . a final alternative that I find as appealing as any is simply to dispense with the objects of the propositional attitudes' (216). Where Scheffler still saw 'said that' as a two-place predicate relating speakers and utterances, though welding content-sentences into one-piece one-place predicates true of utterances, Quine now envisions content-sentence and 'said that' welded directly to form the one-place predicate '*x* said-that-the-earth-moves', true of persons. Of course some inferences inherent in Scheffler's scheme now fall away: we can no longer infer 'Galileo said something' from our sample sentence, nor can we infer from it and 'Someone denied that the earth moves' the sentence 'Someone denied what Galileo said'. Yet as Quine reminds us, inferences like these may fail on Scheffler's analysis too when the analysis is extended along the obvious line to belief and other propositional attitudes, since needed utterances may fail to materialize (215). The advantages of Scheffler's theory over Quine's 'final alternative' are therefore few and uncertain; this is why Quine concludes that the view that invites the fewest inferences is 'as appealing as any'.

This way of eliminating unwanted inferences unfortunately abolishes most of the structure needed by the theory of truth. So it is worth returning for another look at the earlier proposal to analyse indirect discourse in terms of a predicate relating an originating speaker, a sentence, and the present speaker of the sentence in indirect discourse. For that proposal did not cut off any of the simple entailments we have been discussing, and it alone of recent suggestions promised, when coupled with a workable theory of quotation, to yield to standard semantic methods. But there is a subtle flaw.

We tried to bring out the flavour of the analysis to which we have returned by rewording our favourite sentence as 'Galileo uttered a sentence that meant in his mouth what "The earth moves" means now in mine'. We should not think ill of this verbose version of 'Galileo said that the earth moves' because of apparent reference to a meaning ('what "The earth moves" means'); this expression is not treated as a singular term in the theory. We are indeed asked to make sense of a judgement of synonymy between utterances, but not as the foundation of a theory of language, merely as an unanalysed part of the content of the familiar idiom of indirect discourse. The idea that underlies our awkward paraphrase is that of *samesaying*: when I say that Galileo said that the earth moves, I represent Galileo and myself as samesayers.[14]

---

[14] Strictly speaking, the verb 'said' is here analysed as a three-place predicate which holds of a speaker (Galileo), an utterance of the speaker ('Eppur si muove'), and an utterance of the attributer ('The earth moves'). This predicate is from a semantic point of view a primitive. The, fact that an

And now the flaw is this. If I merely *say* we are samesayers, Galileo and I, I have yet to *make* us so; and how am I to do this? Obviously, by saying what he said; not by using his words (necessarily), but by using words the same in import here and now as his then and there. Yet this is just what, on the theory, I cannot do. For the theory brings the content-sentence into the act sealed in quotation marks, and on any standard theory of quotation, this means the content-sentence is mentioned and not used. In uttering the words 'The earth moves' I do not, according to this account, say anything remotely like what Galileo is claimed to have said; I do not, in fact, say anything. My words in the frame provided by 'Galileo said that_____' merely help refer to a sentence. There will be no missing the point if we expand quotation in the style we recently considered. Any intimation that Galileo and I are samesayers vanishes in this version:

Galileo said that 'T'$\cap$'h'$\cap$'e'$\cap$' '$\cap$'e'$\cap$'a'$\cap$'r'$\cap$'t'$\cap$'h'$\cap$' '$\cap$'m' $\cap$'o'$\cap$'v'$\cap$'e'$\cap$'s'

We seem to have been taken in by a notational accident, a way of referring to expressions that when abbreviated produces framed pictures of the very words referred to. The difficulty is odd; let's see if we can circumvent it. Imagine an altered case. Galileo utters his words 'Eppur si muove', I utter my words, 'The earth moves'. There is no problem yet in recognizing that we are samesayers; an utterance of mine matches an utterance of his in purport. I am not now using my words to help refer to a sentence; I speak for myself, and my words refer in their usual way to the earth and to its movement. If Galileo's utterance 'Eppur si muove' made us samesayers, then some utterance or other of Galileo's made us samesayers. The form '$(\exists x)$ (Galileo's utterance x and my utterance y makes us samesayers)' is thus a way of attributing any saying I please to Galileo provided I find a way of replacing 'y' by a word or phrase that refers to an appropriate utterance of mine. And surely there is a way I can do this: I need only produce the required utterance and replace 'y' by a reference to it. Here goes:

The earth moves.

$(\exists x)$ (Galileo's utterance x and my last utterance makes us samesayers).

Definitional abbreviation is all that is needed to bring this little skit down to:

The earth moves.
Galileo said that.

Here the 'that' is a demonstrative singular term referring to an utterance (not a sentence).

informal paraphrase of the predicate appeals to a relation of sameness of content as between utterances introduces no intentional entities or semantics. Some have regarded this as a form of cheating, but the policy is deliberate and principled. For a discussion of the distinction between questions of logical form (which is the present concern) and the analysis of individual predicates, see Essay 8. It is also worth observing that radical interpretation, if it succeeds, yields an adequate concept of synonymy as between utterances. [Footnote added in 1982.]

This form has a small drawback in that it leaves the hearer up in the air about the purpose served by saying 'The earth moves' until the act has been performed. As if, say, I were first to tell a story and then add, 'That's how it was once upon a time'. There's some fun to be had this way, and in any case no amount of telling what the illocutionary force of our utterances is is going to insure that they have that force. But in the present case nothing stands in the way of reversing the order of things, thus:

Galileo said that.
The earth moves.

It is now safe to allow a tiny orthographic change, a change without semantic significance, but suggesting to the eye the relation of introducer and introduced: we may suppress the stop after 'that' and the consequent capitalization:

Galileo said that the earth moves.

Perhaps it should come as no surprise to learn that the form of psychological sentences in English apparently evolved in much the way these ruminations suggest. According to the *Oxford English Dictionary*,

The use of *that* is generally held to have arisen out of the demonstrative pronoun pointing to the clause which it introduces. Cf. (1) He once lived here: we all know *that*; (2) *That* (now *this*) we all know: he once lived here; (3) We all know *that* (or *this*): he once lived here; (4) We all know *that* he once lived here . . . [15]

The proposal then is this: sentences in indirect discourse, as it happens, wear their logical form on their sleeves (except for one small point). They consist of an expression referring to a speaker, the two-place predicate 'said', and a demonstrative referring to an utterance. Period. What follows gives the content of the subject's saying, but has no logical or semantic connection with the original attribution of a saying. This last point is no doubt the novel one, and upon it everything depends: from a semantic point of view the content-sentence in indirect discourse is not contained in the sentence whose truth counts, i.e. the sentence that ends with 'that'.

We would do better, in coping with this subject, to talk of inscriptions and utterances and speech acts, and avoid reference to sentences.[16] For what an utterance of 'Galileo said that' does is announce a further utterance. Like any utterance, this first may be serious or silly, assertive or playful; but if it is true, it must be followed by an utterance synonymous with some other. The second

---

[15] J. A. H. Murray *et al.* (eds.), *The Oxford English Dictionary*, 253. Cf. C. T. Onions, *An Advanced English Syntax*, 154–6. I first learned that 'that' in such contexts evolved from an explicit demonstrative in J. Hintikka, *Knowledge and Belief*, 13. Hintikka remarks that a similar development has taken place in German and Finnish. I owe the *OED* reference to Eric Stiezel.

[16] I assume that a theory of truth for a language containing demonstratives must apply strictly to utterances and not to sentences, or will treat truth as a relation between sentences, speakers, and times. See Essay 2.

utterance, the introduced act, may also be true or false, done in the mode of assertion or of play. But if it is as announced, it must serve at least the purpose of conveying the content of what someone said. The role of the introducing utterance is not unfamiliar: we do the same with words like 'This is a joke', 'This is an order', 'He commanded that', 'Now hear this'. Such expressions might be called performatives, for they are used to usher in performances on the part of the speaker. A certain interesting reflexive effect sets in when performatives occur in the first-person present tense, for then the speaker utters words which if true are made so exclusively by the content and mode of the performance that follows, and the mode of this performance may well be in part determined by that same performative introduction. Here is an example that will also provide the occasion for a final comment on indirect discourse.

'Jones asserted that Entebbe is equatorial' would, if we parallel the analysis of indirect discourse, come to mean something like, 'An utterance of Jones' in the assertive mode had the content of this utterance of mine. Entebbe is equatorial.' The analysis does not founder because the modes of utterance of the two speakers may differ; all that the truth of the performative requires is that the second utterance, in whatever mode (assertive or not), match in content an assertive utterance of Jones. Whether such an asymmetry is appropriate in indirect discourse depends on how much of assertion we read into the concept of saying. Now suppose I try: 'I assert that Entebbe is equatorial.' Of course by saying this I may not assert anything; mood of words cannot guarantee mode of utterance. But if my utterance of the performative is true, then do I say something in the assertive mode that has the content of my second utterance—I do, that is, assert that Entebbe is equatorial. If I do assert it, an element in my success is no doubt my utterance of the performative, which announces an assertion; thus performatives tend to be self-fulfilling. Perhaps it is this feature of performatives that has misled some philosophers into thinking that performatives, or their utterances, are neither true nor false.

On the analysis of indirect discourse here proposed, standard problems seem to find a just solution. The appearance of failure of the laws of extensional substitution is explained as due to our mistaking what are really two sentences for one: we make substitutions in one sentence, but it is the other (the utterance of) which changes in truth. Since an utterance of 'Galileo said that' and any utterance following it are semantically independent, there is no reason to predict, on grounds of form alone, any *particular* effect on the truth of the first from change in the second. On the other hand, if the second utterance had been different in any way at all, the first utterance *might* have had a different truth value, for the reference of the 'that' would have changed.

The paradox, that sentences (utterances) in *oratio obliqua* do not have the logical consequences they should if truth is to be defined, is resolved. What follows the verb 'said' has only the structure of a singular term, usually the demonstrative 'that'. Assuming the 'that' refers, we can infer that Galileo said something from 'Galileo said that'; but this is welcome. The familiar words coming in the train of the performative of indirect discourse do, on my account, have structure, but it is familiar structure and poses no problem for theory of truth not there before indirect discourse was the theme.

Since Frege, philosophers have become hardened to the idea that content-sentences in talk about propositional attitudes may strangely refer to such entities as intensions, propositions, sentences, utterances, and inscriptions. What is strange is not the entities, which are all right in their place (if they have one), but the notion that ordinary words for planets, people, tables, and hippopotami in indirect discourse may give up these pedestrian references for the exotica. If we could recover our pre-Fregean semantic innocence, I think it would seem to us plainly incredible that the words 'The earth moves', uttered after the words 'Galileo said that', mean anything different, or refer to anything else, than is their wont when they come in other environments. No doubt their role in *oratio obliqua* is in some sense special: but that is another story. Language is the instrument it is because the same expression, with semantic features (meaning) unchanged, can serve countless purposes. I have tried to show how our understanding of indirect discourse does not strain this basic insight.

10

Radical Interpretation

Kurt utters the words 'Es regnet' and under the right conditions we know that he has said that it is raining. Having identified his utterance as intentional and linguistic, we are able to go on to interpret his words: we can say what his words, on that occasion, meant. What could we know that would enable us to do this? How could we come to know it? The first of these questions is not the same as the question what we *do* know that enables us to interpret the words of others. For there may easily be something we could know and don't, knowledge of which would suffice for interpretation, while on the other hand it is not altogether obvious that there is anything we actually know which plays an essential role in interpretation. The second question, how we could come to have knowledge that would serve to yield interpretations, does not, of course, concern the actual history of language acquisition. It is thus a doubly hypothetical question: given a theory that would make interpretation possible, what evidence plausibly available to a potential interpreter would support the theory to a reasonable degree? In what follows I shall try to sharpen these questions and suggest answers.

The problem of interpretation is domestic as well as foreign: it surfaces for speakers of the same language in the form of the question, how can it be determined that the language is the same? Speakers of the same language can go on the assumption that for them the same expressions are to be interpreted in the same way, but this does not indicate what justifies the assumption. All understanding of the speech of another involves radical interpretation. But it will help keep assumptions from going unnoticed to focus on cases where interpretation is most clearly called for: interpretation in one idiom of talk in another.[1]

What knowledge would serve for interpretation? A short answer would be, knowledge of what each meaningful expression means. In German, those words Kurt spoke mean that it is raining and Kurt was speaking German. So in uttering the words 'Es regnet', Kurt said that it was raining. This reply does not, as might first be thought, merely restate the problem. For it suggests that in passing from a description that does not interpret (his uttering of the words 'Es regnet') to interpreting description (his saying that it is raining) we must introduce a

---

[1] The term 'radical interpretation' is meant to suggest strong kinship with Quine's 'radical translation'. Kinship is not identity, however, and 'interpretation' in place of 'translation' marks one of the differences: a greater emphasis on the explicitly semantical in the former.

machinery of words and expressions (which may or may not be exemplified in actual utterances), and this suggestion is important. But the reply is no further help, for it does not say what it is to know what an expression means.

There is indeed also the hint that corresponding to each meaningful expression that is an entity, its meaning. This idea, even if not wrong, has proven to be very little help: at best it hypostasizes the problem.

Disenchantment with meanings as implementing a viable account of communication or interpretation helps explain why some philosophers have tried to get along without, not only meanings, but any serious theory at all. It is tempting, when the concepts we summon up to try to explain interpretation turn out to be more baffling than the explanandum, to reflect that after all verbal communication consists in nothing more than elaborate disturbances in the air which form a causal link between the non-linguistic activities of human agents. But although interpretable speeches are nothing but (that is, identical with) actions performed with assorted non-linguistic intentions (to warn, control, amuse, distract, insult), and these actions are in turn nothing but (identical with) intentional movements of the lips and larynx, this observation takes us no distance towards an intelligible general account of what we might know that would allow us to redescribe uninterpreted utterances as the right interpreted ones.

Appeal to meanings leaves us stranded further than we started from the non-linguistic goings-on that must supply the evidential base for interpretation; the 'nothing but' attitude provides no clue as to how the evidence is related to what it surely is evident for.

Other proposals for bridging the gap fall short in various ways. The 'causal' theories of Ogden and Richards and of Charles Morris attempted to analyse the meaning of sentences, taken one at a time, on the basis of behaviouristic data. Even if these theories had worked for the simplest sentences (which they clearly did not), they did not touch the problem of extending the method to sentences of greater complexity and abstractness. Theories of another kind start by trying to connect words rather than sentences with non-linguistic facts. This is promising because words are finite in number while sentences are not, and yet each sentence is no more than a concatenation of words: this offers the chance of a theory that interprets each of an infinity of sentences using only finite resources. But such theories fail to reach the evidence, for it seems clear that the semantic features of words cannot be explained directly on the basis of non-linguistic phenomena. The reason is simple. The phenomena to which we must turn are the extra-linguistic interests and activities that language serves, and these are served by words only in so far as the words are incorporated in (or on occasion happen to be) sentences. But then there is no chance of giving a foundational account of words before giving one of sentences.

For quite different reasons, radical interpretation cannot hope to take as evidence for the meaning of a sentence an account of the complex and delicately discriminated intentions with which the sentence is typically uttered. It is not easy to see how such an approach can deal with the structural, recursive feature of language that is essential to explaining how new sentences can be understood. But the central difficulty is that we cannot hope to attach a sense to the attribution of finely discriminated intentions independently of interpreting speech. The reason is not that we cannot ask necessary questions, but that interpreting an agent's intentions, his beliefs and his words are parts of a single project, no part of which can be assumed to be complete before the rest is. If this is right, we cannot make the full panoply of intentions and beliefs the evidential base for a theory of radical interpretation.

We are now in a position to say something more about what would serve to make interpretation possible. The interpreter must be able to understand any of the infinity of sentences the speaker might utter. If we are to state explicitly what the interpreter might know that would enable him to do this, we must put it in finite form.[2] If this requirement is to be met, any hope of a universal method of interpretation must be abandoned. The most that can be expected is to explain how an interpreter could interpret the utterances of speakers of a single language (or a finite number of languages): it makes no sense to ask for a theory that would yield an explicit interpretation for any utterance in any (possible) language.

It is still not clear, of course, what it is for a theory to yield an explicit interpretation of an utterance. The formulation of the problem seems to invite us to think of the theory as the specification of a function taking utterances as arguments and having interpretations as values. But then interpretations would be no better than meanings and just as surely entities of some mysterious kind. So it seems wise to describe what is wanted of the theory without apparent reference to meanings or interpretations: someone who knows the theory can interpret the utterances to which the theory applies.

The second general requirement on a theory of interpretation is that it can be supported or verified by evidence plausibly available to an interpreter. Since the theory is general—it must apply to a potential infinity of utterances—it would be natural to think of evidence in its behalf as instances of particular interpretations recognized as correct. And this case does, of course, arise for the interpreter dealing with a language he already knows. The speaker of a language normally cannot produce an explicit finite theory for his own language, but he can test a proposed theory since he can tell whether it yields correct interpretations when applied to particular utterances.

In radical interpretation, however, the theory is supposed to supply an understanding of particular utterances that is not given in advance, so the ultimate evidence for the theory cannot be correct sample interpretations. To deal with the general case, the evidence must be of a sort that would be available to someone who does not already know how to interpret utterances the theory

---

[2] See Essay 1 of Davidson, *Inquiries into Truth and Interpretation*.

is designed to cover: it must be evidence that can be stated without essential use of such linguistic concepts as meaning, interpretation, synonymy, and the like.

Before saying what kind of theory I think will do the trick, I want to discuss a last alternative suggestion, namely that a method of translation, from the language to be interpreted into the language of the interpreter, is all the theory that is needed. Such a theory would consist in the statement of an effective method for going from an arbitrary sentence of the alien tongue to a sentence of a familiar language; thus it would satisfy the demand for a finitely stated method applicable to any sentence. But I do not think a translation manual is the best form for a theory of interpretation to take.[3]

When interpretation is our aim, a method of translation deals with a wrong topic, a relation between two languages, where what is wanted is an interpretation of one (in another, of course, but that goes without saying since any theory is in some language). We cannot without confusion count the language used in stating the theory as part of the subject matter of the theory unless we explicitly make it so. In the general case, a theory of translation involves three languages: the object language, the subject language, and the metalanguage (the languages from and into which translation proceeds, and the language of the theory, which says what expressions of the subject language translate which expressions of the object language). And in this general case, we can know which sentences of the subject language translate which sentences of the object language without knowing what any of the sentences of either language mean (in any sense, anyway, that would let someone who understood the theory interpret sentences of the object language). If the subject language happens to be identical with the language of the theory, then someone who understands the theory can no doubt use the translation manual to interpret alien utterances; but this is because he brings to bear two things he knows and that the theory does not state: the fact that the subject language is his own, and his knowledge of how to interpet utterances in his own language.

It is awkward to try to make explicit the assumption that a mentioned sentence belongs to one's own language. We could try, for example, ' "Es regnet" in Kurt's language is translated as "It is raining" in mine', but the indexical self-reference is out of place in a theory that ought to work for any interpreter. If we decide to accept this difficulty, there remains the fact that the method of translation leaves tacit and beyond the reach of theory what we need to know that allows us to interpret our own language. A theory of translation must read some sort of

---

[3] The idea of a translation manual with appropriate empirical constraints as a device for studying problems in the philosophy of language is, of course, Quine's. This idea inspired much of my thinking on the present subject, and my proposal is in important respects very close to Quine's. Since Quine did not intend to answer the questions I have set, the claim that the method of translation is not adequate as a solution to the problem of radical interpretation is not a criticism of any doctrine of Quine's.

structure into sentences, but there is no reason to expect that it will provide any insight into how the meanings of sentences depend on their structure.

A satisfactory theory for interpreting the utterances of a language, our own included, will reveal significant semantic structure: the interpretation of utterances of complex sentences will systematically depend on the interpretation of utterances of simpler sentences, for example. Suppose we were to add to a theory of translation a satisfactory theory of interpretation for our own language. Then we would have exactly what we want, but in an unnecessarily bulky form. The translation manual churns out, for each sentence of the language to be translated, a sentence of the translator's language; the theory of interpretation then gives the interpretation of these familiar sentences. Clearly the reference to the home language is superfluous; it is an unneeded intermediary between interpretation and alien idiom. The only expressions a theory of interpretation has to mention are those belonging to the language to be interpreted.

A theory of interpretation for an object language may then be viewed as the result of the merger of a structurally revealing theory of interpretation for a known language, and a system of translation from the unknown language into the known. The merger makes all reference to the known language otiose; when this reference is dropped, what is left is a structurally revealing theory of interpretation for the object language—couched, of course, in familiar words. We have such theories, I suggest, in theories of truth of the kind Tarski first showed how to give.[4]

What characterizes a theory of truth in Tarski's style is that it entails, for every sentence s of the object language, a sentence of the form:

s is true (in the object language) if and only if p.

Instances of the form (which we shall call T-sentences) are obtained by replacing 's' by a canonical description of s, and 'p' by a translation of s. The important undefined semantical notion in the theory is that of *satisfaction* which relates sentences, open or closed, to infinite sequences of objects, which may be taken to belong to the range of the variables of the object language. The axioms, which are finite in number, are of two kinds: some give the conditions under which a sequence satisfies a complex sentence on the basis of the conditions of satisfaction of simpler sentences, others give the conditions under which the simplest (open) sentences are satisfied. Truth is defined for closed sentences in terms of the notion of satisfaction. A recursive theory like this can be turned into an explicit definition along familiar lines, as Tarski shows, provided the language of the theory contains enough set theory; but we shall not be concerned with this extra step.

Further complexities enter if proper names and functional expressions are irreducible features of the object language. A trickier matter concerns indexical

---

[4] A. Tarski, 'The Concept of Truth in Formalized Languages'.

devices. Tarski was interested in formalized languages containing no indexical or demonstrative aspects. He could therefore treat sentences as vehicles of truth; the extension of the theory to utterances is in this case trivial. But natural languages are indispensably replete with indexical features, like tense, and so their sentences may vary in truth according to time and speaker. The remedy is to characterize truth for a language relative to a time and a speaker. The extension to utterances is again straightforward.[5]

What follows is a defence of the claim that a theory of truth, modified to apply to a natural language, can be used as a theory of interpretation. The defence will consist in attempts to answer three questions:

1. Is it reasonable to think that a theory of truth of the sort described can be given for a natural language?
2. Would it be possible to tell that such a theory was correct on the basis of evidence plausibly available to an interpreter with no prior knowledge of the language to be interpreted?
3. If the theory were known to be true, would it be possible to interpret utterances of speakers of the language?

The first question is addressed to the assumption that a theory of truth can be given for a natural language: the second and third questions ask whether such a theory would satisfy the further demands we have made on a theory of interpretation.

1. *Can a theory of truth be given for a natural language?*

It will help us to appreciate the problem to consider briefly the case where a significant fragment of a language (plus one or two semantical predicates) is used to state its own theory of truth. According to Tarski's Convention T, it is a test of the adequacy of a theory that it entails all the T-sentences. This test apparently cannot be met without assigning something very much like a standard quantificational form to the sentences of the language, and appealing, in the theory, to a relational notion of satisfaction.[6] But the striking thing about T-sentences is that whatever machinery must operate to produce them, and whatever ontological wheels must turn, in the end a T-sentence states the truth conditions of a sentence using resources no richer than, because the same as, those of the sentence itself. Unless the original sentence mentions possible worlds, intensional entities, properties, or propositions, the statement of its truth conditions does not.

There is no equally simple way to make the analogous point about an alien language without appealing, as Tarski does, to an unanalysed notion of translation. But what we can do for our own language we ought to be able to do for another; the problem, it will turn out, will be to know that we are doing it.

---

[5] For a discussion of how a theory of truth can handle demonstratives and how Convention T must be modified, see S. Weinstein, 'Truth and Demonstratives'.
[6] See J. Wallace. 'On the Frame of Reference'.

The restriction imposed by demanding a theory that satisfies Convention T seems to be considerable: there is no generally accepted method now known for dealing, within the restriction, with a host of problems, for example, sentences that attribute attitudes, modalities, general causal statements, counterfactuals, attributive adjectives, quantifiers like 'most', and so on. On the other hand, there is what seems to me to be fairly impressive progress. To mention some examples, there is the work of Tyler Burge on proper names,[7] Gilbert Harman on 'ought',[8] John Wallace on mass terms and comparatives,[9] and there is my own work on attributions of attitudes and performatives,[10] on adverbs, events, and singular causal statements,[11] and on quotation.[12]

If we are inclined to be pessimistic about what remains to be done (or some of what has been done!), we should think of Frege's magnificent accomplishment in bringing what Dummett calls 'multiple generality' under control.[13] Frege did not have a theory of truth in Tarski's sense in mind, but it is obvious that he sought, and found, structures of a kind for which a theory of truth can be given.

The work of applying a theory of truth in detail to a natural language will in practice almost certainly divide into two stages. In the first stage, truth will be characterized, not for the whole language, but for a carefully gerrymandered part of the language. This part, though no doubt clumsy grammatically, will contain an infinity of sentences which exhaust the expressive power of the whole language. The second part will match each of the remaining sentences to one or (in the case of ambiguity) more than one of the sentences for which truth has been characterized. We may think of the sentences to which the first stage of the theory applies as giving the logical form, or deep structure, of all sentences.

2. Can a theory of truth be verified by appeal to evidence available before interpretation has begun?

Convention T says that a theory of truth is satisfactory if it generates a T-sentence for each sentence of the object language. It is enough to demonstrate that a theory of truth is empirically correct, then, to verify that the T-sentences are true (in practice, an adequate sample will confirm the theory to a reasonable degree). T-sentences mention only the closed sentences of the language, so the relevant evidence can consist entirely of facts about the behaviour and attitudes of speakers in relation to sentences (no doubt by way of utterances). A workable theory must, of course, treat sentences as concatenations of expressions of less than sentential length, it must introduce semantical notions like satisfaction and reference, and it must appeal to an ontology of sequences and the objects ordered by the sequences. All this apparatus is properly viewed as theoretical construction,

---

[7] T. Burge, 'Reference and Proper Names'.   [8] G. Harman, 'Moral Relativism Defended'.
[9] J. Wallace, 'Positive, Comparative, Superlative'.   [10] See Essay 9 in this volume.
[11] See Essays 6–10 in Davidson, *Essays on Actions and Events*.
[12] See Essay 6 in Davidson, *Inquiries into Truth and Interpretation*.
[13] M. Dummett, *Frege: Philosophy of Language*.

beyond the reach of direct verification. It has done its work provided only it entails testable results in the form of T-sentences, and these make no mention of the machinery. A theory of truth thus reconciles the demand for a theory that articulates grammatical structure with the demand for a theory that can be tested only by what it says about sentences.

In Tarski's work, T-sentences are taken to be true because the right branch of the biconditional is assumed to be a translation of the sentence truth conditions for which are being given. But we cannot assume in advance that correct translation can be recognized without pre-empting the point of radical interpretation; in empirical applications, we must abandon the assumption. What I propose is to reverse the direction of explanation: assuming translation, Tarski was able to define truth; the present idea is to take truth as basic and to extract an account of translation or interpretation. The advantages, from the point of view of radical interpretation, are obvious. Truth is a single property which attaches, or fails to attach, to utterances, while each utterance has its own interpretation; and truth is more apt to connect with fairly simple attitudes of speakers.

There is no difficulty in rephrasing Convention T without appeal to the concept of translation: an acceptable theory of truth must entail, for every sentence *s* of the object language, a sentence of the form: *s* is true if and only if *p*, where '*p*' is replaced by any sentence that is true if and only if *s* is. Given this formulation, the theory is tested by evidence that T-sentences are simply true; we have given up the idea that we must also tell whether what replaces '*p*' translates *s*. It might seem that there is no chance that if we demand so little of T-sentences, a theory of interpretation will emerge. And of course this would be so if we took the T-sentences in isolation. But the hope is that by putting appropriate formal and empirical restrictions on the theory as a whole, individual T-sentences will in fact serve to yield interpretations.[14]

We have still to say what evidence is available to an interpreter—evidence, we now see, that T-sentences are true. The evidence cannot consist in detailed descriptions of the speaker's beliefs and intentions, since attributions of attitudes, at least where subtlety is required, demand a theory that must rest on much the same evidence as interpretation. The interdependence of belief and meaning is evident in this way: a speaker holds a sentence to be true because of what the sentence (in his language) means, and because of what he believes. Knowing that he holds the sentence to be true, and knowing the meaning, we can infer his belief; given enough information about his beliefs, we could perhaps infer the meaning. But radical interpretation should rest on evidence that does not assume knowledge of meanings or detailed knowledge of beliefs.

A good place to begin is with the attitude of holding a sentence true, of accepting it as true. This is, of course, a belief, but it is a single attitude applicable to all sentences, and so does not ask us to be able to make finely discriminated

---

[14] For essential qualifications, see footnote 11 of Essay 8.

distinctions among beliefs. It is an attitude an interpreter may plausibly be taken to be able to identify before he can interpret, since he may know that a person intends to express a truth in uttering a sentence without having any idea *what* truth. Not that sincere assertion is the only reason to suppose that a person holds a sentence to be true. Lies, commands, stories, irony, if they are detected as attitudes, can reveal whether a speaker holds his sentences to be true. There is no reason to rule out other attitudes towards sentences, such as wishing true, wanting to make true, believing one is going to make true, and so on, but I am inclined to think that all evidence of this kind may be summed up in terms of holding sentences to be true.

Suppose, then, that the evidence available is just that speakers of the language to be interpreted hold various sentences to be true at certain times and under specified circumstances. How can this evidence be used to support a theory of truth? On the one hand, we have T-sentences, in the form:

(T) 'Es regnet' is true-in-German when spoken by x at time t if and only if it is raining near x at t.

On the other hand, we have the evidence, in the form:

(E) Kurt belongs to the German speech community and Kurt holds true 'Es regnet' on Saturday at noon and it is raining near Kurt on Saturday at noon.

We should, I think, consider (E) as evidence that (T) is true. Since (T) is a universally quantified conditional, the first step would be to gather more evidence to support the claim that:

(GE) $(x)(t)$ (if x belongs to the German speech community then (x holds true 'Es regnet' at t if and only if it is raining near x at t)).

The appeal to a speech community cuts a corner but begs no question: speakers belong to the same speech community if the same theories of interpretation work for them.

The obvious objection is that Kurt, or anyone else, may be wrong about whether it is raining near him. And this is of course a reason for not taking (E) as conclusive evidence for (GE) or for (T); and a reason not to expect generalizations like (GE) to be more than generally true. The method is rather one of getting a best fit. We want a theory that satisfies the formal constraints on a theory of truth, and that maximizes agreement, in the sense of making Kurt (and others) right, as far as we can tell, as often as possible. The concept of maximization cannot be taken literally here, since sentences are infinite in number, and anyway once the theory begins to take shape it makes sense to accept intelligible error and to make allowance for the relative likelihood of various kinds of mistake.[15]

---

[15] For more on getting a 'best fit' see Essays 10–12 in Davidson, *Inquiries into Truth and Interpretation*.

The process of devising a theory of truth for an unknown native tongue might in crude outline go as follows. First we look for the best way to fit our logic, to the extent required to get a theory satisfying Convention T, on to the new language; this may mean reading the logical structure of first-order quantification theory (plus identity) into the language, not taking the logical constants one by one, but treating this much of logic as a grid to be fitted on to the language in one fell swoop. The evidence here is classes of sentences always held true or always held false by almost everyone almost all of the time (potential logical truths) and patterns of inference. The first step identifies predicates, singular terms, quantifiers, connectives, and identity; in theory, it settles matters of logical form. The second step concentrates on sentences with indexicals; those sentences sometimes held true and sometimes false according to discoverable changes in the world. This step in conjunction with the first limits the possibilities for interpreting individual predicates. The last step deals with the remaining sentences, those on which there is not uniform agreement, or whose held truth value does not depend systematically on changes in the environment.[16]

This method is intended to solve the problem of the interdependence of belief and meaning by holding belief constant as far as possible while solving for meaning. This is accomplished by assigning truth conditions to alien sentences that make native speakers right when plausibly possible, according, of course, to our own view of what is right. What justifies the procedure is the fact that disagreement and agreement alike are intelligible only against a background of massive agreement. Applied to language, this principle reads: the more sentences we conspire to accept or reject (whether or not through a medium of interpretation), the better we understand the rest, whether or not we agree about them.

The methodological advice to interpret in a way that optimizes agreement should not be conceived as resting on a charitable assumption about human intelligence that might turn out to be false. If we cannot find a way to interpret the utterances and other behaviour of a creature as revealing a set of beliefs largely consistent and true by our own standards, we have no reason to count that creature as rational, as having beliefs, or as saying anything.

Here I would like to insert a remark about the methodology of my proposal. In philosophy we are used to definitions, analyses, reductions. Typically these are intended to carry us from concepts better understood, or clear, or more basic epistemologically or ontologically, to others we want to understand. The method

---

[16] Readers who appreciate the extent to which this account parallels Quine's account of radical translation in Chapter 2 of *Word and Object* will also notice the differences: the semantic constraint in my method forces quantificational structure on the language to be interpreted, which probably does not leave room for indeterminacy of logical form; the notion of stimulus meaning plays no role in my method, but its place is taken by reference to the objective features of the world which alter in conjunction with changes in attitude towards the truth of sentences; the principle of charity, which Quine emphasizes only in connection with the identification of the (pure) sentential connectives, I apply across the board.

I have suggested fits none of these categories. I have proposed a looser relation between concepts to be illuminated and the relatively more basic. At the centre stands a formal theory, a theory of truth, which imposes a complex structure on sentences containing the primitive notions of truth and satisfaction. These notions are given application by the form of the theory and the nature of the evidence. The result is a partially interpreted theory. The advantage of the method lies not in its free-style appeal to the notion of evidential support but in the idea of a powerful theory interpreted at the most advantageous point. This allows us to reconcile the need for a semantically articulated structure with a theory testable only at the sentential level. The more subtle gain is that very thin evidence in support of each of a potential infinity of points can yield rich results, even with respect to the points. By knowing only the conditions under which speakers hold sentences true, we can come out, given a satisfactory theory, with an interpretation of each sentence. It remains to make good on this last claim. The theory itself at best gives truth conditions. What we need to show is that if such a theory satisfies the constraints we have specified, it may be used to yield interpretations.

3. *If we know that a theory of truth satisfies the formal and empirical criteria described, can we interpret utterances of the language for which it is a theory?*
A theory of truth entails a T-sentence for each sentence of the object language, and a T-sentence gives truth conditions. It is tempting, therefore, simply to say that a T-sentence 'gives the meaning' of a sentence. Not, of course, by naming or describing an entity that is a meaning, but simply by saying under what conditions an utterance of the sentence is true.

But on reflection it is clear that a T-sentence does not give the meaning of the sentence it concerns: the T-sentences does fix the truth value relative to certain conditions, but it does not say the object language sentence is true *because* the conditions hold. Yet if truth values were all that mattered, the T-sentence for 'Snow is white' could as well say that it is true if and only if grass is green or $2 + 2 = 4$ as say that it is true if and only if snow is white. We may be confident, perhaps, that no satisfactory theory of truth will produce such anomalous T-sentences, but this confidence does not license us to make more of T-sentences.

A move that might seem helpful is to claim that it is not the T-sentence alone, but the canonical proof of a T-sentence, that permits us to interpret the alien sentence. A canonical proof, given a theory of truth, is easy to construct, moving as it does through a string of biconditionals, and requiring for uniqueness only occasional decisions to govern left and right precedence. The proof does reflect the logical form the theory assigns to the sentence, and so might be thought to reveal something about meaning. But in fact we would know no more than before about how to interpret if all we knew was that a certain sequence of sentences was the proof, from some true theory, of a particular T-sentence.

A final suggestion along these lines is that we can interpret a particular sentence provided we know a correct theory of truth that deals with the language of the sentence. For then we know not only the T-sentence for the sentence to be interpreted, but we also 'know' the T-sentences for all other sentences; and of course, all the proofs. Then we would see the place of the sentence in the language as a whole, we would know the role of each significant part of the sentence, and we would know about the logical connections between this sentence and others.

If we knew that a T-sentence satisfied Tarski's Convention T, we would know that it was true, and we could use it to interpret a sentence because we would know that the right branch of the biconditional translated the sentence to be interpreted. Our present trouble springs from the fact that in radical interpretation we cannot assume that a T-sentence satisfies the translation criterion. What we have been overlooking, however, is that we have supplied an alternative criterion: this criterion is that the totality of T-sentences should (in the sense described above) optimally fit evidence about sentences held true by native speakers. The present idea is that what Tarski assumed outright for each T-sentence can be indirectly elicited by a holistic constraint. If that constraint is adequate, each T-sentence will in fact yield an acceptable interpretation.

A T-sentence of an empirical theory of truth can be used to interpret a sentence, then, provided we also know the theory that entails it, and know that it is a theory that meets the formal and empirical criteria.[17] For if the constraints are adequate, the range of acceptable theories will be such that any of them yields some correct interpretation for each potential utterance. To see how it might work, accept for a moment the absurd hypothesis that the constraints narrow down the possible theories to one, and this one implies the T-sentence (T) discussed previously. Then we are justified in using this T-sentence to interpret Kurt's utterance of 'Es regnet' as his saying that it is raining. It is not likely, given the flexible nature of the constraints, that all acceptable theories will be identical. When all the evidence is in, there will remain, as Quine has emphasized, the trade-offs between the beliefs we attribute to a speaker and the interpretations we give his words. But the resulting indeterminacy cannot be so great but that any theory that passes the tests will serve to yield interpretations.

[17] See footnote 11 of Essay 8.

11

On the Very Idea of a Conceptual Scheme

Philosophers of many persuasions are prone to talk of conceptual schemes. Conceptual schemes, we are told, are ways of organizing experience; they are systems of categories that give form to the data of sensation; they are points of view from which individuals, cultures, or periods survey the passing scene. There may be no translating from one scheme to another, in which case the beliefs, desires, hopes, and bits of knowledge that characterize one person have no true counterparts for the subscriber to another scheme. Reality itself is relative to a scheme: what counts as real in one system may not in another.

Even those thinkers who are certain there is only one conceptual scheme are in the sway of the scheme concept; even monotheists have religion. And when someone sets out to describe 'our conceptual scheme', his homey task assumes, if we take him literally, that there might be rival systems.

Conceptual relativism is a heady and exotic doctrine, or would be if we could make good sense of it. The trouble is, as so often in philosophy, it is hard to improve intelligibility while retaining the excitement. At any rate that is what I shall argue.

We are encouraged to imagine we understand massive conceptual change or profound contrasts by legitimate examples of a familiar sort. Sometimes an idea, like that of simultaneity as defined in relativity theory, is so important that with its addition a whole department of science takes on a new look. Sometimes revisions in the list of sentences held true in a discipline are so central that we may feel that the terms involved have changed their meanings. Languages that have evolved in distant times or places may differ extensively in their resources for dealing with one or another range of phenomena. What comes easily in one language may come hard in another, and this difference may echo significant dissimilarities in style and value.

But examples like these, impressive as they occasionally are, are not so extreme but that the changes and the contrasts can be explained and described using the equipment of a single language. Whorf, wanting to demonstrate that Hopi incorporates a metaphysics so alien to ours that Hopi and English cannot, as he puts it, 'be calibrated', uses English to convey the contents of sample Hopi sentences.[1] Kuhn is brilliant at saying what things were like before the revolution using—what else?—our post-revolutionary idiom.[2] Quine gives us a feel for the 'pre-individuative phase in the evolution of our conceptual scheme',[3] while Bergson tells us where we can go to get a view of a mountain undistorted by one or another provincial perspective.

The dominant metaphor of conceptual relativism, that of differing points of view, seems to betray an underlying paradox. Different points of view make sense, but only if there is a common co-ordinate system on which to plot them; yet the existence of a common system belies the claim of dramatic incomparability. What we need, it seems to me, is some idea of the considerations that set the limits to conceptual contrast. There are extreme suppositions that founder on paradox or contradiction; there are modest examples we have no trouble understanding. What determines where we cross from the merely strange or novel to the absurd?

We may accept the doctrine that associates having a language with having a conceptual scheme. The relation may be supposed to be this: where conceptual schemes differ, so do languages. But speakers of different languages may share a conceptual scheme provided there is a way of translating one language into the other. Studying the criteria of translation is therefore a way of focusing on criteria of identity for conceptual schemes. If conceptual schemes aren't associated with languages in this way, the original problem is needlessly doubled, for then we would have to imagine the mind, with its ordinary categories, operating with a language with *its* organizing structure. Under the circumstances we would certainly want to ask who is to be master.

Alternatively, there is the idea that *any* language distorts reality, which implies that it is only wordlessly if at all that the mind comes to grips with things as they really are. This is to conceive language as an inert (though necessarily distorting) medium independent of the human agencies that employ it; a view of language that surely cannot be maintained. Yet if the mind can grapple without distortion with the real, the mind itself must be without categories and concepts. This featureless self is familiar from theories in quite different parts of the philosophical landscape. There are, for example, theories that make freedom consist in decisions taken apart from all desires, habits, and dispositions of the agent; and theories of knowledge that suggest that the mind can observe the totality of its own perceptions and ideas. In each case, the mind is divorced from the traits that constitute it; an inescapable conclusion from certain lines of reasoning, as I said, but one that should always persuade us to reject the premises.

We may identify conceptual schemes with languages, then, or better, allowing for the possibility that more than one language may express the same scheme, sets

[1] B. L. Whorf, 'The Punctual and Segmentative Aspects of Verbs in Hopi'.
[2] T. S. Kuhn, *The Structure of Scientific Revolutions*.
[3] W. V. Quine, 'Speaking of Objects', 24.

of intertranslatable languages. Languages we will not think of as separable from souls; speaking a language is not a trait a man can lose while retaining the power of thought. So there is no chance that someone can take up a vantage point for comparing conceptual schemes by temporarily shedding his own. Can we then say that two people have different conceptual schemes if they speak languages that fail of intertranslatability?

In what follows I consider two kinds of case that might be expected to arise: complete, and partial, failures of translatability. There would be complete failure if no significant range of sentences in one language could be translated into the other; there would be partial failure if some range could be translated and some range could not (I shall neglect possible asymmetries). My strategy will be to argue that we cannot make sense of total failure, and then to examine more briefly cases of partial failure.

First, then, the purported cases of complete failure. It is tempting to take a very short line indeed: nothing, it may be said, could count as evidence that some form of activity could not be interpreted in our language that was not at the same time evidence that that form of activity was not speech behaviour. If this were right, we probably ought to hold that a form of activity that cannot be interpreted as language in our language is not speech behaviour. Putting matters this way is unsatisfactory, however, for it comes to little more than making translatability into a familiar tongue a criterion of languagehood. As fiat, the thesis lacks the appeal of self-evidence; if it is a truth, as I think it is, it should emerge as the conclusion of an argument.

The credibility of the position is improved by reflection on the close relations between language and the attribution of attitudes such as belief, desire, and intention. On the one hand, it is clear that speech requires a multitude of finely discriminated intentions and beliefs. A person who asserts that perseverance keeps honour bright must, for example, represent himself as believing that perseverance keeps honour bright, and he must intend to represent himself as believing it. On the other hand, it seems unlikely that we can intelligibly attribute attitudes as complex as these to a speaker unless we can translate his words into ours. There can be no doubt that the relation between being able to translate someone's language and being able to describe his attitudes is very close. Still, until we can say more about *what* this relation is, the case against untranslatable languages remains obscure.

It is sometimes thought that translatability into a familiar language, say English, cannot be a criterion of languagehood on the grounds that the relation of translatability is not transitive. The idea is that some language, say Saturnian, may be translatable into English, and some further language, like Plutonian, may be translatable into Saturnian, while Plutonian is not translatable into English. Enough translatable differences may add up to an untranslatable one. By imagining a sequence of languages, each close enough to the one before to be acceptably translated into it, we can imagine a language so different from English as to resist totally translation into it. Corresponding to this distant language would be a system of concepts altogether alien to us.

This exercise does not, I think, introduce any new element into the discussion. For we should have to ask how we recognized that what the Saturnian was doing was *translating* Plutonian (or anything else). The Saturnian speaker might tell us that that was what he was doing or rather we might for a moment assume that that was what he was telling us. But then it would occur to us to wonder whether our translations of Saturnian were correct.

According to Kuhn, scientists operating in different scientific traditions (within different 'paradigms') 'work in different worlds'.[4] Strawson's *The Bounds of Sense* begins with the remark that 'It is possible to imagine kinds of worlds very different from the world as we know it'.[5] Since there is at most one world, these pluralities are metaphorical or merely imagined. The metaphors are, however, not at all the same. Strawson invites us to imagine possible non-actual worlds, worlds that might be described, using our present language, by redistributing truth values over sentences in various systematic ways. The clarity of the contrasts between worlds in this case depends on supposing our scheme of concepts, our descriptive resources, to remain fixed. Kuhn, on the other hand, wants us to think of different observers of the same world who come to it with incommensurable systems of concepts. Strawson's many imagined worlds are seen or heard or described from the same point of view; Kuhn's one world is seen from different points of view. It is the second metaphor we want to work on.

The first metaphor requires a distinction within language of concept and content: using a fixed system of concepts (words with fixed meanings) we describe alternative universes. Some sentences will be true simply because of the concepts or meanings involved, others because of the way of the world. In describing possible worlds, we play with sentences of the second kind only.

The second metaphor suggests instead a dualism of quite a different sort, a dualism of total scheme (or language) and uninterpreted content. Adherence to the second dualism, while not inconsistent with adherence to the first, may be encouraged by attacks on the first. Here is how it may work.

To give up the analytic-synthetic distinction as basic to the understanding of language is to give up the idea that we can clearly distinguish between theory and language. Meaning, as we might loosely use the word, is contaminated by theory, by what is held to be true. Feyerabend puts it this way:

Our argument against meaning invariance is simple and clear. It proceeds from the fact that usually some of the principles involved in the determinations of the meanings of older theories or points of views are inconsistent with the new . . . theories. It points out that it is natural to resolve this contradiction by eliminating the troublesome . . . older principles, and to replace them by principles, or theorems, of a new . . . theory. And it

---

[4] T. S. Kuhn, *The Structure of Scientific Revolutions*, 134.
[5] P. Strawson, *The Bounds of Sense*, 15.

concludes by showing that such a procedure will also lead to the elimination of the old meanings.[6]

We may now seem to have a formula for generating distinct conceptual schemes. We get a new out of an old scheme when the speakers of a language come to accept as true an important range of sentences they previously took to be false (and, of course, vice versa). We must not describe this change simply as a matter of their coming to view old falsehoods as truths, for a truth is a proposition, and what they come to accept, in accepting a sentence as true, is not the same thing that they rejected when formerly they held the sentence to be false. A change has come over the meaning of the sentence because it now belongs to a new language.

This picture of how new (perhaps better) schemes result from new and better science is very much the picture philosophers of science, like Putnam and Feyerabend, and historians of science, like Kuhn, have painted for us. A related idea emerges in the suggestion of some other philosophers, that we could improve our conceptual lot if we were to tune our language to an improved science. Thus both Quine and Smart, in somewhat different ways, regretfully admit that our present ways of talking make a serious science of behaviour impossible. (Wittgenstein and Ryle have said similar things without regret.) The cure, Quine and Smart think, is to change how we talk. Smart advocates (and predicts) the change in order to put us on the scientifically straight path of materialism: Quine is more concerned to clear the way for a purely extensional language. (Perhaps I should add that I think our actual scheme and language are best understood as extensional and materialist.)

If we were to follow this advice, I do not myself think science or understanding would be advanced, though possibly morals would. But the present question is only whether, if such changes were to take place, we should be justified in calling them alterations in the basic conceptual apparatus. The difficulty in so calling them is easy to appreciate. Suppose that in my office of Minister of Scientific Language I want the new man to stop using words that refer, say, to emotions, feelings, thoughts, and intentions, and to talk instead of the physiological states and happenings that are assumed to be more or less identical with the mental riff and raff. How do I tell whether my advice has been heeded if the new man speaks a new language? For all I know, the shiny new phrases, though stolen from the old language in which they refer to physiological stirrings, may in his mouth play the role of the messy old mental concepts.

The key phrase is: for all I know. What is clear is that retention of some or all of the old vocabulary in itself provides no basis for judging the new scheme to be the same as, or different from, the old. So what sounded at first like a thrilling discovery—that truth is relative to a conceptual scheme—has not so far been shown to be anything more than the pedestrian and familiar fact that the truth of

---

[6] P. Feyerabend, 'Explanation, Reduction, and Empiricism', 82.

a sentence is relative to (among other things) the language to which it belongs. Instead of living in different worlds, Kuhn's scientists may, like those who need Webster's dictionary, be only words apart.

Giving up the analytic-synthetic distinction has not proven a help in making sense of conceptual relativism. The analytic-synthetic distinction is however explained in terms of something that may serve to buttress conceptual relativism, namely the idea of empirical content. The dualism of the synthetic and the analytic is a dualism of sentences some of which are true (or false) both because of what they mean and because of their empirical content, while others are true (or false) by virtue of meaning alone, having no empirical content. If we give up the dualism, we abandon the conception of meaning that goes with it, but we do not have to abandon the idea of empirical content: we can hold, if we want, that *all* sentences have empirical content. Empirical content is in turn explained by reference to the facts, the world, experience, sensation, the totality of sensory stimuli, or something similar. Meanings gave us a way to talk about categories, the organizing structure of language, and so on; but it is possible, as we have seen, to give up meanings and analyticity while retaining the idea of language as embodying a conceptual scheme. Thus in place of the dualism of the analytic-synthetic we get the dualism of conceptual scheme and empirical content. The new dualism is the foundation of an empiricism shorn of the untenable dogmas of the analytic-synthetic distinction and reductionism—shorn, that is, of the unworkable idea that we can uniquely allocate empirical content sentence by sentence.

I want to urge that this second dualism of scheme and content, of organizing system and something waiting to be organized, cannot be made intelligible and defensible. It is itself a dogma of empiricism, the third dogma. The third, and perhaps the last, for if we give it up it is not clear that there is anything distinctive left to call empiricism.

The scheme-content dualism has been formulated in many ways. Here are some examples. The first comes from Whorf, elaborating on a theme of Sapir's. Whorf says that:

. . . language produces an organization of experience. We are inclined to think of language simply as a technique of expression, and not to realize that language first of all is a classification and arrangement of the stream of sensory experience which results in a certain world-order . . . In other words, language does in a cruder but also in a broader and more versatile way the same thing that science does . . . We are thus introduced to a new principle of relativity, which holds that all observers are not led by the same physical evidence to the same picture of the universe, unless their linguistic backgrounds are similar, or can in some way be calibrated.[7]

Here we have all the required elements: language as the organizing force, not to be distinguished clearly from science; what is organized, referred to variously as

---

[7] B. L. Whorf, 'The Punctual and Segmentative Aspects of Verbs in Hopi', 55.

'experience', 'the stream of sensory experience', and 'physical evidence'; and finally, the failure of intertranslatability ('calibration'). The failure of inter-translatability is a necessary condition for difference of conceptual schemes; the common relation to experience or the evidence is what is supposed to help us make sense of the claim that it is languages or schemes that are under consideration when translation fails. It is essential to this idea that there be something neutral and common that lies outside all schemes. This common something cannot, of course, be the *subject matter* of contrasting languages, or translation would be possible. Thus Kuhn has recently written:

Philosophers have now abandoned hope of finding a pure sense-datum language . . . but many of them continue to assume that theories can be compared by recourse to a basic vocabulary consisting entirely of words which are attached to nature in ways that are unproblematic and, to the extent necessary, independent of theory . . . Feyerabend and I have argued at length that no such vocabulary is available. In the transition from one theory to the next words change their meanings or conditions of applicability in subtle ways. Though most of the same signs are used before and after a revolution—e.g. force, mass, element, compound, cell—the way in which some of them attach to nature has somehow changed. Successive theories are thus, we say, incommensurable.[8]

'Incommensurable' is, of course, Kuhn and Feyerabend's word for 'not inter-translatable'. The neutral content waiting to be organized is supplied by nature.

Feyerabend himself suggests that we may compare contrasting schemes by 'choosing a point of view outside the system or the language'. He hopes we can do this because 'there is still human experience as an actually existing process'[9] independent of all schemes.

The same, or similar, thoughts are expressed by Quine in many passages: 'The totality of our so-called knowledge or beliefs . . . is a man-made fabric which impinges on experience only along the edges . . .';[10] '. . . total science is like a field of force whose boundary conditions are experience';[11] 'As an empiricist I . . . think of the conceptual scheme of science as a tool . . . for predicting future experience in the light of past experience.'[12] And again:

We persist in breaking reality down somehow into a multiplicity of identifiable and discriminable objects . . . We talk so inveterately of objects that to say we do so seems almost to say nothing at all; for how else is there to talk? It is hard to say how else there is to talk, not because our objectifying pattern is an invariable trait of human nature, but because we are bound to adapt any alien pattern to our own in the very process of understanding or translating the alien sentences.[13]

The test of difference remains failure or difficulty of translation: ' . . . to speak of that remote medium as radically different from ours is to say no more than that

[8] T. S. Kuhn, 'Reflections on my Critics', 266, 267.
[9] P. Feyerabend, 'Problems of Empiricism', 214.
[10] W. V. Quine, 'Two Dogmas of Empiricism', 42.   [11] Ibid.   [12] Ibid., 44.
[13] W. V. Quine, 'Speaking of Objects', 1.

the translations do not come smoothly.'[14] Yet the roughness may be so great that the alien has an 'as yet unimagined pattern beyond individuation'.[15]

The idea is then that something is a language, and associated with a conceptual scheme, whether we can translate it or not, if it stands in a certain relation (predicting, organizing, facing, or fitting) experience (nature, reality, sensory promptings). The problem is to say what the relation is, and to be clearer about the entities related.

The images and metaphors fall into two main groups: conceptual schemes (languages) either *organize* something, or they *fit* it (as in 'he warps his scientific heritage to fit his . . . sensory promptings'[16]).The first group contains also *systematize, divide up* (the stream of experience); further examples of the second group are *predict, account for, face* (the tribunal of experience). As for the entities that get organized, or which the scheme must fit, I think again we may detect two main ideas: either it is reality (the universe, the world, nature), or it is experience (the passing show, surface irritations, sensory promptings, sense-data, the given).

We cannot attach a clear meaning to the notion of organizing a single object (the world, nature, etc.) unless that object is understood to contain or consist in other objects. Someone who sets out to organize a closet arranges the things in it. If you are told not to organize the shoes and shirts, but the closet itself, you would be bewildered. How would you organize the Pacific Ocean? Straighten out its shores, perhaps, or relocate its islands, or destroy its fish.

A language may contain simple predicates whose extensions are matched by no simple predicates, or even by any predicates at all, in some other language. What enables us to make this point in particular cases is an ontology common to the two languages, with concepts that individuate the same objects. We can be clear about breakdowns in translation when they are local enough, for a background of generally successful translation provides what is needed to make the failures intelligible. But we were after larger game: we wanted to make sense of there being a language we could not translate at all. Or, to put the point differently, we were looking for a criterion of languagehood that did not depend on, or entail, translatability into a familiar idiom. I suggest that the image of organizing the closet of nature will not supply such a criterion.

How about the other kind of object, experience? Can we think of a language organizing *it*? Much the same difficulties recur. The notion of organization applies only to pluralities. But whatever plurality we take experience to consist in—events like losing a button or stubbing a toe, having a sensation of warmth or hearing an oboe—we will have to individuate according to familiar principles. A language that organizes *such* entities must be a language very like our own.

Experience (and its classmates like surface irritations, sensations, and sense-data) also makes another and more obvious trouble for the organizing idea. For how could something count as a language that organized *only* experiences,

---

[14] Ibid., 25.   [15] Ibid., 24.   [16] W. V. Quine, 'Two Dogmas of Empiricism', 46.

sensations, surface irritations, or sense-data? Surely knives and forks, railroads and mountains, cabbages and kingdoms also need organizing.

This last remark will no doubt sound inappropriate as a response to the claim that a conceptual scheme is a way of coping with sensory experience; and I agree that it is. But what was under consideration was the idea of *organizing* experience, not the idea of *coping with* (or fitting or facing) experience. The reply was apropos of the former, not the latter, concept. So now let's see whether we can do better with the second idea.

When we turn from talk of organization to talk of fitting we turn our attention from the referential apparatus of language—predicates, quantifiers, variables, and singular terms—to whole sentences. It is sentences that predict (or are used to predict), sentences that cope or deal with things, that fit our sensory promptings, that can be compared or confronted with the evidence. It is sentences also that face the tribunal of experience, though of course they must face it together.

The proposal is not that experiences, sense-data, surface irritations, or sensory promptings are the sole subject matter of language. There is, it is true, the theory that talk about brick houses on Elm Street is ultimately to be construed as being about sense data or perceptions, but such reductionistic views are only extreme, and implausible, versions of the general position we are considering. The general position is that sensory experience provides all the *evidence* for the acceptance of sentences (where sentences may include whole theories). A sentence or theory fits our sensory promptings, successfully faces the tribunal of experience, predicts future experience, or copes with the pattern of our surface irritations, provided it is borne out by the evidence.

In the common course of affairs, a theory may be borne out by the available evidence and yet be false. But what is in view here is not just actually available evidence; it is the totality of possible sensory evidence past, present, and future. We do not need to pause to contemplate what this might mean. The point is that for a theory to fit or face up to the totality of possible sensory evidence is for that theory to be true. If a theory quantifies over physical objects, numbers, or sets, what it says about these entities is true provided the theory as a whole fits the sensory evidence. One can see how, from this point of view, such entities might be called posits. It is reasonable to call something a posit if it can be contrasted with something that is not. Here the something that is not is sensory experience—at least that is the idea.

The trouble is that the notion of fitting the totality of experience, like the notion of fitting the facts, or of being true to the facts, adds nothing intelligible to the simple concept of being true. To speak of sensory experience rather than the evidence, or just the facts, expresses a view about the source or nature of evidence, but it does not add a new entity to the universe against which to test conceptual schemes. The totality of sensory evidence is what we want provided it is all the evidence there is; and all the evidence there is is just what it takes to make our sentences or theories true. Nothing, however, no *thing*, makes sentences and theories true: not experience, not surface irritations, not the world, can make a sentence true. *That* experience takes a certain course, that our skin is warmed or punctured, that the universe is finite, these facts, if we like to talk that way, make sentences and theories true. But this point is put better without mention of facts. The sentence 'My skin is warm' is true if and only if my skin is warm. Here there is no reference to a fact, a world, an experience, or a piece of evidence.[17]

Our attempt to characterize languages or conceptual schemes in terms of the notion of fitting some entity has come down, then, to the simple thought that something is an acceptable conceptual scheme or theory if it is true. Perhaps we better say *largely* true in order to allow sharers of a scheme to differ on details. And the criterion of a conceptual scheme different from our own now becomes: largely true but not translatable. The question whether this is a useful criterion is just the question how well we understand the notion of truth, as applied to language, independent of the notion of translation. The answer is, I think, that we do not understand it independently at all.

We recognize sentences like ' "Snow is white" is true if and only if snow is white' to be trivially true. Yet the totality of such English sentences uniquely determines the extension of the concept of truth for English. Tarski generalized this observation and made it a test of theories of truth: according to Tarski's Convention T, a satisfactory theory of truth for a language L must entail, for every sentence *s* of L, a theorem of the form '*s* is true if and only if *p*' where '*s*' is replaced by a description of *s* and '*p*' by *s* itself if L is English, and by a translation of *s* into English if L is not English.[18] This isn't, of course, a definition of truth, and it doesn't hint that there is a single definition or theory that applies to languages generally. Nevertheless, Convention T suggests, though it cannot state, an important feature common to all the specialized concepts of truth. It succeeds in doing this by making essential use of the notion of translation into a language we know. Since Convention T embodies our best intuition as to how the concept of truth is used, there does not seem to be much hope for a test that a conceptual scheme is radically different from ours if that test depends on the assumption that we can divorce the notion of truth from that of translation.

Neither a fixed stock of meanings, nor a theory-neutral reality, can provide, then, a ground for comparison of conceptual schemes. It would be a mistake to look further for such a ground if by that we mean something conceived as common to incommensurable schemes. In abandoning this search, we abandon the attempt to make sense of the metaphor of a single space within which each scheme has a position and provides a point of view.

I turn now to the more modest approach: the idea of partial rather than total failure of translation. This introduces the possibility of making changes and

---

[17] See Essay 3 in Davidson, *Inquiries into Truth and Interpretation*.
[18] A. Tarski, 'The Concept of Truth in Formalized Languages'.

contrasts in conceptual schemes intelligible by reference to the common part. What we need is a theory of translation or interpretation that makes no assumptions about shared meanings, concepts, or beliefs.

The interdependence of belief and meaning springs from the interdependence of two aspects of the interpretation of speech behaviour: the attribution of beliefs and the interpretation of sentences. We remarked before that we can afford to associate conceptual schemes with languages because of these dependencies. Now we can put the point in a somewhat sharper way. Allow that a man's speech cannot be interpreted except by someone who knows a good deal about what the speaker believes (and intends and wants), and that fine distinctions between beliefs are impossible without understood speech; how then are we to interpret speech or intelligibly to attribute beliefs and other attitudes? Clearly we must have a theory that simultaneously accounts for attitudes and interprets speech, and which assumes neither.

I suggest, following Quine, that we may without circularity or unwarranted assumptions accept certain very general attitudes towards sentences as the basic evidence for a theory of radical interpretation. For the sake of the present discussion at least we may depend on the attitude of accepting as true, directed to sentences, as the crucial notion. (A more full-blooded theory would look to other attitudes towards sentences as well, such as wishing true, wondering whether true, intending to make true, and so on.) Attitudes are indeed involved here, but the fact that the main issue is not begged can be seen from this: if we merely know that someone holds a certain sentence to be true, we know neither what he means by the sentence nor what belief his holding it true represents. His holding the sentence true is thus the vector of two forces: the problem of interpretation is to abstract from the evidence a workable theory of meaning and an acceptable theory of belief.

The way this problem is solved is best appreciated from undramatic examples. If you see a ketch sailing by and your companion says, 'Look at that handsome yawl', you may be faced with a problem of interpretation. One natural possibility is that your friend has mistaken a ketch for a yawl, and has formed a false belief. But if his vision is good and his line of sight favourable it is even more plausible that he does not use the word 'yawl' quite as you do, and has made no mistake at all about the position of the jigger on the passing yacht. We do this sort of off the cuff interpretation all the time, deciding in favour of reinterpretation of words in order to preserve a reasonable theory of belief. As philosophers we are peculiarly tolerant of systematic malapropism, and practised at interpreting the result. The process is that of constructing a viable theory of belief and meaning from sentences held true.

Such examples emphasize the interpretation of anomalous details against a background of common beliefs and a going method of translation. But the principles involved must be the same in less trivial cases. What matters is this: if all we know is what sentences a speaker holds true, and we cannot assume that his language is our own, then we cannot take even a first step towards interpretation without knowing or assuming a great deal about the speaker's beliefs. Since knowledge of beliefs comes only with the ability to interpret words, the only possibility at the start is to assume general agreement on beliefs. We get a first approximation to a finished theory by assigning to sentences of a speaker conditions of truth that actually obtain (in our own opinion) just when the speaker holds those sentences true. The guiding policy is to do this as far as possible, subject to considerations of simplicity, hunches about the effects of social conditioning, and of course our common-sense, or scientific, knowledge of explicable error.

The method is not designed to eliminate disagreement, nor can it; its purpose is to make meaningful disagreement possible, and this depends entirely on a foundation—*some* foundation—in agreement. The agreement may take the form of widespread sharing of sentences held true by speakers of 'the same language', or agreement in the large mediated by a theory of truth contrived by an interpreter for speakers of another language.

Since charity is not an option, but a condition of having a workable theory, it is meaningless to suggest that we might fall into massive error by endorsing it. Until we have successfully established a systematic correlation of sentences held true with sentences held true, there are no mistakes to make. Charity is forced on us; whether we like it or not, if we want to understand others, we must count them right in most matters. If we can produce a theory that reconciles charity and the formal conditions for a theory, we have done all that could be done to ensure communication. Nothing more is possible, and nothing more is needed.

We make maximum sense of the words and thoughts of others when we interpret in a way that optimizes agreement (this includes room, as we said, for explicable error, i.e., differences of opinion). Where does this leave the case for conceptual relativism? The answer is, I think, that we must say much the same thing about differences in conceptual scheme as we say about differences in belief: we improve the clarity and bite of declarations of difference, whether of scheme or opinion, by enlarging the basis of shared (translatable) language or of shared opinion. Indeed, no clear line between the cases can be made out. If we choose to translate some alien sentence rejected by its speakers by a sentence to which we are strongly attached on a community basis, we may be tempted to call this a difference in schemes; if we decide to accommodate the evidence in other ways, it may be more natural to speak of a difference of opinion. But when others think differently from us, no general principle, or appeal to evidence, can force us to decide that the difference lies in our beliefs rather than in our concepts.

We must conclude, I think, that the attempt to give a solid meaning to the idea of conceptual relativism, and hence to the idea of a conceptual scheme, fares no better when based on partial failure of translation than when based on total failure. Given the underlying methodology of interpretation, we could not be in a position to judge that others had concepts or beliefs radically different from our own.

It would be wrong to summarize by saying we have shown how communication is possible between people who have different schemes, a way that works without need of what there cannot be, namely a neutral ground, or a common co-ordinate system. For we have found no intelligible basis on which it can be said that schemes are different. It would be equally wrong to announce the glorious news that all mankind—all speakers of language, at least—share a common scheme and ontology. For if we cannot intelligibly say that schemes are different, neither can we intelligibly say that they are one.

In giving up dependence on the concept of an uninterpreted reality, something outside all schemes and science, we do not relinquish the notion of objective truth—quite the contrary. Given the dogma of a dualism of scheme and reality, we get conceptual relativity, and truth relative to a scheme. Without the dogma, this kind of relativity goes by the board. Of course truth-of sentences remains relative to language, but that is as objective as can be. In giving up the dualism of scheme and world, we do not give up the world, but re-establish unmediated touch with the familiar objects whose antics make our sentences and opinions true or false.

12

What Metaphors Mean

Metaphor is the dreamwork of language and, like all dreamwork, its interpretation reflects as much on the interpreter as on the originator. The interpretation of dreams requires collaboration between a dreamer and a waker, even if they be the same person; and the act of interpretation is itself a work of the imagination. So too understanding a metaphor is as much a creative endeavour as making a metaphor, and as little guided by rules.

These remarks do not, except in matters of degree, distinguish metaphor from more routine linguistic transactions: all communication by speech assumes the interplay of inventive construction and inventive construal. What metaphor adds to the ordinary is an achievement that uses no semantic resources beyond the resources on which the ordinary depends. There are no instructions for devising metaphors; there is no manual for determining what a metaphor 'means' or 'says' there is no test for metaphor that does not call for taste.[1] A metaphor implies a kind and degree of artistic success; there are no unsuccessful metaphors, just as there are no unfunny jokes. There are tasteless metaphors, but these are turns that nevertheless have brought something off, even if it were not worth bringing off or could have been brought off better.

This paper is concerned with that metaphors mean, and its thesis is that metaphors mean what the words, in their most literal interpretation, mean, and nothing more. Since this thesis flies in the face of contemporary views with which I am familiar, much of what I have to say is critical. But I think the picture of metaphor that emerges when error and confusion are cleared away makes metaphor a more, not a less, interesting phenomenon.

The central mistake against which I shall be inveighing is the idea that a metaphor has, in addition to its literal sense or meaning, another sense or meaning. This idea is common to many who have written about metaphor: it is found in the works of literary critics like Richards, Empson, and Winters; philosophers from Aristotle to Max Black; psychologists from Freud and earlier to Skinner and later; and linguists from Plato to Uriel Weinreich and George Lakoff. The idea takes many forms, from the relatively simple in Aristotle to the

---

[1] I think Max Black is wrong when he says, 'The rules of our language determine that some expressions must count as metaphors.' ('Metaphor', 29.) There are no such rules.

relatively complex in Black. The idea appears in writings which maintain that a literal paraphrase of a metaphor can be produced, but it is also shared by those who hold that typically no literal paraphrase can be found. Some stress the special insight metaphor can inspire and make much of the fact that ordinary language, in its usual functioning, yields no such insight. Yet this view too sees metaphor as a form of communication alongside ordinary communication; metaphor conveys truths or falsehoods about the world much as plainer language does, though the message may be considered more exotic, profound, or cunningly garbed.

The concept of metaphor as primarily a vehicle for conveying ideas, even if unusual ones, seems to me as wrong as the parent idea that a metaphor has a special meaning. I agree with the view that metaphors cannot be paraphrased, but I think this is not because metaphors say something too novel for literal expression but because there is nothing there to paraphrase. Paraphrase, whether possible or not, is appropriate to what is *said*: we try, in paraphrase, to say it another way. But if I am right, a metaphor doesn't say anything beyond its literal meaning (nor does its maker say anything, in using the metaphor, beyond the literal). This is not, of course, to deny that a metaphor has a point, nor that that point can be brought out by using further words.

In the past those who have denied that metaphor has a cognitive content in addition to the literal have often been out to show that metaphor is confusing, merely emotive, unsuited to serious, scientific, or philosophic discourse. My views should not be associated with this tradition. Metaphor is a legitimate device not only in literature but in science, philosophy, and the law; it is effective in praise and abuse, prayer and promotion, description and prescription. For the most part I don't disagree with Max Black, Paul Henle, Nelson Goodman, Monroe Beardsley, and the rest in their accounts of what metaphor accomplishes, except that I think it accomplishes more and that what is additional is different in kind.

My disagreement is with the explanation of how metaphor works its wonders. To anticipate: I depend on the distinction between what words mean and what they are used to do. I think metaphor belongs exclusively to the domain of use. It is something brought off by the imaginative employment of words and sentences and depends entirely on the ordinary meanings of those words and hence on the ordinary meanings of the sentences they comprise.

It is no help in explaining how words work in metaphor to posit metaphorical or figurative meanings, or special kinds of poetic or metaphorical truth. These ideas don't explain metaphor, metaphor explains them. Once we understand a metaphor we can call what we grasp the 'metaphorical truth' and (up to a point) say what the 'metaphorical meaning' is. But simply to lodge this meaning in the metaphor is like explaining why a pill puts you to sleep by saying it has a dormative power. Literal meaning and literal truth conditions can be assigned to words and sentences apart from particular contexts of use. This is why adverting to them has genuine explanatory power.

I shall try to establish my negative views about what metaphors mean and introduce my limited positive claims by examining some false theories of the nature of metaphor.

A metaphor makes us attend to some likeness, often a novel or surprising likeness, between two or more things. This trite and true observations leads, or seems to lead, to a conclusion concerning the meaning of metaphors. Consider ordinary likeness or similarity: two roses are similar because they share the property of being a rose; two infants are similar by virtue of their infanthood. Or, more simply, roses are similar because each is a rose, infants, because each is an infant.

Suppose someone says 'Tolstoy was once an infant'. How is the infant Tolstoy like other infants? The answer comes pat: by virtue of exhibiting the property of infanthood, that is, leaving out some of the wind, by virtue of being an infant. If we tire of the phrase 'by virtue of', we can, it seems, be plainer still by saying the infant Tolstoy shares with other infants the fact that the predicate 'is an infant' applies to him; given the word 'infant', we have no trouble saying exactly how the infant Tolstoy resembles other infants. We could do it without the word 'infant'; all we need is other words that mean the same. The end result is the same. Ordinary similarity depends on groupings established by the ordinary meanings of words. Such similarity is natural and unsurprising to the extent that familiar ways of grouping objects are tied to usual meanings of usual words.

A famous critic said that Tolstoy was 'a great moralizing infant'. The Tolstoy referred to here is obviously not the infant Tolstoy but Tolstoy the adult writer; this is metaphor. Now in what sense is Tolstoy the writer similar to an infant? What we are to do, perhaps, is think of the class of objects which includes all ordinary infants and, in addition, the adult Tolstoy and then ask ourselves what special, surprising property the members of this class have in common. The appealing thought is that given patience we could come as close as need be to specifying the appropriate property. In any case, we could do the job perfectly if we found words that meant exactly what the metaphorical 'infant' means. The important point, from my perspective, is not whether we can find the perfect other words but the assumption that there is something to be attempted, a metaphorical meaning to be matched. So far I have been doing no more than crudely sketching how the concept of meaning may have crept into the analysis of metaphor, and the answer I have suggested is that since what we think of as garden variety similarity goes with what we think of as garden variety meanings, it is natural to posit unusual or metaphorical meanings to help explain the similarities metaphor promotes.

The idea, then, is that in metaphor certain words take on new, or what are often called 'extended', meanings. When we read, for example, that 'the Spirit of God moved upon the face of the waters', we are to regard the word 'face' as having an extended meaning (I disregard further metaphor in the passage). The extension applies, as it happens, to what philosophers call the extension of the word, that is, the class of entities to which it refers. Here the word 'face' applies to ordinary faces, and to waters in addition.

This account cannot, at any rate, be complete, for if in these contexts the words 'face' and 'infant' apply correctly to waters and to the adult Tolstoy, then waters really do have faces and Tolstoy literally was an infant, and all sense of metaphor evaporates. If we are to think of words in metaphors as directly going about their business of applying to what they properly do apply to, there is no difference between metaphor and the introduction of a new term into our vocabulary: to make a metaphor is to murder it.

What has been left out is any appeal to the original meaning of the words. Whether or not metaphor depends on new or extended meanings, it certainly depends in some way on the original meanings; an adequate account of metaphor must allow that the primary or original meanings of words remain active in their metaphorical setting.

Perhaps, then, we can explain metaphor as a kind of ambiguity: in the context of a metaphor, certain words have either a new or an original meaning, and the force of the metaphor depends on our uncertainty as we waver between the two meanings. Thus when Melville writes that 'Christ was a chronometer', the effect of metaphor is produced by our taking 'chronometer' first in its ordinary sense and then in some extraordinary or metaphorical sense.

It is hard to see how this theory can be correct. For the ambiguity in the word, if there is any, is due to the fact that in ordinary contexts it means one thing and in the metaphorical context it means something else; but in the metaphorical context we do not necessarily hesitate over its meaning. When we do hesitate, it is usually to decide which of a number of metaphorical interpretations we shall accept; we are seldom in doubt that what we have is a metaphor. At any rate, the effectiveness of the metaphor easily outlasts the end of uncertainty over the interpretation of the metaphorical passage. Metaphor cannot, therefore, owe its effect to ambiguity of this sort.[2]

Another brand of ambiguity may appear to offer a better suggestion. Sometimes a word will, in a single context, bear two meanings where we are meant to remember and to use both. Or, if we think of wordhood as implying sameness of meaning, then we may describe the situation as one in which what appears as a single word is in fact two. When Shakespeare's Cressida is welcomed bawdily into the Grecian camp, Nestor says, 'Our general doth salute you with a kiss.' Here we are to take 'general' two ways: once as applying to Agamemnon, who is

---

[2] Nelson Goodman says metaphor and ambiguity differ chiefly 'in that the several uses of a merely ambiguous term are coeval and independent' while in metaphor 'a term with an extension established by habit is applied elsewhere under the influence of that habit'; he suggests that as our sense of the history of the 'two uses' in metaphor fades, the metaphorical word becomes merely ambiguous (*Languages of Art*, 71). In fact in many cases of ambiguity, one use springs from the other (as Goodman says) and so cannot be coeval. But the basic error, which Goodman shares with others, is the idea that two 'uses' are involved in metaphor in anything like the way they are in ambiguity.

the general; and once, since she is kissing everyone, as applying to no one in particular, but everyone in general. We really have a conjunction of two sentences: our general, Agamemnon, salutes you with a kiss; and everyone in general is saluting you with a kiss.

This is a legitimate device, a pun, but it is not the same device as metaphor. For in metaphor there is no essential need of reiteration; whatever meanings we assign the words, they keep through every correct reading of the passage.

A plausible modification of the last suggestion would be to consider the key word (or words) in a metaphor as having two different kinds of meaning at once, a literal and a figurative meaning. Imagine the literal meaning as latent, something that we are aware of, that can work on us without working in the context, while the figurative meaning carries the direct load. And finally, there must be a rule which connects the two meanings, for otherwise the explanation lapses into a form of the ambiguity theory. The rule, at least for many typical cases of metaphor, says that in its metaphorical role the word applies to everything that it applies to in its literal role, and then some.[3]

This theory may seem complex, but it is strikingly similar to what Frege proposed to account for the behaviour of referring terms in modal sentences and sentences about propositional attitudes like belief and desire. According to Frege, each referring term has two (or more) meanings, one which fixes its reference in ordinary contexts and another which fixes its reference in the special contexts created by modal operators or psychological verbs. The rule connecting the two meanings may be put like this: the meaning of the word in the special contexts makes the reference in those contexts to be identical with the meaning in ordinary contexts.

Here is the whole picture, putting Frege together with a Fregean view of metaphor: we are to think of a word as having, in addition to its mundane field of application or reference, two special or supermundane fields of application, one for metaphor and the other for model contexts and the like. In both cases the original meaning remains to do its work by virtue of a rule which relates the various meanings.

Having stressed the possible analogy between metaphorical meaning and the Fregean meanings for oblique contexts, I turn to an imposing difficulty in maintaining the analogy. You are entertaining a visitor from Saturn by trying to teach him to use the word 'floor'. You go through the familiar dodges, leading him from floor to floor, pointing and stamping and repeating the word. You prompt him to make experiments, tapping objects tentatively with his tentacle while rewarding his right and wrong tries. You want him to come out knowing not only that these particular objects or surfaces are floors but also how to tell a floor when one is in sight or touch. The skit you are putting on doesn't *tell* him what he needs to know, but with luck it helps him to learn it.

---

[3] The theory described is essentially that of Paul Henle, 'Metaphor'.

Should we call this process learning something about the world or learning something about language? An odd question, since what is learned is that a bit of language refers to a bit of the world. Still, it is easy to distinguish between the business of learning the meaning of a word and using the word once the meaning is learned. Comparing these two activities, it is natural to say that the first concerns learning something about language, while the second is typically learning something about the world. If your Saturnian has learned how to use the word 'floor', you may try telling him something new, that *here* is a floor. If he has mastered the word trick, you have told him something about the world.

Your friend from Saturn now transports you through space to his home sphere, and looking back remotely at earth you say to him, nodding at the earth, 'floor'. Perhaps he will think this is still part of the lesson and assume that the word 'floor' applies properly to the earth, at least as seen from Saturn. But what if you thought he already knew the meaning of 'floor', and you were remembering how Dante, from a similar place in the heavens, saw the inhabited earth as 'the small round floor that makes us passionate'? Your purpose was metaphor, not drill in the use of language. What difference would it make to your friend which way he took it? With the theory of metaphor under consideration, very little difference, for according to that theory a word has a new meaning in a metaphorical context; the occasion of the metaphor would, therefore, be the occasion for learning the new meaning. We should agree that in some ways it makes relatively little difference whether, in a given context, we think a word is being used metaphorically or in a previously unknown, but literal way. Empson, in *Some Versions of Pastoral*, quotes these lines from Donne: 'As our blood labours to beget/Spirits, as like souls as it can, . . . / So must pure lover's soules descend. . . .' The modern reader is almost certain, Empson points out, to take the word 'spirits' in this passage metaphorically, as applying only by extension to something spiritual. But for Donne there was no metaphor. He writes in his *Sermons*, 'The Spirits . . . are the thin and active parts of the blood, and are a kind of middle nature, between soul and body.' Learning this does not matter much; Empson is right when he says, 'It is curious how the change in the word [that is, in what we think it means] leaves the poetry unaffected.'[4]

The change may be, in some cases at least, hard to appreciate; but unless there is a change, most of what is thought to be interesting about metaphor is lost. I have been making the point by contrasting learning a new use for an old word with using a word already understood; in one case, I said, our attention is directed to language, in the other, to what language is about. Metaphor, I suggested, belongs in the second category. This can also be seen by considering dead metaphors. Once upon a time, I suppose, rivers and bottles did not, as they do now, literally have mouths. Thinking of present usage, it doesn't matter whether we take the word 'mouth' to be ambiguous because it applies to

---

[4] W. Empson, *Some Versions of Pastoral*, 133.

entrances to rivers and openings of bottles as well as to animal apertures, or we think there is a single wide field of application that embraces both. What does matter is that when 'mouth' applied only metaphorically to bottles, the application made the hearer *notice* a likeness between animal and bottle openings. (Consider Homer's reference to wounds as mouths.) Once one has the present use of the word, with literal application to bottles, there is nothing left to notice. There is no similarity to seek because it consists simply in being referred to by the same word.

Novelty is not the issue. In its context a word once taken for a metaphor remains a metaphor on the hundredth hearing, while a word may easily be appreciated in a new literal role on a first encounter. What we call the element of novelty or surprise in a metaphor is a built-in aesthetic feature we can experience again and again, like the surprise in Haydn's Symphony No. 94, or a familiar deceptive cadence.

If metaphor involved a second meaning, as ambiguity does, we might expect to be able to specify the special meaning of a word in a metaphorical setting by waiting until the metaphor dies. The figurative meaning of the living metaphor should be immortalized in the literal meaning of the dead. But although some philosophers have suggested this idea, it seems plainly wrong. 'He was burned up' is genuinely ambiguous (since it may be true in one sense and false in another), but although the slangish idiom is no doubt the corpse of a metaphor, 'He was burned up' now suggests no more than that he was very angry. When the metaphor was active, we would have pictured fire in the eyes or smoke coming out of the ears.

We can learn much about what metaphors mean by comparing them with similes, for a simile tells us, in part, what a metaphor merely nudges us into noting. Suppose Goneril had said, thinking of Lear, 'Old fools are like babes again'; then she would have used the words to assert a similarity between old fools and babes. What she did say, of course, was 'Old fools are babes again', thus using the words to intimate what the simile declared. Thinking along these lines may inspire another theory of the figurative or special meaning of metaphors: the figurative meaning of a metaphor is the literal meaning of the corresponding simile. Thus 'Christ was a chronometer' in its figurative sense is synonymous with 'Christ was like a chronometer', and the metaphorical meaning once locked up in 'He was burned up' is released in 'He was like someone who was burned up' (or perhaps 'He was like burned up').

There is, to be sure, the difficulty of identifying the simile that corresponds to a given metaphor. Virginia Woolf said that a highbrow is 'a man or woman of thoroughbred intelligence who rides his mind at a gallop across country in pursuit of an idea'. What simile corresponds? Something like this, perhaps: 'A highbrow is a man or woman whose intelligence is like a thoroughbred horse and who persists in thinking about an idea like a rider galloping across country in pursuit of . . . well, something.'

The view that the special meaning of a metaphor is identical with the literal meaning of a corresponding simile (however 'corresponding' is spelled out) should not be confused with the common theory that a metaphor is an elliptical simile.[5] This theory makes no distinction in meaning between a metaphor and some related simile and does not provide any ground for speaking of figurative, metaphorical, or special meanings. It is a theory that wins hands down so far as simplicity is concerned, but it also seems too simple to work. For if we make the literal meaning of the metaphor to be the literal meaning of a matching simile, we deny access to what we originally took to be the literal meaning of the metaphor, and we agreed almost from the start that *this* meaning was essential to the working of the metaphor, whatever else might have to be brought in in the way of a non-literal meaning.

Both the elliptical simile theory of metaphor and its more sophisticated variant, which equates the figurative meaning of the metaphor with the literal meaning of a simile, share a fatal defect. They make the hidden meaning of the metaphor all too obvious and accessible. In each case the hidden meaning is to be found simply by looking to the literal meaning of what is usually a painfully trivial simile. This is like that—Tolstoy like an infant, the earth like a floor. It is trivial because everything is like everything, and in endless ways. Metaphors are often very difficult to interpret and, so it is said, impossible to paraphrase. But with this theory, interpretation and paraphrase typically are ready to the hand of the most callow.

These simile theories have been found acceptable, I think, only because they have been confused with a quite different theory. Consider this remark by Max Black:

When Schopenhauer called a geometrical proof a mousetrap, he was, according to such a view, *saying* (though not explicitly): 'A geometrical proof is *like* a mousetrap, since both offer a delusive reward, entice their victims by degrees, lead to disagreeable surprise, etc.' This is a view of metaphor as a condensed or elliptical *simile*.[6]

Here I discern two confusions. First, if metaphors are elliptical similes, they say *explicitly* what similes say, for ellipsis is a form of abbreviation, not of paraphrase or indirection. But, and this is the more important matter, Black's statement of what the metaphor says goes far beyond anything given by the corresponding simile. The simile simply says a geometrical proof is like a mousetrap. It no more *tells* us what similarities we are to notice than the metaphor does. Black mentions three similarities, and of course we could go on adding to the list forever. But is this list, when revised and supplemented in the right way, supposed to give the *literal* meaning of the simile? Surely not, since the simile declared no more than the similarity. If the list is supposed to provide the figurative meaning of the

---

[5] J. Middleton Murray says a metaphor is a 'compressed simile' (*Countries of the Mind*, 3). Max Black attributes a similar view to Alexander Bain, *English Composition and Rhetoric*.

[6] M. Black, 'Metaphor', 35.

simile, then we learn nothing about metaphor from the comparison with simile—only that both have the same figurative meaning. Nelson Goodman does indeed claim that 'the difference between simile and metaphor is negligible', and he continues, 'Whether the locution be "is like" or "is", the figure *likens* picture to person by picking out a certain common feature. . . .'[7] Goodman is considering the difference between saying a picture is sad and saying it is like a sad person. It is clearly true that both sayings liken picture to person, but it seems to me a mistake to claim that either way of talking 'picks out' a common feature. The simile says there is a likeness and leaves it to us to pick out some common feature or features; the metaphor does not explicitly assert a likeness, but if we accept it as a metaphor, we are again led to seek common features (not necessarily the same features the associated simile suggests; but that is another matter).

Just because a simile wears a declaration of similitude on its sleeve, it is, I think, far less plausible than in the case of metaphor to maintain that there is a hidden second meaning. In the case of simile, we note what it literally says, that two things resemble one another; we then regard the objects and consider what similarity would, in the context, be to the point. Having decided, we might then say the author of the simile intended us—that is, meant us—to notice that similarity. But having appreciated the difference between what the words meant and what the author accomplished by using those words, we should feel little temptation to explain what has happened by endowing the words themselves with a second, or figurative, meaning. The point of the concept of linguistic meaning is to explain what can be done with words. But the supposed figurative meaning of a simile explains nothing; it is not a feature of the word that the word has prior to and independent of the context of use, and it rests upon no linguistic customs except those that govern ordinary meaning.

What words do do with their literal meaning in simile must be possible for them to do in metaphor. A metaphor directs attention to the same sorts of similarity, if not the same similarities, as the corresponding simile. But then the unexpected or subtle parallels and analogies it is the business of metaphor to promote need not depend, for their promotion, on more than the literal meanings of words.

Metaphor and simile are merely two among endless devices that serve to alert us to aspects of the world by inviting us to make comparisons. I quote a few stanzas of T. S. Eliot's 'The Hippopotamus':

> The broad-backed hippopotamus
> Rests on his belly in the mud;
> Although he seems so firm to us
> He is merely flesh and blood.

> Flesh and blood is weak and frail,
> Susceptible to nervous shock;

---

[7] N. Goodman, *Languages of Art*, 77–8.

> While the True Church can never fail
> For it is based upon a rock.
>
> The hippo's feeble steps may err
> In compassing material ends,
> While the True Church need never stir
> To gather in its dividends.
>
> The 'potamus can never reach
> The mango on the mango-tree;
> But fruits of pomegranate and peach
> Refresh the Church from over sea.[8]

Here we are neither told that the Church resembles a hippopotamus (as in simile) nor bullied into making this comparison (as in metaphor), but there can be no doubt the words are being used to direct our attention to similarities between the two. Nor should there be much inclination, in this case, to posit figurative meanings, for in what words or sentences would we lodge them? The hippopotamus really does rest on his belly in the mud; the True Church, the poem says literally, never can fail. The poem does, of course; intimate much that goes beyond the literal meaning of the words. But intimation is not meaning.

The argument so far has led to the conclusion that as much of metaphor as can be explained in terms of meaning may, and indeed must, be explained by appeal to the literal meanings of words. A consequence is that the sentences in which metaphors occur are true or false in a normal, literal way, for if the words in them don't have special meanings, sentences don't have special truth. This is not to deny that there is such a thing as metaphorical truth, only to deny it of sentences. Metaphor does lead us to notice what might not otherwise be noticed, and there is no reason, I suppose, not to say these visions, thoughts, and feelings inspired by the metaphor are true or false.

If a sentence used metaphorically is true or false in the ordinary sense, then it is clear that it is usually false. The most obvious semantic difference between simile and metaphor is that all similes are true and most metaphors are false. The earth is like a floor, the Assyrian did come down like a wolf on the fold, because everything is like everything. But turn these sentences into metaphors, and you turn them false; the earth is like a floor, but it is not a floor; Tolstoy, grown up, was like an infant, but he wasn't one. We use a simile ordinarily only when we know the corresponding metaphor to be false. We say Mr S is like a pig because we know he isn't one. If we had used a metaphor and said he was a pig, this would not be because we changed our mind about the facts but because we chose to get the idea across a different way.

What matters is not actual falsehood but that the sentence be taken to be false. Notice what happens when a sentence we use as a metaphor, believing it false, comes to be thought true because of a change in what is believed about the world.

[8] T. S. Eliot, *Selected Poems*.

When it was reported that Hemingway's plane had been sighted, wrecked, in Africa, the New York *Mirror* ran a headline saying, 'Hemingway Lost in Africa', the word 'lost' being used to suggest he was dead. When it turned out he was alive, the *Mirror* left the headline to be taken literally. Or consider this case: a woman sees herself in a beautiful dress and says, 'What a dream of a dress!'—and then wakes up. The point of the metaphor is that the dress is like a dress one would dream of and therefore isn't a dream-dress. Henle provides a good example from *Antony and Cleopatra* (2.2):

> The barge she sat in, like a burnish'd throne
> Burn'd on the water

Here simile and metaphor interact strangely, but the metaphor would vanish if a literal conflagration were imagined. In much the same way the usual effect of a simile can be sabotaged by taking the comparison too earnestly. Woody Allen writes, 'The trial, which took place over the following weeks, was like a circus, although there was some difficulty getting the elephants into the courtroom'.[9]

Generally it is only when a sentence is taken to be false that we accept it as a metaphor and start to hunt out the hidden implication. It is probably for this reason that most metaphorical sentences are *patently* false, just as all similes are trivially true. Absurdity or contradiction in a metaphorical sentence guarantees we won't believe it and invites us, under proper circumstances, to take the sentence metaphorically.

Patent falsity is the usual case with metaphor, but on occasion patent truth will do as well. 'Business is business' is too obvious in its literal meaning to be taken as having been uttered to convey information, so we look for another use; Ted Cohen reminds us, in the same connection, that no man is an island.[10] The point is the same. The ordinary meaning in the context of use is odd enough to prompt us to disregard the question of literal truth.

Now let me raise a somewhat Platonic issue by comparing the making of a metaphor with telling a lie. The comparison is apt because lying, like making a metaphor, concerns not the meaning of words but their use. It is sometimes said that telling a lie entails what is false; but this is wrong. Telling a lie requires not that what you say be false but that you think it false. Since we usually believe true sentences and disbelieve false, most lies are falsehoods; but in any particular case this is an accident. The parallel between making a metaphor and telling a lie is emphasized by the fact that the same sentence can be used, with meaning unchanged, for either purpose. So a woman who believed in witches but did not think her neighbour a witch might say, 'She's a witch', meaning it metaphorically; the same woman, still believing the same of witches and her

---

[9] Woody Allen, 'Condemned'.
[10] T. Cohen, 'Figurative Speech and Figurative Acts', 671. Since the negation of a metaphor seems always to be a potential metaphor, there may be as many platitudes among the potential metaphors as there are absurds among the actuals.

neighbour but intending to deceive, might use the same words to very different effect. Since sentence and meaning are the same in both cases, it is sometimes hard to prove which intention lay behind the saying of it; thus a man who says 'Lattimore's a Communist' and means to lie can always try to beg off by pleading a metaphor.

What makes the difference between a lie and a metaphor is not a difference in the words used or what they mean (in any strict sense of meaning) but in how the words are used. Using a sentence to tell a lie and using it to make a metaphor are, of course, totally different uses, so different that they do not interfere with one another, as say, acting and lying do. In lying, one must make an assertion so as to represent oneself as believing what one does not; in acting, assertion is excluded. Metaphor is careless of the difference. It can be an insult, and so be an assertion, to say to a man 'You are a pig'. But no metaphor was involved when (let us suppose) Odysseus addressed the same words to his companions in Circe's palace; a story, to be sure, and so no assertion—but the word, for once, was used literally of men.

No theory of metaphorical meaning or metaphorical truth can help explain how metaphor works. Metaphor runs on the same familiar linguistic tracks that the plainest sentences do; this we saw from considering simile. What distinguishes metaphor is not meaning but use—in this it is like assertion, hinting, lying, promising, or criticizing. And the special use to which we put language in metaphor is not—cannot be—to 'say something' special, no matter how indirectly. For a metaphor *says* only what shows on its face—usually a patent falsehood or an absurd truth. And this plain truth or falsehood needs no paraphrase—its meaning is given in the literal meaning of the words.

What are we to make, then, of the endless energy that has been, and is being, spent on methods and devices for drawing out the content of a metaphor? The psychologists Robert Verbrugge and Nancy McCarrell tell us that:

Many metaphors draw attention to common systems of relationships or common transformations, in which the identity of the participants is secondary. For example, consider the sentences: *A car is like an animal, Tree trunks are straws for thirsty leaves and branches.* The first sentence directs attention to systems of relationships among energy consumption, respiration, self-induced motion, sensory systems, and, possibly a homunculus. In the second sentence, the resemblance is a more constrained type of transformation: suction of fluid through a vertically oriented cylindrical space from a source of fluid to a destination.[11]

Verbrugge and McCarrell don't believe there is any sharp line between the literal and metaphorical uses of words; they think many words have a 'fuzzy' meaning that gets fixed, if fixed at all, by a context. But surely this fuzziness, however it is illustrated and explained, cannot erase the line between what a

---

[11] R. R. Verbrugge and N. S. McCarrell, 'Metaphoric Comprehension: Studies in Reminding and Resembling', 499.

sentence literally means (given its context) and what it 'draws our attention to' (given its literal meaning as fixed by the context). The passage I have quoted is not employing such a distinction: what it says the sample sentences direct our attention to are facts expressed by paraphrases of the sentences. Verbrugge and McCarrell simply want to insist that a correct paraphrase may emphasize 'systems of relationships' rather than resemblances between objects.

According to Black's interaction theory, a metaphor makes us apply a 'system of commonplaces' associated with the metaphorical word to the subject of the metaphor: in 'Man is a wolf' we apply commonplace attributes (stereotypes) of the wolf to man. The metaphor, Black says, thus 'selects, emphasizes, suppresses, and organizes features of the principal subject by implying statements about it that normally apply to the subsidiary subject'.[12] If paraphrase fails, according to Black, it is not because the metaphor does not have a special cognitive content, but because the paraphrase 'will not have the same power to inform and enlighten as the original. . . . One of the points I most wish to stress is that the loss in such cases is a loss in cognitive content; the relevant weakness of the literal paraphrase is not that it may be tiresomely prolix or boringly explicit; it fails to be a translation because it fails to give the insight that the metaphor did.'[13]

How can this be right? If a metaphor has a special cognitive content, why should it be so difficult or impossible to set it out? If, as Owen Barfield claims, a metaphor 'says one thing and means another', why should it be that when we try to get explicit about what it means, the effect is so much weaker—'put it that way', Barfield says, 'and nearly all the tanning, and with it half the poetry, is lost.'[14] Why does Black think a literal paraphrase 'inevitably says too much—and with the wrong emphasis'? Why inevitably? Can't we, if we are clever enough, come as close as we please?

For that matter, how is it that a simile gets along without a special intermediate meaning? In general, critics do not suggest that a simile says one thing and means another—they do not suppose it *means* anything but what lies on the surface of the words. It may make us think deep thoughts, just as a metaphor does; how come, then, no one appeals to the 'special cognitive content' of the simile? And remember Eliot's hippopotamus; there there was neither simile nor metaphor, but what seemed to get done was just like what gets done by similes and metaphors. Does anyone suggest that the *words* in Eliot's poem have special meanings?

Finally, if words in metaphor bear a coded meaning, how can this meaning differ from the meaning those same words bear in the case where the metaphor *dies*—that is, when it comes to be part of the language? Why doesn't 'He was burned up' as now used and meant mean *exactly* what the fresh metaphor once

---

[12] M. Black, 'Metaphor', 44–5.   [13] Ibid., 46.
[14] O. Barfield, 'Poetic Diction and Legal Fiction', 55.

meant? Yet all that the dead metaphor means is that he was very angry—a notion not very difficult to make explicit.

There is, then, a tension in the usual view of metaphor. For on the one hand, the usual view wants to hold that a metaphor does something no plain prose can possibly do and, on the other hand, it wants to explain what a metaphor does by appealing to a cognitive content—just the sort of thing plain prose is designed to express. As long as we are in this frame of mind, we must harbour the suspicion that it *can* be done, at least up to a point.

There is a simple way out of the impasse. We must give up the idea that a metaphor carries a message, that it has a content or meaning (except, of course, its literal meaning). The various theories we have been considering mistake their goal. Where they think they provide a method for deciphering an encoded content, they actually tell us (or try to tell us) something about the *effects* metaphors have on us. The common error is to fasten on the contents of the thoughts a metaphor provokes and to read these contents into the metaphor itself. No doubt metaphors often make us notice aspects of things we did not notice before; no doubt they bring surprising analogies and similarities to our attention; they do provide a kind of lens or lattice, as Black says, through which we view the relevant phenomena. The issue does not lie here but in the question of how the metaphor is related to what it makes us see.

It may be remarked with justice that the claim that a metaphor provokes or invites a certain view of its subject rather than saying it straight out is a commonplace; so it is. Thus Aristotle says metaphor leads to a 'perception of resemblances'. Black, following Richards, says a metaphor 'evokes' a certain response: 'a suitable hearer will be led by a metaphor to construct a . . . system.'[15] This view is neatly summed up by what Heracleitus said of the Delphic oracle: 'It does not say and it does not hide, it intimates.'[16]

I have no quarrel with these descriptions of the effects of metaphor, only with the associated views as to *how* metaphor is supposed to produce them. What I deny is that metaphor does its work by having a special meaning, a specific cognitive content. I do not think, as Richards does, that metaphor produces its result by having a meaning which results from the interaction of two ideas; it is wrong, in my view, to say, with Owen Barfield, that a metaphor 'says one thing and means another'; or with Black that a metaphor asserts or implies certain complex things by dint of a special meaning and *thus* accomplishes its job of yielding an 'insight'. A metaphor does its work through other intermediaries—to suppose it can be effective only by conveying a coded message is like thinking a joke or a dream makes some statement which a clever interpreter can restate in plain prose. Joke or dream or metaphor can, like a picture or a bump on

---

[15] M. Black, 'Metaphor', 41.

[16] I use Hannah Arendt's attractive translation of '$\sigma\eta\mu\alpha\acute{\iota}\nu\epsilon\iota$'; it clearly should not be rendered as 'means' in this context.

the head, make us appreciate some fact—but not by standing for, or expressing, the fact.

If this is right, what we attempt in 'paraphrasing' a metaphor cannot be to give its meaning, for that lies on the surface; rather we attempt to evoke what the metaphor brings to our attention. I can imagine someone granting this and shrugging it off as no more than an insistence on restraint in using the word 'meaning'. This would be wrong. The central error about metaphor is most easily attacked when it takes the form of a theory of metaphorical meaning, but behind that theory, and statable independently, is the thesis that associated with a metaphor is a definite cognitive content that its author wishes to convey and that the interpreter must grasp if he is to get the message. This theory is false as a full account of metaphor, whether or not we call the purported cognitive content a meaning.

It should make us suspect the theory that it is so hard to decide, even in the case of the simplest metaphors, exactly what the content is supposed to be. The reason it is often so hard to decide is, I think, that we imagine there is a content to be captured when all the while we are in fact focusing on what the metaphor makes us notice. If what the metaphor makes us notice were finite in scope and propositional in nature, this would not in itself make trouble; we would simply project the content the metaphor brought to mind on to the metaphor. But in fact there is no limit to what a metaphor calls to our attention, and much of what we are caused to notice is not propositional in character. When we try to say what a metaphor 'means', we soon realize there is no end to what we want to mention.[17] If someone draws his finger along a coastline on a map, or mentions the beauty and deftness of a line in a Picasso etching, how many things are drawn to your attention? You might list a great many, but you could not finish since the idea of finishing would have no clear application. How many facts or propositions are conveyed by a photograph? None, an infinity, or one great unstatable fact? Bad question. A picture is not worth a thousand words, or any other number. Words are the wrong currency to exchange for a picture.

It's not only that we can't provide an exhaustive catalogue of what has been attended to when we are led to see something in a new light; the difficulty is more fundamental. What we notice or see is not, in general, propositional in character. Of course it *may* be, and when it is, it usually may be stated in fairly plain words. But if I show you Wittgenstein's duck-rabbit, and I say, 'It's a duck', then with luck you see it as a duck; if I say, 'It's a rabbit', you see it as a rabbit. But no

---

[17] Stanley Cavell mentions the fact that most attempts at paraphrase end with 'and so on' and refers to Empson's remark that metaphors are 'pregnant' ('Aesthetic Problems of Modern Philosophy', 79). But Cavell doesn't explain the endlessness of paraphrase as I do, as can be learned from the fact that he thinks it distinguishes metaphor from some ('but perhaps not all') literal discourse. I hold that the endless character of what we call the paraphrase of a metaphor springs from the fact that it attempts to spell out what the metaphor makes us notice, and to this there is no clear end. I would say the same for any use of language.

proposition expresses what I have led you to see. Perhaps you have come to realize that the drawing can be seen as a duck or as a rabbit. But one could come to know this without ever seeing the drawing as a duck or as a rabbit. Seeing as is not seeing that. Metaphor makes us see one thing as another by making some literal statement that inspires or prompts the insight. Since in most cases what the metaphor prompts or inspires is not entirely, or even at all, recognition of some truth or fact, the attempt to give literal expression to the content of the metaphor is simply misguided.

The theorist who tries to explain a metaphor by appealing to a hidden message, like the critic who attempts to state the message, is then fundamentally confused. No such explanation or statement can be forthcoming because no such message exists.

Not, of course, that interpretation and elucidation of a metaphor are not in order. Many of us need help if we are to see what the author of a metaphor wanted us to see and what a more sensitive or educated reader grasps. The legitimate function of so-called paraphrase is to make the lazy or ignorant reader have a vision like that of the skilled critic. The critic is, so to speak, in benign competition with the metaphor maker. The critic tries to make his own art easier or more transparent in some respects than the original, but at the same time he tries to reproduce in others some of the effects the original had on him. In doing this the critic also, and perhaps by the best method at his command, calls attention to the beauty or aptness, the hidden power, of the metaphor itself.

13

A Coherence Theory of Truth
and Knowledge

In this essay I defend what may as well be called a coherence theory of truth and knowledge. The theory I defend is not in competition with a correspondence theory, but depends for its defense on an argument that purports to show that coherence yields correspondence.

The importance of the theme is obvious. If coherence is a test of truth, there is a direct connection with epistemology, for we have reason to believe many of our beliefs cohere with many others, and in that case we have reason to believe many of our beliefs are true. When the beliefs are true, then the primary conditions for knowledge would seem to be satisfied.

Someone might try to defend a coherence theory of truth without defending a coherence theory of knowledge, perhaps on the ground that the holder of a coherent set of beliefs might lack a reason to believe his beliefs coherent. This is not likely, but it may be that someone, though he has true beliefs, and good reasons for holding them, does not appreciate the relevance of reason to belief. Such a one may best be viewed as having knowledge he does not know he has: he thinks he is a skeptic. In a word, he is a philosopher.

Setting aside aberrant cases, what brings truth and knowledge together is meaning. If meanings are given by objective truth conditions, there is a question how we can know that the conditions are satisfied, for this would appear to require a confrontation between what we believe and reality; and the idea of such a confrontation is absurd. But if coherence is a test of truth, then coherence is a test for judging that objective truth conditions are satisfied, and we no longer need to explain meaning on the basis of possible confrontation. My slogan is: correspondence without confrontation. Given a correct epistemology, we can be realists in all departments. We can accept objective truth conditions as the key to meaning, a realist view of truth, and we can insist that knowledge is of an objective world independent of our thought or language.

Since there is not, as far as I know, a theory that deserves to be called 'the' coherence theory, let me characterize the sort of view I want to defend. It is obvious that not every consistent set of interpreted sentences contains only true sentences, since one such set might contain just the consistent sentence *s* and another just the negation of *s*. And adding more sentences, while maintaining consistency, will not help. We can imagine endless state-descriptions—maximal consistent descriptions—which do not describe our world.

My coherence theory concerns beliefs, or sentences held true by someone who understands them. I do not want to say, at this point, that every possible coherent set of beliefs is true (or contains mostly true beliefs). I shy away from this because it is so unclear what is possible. At one extreme, it might be held that the range of possible maximal sets of beliefs is as wide as the range of possible maximal sets of sentences, and then there would be no point to insisting that a defensible coherence theory concerns beliefs and not propositions or sentences. But there are other ways of conceiving what it is possible to believe which would justify saying not only that all actual coherent belief systems are largely correct but that all possible ones are also. The difference between the two notions of what it is possible to believe depends on what we suppose about the nature of belief, its interpretation, its causes, its holders, and its patterns. Beliefs for me are states of people with intentions, desires, sense organs; they are states that are caused by, and cause, events inside and outside the bodies of their entertainers. But even given all these constraints, there are many things people do believe, and many more that they could. For all such cases, the coherence theory applies.

Of course some beliefs are false. Much of the point of the concept of belief is the potential gap it introduces between what is held to be true and what is true. So mere coherence, no matter how strongly coherence is plausibly defined, cannot guarantee that what is believed is so. All that a coherence theory can maintain is that most of the beliefs in a coherent total set of beliefs are true.

This way of stating the position can at best be taken as a hint, since there is no useful way to count beliefs, and so no clear meaning to the idea that most of a person's beliefs are true. A somewhat better way to put the point is to say there is a presumption in favor of the truth of a belief that coheres with a significant mass of belief. Every belief in a coherent total set of beliefs is justified in the light of this presumption, much as every intentional action taken by a rational agent (one whose choices, beliefs, and desires cohere in the sense of Bayesian decision theory) is justified. So to repeat, if knowledge is justified true belief, then it would seem that all the true beliefs of a consistent believer constitute knowledge. This conclusion, though too vague and hasty to be right, contains an important core of truth, as I shall argue. Meanwhile I merely note the many problems asking for treatment: What exactly does coherence demand? How much of inductive practice should be included, how much of the true theory (if there is one) of evidential support must be in there? Since no person has a completely consistent body of convictions, coherence with *which* beliefs creates a presumption of truth? Some of these problems will be put in better perspective presently.

It should be clear that I do not hope to define truth in terms of coherence and belief. Truth is beautifully transparent compared to belief and coherence, and I take it as a primitive concept. Truth, as applied to utterances of sentences, shows the disquotational feature enshrined in Tarski's Convention T, and that is enough to fix its domain of application. Relative to a language or a speaker, of course, so there is more to truth than Convention T, there is whatever carries over from language to language or speaker to speaker. What Convention T, and the trite sentences it declares true, like ' "Grass is green", spoken by an English speaker, is true if and only if grass is green', reveal is that the truth of an utterance depends on just two things: what the words as spoken mean, and how the world is arranged. There is no further relativism to a conceptual scheme, a way of viewing things, or a perspective. Two interpreters, as unlike in culture, language, and point of view as you please, can disagree over whether an utterance is true, but only if they differ on how things are in the world they share, or what the utterance means.

I think we can draw two conclusions from these simple reflections. First, truth is correspondence with the way things are. (There is no straightforward and nonmisleading way to state this; to get things right, a detour is necessary through the concept of satisfaction in terms of which truth is characterized.[1]) So if a coherence theory of truth is acceptable, it must be consistent with a correspondence theory. Second, a theory of knowledge that allows that we can know the truth must be a nonrelativized, noninternal form of realism. So if a coherence theory of knowledge is acceptable, it must be consistent with such a form of realism. My form of realism seems to be neither Hilary Putnam's internal realism nor his metaphysical realism.[2] It is not internal realism because internal realism makes truth relative to a scheme, and this is an idea I do not think is intelligible.[3] A major reason, in fact, for accepting a coherence theory is the unintelligibility of the dualism of a conceptual scheme and a 'world' waiting to be coped with. But my realism is certainly not Putnam's metaphysical realism, for *it* is characterized by being 'radically non-epistemic', which implies that all our best-researched and -established thoughts and theories may be false. I think the independence of belief and truth requires only that *each* of our beliefs may be false. But of course a coherence theory cannot allow that all of them can be wrong.

But why not? Perhaps it is obvious that the coherence of a belief with a substantial body of belief enhances its chance of being true, provided there is reason to suppose the body of belief is true, or largely so. But how can coherence alone supply grounds for belief? Mayhap the best we can do to justify one belief is to appeal to other beliefs. But then the outcome would seem to be that we must accept philosophical skepticism, no matter how unshaken in practice our beliefs remain.

This is skepticism in one of its traditional garbs. It asks: why couldn't all my beliefs hang together and yet be comprehensively false about the actual world?

---

[1] See my 'True to the Facts', Essay 3 in *Inquiries into Truth and Interpretation*, and 'Afterthoughts' in this volume.   [2] Hilary Putnam, *Meaning and the Moral Sciences*, 125.
[3] See my 'On the Very Idea of a Conceptual Scheme', Essay 13 in *Inquiries into Truth and Interpretation*.

Mere recognition of the fact that it is absurd or worse to try to *confront* our beliefs, one by one, or as a whole, with what they are about does not answer the question nor show the question unintelligible. In short, even a mild coherence theory like mine must provide a skeptic with a reason for supposing coherent beliefs are true. The partisan of a coherence theory can't allow assurance to come from outside the system of belief, while nothing inside can produce support except as it can be shown to rest, finally or at once, on something independently trustworthy.

It is natural to distinguish coherence theories from others by reference to the question whether or not justification can or must come to an end. But this does not define the positions, it merely suggests a form the argument may take. For there are coherence theorists who hold that some beliefs can serve as the basis for the rest, while it would be possible to maintain that coherence is not enough, although giving reasons never comes to an end. What distinguishes a coherence theory is simply the claim that nothing can count as a reason for holding a belief except another belief. Its partisan rejects as unintelligible the request for a ground or source of justification of another ilk. As Rorty has put it, 'nothing counts as justification unless by reference to what we already accept, and there is no way to get outside our beliefs and our language so as to find some test other than coherence'.[4] About this I am, as you see, in agreement with Rorty. Where we differ, if we do, is on whether there remains a question how, given that we cannot 'get outside our beliefs and our language so as to find some test other than coherence', we nevertheless can have knowledge of, and talk about, an objective public world which is not of our own making. I think this question does remain, while I suspect that Rorty doesn't think so. If this is his view, then he must think I am making a mistake in trying to answer the question. Nevertheless, here goes.

It will promote matters at this point to review very hastily some of the reasons for abandoning the search for a basis for knowledge outside the scope of our beliefs. By 'basis' here I mean specifically an epistemological basis, a source of justification.

The attempts worth taking seriously attempt to ground belief in one way or another on the testimony of the senses: sensation, perception, the given, experience, sense data, the passing show. All such theories must explain at least these two things: what, exactly, is the relation between sensation and belief that allows the first to justify the second? and, why should we believe our sensations are reliable, that is, why should we trust our senses?

The simplest idea is to identify certain beliefs with sensations. Thus Hume seems not to have distinguished between perceiving a green spot and perceiving that a spot is green. (An ambiguity in the word 'idea' was a great help here.) Other philosophers noted Hume's confusion, but tried to attain the same results by reducing the gap between perception and judgement to zero by attempting to

---

[4] Richard Rorty, *Philosophy and the Mirror of Nature*, 178.

formulate judgements that do not go beyond stating that the perception or sensation or presentation exists (whatever that may mean). Such theories do not justify beliefs on the basis of sensations, but try to justify certain beliefs by claiming that they have exactly the same epistemic content as a sensation. There are two difficulties with such a view: first, if the basic beliefs do not exceed in content the corresponding sensation, they cannot support any inference to an objective world; and second, there are no such beliefs.

A more plausible line is to claim that we cannot be wrong about how things appear to us to be. If we believe we have a sensation, we do; this is held to be an analytic truth, or a fact about how language is used.

It is difficult to explain this supposed connection between sensations and some beliefs in a way that does not invite skepticism about other minds, and in the absence of an adequate explanation, there should be a doubt about the implications of the connection for justification. But in any case, it is unclear how, on this line, sensations justify the belief in those sensations. The point is rather that such beliefs require no justification, for the existence of the belief entails the existence of the sensation, and so the existence of the belief entails its own truth. Unless something further is added, we are back to another form of coherence theory.

Emphasis on sensation or perception in matters epistemological springs from the obvious thought: sensations are what connect the world and our beliefs, and they are candidates for justifiers because we often are aware of them. The trouble we have been running into is that the justification seems to depend on the awareness, which is just another belief.

Let us try a bolder tack. Suppose we say that sensations themselves, verbalized or not, justify certain beliefs that go beyond what is given in sensation. So, under certain conditions, having the sensation of seeing a green light flashing may justify the belief that a green light is flashing. The problem is to see how the sensation justifies the belief. Of course if someone has the sensation of seeing a green light flashing, it is likely, under certain circumstances, that a green light is flashing. *We* can say this, since we know of his sensation, but *he* can't say it, since we are supposing he is justified without having to depend on believing he has the sensation. Suppose he believed he didn't have the sensation. Would the sensation still justify him in the belief in an objective flashing green light?

The relation between a sensation and a belief cannot be logical, since sensations are not beliefs or other propositional attitudes. What then is the relation? The answer is, I think, obvious: the relation is causal. Sensations cause some beliefs and in *this* sense are the basis or ground of those beliefs. But a causal explanation of a belief does not show how or why the belief is justified.

The difficulty of transmuting a cause into a reason plagues the anticoherentist again if he tries to answer our second question: what justifies the belief that our senses do not systematically deceive us? For even if sensations justify belief in sensation, we do not yet see how they justify belief in external events and objects.

According to Quine, science tells us that 'our only source of information about the external world is through the impact of light rays and molecules upon our sensory surfaces'.[5] What worries me is how to read the words 'source' and 'information'. Certainly it is true that events and objects in the external world cause us to believe things about the external world, and much, if not all, of the causality takes a route through the sense organs. The notion of information, however, applies in a nonmetaphorical way only to the engendered beliefs. So 'source' has to be read simply as 'cause' and 'information' as 'true belief' or 'knowledge'. Justification of beliefs caused by our senses is not yet in sight.

The approach to the problem of justification we have been tracing must be wrong. We have been trying to see it this way: a person has all his beliefs about the world—that is, all his beliefs. How can he tell if they are true, or apt to be true? This is possible, we have been assuming, only by connecting his beliefs to the world, confronting certain of his beliefs with the deliverances of the senses one by one, or perhaps confronting the totality of his beliefs with the tribunal of experience. No such confrontation makes sense, for of course we can't get outside our skins to find out what is causing the internal happening of which we are aware. Introducing intermediate steps or entities into the causal chain, like sensations or observations, serves only to make the epistemological problem more obvious. For if the intermediaries are merely causes, they don't justify the beliefs they cause, while if they deliver information, they may be lying. The moral is obvious. Since we can't swear intermediaries to truthfulness, we should allow no intermediaries between our beliefs and their objects in the world. Of course there are causal intermediaries. What we must guard against are epistemic intermediaries.

There are common views of language that encourage bad epistemology. This is no accident, of course, since theories of meaning are connected with epistemology through attempts to answer the question how one determines that a sentence is true. If knowing the meaning of a sentence (knowing how to give a correct interpretation of it) involves, or is, knowing how it could be recognized to be true, then the theory of meaning raises the same question we have been struggling with, for giving the meaning of a sentence will demand that we specify what

---

[5] W. V. Quine, 'The Nature of Natural Knowledge', 68. Many other passages in Quine suggest that he hopes to assimilate sensory causes to evidence. In *Word and Object*, 22, he writes that 'surface irritations . . . exhaust our clues to an external world'. In *Ontological Relativity*, 75, we find that 'The stimulation of his sensory receptors is all the evidence anybody has had to go on, ultimately, in arriving at his picture of the world.' On the same page: 'Two cardinal tenets of empiricism remain unassailable . . . One is that whatever evidence there *is* for science *is* sensory evidence. The other . . . is that all inculcation of meanings of words, must rest ultimately on sensory evidence.' In *The Roots of Reference*, 37–8, Quine says 'observations' are basic 'both in the support of theory and in the learning of language', and then goes on, 'What are observations? They are visual, auditory, tactual, olfactory. They are sensory, evidently, and thus subjective . . . Should we say then that the observation is not the sensation . . . ? No . . .'. Quine goes on to abandon talk of observations in favor of talk of observation sentences. But of course observation sentences, unlike observations, cannot play the role of evidence unless we have reason to believe they are true.

would justify asserting it. Here the coherentist will hold that there is no use looking for a source of justification outside of other sentences held true, while the foundationalist will seek to anchor at least some words or sentences to non-verbal rocks. This view is held, I think, both by Quine and by Michael Dummett.

Dummett and Quine differ, to be sure. In particular, they disagree about holism, the claim that the truth of our sentences must be tested together rather than one by one. And they disagree also, and consequently, about whether there is a useful distinction between analytic and synthetic sentences, and about whether a satisfactory theory of meaning can allow the sort of indeterminacy Quine argues for. (On all these points, I am Quine's faithful student.)

But what concerns me here is that Quine and Dummett agree on a basic principle, which is that whatever there is to meaning must be traced back somehow to experience, the given, or patterns of sensory stimulation, something intermediate between belief and the usual objects our beliefs are about. Once we take this step, we open the door to skepticism, for we must then allow that a very great many—perhaps most—of the sentences we hold to be true may in fact be false. It is ironical. Trying to make meaning accessible has made truth inaccessible. When meaning goes epistemological in this way, truth and meaning are necessarily divorced. One can, of course, arrange a shotgun wedding by redefining truth as what we are justified in asserting. But this does not marry the original mates.

Take Quine's proposal that whatever there is to the meaning (information value) of an observation sentence is determined by the patterns of sensory stimulation that would cause a speaker to assent to or dissent from the sentence. This is a marvelously ingenious way of capturing what is appealing about verificationist theories without having to talk of meanings, sense data, or sensations; for the first time it made plausible the idea that one could, and should, do what I call the theory of meaning without need of what Quine calls meanings. But Quine's proposal, like other forms of verificationism, makes for skepticism. For clearly a person's sensory stimulations could be just as they are and yet the world outside very different. (Remember the brain in the vat.)

Quine's way of doing without meanings is subtle and complicated. He ties the meanings of some sentences directly to patterns of stimulation (which also constitute the evidence, Quine thinks, for assenting to the sentence), but the meanings of further sentences are determined by how they are conditioned to the original, or observation, sentences. The facts of such conditioning do not permit a sharp division between sentences held true by virtue of meaning and sentences held true on the basis of observation. Quine made this point by showing that if one way of interpreting a speaker's utterances was satisfactory, so were many others. This doctrine of the indeterminacy of translation, as Quine called it, should be viewed as neither mysterious nor threatening. It is no more mysterious than the fact that temperature can be measured in centigrade or Fahrenheit (or any linear transformation of those numbers). And it is not threatening because the very procedure that demonstrates the degree of indeterminacy at the same time demonstrates that what is determinate is all we need.

In my view, erasing the line between the analytic and synthetic saved philosophy of language as a serious subject by showing how it could be pursued without what there cannot be: determinate meanings. I now suggest also giving up the distinction between observation sentences and the rest. For the distinction between sentences belief in whose truth is justified by sensations and sentences belief in whose truth is justified only by appeal to other sentences held true is as anathema to the coherentist as the distinction between beliefs justified by sensations and beliefs justified only by appeal to further beliefs. Accordingly, I suggest we give up the idea that meaning or knowledge is grounded on something that counts as an ultimate source of evidence. No doubt meaning and knowledge depend on experience, and experience ultimately on sensation. But this is the 'depend' of causality, not of evidence or justification.

I have now stated my problem as well as I can. The search for an empirical foundation for meaning or knowledge leads to skepticism, while a coherence theory seems at a loss to provide any reason for a believer to believe that his beliefs, if coherent, are true. We are caught between a false answer to the skeptic, and no answer.

The dilemma is not a true one. What is needed to answer the skeptic is to show that someone with a (more or less) coherent set of beliefs has a reason to suppose his beliefs are not mistaken in the main. What we have shown is that it is absurd to look for a justifying ground for the totality of beliefs, something outside this totality which we can use to test or compare with our beliefs. The answer to our problem must then be to find a *reason* for supposing most of our beliefs are true that is not a form of *evidence*.

My argument has two parts. First I urge that a correct understanding of the speech, beliefs, desires, intentions, and other propositional attitudes of a person leads to the conclusion that most of a person's beliefs must be true, and so there is a legitimate presumption that any one of them, if it coheres with most of the rest, is true. Then I go on to claim that anyone with thoughts, and so in particular anyone who wonders whether he has any reason to suppose he is generally right about the nature of his environment, must know what a belief is, and how in general beliefs are to be detected and interpreted. These being perfectly general facts we cannot fail to use when we communicate with others, or when we try to communicate with others, or even when we merely think we are communicating with others, there is a pretty strong sense in which we can be said to know that there is a presumption in favor of the overall truthfulness of anyone's beliefs, including our own. So it is bootless for someone to ask for some *further* reassurance; that can only add to his stock of beliefs. All that is needed is that he recognize that belief is in its nature veridical.

Belief can be seen to be veridical by considering what determines the existence and contents of a belief. Belief, like the other so-called propositional attitudes, is supervenient on facts of various sorts, behavioral, neurophysiological, biological, and physical. The reason for pointing this out is not to encourage definitional or nomological reduction of psychological phenomena to something more basic, and certainly not to suggest epistemological priorities. The point is rather understanding. We gain one kind of insight into the nature of the propositional attitudes when we relate them systematically to one another and to phenomena on other levels. Since the propositional attitudes are deeply interlocked, we cannot learn the nature of one by first winning understanding of another. As interpreters, we work our way into the whole system, depending much on the pattern of interrelationships.

Take, for example, the interdependence of belief and meaning. What a sentence means depends partly on the external circumstances that cause it to win some degree of conviction; and partly on the relations, grammatical or logical, that the sentence has to other sentences held true with varying degrees of conviction. Since these relations are themselves translated directly into beliefs, it is easy to see how meaning depends on belief. Belief, however, depends equally on meaning, for the only access to the fine structure and individuation of beliefs is through the sentences speakers and interpreters of speakers use to express and describe beliefs. If we want to illuminate the nature of meaning and belief, therefore, we need to start with something that assumes neither. Quine's suggestion, which I shall essentially follow, is to take *prompted assent* as basic, the causal relation between assenting to a sentence and the cause of such assent. This is a fair place to start the project of identifying beliefs and meanings, since a speaker's assent to a sentence depends both on what he means by the sentence and on what he believes about the world. Yet it is possible to know that a speaker assents to a sentence without knowing either what the sentence, as spoken by him, means, or what belief is expressed by it. Equally obvious is the fact that once an interpretation has been given for a sentence assented to, a belief has been attributed. If correct theories of interpretation are not unique (do not lead to uniquely correct interpretations), the same will go for attributions of belief, of course, as tied to acquiescence in particular sentences.

A speaker who wishes his words to be understood cannot systematically deceive his would-be interpreters about when he assents to sentences—that is, holds them true. As a matter of principle, then, meaning, and by its connection with meaning, belief also, are open to public determination. I shall take advantage of this fact in what follows and adopt the stance of a radical interpreter when asking about the nature of belief. What a fully informed interpreter could learn about what a speaker means is all there is to learn; the same goes for what the speaker believes.[6]

---

[6] I now think it is essential, in doing radical interpretation, to include the desires of the speaker from the start, so that the springs of action and intention, both belief and desire, are related to meaning. But in the present essay it is not necessary to introduce this further factor.

The interpreter's problem is that what he is assumed to know—the causes of assents to sentences of a speaker—is, as we have seen, the product of two things he is assumed not to know, meaning and belief. If he knew the meanings he would know the beliefs, and if he knew the beliefs expressed by sentences assented to, he would know the meanings. But how can he learn both at once, since each depends on the other?

The general lines of the solution, like the problem itself, are owed to Quine. I will, however, introduce some changes into Quine's solution, as I have into the statement of the problem. The changes are directly relevant to the issue of epistemological skepticism.

Radical interpretation (which is much, but not entirely, like Quine's radical translation) aims at producing a Tarski-style characterization of truth for the speaker's language, and a theory of his beliefs. (The second follows from the first plus the presupposed knowledge of sentences held true.) This adds little to Quine's program of translation, since translation of the speaker's language into one's own plus a theory of truth for one's own language add up to a theory of truth for the speaker. But the shift to the semantic notion of truth from the syntactic notion of translation puts the formal restrictions of a theory of truth in the foreground, and emphasizes one aspect of the close relation between truth and meaning.

The principle of charity plays a crucial role in Quine's method, and an even more crucial role in my variant. In either case, the principle directs the interpreter to translate or interpret so as to read some of his own standards of truth into the pattern of sentences held true by the speaker. The point of the principle is to make the speaker intelligible, since too great deviations from consistency and correctness leave no common ground on which to judge either conformity or difference. From a formal point of view, the principle of charity helps solve the problem of the interaction of meaning and belief by restraining the degrees of freedom allowed belief while determining how to interpret words.

We have no choice, Quine has urged, but to read our own logic into the thoughts of a speaker; Quine says this for the sentential calculus, and I would add the same for first-order quantification theory. This leads directly to the identification of the logical constants, as well as to the assignment of a logical form to each sentence.

Something like charity operates in the interpretation of those sentences whose causes of assent come and go with time and place: when the interpreter finds a sentence of the speaker the speaker assents to regularly under conditions the interpreter recognizes, the interpreter takes those conditions to be the truth conditions of the speaker's sentence. This is only roughly right, as we shall see in a moment.

Sentences and predicates less directly geared to easily detected goings-on can, in Quine's canon, be interpreted at will, given only the constraints of interconnections with sentences conditioned directly to the world. Here I would extend the principle of charity to favor interpretations that as far as possible preserve truth: I think it makes for mutual understanding, and hence for better interpretation, to interpret what the speaker accepts as true as true when we can. In this matter, I have less choice than Quine, because I do not see how to draw the line between observation sentences and theoretical sentences at the start. There are several reasons for this, but the one most relevant to the present topic is that this distinction is ultimately based on an epistemological consideration of a sort I have renounced: observation sentences are directly based on something like sensation—patterns of sensory stimulation—and this is an idea I have been urging leads to skepticism. Without the direct tie to sensation or stimulation, the distinction between observation sentences and others can't be drawn on epistemologically significant grounds. The distinction between sentences whose causes to assent come and go with observable circumstances and those a speaker clings to through change remains, however, and offers the possibility of interpreting the words and sentences beyond the logical.

The details are not here to the point. What should be clear is that if the account I have given of how belief and meaning are related and understood by an interpreter is right, then most of the sentences a speaker holds to be true—especially the ones he holds to most stubbornly, the ones most central to the system of his beliefs—most of these sentences *are* true, at least in the opinion of the interpreter. For the only, and therefore unimpeachable, method available to the interpreter automatically puts the speaker's beliefs in accord with the standards of logic of the interpreter, and hence credits the speaker with the plain truths of logic. Needless to say, there are degrees of logical and other consistency, and perfect consistency is not to be expected. What needs emphasis is only the methodological necessity for finding consistency enough.

Analogously, it is impossible for an interpreter to understand a speaker and at the same time discover the speaker to be largely wrong about the world. For the interpreter interprets sentences held true (which is not to be distinguished from attributing beliefs) according to the events and objects in the outside world that cause the sentence to be held true.

What I take to be the important aspect of this approach is apt to be missed because the approach reverses our natural way of thinking of communication derived from situations in which understanding has already been secured. Once understanding has been secured, we are able, often, to learn what a person believes quite independently of what caused him to believe it. This may lead us to the crucial, indeed fatal, conclusion that we can in general fix what someone means independently of what he believes and independently of what caused the belief. But if I am right, we can't in general first identify beliefs and meanings and then ask what caused them. The causality plays an indispensable role in determining the content of what we say and believe. This is a fact we can be led to recognize by taking up, as we have, the interpreter's point of view.

It is an artifact of the interpreter's correct interpretation of a person's speech and attitudes that there is a large degree of truth and consistency in the thought and speech of an agent. But this is truth and consistency by the interpreter's standards. Why couldn't it happen that speaker and interpreter understand one another on the basis of shared but erroneous beliefs? This can, and no doubt often does, happen. But it cannot be the rule. For imagine for a moment an interpreter who is omniscient about the world, and about what does and would cause a speaker to assent to any sentence in his (potentially unlimited) repertoire. The omniscient interpreter, using the same method as the fallible interpreter, finds the fallible speaker largely consistent and correct. By his own standards, of course, but since these are objectively correct, the fallible speaker is seen to be largely correct and consistent by objective standards. We may also, if we want, let the omniscient interpreter turn his attention to the fallible interpreter of the fallible speaker. It turns out that the fallible interpreter can be wrong about some things, but not in general; and so he cannot share universal error with the agent he is interpreting. Once we agree to the general method of interpretation I have sketched, it becomes impossible correctly to hold that anyone could be mostly wrong about how things are.

There is, as I noted above, a key difference between the method of radical interpretation I am now recommending, and Quine's method of radical translation. The difference lies in the nature of the choice of causes that govern interpretation. Quine makes interpretation depend on patterns of sensory stimulation, while I make it depend on the external events and objects the sentence is interpreted as being about. Thus Quine's notion of meaning is tied to sensory criteria, something he thinks can be treated also as evidence. This leads Quine to give epistemic significance to the distinction between observation sentences and others, since observation sentences are supposed, by their direct conditioning to the senses, to have a kind of extralinguistic justification. This is the view against which I argued in the first part of my essay, urging that sensory stimulations are indeed part of the causal chain that leads to belief, but cannot, without confusion, be considered to be evidence, or a source of justification, for the stimulated beliefs.

What stands in the way of global skepticism of the senses is, in my view, the fact that we must, in the plainest and methodologically most basic cases, take the objects of a belief to be the causes of that belief. And what we, as interpreters, must take them to be is what they in fact are. Communication begins where causes converge: your utterance means what mine does if belief in its truth is systematically caused by the same events and objects.[7]

---

[7] It is clear that the causal theory of meaning has little in common with the causal theories of reference of Kripke and Putnam. Those theories look to causal relations between names and objects of which speakers may well be ignorant. The chance of systematic error is thus increased. My causal theory does the reverse by connecting the cause of a belief with its object.

The difficulties in the way of this view are obvious, but I think they can be overcome. The method applies directly, at best, only to occasion sentences—the sentences assent to which is caused systematically by common changes in the world. Further sentences are interpreted by their conditioning to occasion sentences, and the appearance in them of words that appear also in occasion sentences. Among occasion sentences, some will vary in the credence they command not only in the face of environmental change, but also in the face of change of credence awarded related sentences. Criteria can be developed on this basis to distinguish degrees of observationality on internal grounds, without appeal to the concept of a basis for belief outside the circle of beliefs.

Related to these problems, and easier still to grasp, is the problem of error. For even in the simplest cases it is clear that the same cause (a rabbit scampers by) may engender different beliefs in speaker and observer, and so encourage assent to sentences which cannot bear the same interpretation. It is no doubt this fact that made Quine turn from rabbits to patterns of stimulation as the key to interpretation. Just as a matter of statistics, I'm not sure how much better one approach is than the other. Is the relative frequency with which identical patterns of stimulation will touch off assent to 'Gavagai' and 'Rabbit' greater than the relative frequency with which a rabbit touches off the same two responses in speaker and interpreter? Not an easy question to test in a convincing way. But let the imagined results speak for Quine's method. Then I must say, what I must say in any case, the problem of error cannot be met sentence by sentence, even at the simplest level. The best we can do is cope with error holistically, that is, we interpret so as to make an agent as intelligible as possible, given his actions, his utterances, and his place in the world. About some things we will find him wrong, as the necessary cost of finding him elsewhere right. As a rough approximation, finding him right means identifying the causes with the objects of his beliefs, giving special weight to the simplest cases, and countenancing error where it can be best explained.

Suppose I am right that an interpreter must so interpret as to make a speaker or agent largely correct about the world. How does this help the person himself who wonders what reason he has to think his beliefs are mostly true? How can he learn about the causal relations between the real world and his beliefs that lead the interpreter to interpret him as being on the right track?

The answer is contained in the question. In order to doubt or wonder about the provenance of his beliefs, an agent must know what belief is. This brings with it the concept of objective truth, for the notion of a belief is the notion of a state that may or may not jibe with reality. But beliefs are also identified, directly and indirectly, by their causes. What an omniscient interpreter knows a fallible interpreter gets right enough if he understands a speaker, and this is just the complicated causal truth that makes us the believers we are, and fixes the contents of our beliefs. The agent has only to reflect on what a belief is to appreciate that most of his basic beliefs are true, and among his beliefs, those most securely held and that cohere with the main body of his beliefs are the most apt to be true. The question 'how do I know my beliefs are generally true?' thus answers itself, simply because beliefs are by nature generally true. Rephrased or expanded, the question becomes, 'How can I tell whether my beliefs, which are by their nature generally true, are generally true?'

All beliefs are justified in this sense: they are supported by numerous other beliefs (otherwise they wouldn't be the beliefs they are), and have a presumption in favor of their truth. The presumption increases the larger and more significant the body of beliefs with which a belief coheres and, there being no such thing as an isolated belief, there is no belief without a presumption in its favor. In this respect, interpreter and interpreted differ. From the interpreter's point of view, methodology enforces a general presumption of truth for the body of beliefs as a whole, but the interpreter does not need to presume each particular belief of someone else is true. The general presumption applied to others does not make them globally right, as I have emphasized, but provides the background against which to accuse them of error. But from each person's own vantage point, there must be a graded presumption in favor of each of his own beliefs.

We cannot, alas, draw the picturesque and pleasant conclusion that all true beliefs constitute knowledge. For though all of a believer's beliefs are to some extent justified to him, some may not be justified enough, or in the right way, to constitute knowledge. The general presumption in favor of the truth of belief serves to rescue us from a standard form of skepticism by showing why it is impossible for all our beliefs to be false together. This leaves almost untouched the task of specifying the conditions of knowledge. I have not been concerned with the canons of evidential support (if such there be), but to show that all that counts as evidence or justification for a belief must come from the same totality of belief to which it belongs.

AFTERTHOUGHTS

A few aging philosophes, which category may include Quine, Putnam, and Dummett, and certainly includes me, are still puzzling over the nature of truth and its connections or lack of connections with meaning and epistemology. Rorty thinks we should stop worrying; he believes philosophy has seen through or outgrown the puzzles and should turn to less heavy and more interesting matters. He is particularly impatient with me for not conceding that the old game is up because he finds in my work useful support for his enlightened stance; underneath my 'out-dated rhetoric' he detects the outlines of a largely correct attitude.

In 'Pragmatism, Davidson, and Truth' Rorty urges two things: that my view of truth amounts to a rejection of both coherence and correspondence theories and should properly be classed as belonging to the pragmatist tradition, and that I should not pretend that I am answering the skeptic when I am really telling him to get lost. I pretty much concur with him on both points.

In our 1983 discussion at the Pacific Division Meeting of the American Philosophical Association I agreed to stop calling my position either a coherence or a correspondence theory if he would give up the pragmatist theory of truth. He has done his part; he now explicitly rejects both James and Peirce on truth. I am glad to hold to my side of the bargain. If it had not already been published, I would now change the title of 'A Coherence Theory of Truth and Knowledge', and I would not describe the project as showing how 'coherence yields correspondence'. On internal evidence alone, as Rorty points out, my view cannot be called a correspondence theory. As long ago as 1969 ('True to the Facts'[8]) I argued that nothing can usefully and intelligibly be said to correspond to a sentence; and I repeated this in 'A Coherence Theory of Truth and Knowledge'. I thought then the fact that in characterizing truth for a language it is necessary to put words into relation with objects was enough to give some grip for the idea of correspondence; but this now seems to me a mistake. The mistake is in a way only a misnomer, but terminological infelicities have a way of breeding conceptual confusion, and so it is here. Correspondence theories have always been conceived as providing an explanation or analysis of truth, and this a Tarski-style theory of truth certainly does not do. I would also now reject the point generally made against correspondence theories that there is no way we could ever tell whether our sentences or beliefs correspond to reality. This criticism is at best misleading, since no one has ever explained in what such a correspondence could consist; and, worse, it is predicated on the false assumption that truth is transparently epistemic.

I also regret having called my view a 'coherence theory'. My emphasis on coherence was properly just a way of making a negative point, that 'all that counts as evidence or justification for a belief must come from the same totality of belief to which it belongs'. Of course this negative claim has typically led those philosophers who held it to conclude that reality and truth are constructs of thought; but it does not lead me to this conclusion, and for this reason if no other I ought not to have called my view a coherence theory. There is also a less weighty reason for not stressing coherence. Coherence is nothing but consistency. It is certainly in favor of a set of beliefs that they are consistent, but there is no chance that a person's beliefs will not tend to be consistent, since beliefs are individuated in part by their logical properties; what is not largely consistent with many other beliefs cannot be identified as a belief. The main thrust of 'A Coherence Theory of Truth and Knowledge' has little to do with consistency; the important thesis for which I argue is that belief is intrinsically veridical. This is the ground on which I maintain that while truth is not an epistemic concept, neither is it wholly

---

[8] Repr. in *Inquiries into Truth and Interpretation*.

severed from belief (as it is in different ways by both correspondence and coherence theories).

My emphasis on coherence was misplaced; calling my view a 'theory' was a plain blunder. In his paper Rorty stressed a minimalist attitude towards truth that he correctly thought we shared. It could be put this way: truth is as clear and basic a concept as we have. Tarski has given us an idea of how to apply the general concept (or try to apply it) to particular languages on the assumption that we already understand it; but of course he didn't show how to define it in general (he proved, rather, that this couldn't be done). Any further attempt to explain, define, analyze, or explicate the concept will be empty or wrong: correspondence theories, coherence theories, pragmatist theories, theories that identify truth with warranted assertability (perhaps under 'ideal' or 'optimum' conditions), theories that ask truth to explain the success of science, or serve as the ultimate outcome of science or the conversations of some élite, all such theories either add nothing to our understanding of truth or have obvious counterexamples. Why on earth should we expect to be able to reduce truth to something clearer or more fundamental? After all, the only concept Plato succeeded in defining was mud (dirt and water). Putnam's comparison of various attempts to characterize truth with the attempts to define 'good' in naturalistic terms seems to me, as it does to Rorty, apt. It also seems to apply to Putnam's identification of truth with idealized warranted assertability.[9]

A theory of truth for a speaker, or group of speakers, while not a definition of the general concept of truth, does give a firm sense of what the concept is good for; it allows us to say, in a compact and clear way, what someone who understands that speaker, or those speakers, knows. Such a theory also invites the question how an interpreter could confirm its truth—a question which without the theory could not be articulated. The answer will, as I try to show in 'A Coherence Theory of Truth and Knowledge', bring out essential relations among the concepts of meaning, truth, and belief. If I am right, each of these concepts requires the others, but none is subordinate to, much less definable in terms of, the others. Truth emerges not as wholly detached from belief (as a correspondence theory would make it) nor as dependent on human methods and powers of discovery (as epistemic theories of truth would make it). What saves truth from being 'radically non-epistemic' (in Putnam's words) is not that truth is epistemic but that belief, through its ties with meaning, is intrinsically veridical.

Finally, how about Rorty's admonition to stop trying to answer the skeptic, and tell him to get lost? A short response would be that the skeptic has been told this again and again over the millennia and never seems to listen; like the philosopher he is, he wants an argument. To spell this out a bit: there is perhaps the suggestion in Rorty's 'Pragmatism, Davidson, and Truth' that a 'naturalistic' approach to the

---

[9] Hilary Putnam, *Realism and Reason*, p. xviii.

problems of meaning and the propositional attitudes will automatically leave the skeptic no room for maneuver. This thought, whether or not it is Rorty's, is wrong. Quine's naturalized epistemology, because it is based on the empiricist premise that what we mean and what we think is conceptually (and not merely causally) founded on the testimony of the senses, is open to standard skeptical attack. I was much concerned in 'A Coherence Theory of Truth and Knowledge' to argue for an alternative approach to meaning and knowledge, and to show that if this alternative were right, skepticism could not get off the ground. I agree with Rorty to this extent; I set out not to 'refute' the skeptic, but to give a sketch of what I think to be a correct account of the foundations of linguistic communication and its implications for truth, belief, and knowledge. If one grants the correctness of this account, one can tell the skeptic to get lost.

Where Rorty and I differ, if we do, is in the importance we attach to the arguments that lead to the skeptic's undoing, and in the interest we find in the consequences for knowledge, belief, truth, and meaning. Rorty wants to dwell on where the arguments have led: to a position which allows us to dismiss the skeptic's doubts, and so to abandon the attempt to provide a general justification for knowledge claims—a justification that is neither possible nor needed. Rorty sees the history of Western philosophy as a confused and victorless battle between unintelligible skepticism and lame attempts to answer it. Epistemology from Descartes to Quine seems to me just one complex, and by no means uni-illuminating, chapter in the philosophical enterprise. If that chapter is coming to a close, it will be through recourse to modes of analysis and adherence to standards of clarity that have always distinguished the best philosophy, and will, with luck and enterprise, continue to do so.

14

First Person Authority

When a speaker avers that he has a belief, hope, desire or intention, there is a presumption that he is not mistaken, a presumption that does not attach to his ascriptions of similar mental states to others. Why should there be this asymmetry between attributions of attitudes to our present selves and attributions of the same attitudes to other selves? What accounts for the authority accorded first person present tense claims of this sort, and denied second or third person claims?

The point may be made, and the question asked, in the modality either of language or of epistemology. For if one can speak with special authority, the status of one's knowledge must somehow accord; while if one's knowledge shows some systematic difference, claims to know must reflect the difference. I assume therefore that if first person authority in speech can be explained, we will have done much, if not all, of what needs to be done to characterize and account for the epistemological facts.

The connection between the problem of first person authority and the traditional problem of other minds is obvious, but as I pose the former problem, there are two important differences. First person authority is the narrower problem, since I shall consider it only as it applies to propositional attitudes like belief, desire, intention; being pleased, astonished, afraid, or proud that something is the case; or knowing, remembering, noticing, or perceiving that something is the case. But I shall not discuss what are often taken to be central to the problem of other minds: pains and other sensations, and knowledge, memory, attention, and perception as directed to objects like people, streets, cities, comets, and other non-propositional entities. What holds for the propositional attitudes ought, it seems, to be relevant to sensations and the rest, but I do not explore the connections here.

All propositional attitudes exhibit first person authority, but in various degrees and kinds. Belief and desire are relatively clear and simple examples, while intention, perception, memory, and knowledge are in one way or another more complex. Thus in evaluating someone's claim to have noticed that the house is on fire, there are at least three things to consider: whether the house is on fire, whether the speaker believes the house is on fire, and how the fire caused the belief. With respect to the first, the speaker has no special authority; with respect to the second, he does; and with respect to the third, responsibility is mixed and complex. The question whether someone intends to lock the door by turning the key depends in part on whether he wants to lock the door and believes that turning the key will lock the door; and whether this belief and desire have caused, in the right way, a desire to turn the key. Special authority attaches directly to claims about the desire and belief, less directly to claims about the necessary causal connection. These differences among the ways in which first person authority may apply to propositional attitudes are important and worth exploring. But in every case, first person authority is relevant, and it is the general case I wish to consider here. Since in almost every instance, if not in all, first person authority rests at least partially on a belief component, I shall concentrate on the case of belief.

Though there is first person authority with respect to beliefs and other propositional attitudes, error is possible; this follows from the fact that the attitudes are dispositions that manifest themselves in various ways, and over a span of time. Error is possible; so is doubt. So we do not always have indubitable or certain knowledge of our own attitudes. Nor are our claims about our own attitudes incorrigible. It is possible for the evidence available to others to overthrow self-judgements.

It comes closer to characterizing first person authority to note that the self-attributer does not normally base his claims on evidence or observation, nor does it normally make sense to ask the self-attributer why he believes he has the beliefs, desires, or intentions he claims to have. This feature of self-attributions was remarked by Wittgenstein: 'What is the criterion for the redness of an image? For me, when it is someone else's image: what he says or does. For myself, when it is my image: nothing.'[1] Most philosophers have followed Wittgenstein in this, and have extended the criterion to the propositional attitudes, as we shall see.

This feature of first person authority, suggestive as it may be, does not help explain the authority. This is so partly because of the caveats—'normally' we do not make self-attributions on the basis of evidence, but sometimes we do; 'usually' it doesn't make sense to ask someone why he believes he has a certain belief or desire or intention, but sometimes it does. Even in the exceptional cases, however, first person authority persists; even when a self-attribution is in doubt, or a challenge is proper, the person with the attitude speaks about it with special weight.

But the existence of exceptions is not the chief reason first person authority isn't explained by the fact that self-attributions are not based on evidence; the chief reason is simply that claims that are not based on evidence do not in general carry more authority than claims that are based on evidence, nor are they more apt to be correct.

Contemporary philosophers who have discussed first person authority have made little attempt to answer the question why self-ascriptions are privileged. It

---

[1] Ludwig Wittgenstein, *Philosophical Investigations*, §377.

is long out of fashion to explain self-knowledge on the basis of introspection. And it is easy to see why, since this explanation leads only to the question why we should see any better when we inspect our own minds than when we inspect the minds of others.

A few philosophers have denied that the asymmetry exists; Ryle is a sturdy example. In *The Concept of Mind* Ryle suggests that what we take for 'privileged access' is due to nothing more than the fact that we are generally better placed to observe ourselves than others are. Ryle writes, 'in principle, as distinct from practice, John Doe's ways of finding out about John Doe are the same as John Doe's ways of finding out about Richard Roe'. He continues,

the differences are differences of degree, not of kind. The superiority of the speaker's knowledge of what he's doing over that of the listener does not indicate that he has Privileged Access to facts of a type inevitably inaccessible to the listener, but only that he is in a very good position to know what the listener is often in a very poor position to know. The turns taken by a man's conversation do not startle or perplex his wife as much as they had surprised and puzzled his fiancée, nor do close colleagues have to explain themselves to each other as much as they have to explain themselves to their new pupils.[2]

I agree with Ryle that any attempt to explain the asymmetry between first person present tense claims about attitudes, and other person or other tense claims, by reference to a special way of knowing or a special kind of knowledge must lead to a skeptical result. Any such account must accept the asymmetry, but cannot explain it. But Ryle neither accepts nor explains the asymmetry; he simply denies that it exists. Since I think it is obvious that the asymmetry exists, I believe it is a mistake to argue from the absence of a special way of knowing or a special mode or kind of knowledge to the absence of special authority; instead, we should look for another source of the asymmetry.

Ayer at one time took a line similar to Ryle's. In *The Concept of a Person* he emphasizes that first person ascriptions can be in error; and he allows that such ascriptions are privileged.[3] But when he comes to describe the authority of self-ascriptions, he compares it to the authority we sometimes allow an eyewitness when compared with secondhand reports. This analogy seems to me unsatisfactory for two reasons. First, it fails to tell us why a person is like an eyewitness with respect to his own mental states and events while others are not. And second, it does not suggest an accurate description of what first person authority is like. For first person attributions are not based on better evidence but often on no evidence at all. The authority of the eyewitness is at best based on inductive probabilities easily overridden in particular cases: an eyewitness is discredited and his evidence discounted if he is a notoriously unreliable observer, prejudiced, or myopic. But a person never loses his special claim to be right about his own attitudes, even when his claim is challenged or overturned.

<hr/>

[2] Gilbert Ryle, *The Concept of Mind*, 156, 179.   [3] A. J. Ayer, 'Privacy'.

Joseph Agassi has actually maintained that we know the mental states and events in other minds better than those in our own mind. He distinguishes privileged access from the commonsense truth that 'every person has access to some information available to that person alone, and it involves one's self, at least as an eye-witness'. He goes on:

The doctrine of privileged access is that I am the authority on all my own experiences . . . The thesis was refuted by Freud (I know your dreams better than you), Duhem (I know your methods of scientific discovery better than you), Malinowski (I know your customs and habits better than you), and perception theorists (I can make you see things which are not there and describe your perceptions better than you can).[4]

Aside from Freud's case, there is little here to threaten first person authority. Freud's views, by extending the concepts of intention, belief, desire, and the rest to include the unconscious, do mean that with respect to some propositional attitudes a person loses direct authority. Indeed, loss of authority is the main distinguishing feature of unconscious mental states. Of course, the pre-Freudian attitudes remain as subject as ever to first person authority. But more interesting is the fact that in psychoanalytic practice, recovery of authority over an attitude is often considered the only solid evidence that the attitude was there before being noninferentially appreciated by its holder. Thus those cases of unconscious mental states that were unsystematically recognized to exist before Freud are indirectly included in the scope of first person authority by psychoanalysis. So I do not think the existence of unconscious attitudes threatens the importance of first person authority.

I turn now to philosophers who have assumed that there is such a thing as first person authority, and have accepted Wittgenstein's description of the difference between first and third person attributions.

Strawson discusses first person authority in the context of trying to answer skepticism about other minds. According to Strawson, if the skeptic understands his own question ('How does anyone know what is going on in someone else's mind?'), he knows the answer. For if the skeptic knows what a mind is, he knows it must be in a body, and that it has thoughts. He also knows that we attribute thoughts to others on the basis of observed behaviour, but to ourselves without such a basis. Strawson writes:

In order to *have* this type of concept [of a mental property], one must be both a self-ascriber and an other-ascriber of such predicates [which ascribe mental properties], and must see every other as a self-ascriber. In order to *understand* this type of concept, one must acknowledge that there is a kind of predicate which is unambiguously and adequately ascribable *both* on the basis of observation of the subject of the predicate *and* not on that basis, i.e. independently of observation of the subject.[5]

⁴ Joseph Agassi, *Science in Flux*, 120.
⁵ Peter Strawson, *Individuals*, 108. (Anita Avramides has pointed out that Strawson has contributed more to this issue than I allow. See her 'Davidson and the New Sceptical Problem'.)

This cannot be deemed a satisfactory answer to the skeptic. For the skeptic will reply that though Strawson may have correctly described the asymmetry between first and other person ascriptions of mental predicates, he has done nothing to explain it. In the absence of an explanation, the skeptic is surely justified in asking how we know that the description is correct. In particular, why should we think that a predicate that is sometimes applied on the basis of observation, and sometimes not, is unambiguous? This question, to which Strawson has not addressed himself, is a major source of skepticism about knowledge of other minds.

Richard Rorty has attempted an explanation. We are asked to imagine that originally self-ascriptions were made on the basis of the same sort of observation or behavioral evidence as other-ascriptions. It was then noticed that people could ascribe mental properties to themselves without making observations or using behavioral evidence, and that self-ascriptions turned out in the long run to provide better explanations of behavior than third person ascriptions. So it became a linguistic convention to treat self-ascriptions as privileged: 'it became a constraint on explanations of behavior that they should fit all reported thoughts or sensations into the overall account being offered'.[6]

This account is not meant to be taken seriously as a piece of folk anthropology, but it is meant to make it seem reasonable that we should treat self-ascriptions as having special authority. But the question remains: what reason has Rorty given to show that self-ascriptions not based on evidence concern the same states and events as ascriptions of the same mental predicates based on observation or evidence? There is a difference in kind in the ways the two sorts of ascription are made, and how they explain behavior is different. What Rorty describes as the discovery that self-ascriptions not based on evidence explain behavior better will be described by the skeptic as the fact that what is being ascribed is on every count apparently different.

It may come as a surprise to realize that the philosophers I am discussing have not really dealt with the ancient problem of skepticism concerning knowledge of other minds. But I think it is easy to explain. Historically the problem has been seen from either a Cartesian or an empiricist point of view, and both venues assume that each person knows what is in his own mind. The problem has therefore seemed to be that of supplying a basis for knowledge of other minds (and, of course, the external world). Philosophers now realize that part of understanding mental concepts (or predicates) consists in knowing what kind of observable behavior justifies the ascription of these concepts to others. But this answer to the skeptic does nothing to explain first person authority, or the asymmetry between self-ascriptions and other-ascriptions. We can still ask why we believe these two sorts of ascription pertain to the same subject matter. And

    [6] Richard Rorty, 'Incorrigibility as the Mark of the Mental', 416. Rorty's account is derived from Wilfred Sellars, 'Empiricism and the Philosophy of Mind'. With respect to the point at issue. Sellars's account does not differ from Rorty's.

this question is a good one, whether or not we recognize its traditional skeptical ancestry.

Perhaps it should be pointed out that no concepts aside from those applying to sensations, propositional attitudes, and the positions of our limbs show the sort of asymmetry we are discussing. Many concepts can be applied on the basis of multiple criteria, but no others are such that ascribers *must*, on particular occasions, use different criteria. If we are to explain this anomaly and avoid an invitation to skepticism, the explanation should point to a natural asymmetry between other observers and ourselves, an asymmetry not simply invented to solve the problem.

The first step towards a solution depends on becoming clear about the entities to which first person authority applies. William Alston proposes this principle to characterize the special status of self-attributions: 'Each person is so related to propositions ascribing current mental states to himself that it is logically impossible both for him to believe that such a proposition is true and not to be justified in holding this belief while no one else is so related to such propositions.'[7]

For this suggestion to be plausible, we must suppose that the proposition Jones expresses by the sentence 'I believe Wagner died happy' is the same proposition as the proposition Smith expresses by the sentence 'Jones believes Wagner died happy.' This is, of course, a highly questionable supposition. Once more, the epistemic contrast goes unexplained; and in the absence of an explanation, the question arises what *reason* one has in any particular case to believe that the proposition entertained by Jones and Smith *is* the same. Given only a description of an epistemic difference, the natural conclusion is that the propositions differ.

I turn, then, to a formulation of Sidney Shoemaker's, which makes explicit mention of language: 'Among the incorrigible statements are statements about . . . mental events, e.g. . . . reports of thoughts . . . These are incorrigible in the sense that if a person sincerely asserts such a statement it does not make sense to suppose, and nothing could be accepted as showing, that he is mistaken; i.e. that what he says is false.'[8]

I shall ignore the incorrigibility condition and substitute something less strong—something that amounts to first person authority. (This is perhaps reasonable, since Shoemaker is mainly concerned with sensations such as pain, while I am exclusively concerned with propositional attitudes.) What is important here is that Shoemaker assigns the presumption of correctness not to a kind of knowledge, but to a class of utterances. This idea might lead to an explanation of first person authority if the class of utterances could be specified in syntactic terms. Unfortunately it cannot. If Shoemaker is right, a speaker who sincerely uses a certain sort of sentence must be presumed to be right in what he

---

[7] William Alston, 'Varieties of Privileged Access', 235.
[8] Sidney Shoemaker, *Self-Knowledge and Self-Identity*, 215–16.

says. But of course this holds only if the speaker knows he is using the privileged sort of sentence; if he is not, he is misusing language. What would constitute a misuse here? Above all, one wants to say, sincerely asserting a sentence one has no special authority to assert. Perhaps so; but this is just to reiterate the uninformative and unexplained claim that it is a convention of language to treat self-ascriptions with special respect. Seen from the point of view of the interpreter, this implies that he should interpret self-ascriptions in such a way as to make them true—or to assign a special priority to their truth. The point of view of the interpreter is the only one we can take, given Shoemaker's principle, and this deprives the principle of independent application: our only reason for saying the speaker has special authority on occasion is that we are prepared to treat his utterance as a self-ascription. In other words, self-ascriptions have special authority: true; and that is where we began.

No satisfactory explanation of the asymmetry between first and other person attributions of attitudes has yet emerged. Still, focusing on sentences and utterances rather than propositions or meanings is a step in a promising direction. The reason for this is relatively simple. As long as we pose the problem in terms of the kind of warrant or authority someone has with respect to claims about an agent's attitude to a proposition (or a sentence with a given interpretation), we seem constrained to account for differences by simply postulating different kinds or sources of information. Alternatively, we may postulate different criteria of application for the key concepts or words ('believes that', 'intends to','wishes that', etc.). But these moves do no more than restate the problem, as we have seen, and thereby invite skepticism about knowledge of the minds of others (or of our own mind). But if we pose the problem in terms of relations between agents and utterances, we can avoid the impasse.

We now need to distinguish two related but different asymmetries. On the one hand, there is the familiar difference between self- and other-attributions of the same attitude to the same person: my claim that I believe Wagner died happy and your claim that I believe Wagner died happy. If these claims are put into words, we have the difficulty of deciding what pairs of utterances are suitably related in order to guarantee that the claims have the 'same content'. On the other hand, we may consider my utterance of the sentence 'I believe Wagner died happy', and then contrast my warrant for thinking I have said something true, and your warrant for thinking I have said something true. These two asymmetries are of course connected since we are inclined to say your warrant for thinking I speak the truth when I say 'I believe Wagner died happy' must be closely related to your warrant for thinking you would be speaking the truth if you said 'Davidson believes Wagner died happy'. But for reasons that will soon be evident, I shall deal with the second version of the asymmetry.

The question then comes to this: what explains the difference in the sort of assurance you have that I am right when I say 'I believe Wagner died happy' and the sort of assurance I have? We know by now that it is no help to say I have access to a way of knowing about my own beliefs that you do not have; nor that we use different criteria in applying the concept of belief (or the word 'believes'). So let us simply consider a shorter utterance of mine: I utter the sentence 'Wagner died happy'. Clearly, if you or I or anyone knows that I hold this sentence true on this occasion of utterance, and she knows what I meant by this sentence on this occasion of utterance, then she knows what I believe—what belief I expressed.

It would once more make the account circular to explain the basic asymmetry by assuming an asymmetry in the assurance you and I have that I hold the sentence I have just uttered to be a true sentence. There must *be* such an asymmetry, of course, but it cannot be allowed to contribute to the desired explanation. But we can assume without prejudice that we both know, whatever the source or nature of our knowledge, that on this occasion I do hold the sentence I uttered to be true. Similarly, it would beg the question to explain the basic asymmetry by appeal to some asymmetry in our knowledge of the fact that I know what my sentence, as uttered on this occasion, meant. So again, let us simply assume we both know this, whatever the source or character of our knowledge.

So far, then, we have not postulated or assumed any asymmetry at all. The assumptions are just these: you and I both know that I held the sentence 'Wagner died happy' to be a true sentence when I uttered it; and that I knew what that sentence meant on the occasion of its utterance. And now there is this difference between us, which is what was to be explained: on these assumptions, I know what I believe, while you may not.

The difference follows, of course, from the fact that the assumption that I know what I mean necessarily gives me, but not you, knowledge of what belief I expressed by my utterance. It remains to show why there must be a presumption that speakers, but not their interpreters, are not wrong about what their words mean. The presumption is essential to the nature of interpretation—the process by which we understand the utterances of a speaker. This process cannot be the same for the utterer and for his hearers.

To put the matter in its simplest form: there can be no general guarantee that a hearer is correctly interpreting a speaker; however easily, automatically, unreflectively, and successfully a hearer understands a speaker, he is liable to serious error. In this special sense, he may always be regarded as interpreting a speaker. The speaker cannot, in the same way, interpret his own words. A hearer interprets (normally without thought or pause) on the basis of many clues: the actions and other words of the speaker, what he assumes about the education, birthplace, wit, and profession of the speaker, the relation of the speaker to objects near and far, and so forth. The speaker, though he must bear many of these things in mind when he speaks, since it is up to him to try to be understood, cannot wonder whether he generally means what he says.

The contrast between the grounds a self-ascriber has for his self-ascription, and the grounds an interpreter has for accepting that same ascription, would be stark if we were to assume that no question can arise concerning a speaker's interpretation of his own words. But of course it can, since what his words mean depends in part on the clues to interpretation he has given the interpreter, or other evidence that he justifiably believes the interpreter has. The speaker can be wrong about what his own words mean. This is one of the reasons first person authority is not infallible. But the possibility of error does not eliminate the asymmetry. The asymmetry rests on the fact that the interpreter must, while the speaker doesn't, rely on what, if it were made explicit, would be a difficult inference in interpreting the speaker.

Neither speaker nor hearer knows in a special or mysterious way what the speaker's words mean; and both can be wrong. But there is a difference. The speaker, after bending whatever knowledge and craft he can to the task of saying what his words mean, cannot improve on the following sort of statement: 'My utterance of "Wagner died happy" is true if and only if Wagner died happy'. An interpreter has no reason to assume this will be *his* best way of stating the truth conditions of the speaker's utterance.

The best way to appreciate this difference is by imagining a situation in which two people who speak unrelated languages, and are ignorant of each other's languages, are left alone to learn to communicate. Deciphering a new language is not like learning a first language, for a true beginner has neither the reasoning power nor the stock of concepts the participants in the imagined situation have to draw on. This does not, however, affect the point I wish to stress, since what my imagined interpreter can treat consciously as evidence is exactly what conditions the first learner to be a language user. Let one of the imagined pair speak and the other try to understand. It will not matter whether the speaker speaks his 'native' tongue, since his past social situation is irrelevant. (I assume the speaker has no interest in training the hearer to cope with the speaker's original speech community.) The best the speaker can do is to be *interpretable*, that is, to use a finite supply of distinguishable sounds applied consistently to objects and situations he believes are apparent to his hearer. Obviously the speaker may fail in this project from time to time; in that case we can say if we please that he does not know what his words mean. But it is equally obvious that the interpreter has nothing to go on but the pattern of sounds the speaker exhibits in conjunction with further events (including, of course, further actions on the part of both speaker and interpreter). It makes no sense in this situation to wonder whether the speaker is generally getting things wrong. His behaviour may simply not be interpretable. But if it is, then what his words mean is (generally) what he intends them to mean. Since the 'language' he is speaking has no other hearers, the idea of the speaker misusing his language has no application. There is a presumption—an unavoidable presumption built into the nature of interpretation—that the speaker usually knows what he means. So there is a presumption that if he knows that he holds a sentence true, he knows what he believes.

15

A Nice Derangement of Epitaphs

Goodman Ace wrote radio sitcoms. According to Mark Singer, Ace often talked the way he wrote:

Rather than take for granite that Ace talks straight, a listener must be on guard for an occasional entre nous and me... or a long face no see. In a roustabout way, he will maneuver until he selects the ideal phrase for the situation, hitting the nail right on the thumb. The careful conversationalist might try to mix it up with him in a baffle of wits. In quest of this pinochle of success, I have often wrecked my brain for a clowning achievement, but Ace's chickens always come home to roast. From time to time, Ace will, in a jersksome way, monotonise the conversation with witticisms too humorous to mention. It's high noon someone beat him at his own game, but I have never done it; cross my eyes and hope to die, he always wins thumbs down.[1]

I quote at length because philosophers have tended to neglect or play down the sort of language-use this passage illustrates. For example, Jonathan Bennett writes,

I doubt if I have ever been present when a speaker did something like shouting 'Water!' as a warning of fire, knowing what 'Water!' means and knowing that his hearers also knew, but thinking that they would expect him to give to 'Water!' the normal meaning of 'Fire!'[2]

Bennett adds that, 'Although such things could happen, they seldom do.' I think such things happen all the time; in fact, if the conditions are generalized in a natural way, the phenomenon is ubiquitous.

Singer's examples are special in several ways. A malapropism does not have to be amusing or surprising. It does not have to be based on a cliché, and of course it does not have to be intentional. There need be no play on words, no hint of deliberate pun. We may smile at someone who says 'Lead the way and we'll precede', or, with Archie Bunker, 'We need a few laughs to break up the monogamy', because he has said something that, given the usual meanings of the words, is ridiculous or fun. But the humour is adventitious.

---

[1] *The New Yorker*, 4 April 1977, p. 56. Reprinted by permission, 1977, The New Yorker Magazine, Inc.
[2] Jonathan Bennett, *Linguistic Behaviour*, Cambridge, 1976, p. 186. Donald Davidson, 1985.

Ace's malaprops generally make some sort of sense when the words are taken in the standard way, as in 'Familiarity breeds attempt', or 'We're all cremated equal', but this is not essential ('the pinochle of success'). What is interesting is the fact that in all these cases the hearer has no trouble understanding the speaker in the way the speaker intends.

It is easy enough to explain this feat on the hearer's part: the hearer realizes that the 'standard' interpretation cannot be the intended interpretation; through ignorance, inadvertence, or design the speaker has used a word similar in sound to the word that would have 'correctly' expressed his meaning. The absurdity or inappropriateness of what the speaker would have meant had his words been taken in the 'standard' way alerts the hearer to trickery or error; the similarity in sound tips him off to the right interpretation. Of course there are many other ways the hearer might catch on; similarity of sound is not essential to the malaprop. Nor for that matter does the general case require that the speaker use a real word: most of 'The Jabberwock' is intelligible on first hearing.

It seems unimportant, so far as understanding is concerned, who makes a mistake, or whether there is one. When I first read Singer's piece on Goodman Ace, I thought that the word 'malaprop', though the name of Sheridan's character, was not a common noun that could be used in place of 'malapropism'. It turned out to be my mistake. Not that it mattered: I knew what Singer meant, even though I was in error about the word; I would have taken his meaning in the same way if he had been in error instead of me. We could both have been wrong and things would have gone as smoothly.

This talk of error or mistake is not mysterious nor open to philosophical suspicions. I was wrong about what a good dictionary would say, or what would be found by polling a pod of experts whose taste or training I trust. But error or mistake of this kind, with its associated notion of correct usage, is not philosophically interesting. We want a deeper notion of what words, when spoken in context, mean; and like the shallow notion of correct usage, we want the deep concept to distinguish between what a speaker, on a given occasion, means, and what his words mean. The widespread existence of malapropisms and their kin threatens the distinction, since here the intended meaning seems to take over from the standard meaning.

I take for granted, however, that nothing should be allowed to obliterate or even blur the distinction between speaker's meaning and literal meaning. In order to preserve the distinction we must, I shall argue, modify certain commonly accepted views about what it is to 'know a language', or about what a natural language is. In particular, we must pry apart what is literal in language from what is conventional or established.

Here is a preliminary stab at characterizing what I have been calling literal meaning. The term is too incrusted with philosophical and other extras to do much work, so let me call what I am interested in *first meaning*. The concept applies to words and sentences as uttered by a particular speaker on a particular occasion. But if the occasion, the speaker, and the audience are 'normal' or 'standard' (in a sense not to be further explained here), then the first meaning of an utterance will be what should be found by consulting a dictionary based on actual usage (such as *Webster's Third*). Roughly speaking, first meaning comes first in the order of interpretation. We have no chance of explaining the image in the following lines, for example, unless we know what 'foison' meant in Shakespeare's day:

> Speak of the spring and foison of the year,
> The one doth shadow of your beauty show,
> The other as your bounty doth appear . . . [3]

Little here is to be taken literally, but unless we know the literal, or first, meaning of the words we do not grasp and cannot explain the image.

But 'the order of interpretation' is not at all clear. For there are cases where we may first guess at the image and so puzzle out the first meaning. This might happen with the word 'tires' in the same sonnet:

> On Helen's cheek all art of beauty set,
> And you in Grecian tires are painted new.

And of course it often happens that we can descry the literal meaning of a word or phrase by first appreciating what the speaker was getting at.

A better way to distinguish first meaning is through the intentions of the speaker. The intentions with which an act is performed are usually unambiguously ordered by the relation of means to ends (where this relation may or may not be causal). Thus the poet wants (let us say) to praise the beauty and generosity of his patron. He does this by using images that say the person addressed takes on every good aspect to be found in nature or in man or woman. This he does in turn by using the word 'tire' to mean 'attire' and the word 'foison' to mean 'harvest'. The order established here by 'by' can be reversed by using the phrase 'in order to'. In the 'in order to' sequence, first meaning is the first meaning referred to. ('With the intention of' with 'ing' added to the verb does as well.)

Suppose Diogenes utters the words 'I would have you stand from between me and the sun' (or their Greek equivalent) with the intention of uttering words that will be interpreted by Alexander as true if and only if Diogenes would have him stand from between Diogenes and the sun, and this with the intention of getting Alexander to move from between him and the sun, and this with the intention of leaving a good anecdote to posterity. Of course these are not the only intentions involved; there will also be the Gricean intentions to achieve certain of these ends through Alexander's recognition of some of the intentions involved. Diogenes' intention to be interpreted in a certain way requires such a self-referring intention,

---

[3] Shakespeare, Sonnet 53.

as does his intention to ask Alexander to move. In general, the first intention in the sequence to require this feature specifies the first meaning.

Because a speaker necessarily intends first meaning to be grasped by his audience, and it is grasped if communication succeeds, we lose nothing in the investigation of first meaning if we concentrate on the knowledge or ability a hearer must have if he is to interpret a speaker. What the speaker knows must correspond to something the interpreter knows if the speaker is to be understood, since if the speaker is understood he has been interpreted as he intended to be interpreted. The abilities of the speaker that go beyond what is required of an interpreter—invention and motor control—do not concern me here.

Nothing said so far limits first meaning to language; what has been characterised is (roughly) Grice's non-natural meaning, which applies to any sign or signal with an intended interpretation. What should be added if we want to restrict first meaning to linguistic meaning? The usual answer would, I think, be that in the case of language the hearer shares a complex system or theory with the speaker, a system which makes possible the articulation of logical relations between utterances, and explains the ability to interpret novel utterances in an organized way.

This answer has been suggested, in one form or another, by many philosophers and linguists, and I assume it must in some sense be right. The difficulty lies in getting clear about what this sense is. The particular difficulty with which I am concerned in this paper (for there are plenty of others) can be brought out by stating three plausible principles concerning first meaning in language: we may label them by saying they require that first meaning be systematic, shared, and prepared.

(1) *First meaning is systematic.* A competent speaker or interpreter is able to interpret utterances, his own or those of others, on the basis of the semantic properties of the parts, or words, in the utterance, and the structure of the utterance. For this to be possible, there must be systematic relations between the meanings of utterances.

(2) *First meanings are shared.* For speaker and interpreter to communicate successfully and regularly, they must share a method of interpretation of the sort described in (1).

(3) *First meanings are governed by learned conventions or regularities.* The systematic knowledge or competence of the speaker or interpreter is learned in advance of occasions of interpretation and is conventional in character.

Probably no one doubts that there are difficulties with these conditions. Ambiguity is an example: often the 'same' word has more than one semantic role, and so the interpretation of utterances in which it occurs is not uniquely fixed by the features of the interpreter's competence so far mentioned. Yet, though the verbal and other features of the context of utterance often determine a correct interpretation, it is not easy or perhaps even possible to specify clear rules for disambiguation. There are many more questions about what is required of the competent interpreter. It does not seem plausible that there is a strict rule fixing the occasions on which we should attach significance to the order in which conjoined sentences appear in a conjunction: the difference between 'They got married and had a child' and 'They had a child and got married'. Interpreters certainly can make these distinctions. But part of the burden of this paper is that much that they can do ought not to count as part of their basic *linguistic* competence. The contrast in what is meant or implied by the use of 'but' instead of 'and' seems to me another matter, since no amount of common sense unaccompanied by linguistic lore would enable an interpreter to figure it out.

Paul Grice has done more than anyone else to bring these problems to our attention and to help sort them out. In particular, he has shown why it is essential to distinguish between the literal meaning (perhaps what I am calling first meaning) of words and what is often implied (or implicated) by someone who uses those words. He has explored the general principles behind our ability to figure out such implicatures, and these principles must, of course, be known to speakers who expect to be taken up on them. Whether knowledge of these principles ought to be included in the description of linguistic competence may not have to be settled: on the one hand they are things a clever person could often figure out without previous training or exposure and they are things we could get along without. On the other hand they represent a kind of skill we expect of an interpreter and without which communication would be greatly impoverished.

I dip into these matters only to distinguish them from the problem raised by malapropisms and the like. The problems touched on in the last two paragraphs all concern the ability to interpret words and constructions of the kind covered by our conditions (1)–(3); the questions have been what is required for such interpretation, and to what extent various competencies should be considered linguistic. Malapropisms introduce expressions not covered by prior learning, or familiar expressions which cannot be interpreted by any of the abilities so far discussed. Malapropisms fall into a different category, one that may include such things as our ability to perceive a well-formed sentence when the actual utterance was incomplete or grammatically garbled, our ability to interpret words we have never heard before, to correct slips of the tongue, or to cope with new idiolects. These phenomena threaten standard descriptions of linguistic competence (including descriptions for which I am responsible).

How should we understand or modify (1)–(3) to accommodate malapropisms? Principle (1) requires a competent interpreter to be prepared to interpret utterances of sentences he or she has never heard uttered before. This is possible because the interpreter can learn the semantic role of each of a finite number of words or phrases and can learn the semantic consequences of a finite number of modes of composition. This is enough to account for the ability to interpret utterances of novel sentences. And since the modes of composition can be iterated, there is no clear upper limit to the number of sentences utterances of which can be interpreted. The interpreter thus has a system for interpreting what he hears or says. You might think of this system as a machine which, when fed an arbitrary utterance (and certain parameters provided by the circumstances of the utterance), produces an interpretation. One model for such a machine is a theory of truth, more or less along the lines of a Tarski truth definition. It provides a recursive characterisation of the truth conditions of all possible utterances of the speaker, and it does this through an analysis of utterances in terms of sentences made up from the finite vocabulary and the finite stock of modes of composition. I have frequently argued that command of such a theory would suffice for interpretation.[4] Here however there is no reason to be concerned with the details of the theory that can adequately model the ability of an interpreter. All that matters in the present discussion is that the theory has a finite base and is recursive, and these are features on which most philosophers and linguists agree.

To say that an explicit theory for interpreting a speaker is a model of the interpreter's linguistic competence is not to suggest that the interpreter knows any such theory. It is possible, of course, that most interpreters could be brought to acknowledge that they know some of the axioms of a theory of truth; for example, that a conjunction is true if and only if each of the conjuncts is true. And perhaps they also know theorems of the form 'An utterance of the sentence "There is life on Mars" is true if and only if there is life on Mars at the time of the utterance.' On the other hand, no one now has explicit knowledge of a fully satisfactory theory for interpreting the speakers of any natural language.

In any case, claims about what would constitute a satisfactory theory are not, as I said, claims about the propositional knowledge of an interpreter, nor are they claims about the details of the inner workings of some part of the brain. They are rather claims about what must be said to give a satisfactory description of the competence of the interpreter. *We* cannot describe what an interpreter can do except by appeal to a recursive theory of a certain sort. It does not add anything to this thesis to say that if the theory does correctly describe the competence of an interpreter, some mechanism in the interpreter must correspond to the theory.

Principle (2) says that for communication to succeed, a systematic method of interpretation must be shared. (I shall henceforth assume there is no harm in calling such a method a theory, as if the interpreter were using the theory we use to describe his competence.) The sharing comes to this: the interpreter uses his theory to understand the speaker; the speaker uses the same (or an equivalent) theory to guide his speech. For the speaker, it is a theory about how the interpreter will interpret him. Obviously this principle does not demand that speaker and interpreter speak the same language. It is an enormous convenience that

---

[4] See the essays on radical interpretation in my *Inquiries into Truth and Interpretation*, Oxford University Press, 1984.

many people speak in similar ways, and therefore can be interpreted in more or less the same way. But in principle communication does not demand that any two people speak the same language. What must be shared is the interpreter's and the speaker's understanding of the speaker's words.

For reasons that will emerge, I do not think that principles (1) and (2) are incompatible with the existence of malapropisms; it is only when they are combined with principle (3) that there is trouble. Before discussing principle (3) directly, however, I want to introduce an apparent diversion.

The perplexing issue that I want to discuss can be separated off from some related matters by considering a distinction made by Keith Donnellan, and something he said in its defence. Donnellan famously distinguished between two uses of definite descriptions. The *referential* use is illustrated as follows: Jones says 'Smith's murderer is insane', meaning that a certain man, whom he (Jones) takes to have murdered Smith, is insane. Donnellan says that even if the man that Jones believes to have murdered Smith did not murder Smith, Jones has referred to the man he had in mind; and if that man is insane, Jones has said something true. The same sentence may be used *attributively* by someone who wants to assert that the murderer of Smith, whoever he may be, is insane. In this case, the speaker does not say something true if no one murdered Smith, nor has the speaker referred to anyone.

In reply, Alfred MacKay objected that Donnellan Shared Humpty Dumpty's theory of meaning: ' "When *I* use a word", Humpty Dumpty said, . . . "it means just what I choose it to mean." ' In the conversation that went before, he had used the word 'glory' to mean 'a nice knockdown argument'. Donnellan, in answer, explains that intentions are connected with expectations and that you cannot intend to accomplish something by a certain means unless you believe or expect that the means will, or at least could, lead to the desired outcome. A speaker cannot, therefore, intend to mean something by what he says unless he believes his audience will interpret his words as he intends (the Gricean circle). Donnellan says,

If I were to end this reply to MacKay with the sentence 'There's glory for you' I would be guilty of arrogance and, no doubt, of overestimating the strength of what I have said, but given the background I do not think I could be accused of saying something unintelligible. I would be understood, and would I not have meant by 'glory' 'a nice knockdown argument'?[5]

I like this reply, and I accept Donnellan's original distinction between two uses of descriptions (there are many more than two). But apparently I disagree with *some* view of Donnellan's, because unlike him I see almost no connection between the answer to MacKay's objection and the remarks on reference. The

[5] Keith Donnellan, 'Putting Humpty Dumpty Together Again', *The Philosophical Review*, 77 (1968), p. 213. Alfred MacKay's article, 'Mr Donnellan and Humpty Dumpty on Referring', appeared in the same issue of *The Philosophical Review*, pp. 197–202.

reason is this. MacKay says you cannot change what words mean (and so their reference if that is relevant) merely by intending to; the answer is that this is true, but you can change the meaning provided you believe (and perhaps are justified in believing) that the interpreter has adequate clues for the new interpretation. You may deliberately provide those clues, as Donnellan did for his final 'There's glory for you'.

The trouble is that Donnellan's original distinction had nothing to do with words changing their meaning or reference. If, in the referential use, Jones refers to someone who did not murder Smith by using the description 'Smith's murderer', the reference is none the less achieved by way of the normal meanings of the words. The words therefore must have their usual reference. All that is needed, if we are to accept this way of describing the situation, is a firm sense of the difference between what *words* mean or refer to and what *speakers* mean or refer to. Jones may have referred to someone else by using words that referred to Smith's murderer; this is something he may have done in ignorance or deliberately. Similarly for Donnellan's claim that Jones has said something true when he says 'Smith's murderer is insane', provided the man he believes (erroneously) to have murdered Smith is insane. Jones has said something true by using a sentence that is false. This is done intentionally all the time, for example in irony or metaphor. A coherent theory could not allow that under the circumstances Jones' sentence was true; nor would Jones think so if he knew the facts. Jones' belief about who murdered Smith cannot change the truth of the sentence he uses (and for the same reason cannot change the reference of the words in the sentence).

Humpty Dumpty is out of it. He cannot mean what he says he means because he knows that 'There's glory for you' cannot be interpreted by Alice as meaning 'There's a nice knockdown argument for you'. We know he knows this because Alice says 'I don't know what you mean by "glory"', and Humpty Dumpty retorts, 'Of course you don't—til I tell you'. It is Mrs Malaprop and Donnellan who interest me; Mrs Malaprop because she gets away with it without even trying or knowing, and Donnellan because he gets away with it on purpose.

Here is what I mean by 'getting away with it': the interpreter comes to the occasion of utterance armed with a theory that tells him (or so he believes) what an arbitrary utterance of the speaker means. The speaker then says something with the intention that it will be interpreted in a certain way, and the expectation that it will be so interpreted. In fact this way is not provided for by the interpreter's theory. But the speaker is nevertheless understood; the interpreter adjusts his theory so that it yields the speaker's intended interpretation. The speaker has 'gotten away with it'. The speaker may or may not (Donnellan, Mrs Malaprop) know that he has got away with anything; the interpreter may or may not know that the speaker intended to get away with anything. What is common to the cases is that the speaker expects to be, and is, interpreted as the speaker intended although the interpreter did not have a correct theory in advance.

We do not need bizarre anecdotes or wonderlands to make the point. We all get away with it all the time; understanding the speech of others depends on it. Take proper names. In small, isolated groups everyone may know the names everyone else knows, and so have ready in advance of a speech encounter a theory that will, without correction, cope with the names to be employed. But even this semantic paradise will be destroyed by each new nickname, visitor, or birth. If a taboo bans a name, a speaker's theory is wrong until he learns of this fact; similarly if an outrigger canoe is christened.

There is not, so far as I can see, any theory of names that gets around the problem. If some definite description gives the meaning of a name, an interpreter still must somehow add to his theory the fact that the name new to him is to be matched with the appropriate description. If understanding a name is to give some weight to an adequate number of descriptions true of the object named, it is even more evident that adding a name to one's way of interpreting a speaker depends on no rule clearly stated in advance. The various theories that discover an essential demonstrative element in names do provide at least a partial rule for adding new names. But the addition is still an addition to the method of interpretation—what we may think of as the interpreter's view of the current language of the speaker. Finding a demonstrative element in names, or for that matter in mass nouns or words for natural kinds, does not reduce these words to pure demonstratives; that is why a new word in any of these categories requires a change in the interpreter's theory, and therefore a change in our description of his understanding of the speaker.

Mrs Malaprop and Donnellan make the case general. There is no word or construction that cannot be converted to a new use by an ingenious or ignorant speaker. And such conversion, while easier to explain because it involves mere substitution, is not the only kind. Sheer invention is equally possible, and we can be as good at interpreting it (say in Joyce or Lewis Carroll) as we are at interpreting the errors or twists of substitution. From the point of view of an ultimate explanation of how new concepts are acquired, learning to interpret a word that expresses a concept we do not already have is a far deeper and more interesting phenomenon than explaining the ability to use a word new to us for an old concept. But both require a change in one's way of interpreting the speech of another, or in speaking to someone who has the use of the word.

The contrast between acquiring a new concept or meaning along with a new word and merely acquiring a new word for an old concept would be salient if I were concerned with the infinitely difficult problem of how a first language is learned. By comparison, my problem is simple. I want to know how people who already have a language (whatever exactly that means) manage to apply their skill or knowledge to actual cases of interpretation. All the things I assume an interpreter knows or can do depend on his having a mature set of concepts, and being at home with the business of linguistic communication. My problem is to describe what is involved in the idea of 'having a language' or of being at home with the business of linguistic communication.

Here is a highly simplified and idealised proposal about what goes on. An interpreter has, at any moment of a speech transaction, what I persist in calling a theory. (I call it a theory, as remarked before, only because a description of the interpreter's competence requires a recursive account.) I assume that the interpreter's theory has been adjusted to the evidence so far available to him: knowledge of the character, dress, role, sex, of the speaker, and whatever else has been gained by observing the speaker's behaviour, linguistic or otherwise. As the speaker speaks his piece the interpreter alters his theory, entering hypotheses about new names, altering the interpretation of familiar predicates, and revising past interpretations of particular utterances in the light of new evidence.

Some of what goes on may be described as improving the method of interpretation as the evidential base enlarges. But much is not like that. When Donnellan ends his reply to MacKay by saying 'There's glory for you', not only he, but his words, are correctly interpreted as meaning 'There's a nice knock-down argument for you'. That's how he intends us to interpret his words, and we know this, since we have, and he knows we have, and we know he knows we have (etc.), the background needed to provide the interpretation. But up to a certain point (before MacKay came on the scene) this interpretation of an earlier utterance by Donnellan of the same words would have been wrong. To put this differently: the theory we actually use to interpret an utterance is geared to the occasion. We may decide later we could have done better by the occasion, but this does not mean (necessarily) that we now have a better theory for the next occasion. The reason for this is, as we have seen, perfectly obvious: a speaker may provide us with information relevant to interpreting an utterance in the course of making the utterance.

Let us look at the process from the speaker's side. The speaker wants to be understood, so he intends to speak in such a way that he will be interpreted in a certain way. In order to judge how he will be interpreted, he forms, or uses, a picture of the interpreter's readiness to interpret along certain lines. Central to this picture is what the speaker believes is the starting theory of interpretation the interpreter has for him. The speaker does not necessarily speak in such a way as to prompt the interpreter to apply this prior theory; he may deliberately dispose the interpreter to modify his prior theory. But the speaker's view of the interpreter's prior theory is not irrelevant to what he says, nor to what he means by his words; it is an important part of what he has to go on if he wants to be understood.

I have distinguished what I have been calling the *prior theory* from what I shall henceforth call the *passing theory*. For the hearer, the prior theory expresses how he is prepared in advance to interpret an utterance of the speaker, while the passing theory is how he *does* interpret the utterance. For the speaker, the prior theory is what he *believes* the interpreter's prior theory to be, while his passing theory is the theory he *intends* the interpreter to use.

I am now in a position to state a problem that arises if we accept the distinction between the prior and the passing theory and also accept the account of linguistic competence given by principles (1)–(2). According to that account, each interpreter (and this includes speakers, since speakers must be interpreters) comes to a successful linguistic exchange prepared with a 'theory' which constitutes his basic linguistic competence, and which he shares with those with whom he communicates. Because each party has such a shared theory and knows that others share his theory, and knows that others know he knows (etc.), some would say that the knowledge or abilities that constitute the theory may be called conventions.

I think that the distinction between the prior and the passing theory, if taken seriously, undermines this commonly accepted account of linguistic competence and communication. Here is why. What must be shared for communication to succeed is the passing theory. For the passing theory is the one the interpreter actually uses to interpret an utterance, and it is the theory the speaker intends the interpreter to use. Only if these coincide is understanding complete. (Of course, there are degrees of success in communication; much may be right although something is wrong. This matter of degree is irrelevant to my argument.)

The passing theory is where, accident aside, agreement is greatest. As speaker and interpreter talk, their prior theories become more alike; so do their passing theories. The asymptote of agreement and understanding is when passing theories coincide. But the passing theory cannot in general correspond to an interpreter's linguistic competence. Not only does it have its changing list of proper names and gerrymandered vocabulary, but it includes every successful— i.e. correctly interpreted—use of any other word or phrase, no matter how far out of the ordinary. Every deviation from ordinary usage, as long as it is agreed on for the moment (knowingly deviant, or not, on one, or both, sides), is in the passing theory as a feature of what the words mean on that occasion. Such meanings, transient though they may be, are literal; they are what I have called first meanings. A passing theory is not a theory of what anyone (except perhaps a philosopher) would call an actual natural language. 'Mastery' of such a language would be useless, since knowing a passing theory is only knowing how to interpret a particular utterance on a particular occasion. Nor could such a language, if we want to call it that, be said to have been learned, or to be governed by conventions. Of course things previously learned were essential to arriving at the passing theory, but what was learned could not have been the passing theory.

Why should a passing theory be called a theory at all? For the sort of theory we have in mind is, in its formal structure, suited to be the theory for an entire language, even though its expected field of application is vanishingly small. The answer is that when a word or phrase temporarily or locally takes over the role of some other word or phrase (as treated in a prior theory, perhaps), the entire burden of that role, with all its implications for logical relations to other words, phrases, and sentences, must be carried along by the passing theory. Someone who grasps the fact that Mrs Malaprop means 'epithet' when she says 'epitaph' must give 'epithet' all the powers 'epitaph' has for many other people. Only a full recursive theory can do justice to these powers. These remarks do not depend on supposing Mrs Malaprop will always make this 'mistake'; once is enough to summon up a passing theory assigning a new role to 'epitaph'.

An interpreter's prior theory has a better chance of describing what we might think of as a natural language, particularly a prior theory brought to a first conversation. The less we know about the speaker, assuming we know he belongs to our language community, the more nearly our prior theory will simply be the theory we expect someone who hears our unguarded speech to use. If we ask for a cup of coffee, direct a taxi driver, or order a crate of lemons, we may know so little about our intended interpreter that we can do no better than to assume that he will interpret our speech along what we take to be standard lines. But all this is relative. In fact we always have the interpreter in mind; there is no such thing as how we expect, in the abstract, to be interpreted. We inhibit our higher vocabulary, or encourage it, depending on the most general considerations, and we cannot fail to have premonitions as to which of the proper names we know are apt to be correctly understood.

In any case, my point is this: most of the time prior theories will not be shared, and there is no reason why they should be. Certainly it is not a condition of successful communication that prior theories be shared: consider the malaprop from ignorance. Mrs Malaprop's theory, prior and passing, is that 'A nice derangement of epitaphs' means a nice arrangement of epithets. An interpreter who, as we say, knows English, but does not know the verbal habits of Mrs Malaprop, has a prior theory according to which 'A nice derangement of epitaphs' means a nice derangement of epitaphs; but his passing theory agrees with that of Mrs Malaprop if he understands her words.

It is quite clear that in general the prior theory is neither shared by speaker and interpreter nor is it what we would normally call a language. For the prior theory has in it all the features special to the idiolect of the speaker that the interpreter is in a position to take into account before the utterance begins. One way to appreciate the difference between the prior theory and our ordinary idea of a person's language is to reflect on the fact that an interpreter must be expected to have quite different prior theories for different speakers—not as different, usually, as his passing theories; but these are matters that depend on how well the interpreter knows his speaker.

Neither the prior theory nor the passing theory describes what we would call the language a person knows, and neither theory characterizes a speaker's or interpreter's linguistic competence. Is there any theory that would do better?

Perhaps it will be said that what is essential to the mastery of a language is not knowledge of any particular vocabulary, or even detailed grammar, much less knowledge of what any speaker is apt to succeed in making his words and sentences mean. What is essential is a basic framework of categories and rules, a sense of the way English (or any) grammars may be constructed, plus a skeleton list of interpreted words for fitting into the basic framework. If I put all this vaguely, it is only because I want to consider a large number of actual or possible proposals in one fell swoop; for I think they all fail to resolve our problem. They fail for the same reasons the more complete and specific prior theories fail: none of them satisfies the demand for a description of an ability that speaker and interpreter share and that is adequate to interpretation.

First, any general framework, whether conceived as a grammar for English, or a rule for accepting grammars, or a basic grammar plus rules for modifying or extending it—any such general framework, by virtue of the features that make it general, will by itself be insufficient for interpreting particular utterances. The general framework or theory, whatever it is, may be a key ingredient in what is needed for interpretation, but it can't be all that is needed since it fails to provide the interpretation of particular words and sentences as uttered by a particular speaker. In this respect it is like a prior theory, only worse because it is less complete.

Second, the framework theory must be expected to be different for different speakers. The more general and abstract it is, the more difference there can be without it mattering to communication. The theoretical possibility of such divergence is obvious; but once one tries to imagine a framework rich enough to serve its purpose, it is clear that such differences must also be actual. It is impossible to give examples, of course, until it is decided what to count in the framework: a sufficiently explicit framework could be discredited by a single malapropism. There is some evidence of a more impressive sort that internal grammars do differ among speakers of 'the same language'. James McCawley reports that recent work by Haber shows

> ... that there is appreciable variation as to what rules of plural formation different speakers have, the variation being manifested in such things as the handling of novel words that an investigator has presented his subjects with, in the context of a task that will force them to use the word in the plural ... Haber suggests that her subjects, rather than having a uniformly applicable process of plural formation, each have a 'core' system, which covers a wide range of cases, but not necessarily everything, plus strategies ... for handling cases that are not covered by the 'core' system ... Haber's data suggest that speakers of what are to the minutest details 'the same dialect' often have acquired grammars that differ in far more respects than their speech differs in.[6]

I have been trying to throw doubt on how clear the idea of 'speaking the same dialect' is, but here we may assume that it at least implies the frequent sharing of passing theories.

---

[6] James McCawley, 'Some Ideas Not to Live By', *Die Neuern Sprachen*, 75 (1976), p. 157. These results are disputed by those who believe the relevant underlying rules and structures are prewired. My point obviously does not depend on the example, or the level at which deviations are empirically possible.

Bringing in grammars, theories, or frameworks more general than, and prior to, prior theories just emphasises the problem I originally presented in terms of the contrast between prior theories and passing theories. Stated more broadly now, the problem is this: what interpreter and speaker share, to the extent that communication succeeds, is not learned and so is not a language governed by rules or conventions known to speaker and interpreter in advance; but what the speaker and interpreter know in advance is not (necessarily) shared, and so is not a language governed by shared rules or conventions. What is shared is, as before, the passing theory; what is given in advance is the prior theory, or anything on which it may in turn be based.

What I have been leaving out of account up to now is what Haber calls a 'strategy', which is a nice word for the mysterious process by which a speaker or hearer uses what he knows in advance plus present data to produce a passing theory. What two people need, if they are to understand one another through speech, is the ability to converge on passing theories from utterance to utterance. Their starting points, however far back we want to take them, will usually be very different—as different as the ways in which they acquired their linguistic skills. So also, then, will the strategies and stratagems that bring about convergence differ.

Perhaps we can give content to the idea of two people 'having the same language' by saying that they tend to converge on passing theories; degree or relative frequency of convergence would then be a measure of similarity of language. What use can we find, however, for the concept of a language? We could hold that any theory on which a speaker and interpreter converge is a language; but then there would be a new language for every unexpected turn in the conversation, and languages could not be learned and no one would want to master most of them.

We just made a sort of sense of the idea of two people 'having the same language', though we could not explain what a language is. It is easy to see that the idea of 'knowing' a language will be in the same trouble, as will the project of characterising the abilities or capacities a person must have if he commands a language. But we might try to say in what a person's ability to interpret or speak to another person consists: it is the ability that permits him to construct a correct, that is, convergent, passing theory for speech transactions with that person. Again, the concept allows of degrees of application.

This characterization of linguistic ability is so nearly circular that it cannot be wrong: it comes to saying that the ability to communicate by speech consists in the ability to make oneself understood, and to understand. It is only when we look at the structure of this ability that we realize how far we have drifted from standard ideas of language mastery. For we have discovered no learnable common core of consistent behaviour, no shared grammar or rules, no portable interpreting machine set to grind out the meaning of an arbitrary utterance. We may say that linguistic ability is the ability to converge on a passing theory from time to time—this is what I have suggested, and I have no better proposal. But if we do say this, then we should realize that we have abandoned not only the ordinary notion of a language, but we have erased the boundary between knowing a language and knowing our way around in the world generally. For there are no rules for arriving at passing theories, no rules in any strict sense, as opposed to rough maxims and methodological generalities. A passing theory really is like a theory at least in this, that it is derived by wit, luck, and wisdom from a private vocabulary and grammar, knowledge of the ways people get their point across, and rules of thumb for figuring out what deviations from the dictionary are most likely. There is no more chance of regularizing, or teaching, this process than there is of regularizing or teaching the process of creating new theories to cope with new data in any field—for that is what this process involves.

The problem we have been grappling with depends on the assumption that communication by speech requires that speaker and interpreter have learned or somehow acquired a common method or theory of interpretation—as being able to operate on the basis of shared conventions, rules, or regularities. The problem arose when we realized that no method or theory fills this bill. The solution to the problem is clear. In linguistic communication nothing corresponds to a linguistic competence as often described: that is, as summarized by principles (1)–(3). The solution is to give up the principles. Principles (1) and (2) survive when understood in rather unusual ways, but principle (3) cannot stand, and it is unclear what can take its place. I conclude that there is no such thing as a language, not if a language is anything like what many philosophers and linguists have supposed. There is therefore no such thing to be learned, mastered, or born with. We must give up the idea of a clearly defined shared structure which language-users acquire and then apply to cases. And we should try again to say how convention in any important sense is involved in language; or, as I think, we should give up the attempt to illuminate how we communicate by appeal to conventions.

Contents List of Volumes of Essays

by Donald Davidson

Volume 1
Essays on Actions and Events

Intention and Action
1. Actions, Reasons, and Causes (1963)
2. How is Weakness of the Will Possible? (1969)
3. Agency (1971)
4. Freedom to Act (1973)
5. Intending (1978)

Event and Cause
6. The Logical Form of Action Sentences (1967)
7. Causal Relations (1967)
8. The Individuation of Events (1969)
9. Events as Particulars (1970)
10. Eternal *vs.* Ephemeral Events (1971)

Philosophy of Psychology
11. Mental Events (1970)
12. Psychology as Philosophy (1974)
13. The Material Mind (1973)
14. Hempel on Explaining Action (1976)
15. Hume's Cognitive Theory of Pride (1976)

Appendices
A. Adverbs of Action (1985)
B. Reply to Quine on Events (1985)

Volume 2

Inquiries into Truth and Interpretation

Truth and Meaning
1. Theories of Meaning and Learnable Languages (1965)
2. Truth and Meaning (1967)
3. True to the Facts (1969)
4. Semantics for Natural Languages (1970)
5. In Defence of Convention T (1973)

Applications
6. Quotation (1979)
7. On Saying That (1968)
8. Moods and Performances (1979)

Radical Interpretation
9. Radical Interpretation (1973)
10. Belief and the Basis of Meaning (1974)
11. Thought and Talk (1975)
12. Reply to Foster (1976)

Language and Reality
13. On the Very Idea of a Conceptual Scheme (1974)
14. The Method of Truth in Metaphysics (1977)
15. Reality Without Reference (1977)
16. The Inscrutability of Reference (1979)

Limits of the Literal
17. What Metaphors Mean (1978)
18. Communication and Convention (1982)

Appendix to Essay 10
Replies to Quine and Lewis (1974)

Volume 3
Subjective, Intersubjective, Objective

Subjective
  1. First Person Authority (1984)
  2. Knowing One's Own Mind (1987)
  3. The Myth of the Subjective (1988)
  4. What is Present to the Mind? (1989)
  5. Indeterminism and Antirealism (1997)
  6. The Irreducibility of the Concept of the Self (1998)

Intersubjective
  7. Rational Animals (1982)
  8. The Second Person (1992)
  9. The Emergence of Thought (1997)

Objective
  10. A Coherence Theory of Truth and Knowledge (1983)
      Afterthoughts (1987)
  11. Empirical Content (1982)
  12. Epistemology and Truth (1988)
  13. Epistemology Externalized (1990)
  14. Three Varieties of Knowledge (1991)

Volume 4
Problems of Rationality

Rationality and Value
 1. The Problem of Objectivity (1995)
 2. Expressing Evaluations (1984)
 3. The Objectivity of Values (1995)
    Appendix: Objectivity and Practical Reason (1999)
 4. The Interpersonal Comparison of Values (1996)

Problems and Proposals
 5. Turing's Test (1990)
 6. Representation and Interpretation (1990)
 7. Problems in the Explanation of Action (1987)
 8. Could There be a Science of Rationality? (1995)
 9. What Thought Requires (2001)
10. A Unified Theory of Thought, Meaning, and Action (1980)

Irrationality
11. Paradoxes of Irrationality (1974)
12. Incoherence and Irrationality (1985)
13. Deception and Division (1986)
14. Who is Fooled? (1997)

Volume 5
Truth, Language, and History

Truth
1. Truth Rehabilitated (1997)
2. The Folly of Trying to Define Truth (1996)
3. Method and Metaphysics (1993)
4. Meaning, Truth, and Evidence (1990)
5. Pursuit of the Concept of Truth (1995)
6. What is Quine's View of Truth? (1994)

Language
7. A Nice Derangement of Epitaphs (1986)
8. The Social Aspect of Language (1994)
9. Seeing Through Language (1997)
10. Joyce and Humpty Dumpty (1989)
11. The Third Man (1992)
12. Locating Literary Language (1993)

Anomalous Monism
13. Thinking Causes (1993)
14. Laws and Cause (1995)

Historical Thoughts
15. Plato's Philosopher (1985)
16. The Socratic Concept of Truth (1992)
17. Dialectic and Dialogue (1994)
18. Gadamer and Plato's *Philebus* (1997)
19. Aristotle's Action (2001)
20. Spinoza's Causal Theory of the Affects (1993)

Appendix
Replies to Rorty, Stroud, McDowell, and Pereda (1998)

Bibliography

AGASSI, JOSEPH (1975). *Science in Flux* (Dordrecht: Reidel), 120.

ALLEN, WOODY (1977). 'Condemned', *New Yorker*, 21 November 1977: 59.

ALSTON, WILLIAM (1971). 'Varieties of Privileged Access', *American Philosophical Quarterly* 9: 235.

ANSCOMBE, G. E. M. (1965). 'Thought and Action in Aristotle', in R. Bamboroughed., *New Essays on Plato and Aristotle* (London: Routledge and Kegan Paul), 143–58.

ANSCOMBE, G. E. M. (1959). *Intention* (Oxford: Blackwell).

AUSTIN, J. L. (1961). 'A Plea for Excuses', in *Philosophical Papers* (Oxford: Clarendon Press), 123–52.

——(1961). 'Unfair to Facts', in *Philosophical Papers* (Oxford: Clarendon Press), 102–22.

—— and STRAWSON, P. F. (1950). 'Symposium on "Truth"', in *Proceedings of the Aristotelian Society*, Supplementary Volume 24.

AVRAMIDES, ANITA (1999). 'Davidson and the New Sceptical Problem', in U. Zeglen, ed., *Donald Davidson: Truth, Meaning and Knowledge* (London: Routledge).

AYER, A. J. (1963). 'Privacy', in *The Concept of a Person and Other Essays* (NY: Macmillan).

BAIER, KURT (1958). *The Moral Point of View* (Ithaca, NY: Cornell University Press).

BAIN, ALEXANDER (1867). *English Composition and Rhetoric* (NY: D. Appleton).

BARFIELD, O. (1962). 'Poetic Diction and Legal Fiction', in M. Black, ed., *The Importance of Language* (Englewood Cliffs, NJ: Prentice-Hall), 55.

BAR-HILLEL, Y. (1954). 'Logical Syntax and Semantics', *Language* 30: 230–7.

——(1963). 'Remarks on Carnap's Logical Syntax of Language', in P. A. Schilpp. ed., *The Philosophy of Rudolph Carnap* (La Salle, IL: Open Court).

BENNETT, JONATHAN (1976). *Linguistic Behaviour* (Cambridge: Cambridge University Press), 186.

BETH, E. W. (1963). 'Carnap's Views on the Advantages of Constructed Systems Over Natural Languages in the Philosophy of Science', in P. A. Schilpp. ed., *The Philosophy of Rudolph Carnap* (La Salle, IL: Open Court).

BLACK, MAX (1962). 'Metaphor', in *Models and Metaphors* (Ithaca, NY: Cornell University Press), 29.

BRANDT, RICHARD, and KIM, JAEGWON (1967). 'The Logic of the Identity Theory', *Journal of Philosophy* 64: 515–37.

BULLARD, E. C. (1966). 'The Detection of Underground Explosions', *Scientific American* 215: 19–29.

BURGE, T. (1973). 'Reference and Proper Names', *Journal of Philosophy* 70: 425–39.

CARGILE, JAMES (1970). 'Davidson's Notion of Logical Form', *Inquiry* 13: 129–39.

CARNAP, R. (1937). *The Logical Syntax of Language* (London: Routledge and Kegan Paul), 248.

——(1947; enlarged edn. 1956). *Meaning and Necessity* (Chicago: University of Chicago Press).

CASTENEDA, H.-N. (1967). 'Comments', in N. Rescher, ed., *The Logic of Decision and Action* (Pittsburgh: University of Pittsburgh Press), 104–12.

CAVELL, STANLEY (1969). 'Aesthetic Problems of Modern Philosophy', in *Must We Lean What We Say?* (NY: Charles Scribner).

CHAPPELL, V. C. (ed.) (1962). *The Philosophy of Mind* (Englewood Cliffs, NJ: Spectrum).

CHISHOLM, RODERICK (1957). *Perceiving* (Ithaca, NY: Cornell University Press).

—— (1964). 'The Descriptive Element in the Concept of Action', *Journal of Philosophy* 61: 613–24.

—— (1964). 'The Ethics of Requirement', *American Philosophical Quarterly* 1: 1–7.

CHOMSKY, NOAM (1966). 'Topics in the Theory of Generative Grammar', in T. A. Sebeok, ed., *Current Trends in Linguistics*, vol. 3 (The Hague: Mouton).

CHURCH, A. (1950). 'On Carnap's Analysis of Statements of Assertion and Belief', *Analysis* 10: 97–9.

—— (1951). 'A Formulation of the Logic of Sense and Denotation', in P. Henle, H. M. Kallen, and S. K. Langer, eds, *Structure, Method, and Meaning: Essays in Honour of H. M. Sheffer* (NY: Liberal Arts Press).

—— (1954). 'Intentional Isomorphism and Identity of Belief', *Philosophical Studies* 5: 65–73.

—— (1956). *Introduction to Mathematical Logic* (Princeton, NJ: Princeton University Press).

COHEN, T. (1975). 'Figurative Speech and Figurative Acts', *Journal of Philosophy* 72: 669–84 at 671.

DAVIDSON, DONALD (1965). 'Theories of Meaning and Learnable Languages', in *Proceedings of the 1964 International Congress of Logic, Methodology and the Philosophy of Science* (Amsterdam: North-Holland Publishing Company), 383–94.

—— (1980, 2nd edn. 2001). *Essays on Actions and Events* (Oxford: Oxford University Press).

—— (1980, 2nd edn. 2001). *Inquiries into Truth and Interpretation* (Oxford: Oxford University Press).

DONNELLAN, KEITH (1968). 'Putting Humpty Dumpty Together Again', *The Philosophical Review* 77: 213.

DRAY, WILLIAM (1957). *Laws and Explanation in History* (London: Oxford University Press).

DRETSKE, F. I. (1967). 'Can Events Move?', *Mind* 76: 479–92.

DUMMETT, M. (1973). *Frege: Philosophy of Language* (London: Duckworth), Ch. 9.

ELIOT, T. S. (1967). *Selected Poems* (NY: Harcourt, Brace, Jovanovich).

EMPSON, WILLIAM (1935). *Some Versions of Pastoral* (London: Chatto and Windus), 133.

FEIGL, HERBERT (1958). 'The "Mental" and the "Physical"', in H. Feigl, M. Scriven, and G. Maxwell, eds, *Minnesota Studies in the Philosophy of Science* 2 (Minneapolis: University of Minnesota Press), 370–497.

FEYERABEND, P. (1962). 'Explanation, Reduction, and Empiricism', in *Scientific Explanation, Space and Time: Minnesota Studies in the Philosophy of Science, 3* (Minneapolis: University of Minnesota Press), 82.

—— (1965). 'Problems of Empiricism', in R. G. Colodny, ed., *Beyond the Edge of Certainty* (Englewood Cliffs, NJ: Prentice-Hall).

FLEW, ANTHONY (1956). 'Motives and the Unconscious', in H. Feigl and M. Scriven, eds, *Minnesota Studies in the Philosophy of Science*, vol. 1 (Minneapolis: University of Minnesota Press).

FØLLESDAL, DAGFINN (1969). 'Quine on Modality', in D. Davidson and J. Hintikka, eds, *Words and Objections: Essays on the Work of W. V. Quine* (London: Reidel Publishing Company), 175–85.

FREGE, G. (1962). 'On Sense and Reference', in M. Black and P. T. Geach, eds, *Philosophical Writings* (Oxford: Blackwell), 56–78.

GEACH, P. T. (1957). *Mental Acts* (London: Routledge and Kegan Paul).

GOODMAN, N. (1966). 'Comments', *Journal of Philosophy* 63: 328–31.

—— (1983, 4th edn.). *Fact, Fiction and Forecast* (Cambridge, MA: Harvard University Press).

—— *Languages of Art* (Indianapolis: Bobbs-Merrill), 71, 77–8.

GRICE, H. P. (1979). 'Intention and Uncertainty', *British Academy Lecture* (London: Oxford University Press).

HAMPSHIRE, S. (1959). *Thought and Action* (London: Chatto and Windus).

—— (1965). *Freedom of the Individual* (Princeton, NJ: Princeton University Press).

HARE, R. M. (1952). *The Language of Morals* (Oxford: Clarendon Press).

—— (1963). *Freedom and Reason* (Oxford: Clarendon Press).

HARMAN, G. (1975). 'Moral Relativism Defended', *Philosophical Review* 84: 3–22.

HART, H. L. A, and HONORÉ, A. M. (1959). *Causation in the Law* (Oxford: Clarendon Press).

HEDMAN, C. (1970). 'On the Individuation of Action', *Inquiry* 13: 125–8.

HEMPEL, C. G. (1965). *Aspects of Scientific Explanation* (NY: Free Press).

HENLE, PAUL (1958). 'Metaphor', in P. Henle, ed., *Language, Thought and Culture* (Ann Arbor: University of Michigan Press).

HINTIKKA, J. (1962). *Knowledge and Belief* (Ithaca, NY: Cornell University Press), 13.

HOLLAND, R. F. (ed.) (1960). *Studies in Philosophical Psychology* (London: Routledge and Kegan Paul).

HUME, DAVID (1757; reproduced by facsimile 1970). 'A Dissertation of the Passions', in *Four Dissertations* (NY: Garland), 121–81.

HUME, DAVID (1957 edn.). *An Inquiry Concerning the Principle of Morals*, L. A. Selby Bigg, ed. (Oxford: Clarendon Press), Appendix I, 293.

JACKSON, H. (1922). *The Eighteen-Nineties* (NY: Knopf), 73.

JEFFREY, RICHARD C. (1966). 'Goodman's Query', *Journal of Philosophy* 63: 281–8.

KANT, IMMANUEL (1909 edn.). *Fundamental Principles of the Metaphysics of Morals*, T. K. Abbott, trans. (London: Longman, Green and Co.).

KENNY, A. J. P. (1963). *Action, Emotion and Will* (London: Routledge and Kegan Paul).

KIM, JAEGWON (1966). 'On the Psycho-Physical Identity Theory', *American Philosophical Quarterly* 3: 277–85.

KUHN, T. S. (1962). *The Structure of Scientific Revolutions* (Chicago: University of Chicago Press).

—— (1970). 'Reflections on my Critics', in I. Lakatos and A. Musgrave, eds, *Criticism and the Growth of Knowledge* (Cambridge: Cambridge University Press).

LEMMON, E. J. (1962). 'Moral Dilemmas', *Philosophical Review* 71: 138–58.

—— (1967). 'Comments on D. Davidson's "The Logical Form of Action Sentences"', in N. Rescher, ed., *The Logic of Decision and Action* (Pittsburgh: University of Pittsburgh Press), 96–103.

LEVIN, HARRY (1959). *The Question of Hamlet* (New York: Oxford University Press).

LEWIS, DAVID K. (1966). 'An Argument for the Identity Theory', *Journal of Philosophy* 63: 17–25.

LUCE, DAVID RANDALL (1966). 'Mind–Body Identity and Psycho-Physical Correlation', *Philosophical Studies* 17: 1–7.

MACINTRYRE, ALASDAIR (1958). *The Unconscious* (London: Routledge).

MALCOLM, NORMAN (1964–5). 'Scientific Materialism and the Identity Theory', *Dialogue* 3: 115–25.

MARTIN, R. M. (1969). 'On Events and Event-Descriptions', in J. Margolis, ed., *Fact and Existence* (Oxford: Blackwell), 63–73.

MATES, B. (1952). 'Synonymity', in L. Linsky, ed., *Semantics and the Philosophy of Language* (Urbana: University of Illinois Press).

MCCAWLEY, JAMES (1976). 'Some Ideas Not to Live By', *Die Neuern Sprachen* 75: 157.

MCKAY, ALFRED (1968). 'Mr Donnellan and Humpty Dumpty on Referring', *The Philosophical Review* 77: 197–202.

MELDEN, A. I. (1961). *Free Action* (London: Routledge and Kegan Paul).

MORAVSCIK, J. (1965). 'Strawson and Ontological Priority', in P. J. Butler, ed., *Analytical Philosophy*, Second Series (NY: Barnes and Noble), 106–19.

MURRAY, J. MIDDLETON (1922). *Countries of the Mind* (London: Collins).

NAGEL, THOMAS (1965). 'Physicalism', *Philosophical Review* 74: 339–56.

NOWELL-SMITH, P. H. (1954). *Ethics* (London: Penguin Books).

ONIONS, C. T. (1965). *An Advances English Syntax* (London: Routledge and Kegan Paul), 154–6.

PETERS. R. S. (1958). *The Concept of Motivation* (London: Routledge and Kegan Paul).

PUTNAM, HILARY (1978). *Meaning and the Moral Sciences* (London: Routledge and Kegan Paul), 125.

PUTNAM, HILARY (1983). *Realism and Reason* (Cambridge: Cambridge University Press), xviii.

QUINE, W. V. O. (1969). 'Existence and Quantification', in J. Margolis, ed., *Fact and Existence* (Oxford: Blackwell), 1–17.

—— (1950). *Methods of Logic* (NY: Holt).

—— (1960). *Word and Object* (Cambridge, MA: M.I.T. Press).

—— (1961). 'Two Dogmas of Empiricism', in *From a Logical Point of View* (Cambridge, MA: Harvard University Press), 42, 44, 46.

—— (1966). 'Ontological Reduction and the World of Numbers', in *Ways of Paradox* (NY: Random House), 199–207.

—— (1966). 'Truth by Convention', in *The Ways of Paradox* (NY: Random House), 70–99 at 82.

—— (1969). 'Speaking of Objects', in *Ontological Reality and Other Essays* (NY: University of Columbia Press), 1, 24, 25.

—— (1969). *Ontological Relativity and Other Essays* (NY: Columbia University Press), 75.

—— (1974). *The Roots of Reference* (La Salle, IL: Open Court), 37–8.

QUINE, W. V. O. (1975). 'The Nature of Natural Knowledge', in S. Guttenplan, ed., *Mind and Language* (Oxford University Press), 68.

RAMSEY, F. P. (1950). *Foundations of Mathematics* (NY: Humanities Press).

—— (1950). 'Facts and Propositions', reprinted in *Foundations of Mathematics* (NY: Humanities Press), 138–55.

REICHENBACH, HANS (1947). *Elements of Symbolic Logic* (NY: Macmillan Co.).

RORTY, RICHARD (1970). 'Incorrigibility as the Mark of the Mental', *Journal of Philosophy* 67: 416.

—— (1979). *Philosophy and the Mirror of Nature* (Princeton, NJ: Princeton University Press), 178.

—— (1986). 'Pragmatism, Davidson, and Truth', in E. Lepore, ed., *Truth and Interpretation: Perspectives on the Philosophy of Donald Davidson* (Oxford: Blackwell).

RYLE, GILBERT (1949). *The Concept of Mind* (NY: Barnes and Noble).

SANTAS, G. (1964). 'The Socratic Paradoxes', *Philosophical Review* 73: 147–64.

—— (1966). 'Plato's *Protagoras* and Explanations of Weakness', *Philosophical Review* 75: 3–33.

SCHEFFLER, I. (1954). 'An Inscriptional Approach to Indirect Quotation', *Analysis* 10: 83–90.

—— ISRAEL (1963). *The Anatomy of Inquiry* (NY: Knopf).

SELLARS, W. (1955). 'Putnam on Synonymity and Belief', *Analysis* 15: 117–20.

—— (1956). 'Empiricism and the Philosophy of Mind', in H. Feigl and Scriven, eds, *Minnesota Studies in the Philosophy of Science* (Minneapolis: University of Minnesota Press).

SHOEMAKER, SIDNEY (1963). *Self-Knowledge and Self-Identity* (Ithaca, NY: Cornell University Press), 215–16.

—— (1965). 'Ziff's Other Minds', *Journal of Philosophy* 62: 587–9.

SINGER, M. (1958). 'Moral Rules and Principles', in A. J. Melden, ed., *Essays in Moral Philosophy* (Seattle: University of Washington Press), 160–97.

—— (1977). *The New Yorker*, 4 April 1977: 56.

SMART, J. J. (1959). 'Sensations and Brain Processes', *Philosophical Review* 68: 141–56.

STRAWSON, P. F. (1959). *Individuals* (London: Methuen), 108.

—— (1959). *Individuals* (London: Methuen).

—— (1963). 'Contribution to a Symposium on "Determinism"', in D. F. Pears, ed., *Freedom and the Will* (London: St. Martin's Press), 48–58.

—— (1966). *The Bounds of Sense* (London: Methuen).

TARSKI, A. (1956). 'The Concept of Truth in Formalized Languages', in *Logic, Semantics, Metamathematics* (Oxford: Clarendon Press).

TAYLOR, CHARLES (1965). *The Explanation of Behaviour* (London: Routledge).

—— (1967). 'Mind-Body Identity, a Side Issue?', *Philosophical Review* 76: 201–13.

THALBERG, IRVING (1982). 'Freud's Anatomies of the Self', in R. Wollheim and J. Hopkins, eds, *Philosophical Essays on Freud* (Cambridge: Cambridge University Press).

VENDLER, Z. (1965). 'Comments', *Journal of Philosophy* 62: 602–4.

VERBRUGGE, R. R., and McCARRELL, N. S. (1977). 'Metaphoric Comprehension: Studies in Reminding and Resembling', *Cognitive Psychology* 9: 494–533 at 499.

VICKERS, JOHN M. (1967). 'Characteristics of Projectible Predicates', *Journal of Philosophy* 64: 280–5.

von WRIGHT, GEORG HENRIK (1963). *Norm and Action* (London: Routledge and Kegan Paul).

WALLACE, J. (1970). 'On the Frame of Reference', *Synthèse* 22: 61–94.

—— (1972). 'Positive, Comparative, Superlative', *Journal of Philosophy* 69: 773–82.

WALLACE, JOHN R. (1966). 'Goodman, Logic, Induction', *Journal of Philosophy* 62: 310–28.

WEINSTEIN, S. (1974). 'Truth and Demonstratives', *Noûs* 8: 179–84.

WHORF, B. L. 'The Punctual and Segmentative Aspects of Verbs in Hopi', in J. B. Carroll, ed., *Language, Thought, and Reality: Selected Writings of Benjamin Lee Whorf* (Cambridge, MA: The Technology Press of the Massachusetts Institute of Technology).

WILLIAMS, C. (1943). *The Figure of Beatrice* (London: Faber and Faber).

WINCH, P. (1958). *The Idea of a Social Science* (London: Routledge and Kegan Paul).

WITTGENSTEIN, LUDWIG. *Philosophical Investigations* (NY: Macmillan), §377.

Index

Ace, G. 251–2
action
  and meaning 185
  causal explanation of, *see* causal
    explanation of action
  causal theory of 31, 80
  description of 24n, 25n, 27, 28, 32,
    42, 43, 49, 55, 123, 124, 125, 145
  quasi-intensional character of 25, 50
  rationalization of 23–5, 28, 33, 34
  reason explanation of 3, 4, 138–52
  see also agency; decision theory; intention;
    logical form; primary reasons
adverbial modification 5, 37–40, 47–8, 62
Agassi, J. 245
agency 1, 36, 39, 42, 44, 49–50, 55, 56
akrasia, *see* weakness of will
Allen, W. 219
Alston, W. P. 247
ambiguity 56, 74, 146, 164, 165, 166, 190,
  212–13, 215, 228, 246
analytic–synthetic distinction 199, 201
  see also meanings as entities
anomalous dualism 110
anomalous monism 5, 9, 110, 111–19
Anscombe, G. E. M. 23n, 27, 70, 73, 88n, 133
Aquinas, T. 73, 77n, 81, 83, 84n
Aristotle 27n, 28n, 29, 30, 32, 75, 77, 78, 79n,
  80–3, 86, 88n, 132, 133, 142–3, 151,
  209, 222
assent, *see* holding true
assertion 33, 103, 104, 175, 182, 192, 220
Augustine 88
Austin, J. L. 40, 58, 61n, 78, 169n
Avramides, A. 245n
Ayer, A. J. 244

Baier, K. 82n
Bain, A. 216n
Barfield, O. 221, 222
Bar-Hillel, Y. 163n
Beardsley, M. 210
behaviourism 113
belief
  and intention 128–32

and meaning 205–7
sentences about 2, 158, 166–7
see also propositional attitudes
Bennett, D. 3, 62n
Bennett, J. 251
Bergson, H. 197
Beth, E. 163n
Black, M. 209, 210, 216, 221–2
Bowie, L. 108n
Brandt, R. 110n
Burge, T. 190
Butler, S. 79n, 83

Cargile, J. 51, 62–9
Carnap, R. 2, 88, 163n, 166, 174, 175n, 176
Carroll, L. 259
Cartesianism 110
Castañeda, H.-N. 51, 53–4
causal explanation
  of action 3, 4, 10, 23, 24, 27–36,
    40, 96, 142, 147
  see also causal theory of action; laws
causal relations, *see* causal explanation; causal
    statements; cause; laws
causal statements 31–3, 34, 190
cause
  as involving laws 33–6, 105–6, 118–19
  deviant causal chains 125
  states as causes 30–1
Charity, Principle of 15, 116, 150, 163, 177,
  193n, 207, 234, 235
Chisholm, R. 42–4, 51, 55, 113n
Church, A. 58n, 157n, 175n, 176, 178, 218
Cohen, T. 219
coherence theories 16, 115, 139, 225–41
Coherence, Principle of 15–16
commands, *see* imperatives
conceptual relativism 16, 196–208
  as depending on scheme–content distinction,
    199–203, 208
  as reflected in language 196–203
Convention-T 12, 14, 15, 16, 160, 189, 190,
  191, 193, 195, 205, 227
  see also Taski; Tarski-style theories
    of truth; truth

conventions 17, 23, 28, 63, 100, 127, 246, 248, 254, 261, 264, 265
  see also assertion; imperatives; interrogatives
correspondence theory of truth, *see* Tarski-style theories of truth, as correspondence theories; truth, as correspondence to fact
Correspondence, Principle of 15–16
counterfactuals 34, 113, 170, 190

Dante 74, 83, 214
decision theory 2, 3, 15, 226
deep structure 63, 190
descriptions
  of actions, *see* actions
  of events, *see* events, descriptions
demonstratives 18, 51, 52, 54, 98, 133, 162n, 163n, 168–9, 175, 180, 181, 182, 189, 259
Descartes, R. 241
desire
  as disposition to act 32
  unconscious 77, 139, 143, 151, 152, 245
determinism 105
disposition 3, 14, 17, 27, 30, 31, 32, 126, 139, 149, 197, 243
Donne, J. 75n, 132, 214
Donnellan, K. 257, 258, 259, 260
Dostoevsky 78n
Dray, W. 23n
Dretske, F. I. 95n
dualism 110, 199, 201, 208, 227
Duhem, P. M. M. 245
Dummett, M. 176n, 190, 231, 238

Eliot, T. S. 78n, 217, 218n, 221
emotions 26, 77–9, 88, 138–52, 200
empiricism 230n
Empson, W. 209, 214, 223n
epiphenomenalism 110
evaluative terms 166–7
events
  conflated with facts 45–8, 61, 94
  criteria of identity for 37, 39–49, 102–3, 111
  description of 42–3, 91–7, 103, 108, 114, 118
  falling under laws as described 97–8
  location of 9, 52, 99–100, 103, 107n, 150
  not secondary to objects 97–9
  temporal span of 101
  see also actions; descriptions of; adverbial modification
excuse 40, 44, 64, 75, 91, 161, 167

extensionality 48, 64, 65n, 108
extensions 58, 95, 176, 203

facts 45–8, 56, 57, 58, 60
  and states of affairs 41–3
  see also events, conflating facts with
Feigl, H. 110n, 140n
Feyerabend, P. 199–200, 202
finiteness requirement 172, 176, 186
first-person knowledge 34–5
Flew, A. 140
Føllesdal, D. 65n, 138n
force 212, *see* assertion; convention; imperatives
freedom 105, 119, 152, 197, 234
Frege, G. 11, 18, 58, 63, 64, 91, 95, 155–7, 158, 159, 165, 176, 183, 190, 213
Freud, S. 138, 139, 140, 141n, 142, 148n, 151, 152, 209, 245

Geach, P. 127n, 174n
Goodman, N. 114, 119–21, 210, 212n, 217
Grice, H. P. 129–31, 253, 254, 255, 257
grue 113–14, 119–212

Haber, L. 263–4
Hampshire, S. 23n, 29, 31n, 73
Hare, R. M. 76, 77, 82n, 83
Harman, G. 190
Hart, H. L. A. 23n, 33–4
Hedman, C. G. 51, 70–1
Hempel, C. G. 58, 84, 88
Henle, P. 210, 213n, 219
Hintikka, M. 181n
Hobbes, T. 138
holding true 14, 16, 17, 163, 169, 192–3, 195, 196, 206, 207, 226, 232–5
holism 14, 113, 116–17, 150, 159, 195, 231, 237
Holland, R. F. 23n
Honoré, A. M. 33–4
Hopkins, J. 140n
Hume, D. 33–5, 64, 133, 141, 228

illocutionary force, *see* assertion; convention; imperatives
imperatives 88, 170
incontinence, *see* weakness of will
indeterminacy of translation 117, 177, 193n, 195, 231–2
indexicals, *see* demonstratives
indicative sentences 173
  see also assertion

indirect discourse 2, 18, 174, 175, 177, 178, 179,
    181, 182, 183
  logical form of 18, 171–3
  quotational theory of 173–80
  paratactic analysis of 180–1
induction 34, 35, 142
instrumentalism 113
intending
  as a state not a mental act 126–8
  as unconditional judgment 134–7
  avowals of intention 126–8
  compared to wants and desires 132–7
  compared to wishes 136
  in relation to belief 128–32
  pure intending 122–8
  reasons for vs. reasons for belief 131–2
inscrutability of reference, *see* reference,
    inscrutability of
intensional contexts 45, 50, 159, 171–83, 189
  see also, belief, sentences about; indirect
    discourse
intensionality 2, 25, 45, 50, 96, 107–8,
    159, 176, 183, 189
intensions 2, 176, 183, 189
intention 7–8, 24n, 26–7, 31, 41, 50, 54–5, 70,
    80, 122–37, 138–52, 220, 253–4, 258
  connection with desired 72–3
  conditional 129–31
  in acting 25–6, 125
  logical form of sentences about, *see* actions,
    descriptions of
  ontological status of 31, 126
  related to reasons 123–4
  self-knowledge of 34–5
  unconscious 77
  see also agency, intention and; belief, connection
    with intention; reasons; primary reasons;
    intending
interactionism 110
interrogatives 170
irrationality 8, 116, 138–52

Jackson, H. 171n
James, W. 239
Jeffrey, R. C. 114n, 120n
Joyce, J. 259
judgments
  evaluative 8, 72, 76–7, 87, 124, 134n, 166
  intention as form of 134–7
  prima facie vs. unconditional 8, 81–7,
    133–7, 145

Kant, I. 105, 119
Katz, J. 61n
Kenny, A. J. P. 23n, 31n, 38–49, 92n
Kim, J. 59n, 61, 92n, 95–6, 110
Kuhn, T. 197–202

Lakoff, G. 209
language, *see* Taski-style theories of truth, as
    applied to natural languages
Larson, S. 138n
laws
  lawlike vs. statistical correlations 10, 26,
    112, 113, 114, 116, 118, 119, 120,
    121, 162n
  causal 5, 33, 34, 35, 90, 91, 97, 140
  homonomic vs. heteronomic 115, 117,
    118, 119
  lawlike vs. statistical correlations 91
  psychophysical 106, 107, 110, 111, 112,
    114, 117
Lemmon, E. J. 51, 52, 53, 54, 74, 101
Lewis, D. K. 109n
logical form 2, 166–8, 171–3
  and agency 5–7, 9, 39–40, 44, 49–50
  and intentionality 37
  and the 'logic of action' 43
  and meaning 37–8
  and ontology 91–2
  of indirect discourse, *see* indirect discourse,
    logical form of
Luce, D. R. 110n

MacIntyre, A. 140
Malcolm, N. 111n
MacKay, A. 257–8, 260
Martin, R. M. 51, 56, 57, 58, 59,
    60, 61, 94n, 95n
materialism 9, 107–11, 118–19, 200
Mates, B. 166, 177, 178n
McCarrell, N. S. 220–1
McCawley, J. 263
meaning
  causal theory of 113, 236n
  see also meaning as entities; Tarski-style theories
    of truth, as theories of meaning
meanings as entities 155–9
Melden, A. I. 23n, 24n, 29–31, 35
mental events 9, 10, 30, 31, 92, 100, 105–21,
    140, 147, 149–52, 247
  see also materialism; mental-physical;
    psychology; laws; psychophysical